YOTSUBA&!

10

KIYOHIKO AZUMA

YOTSUBA&!
KIYOHIKO AZUMA

CONTENTS

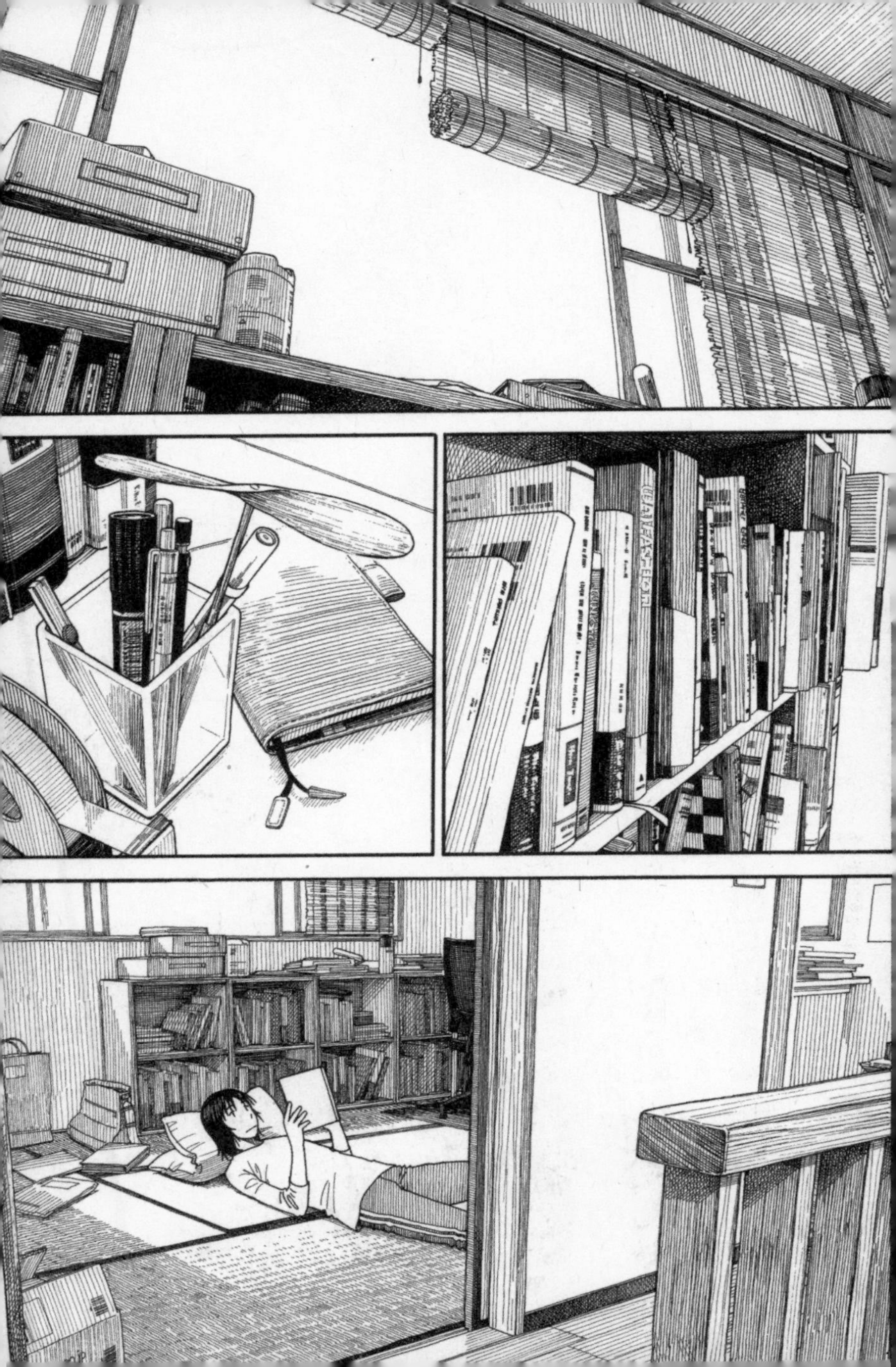

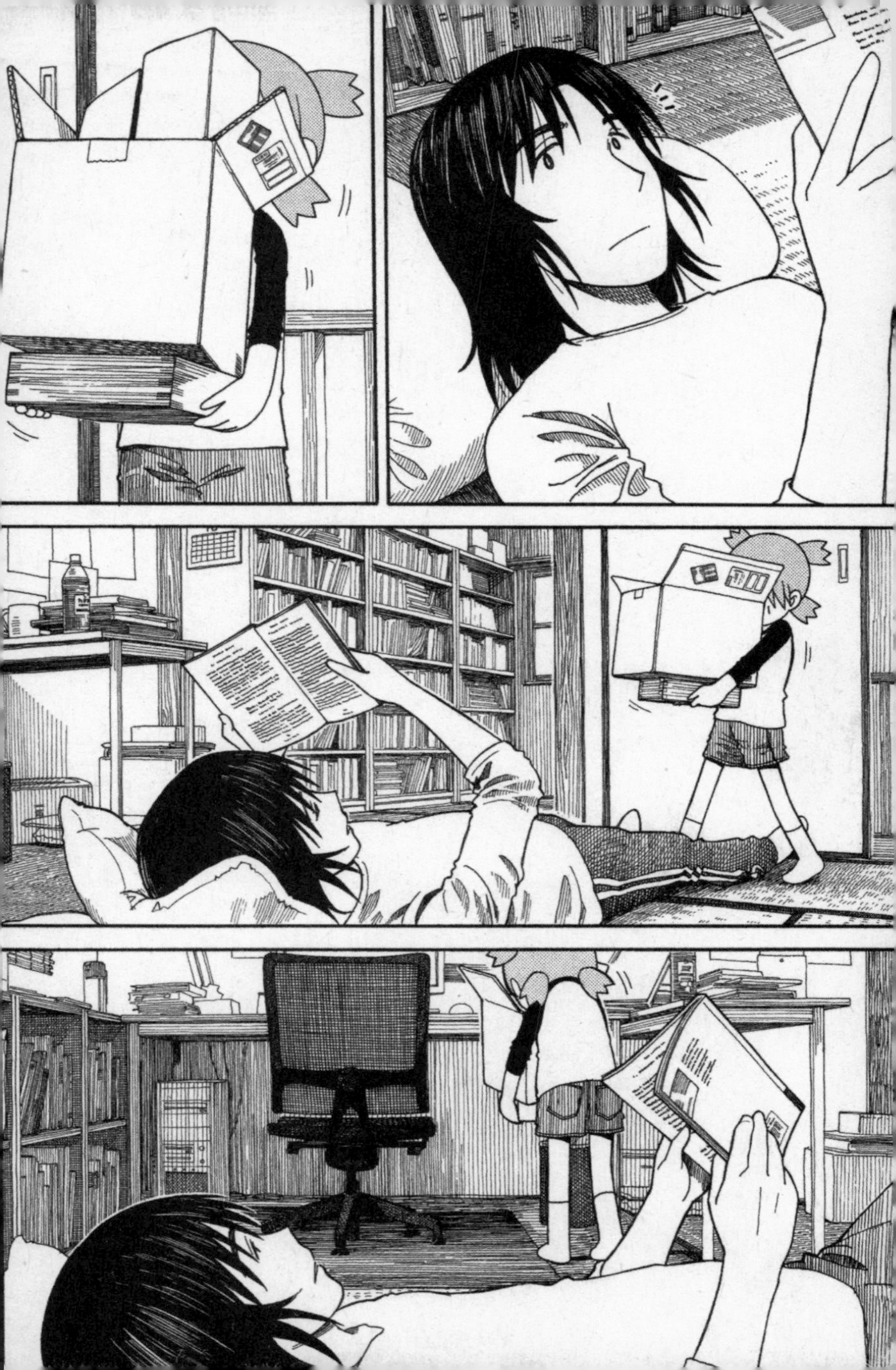

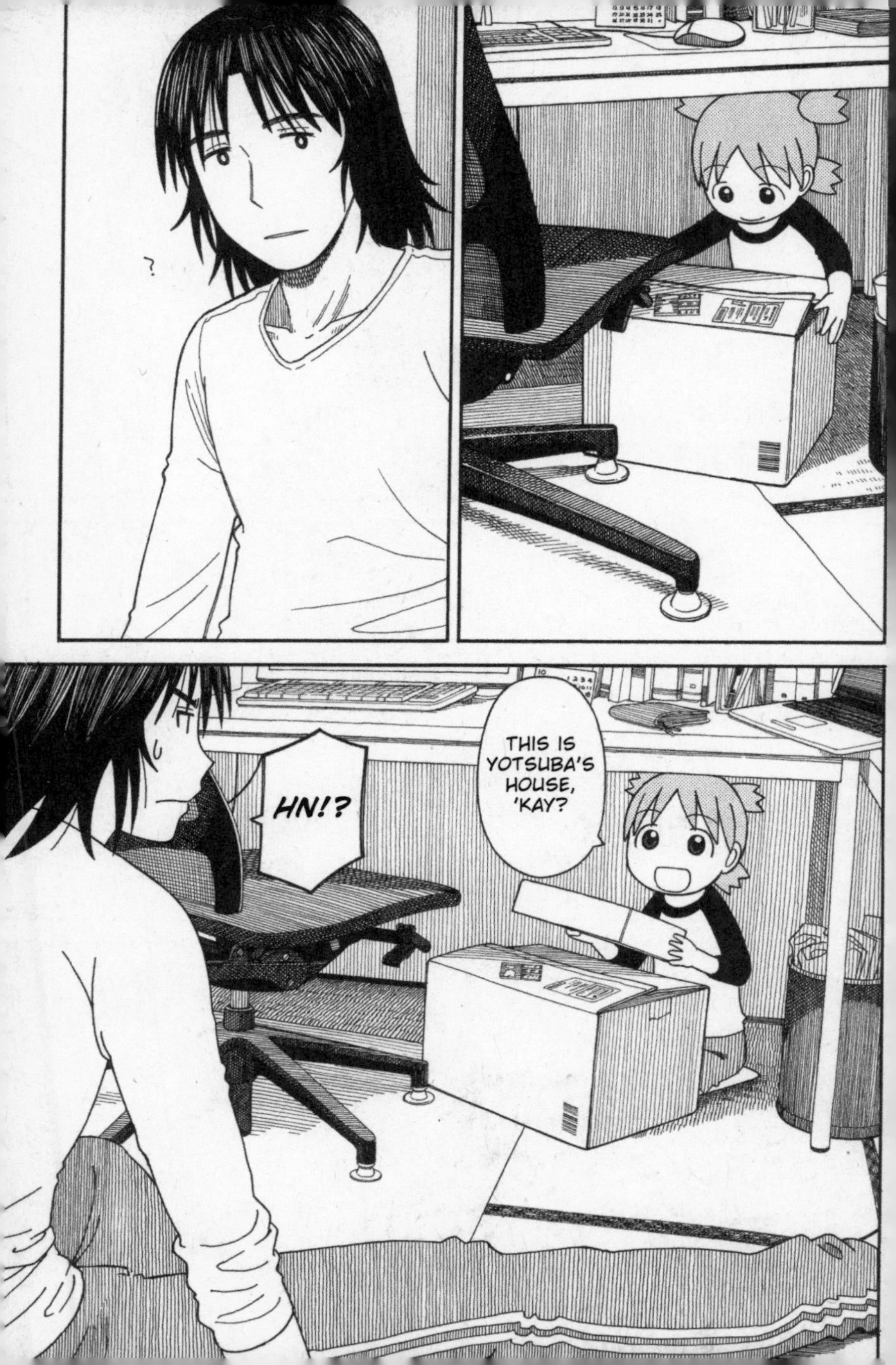
?
THIS IS YOTSUBA'S HOUSE, 'KAY?
HN!?

YOTSUBA& PLAYTIME #63

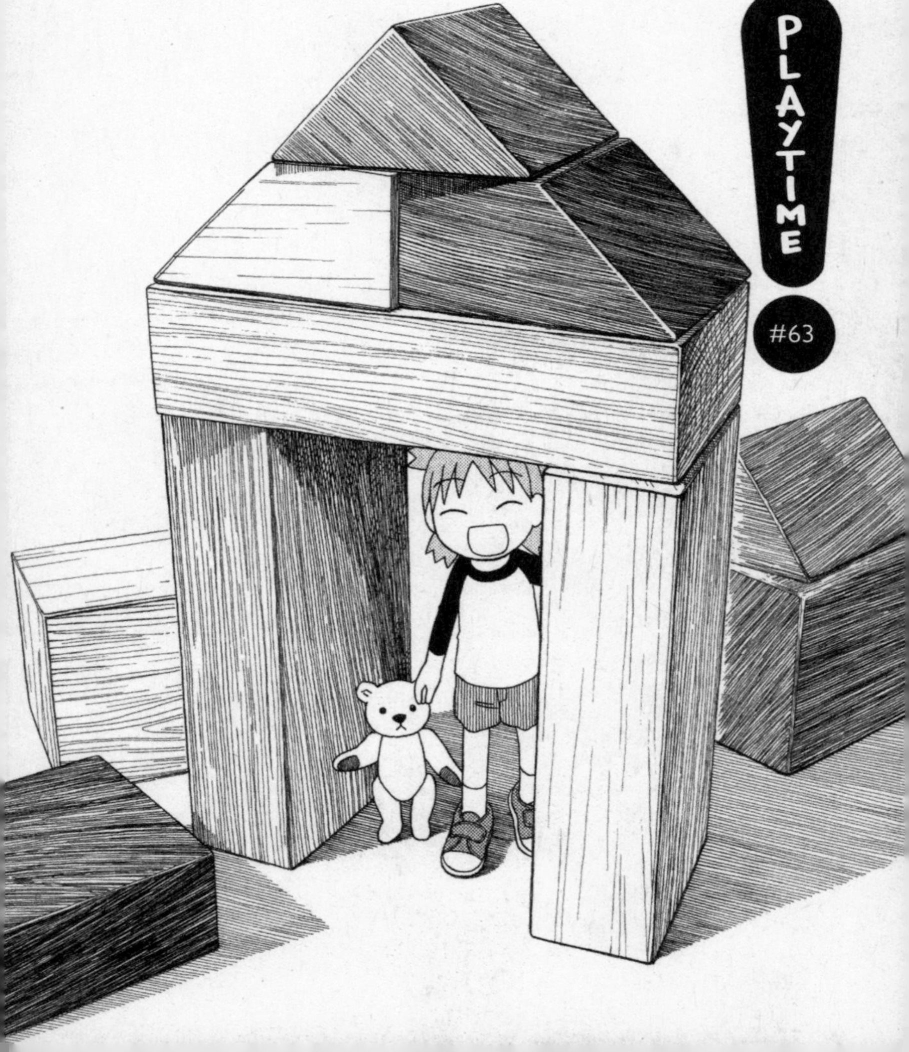

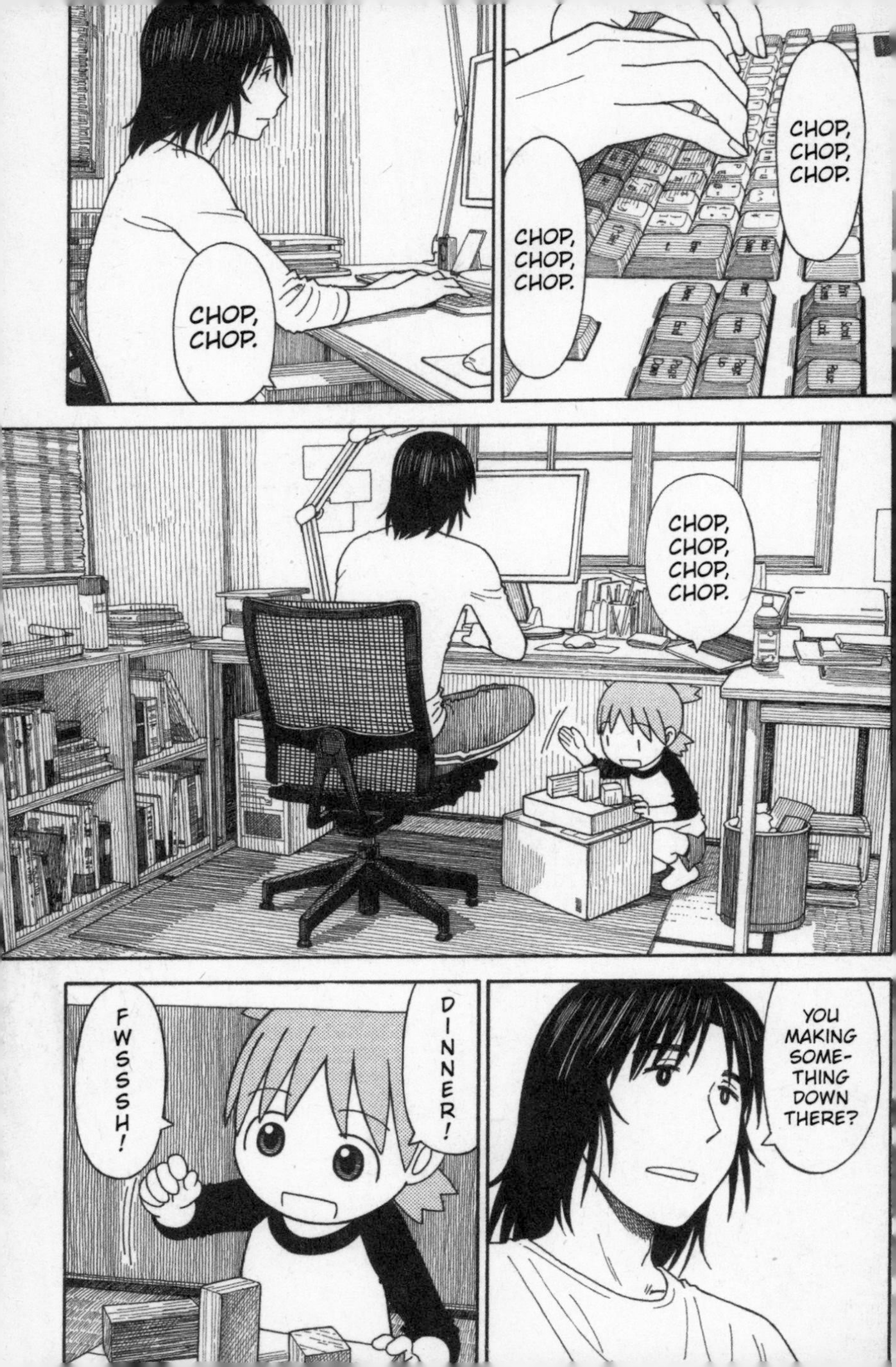
CHOP, CHOP, CHOP.
CHOP, CHOP, CHOP.
CHOP, CHOP.
CHOP, CHOP, CHOP, CHOP.
YOU MAKING SOME-THING DOWN THERE?
DINNER!
FWSSSH!

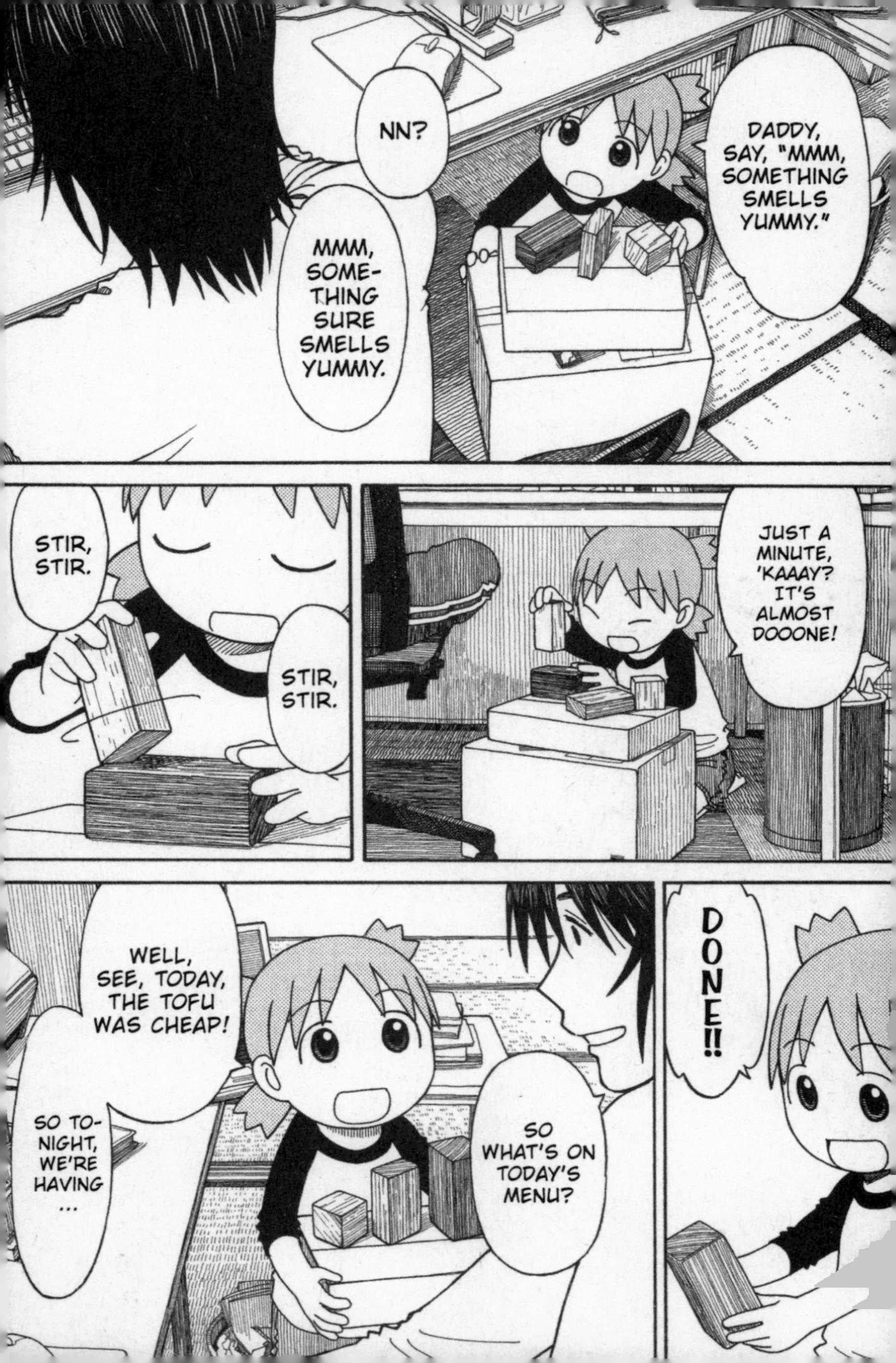
DADDY, SAY, "MMM, SOMETHING SMELLS YUMMY."
NN?
MMM, SOME-THING SURE SMELLS YUMMY.
JUST A MINUTE, 'KAAAY? IT'S ALMOST DOOONE!
STIR, STIR.
STIR, STIR.
DONE!!
SO WHAT'S ON TODAY'S MENU?
WELL, SEE, TODAY, THE TOFU WAS CHEAP!
SO TO-NIGHT, WE'RE HAVING ...

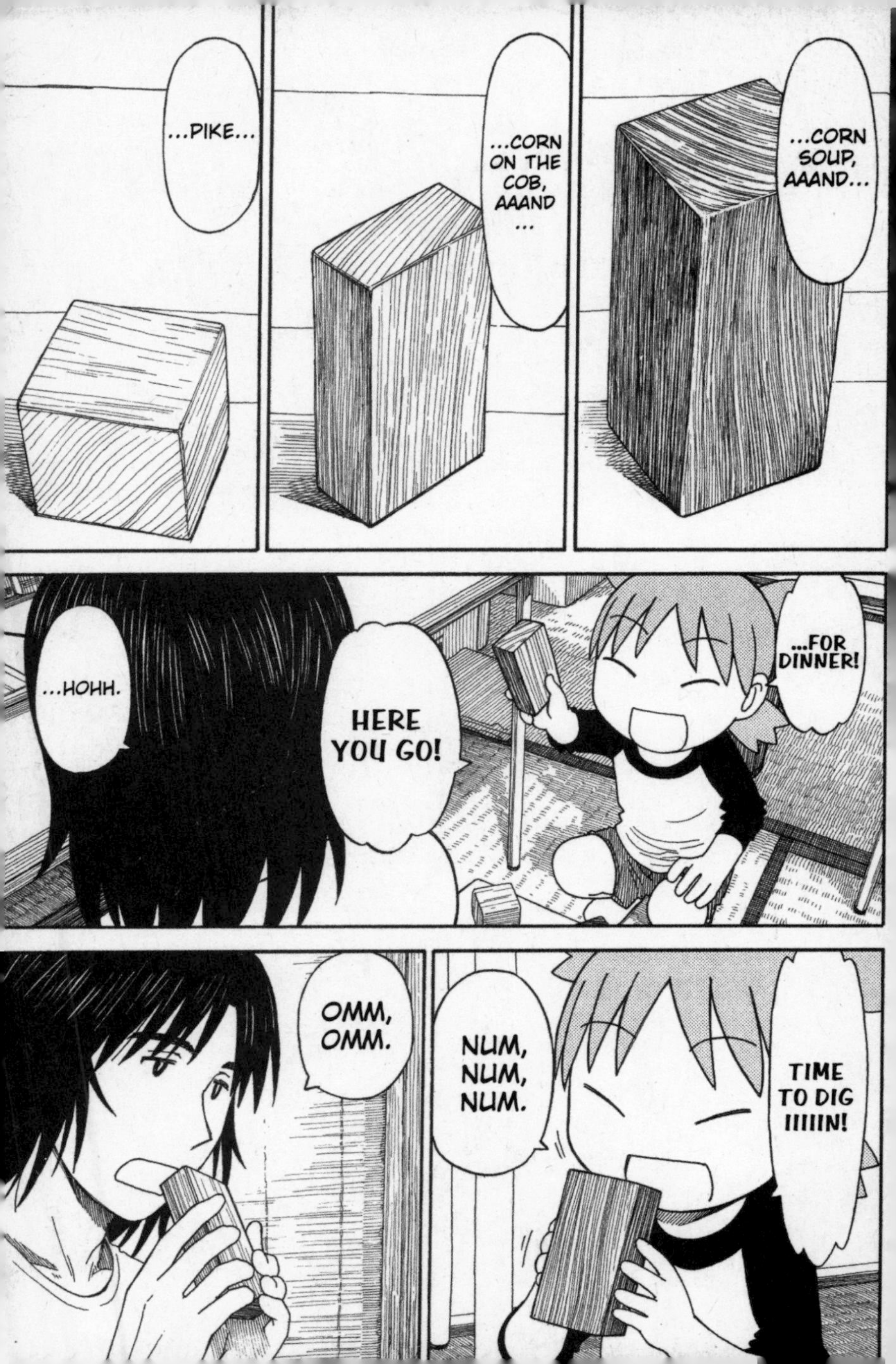
...CORN SOUP, AAAND...
...CORN ON THE COB, AAAND ...
...PIKE...
...FOR DINNER!
HERE YOU GO!
...HOHH.
TIME TO DIG IIIIIN!
NUM, NUM, NUM.
OMM, OMM.

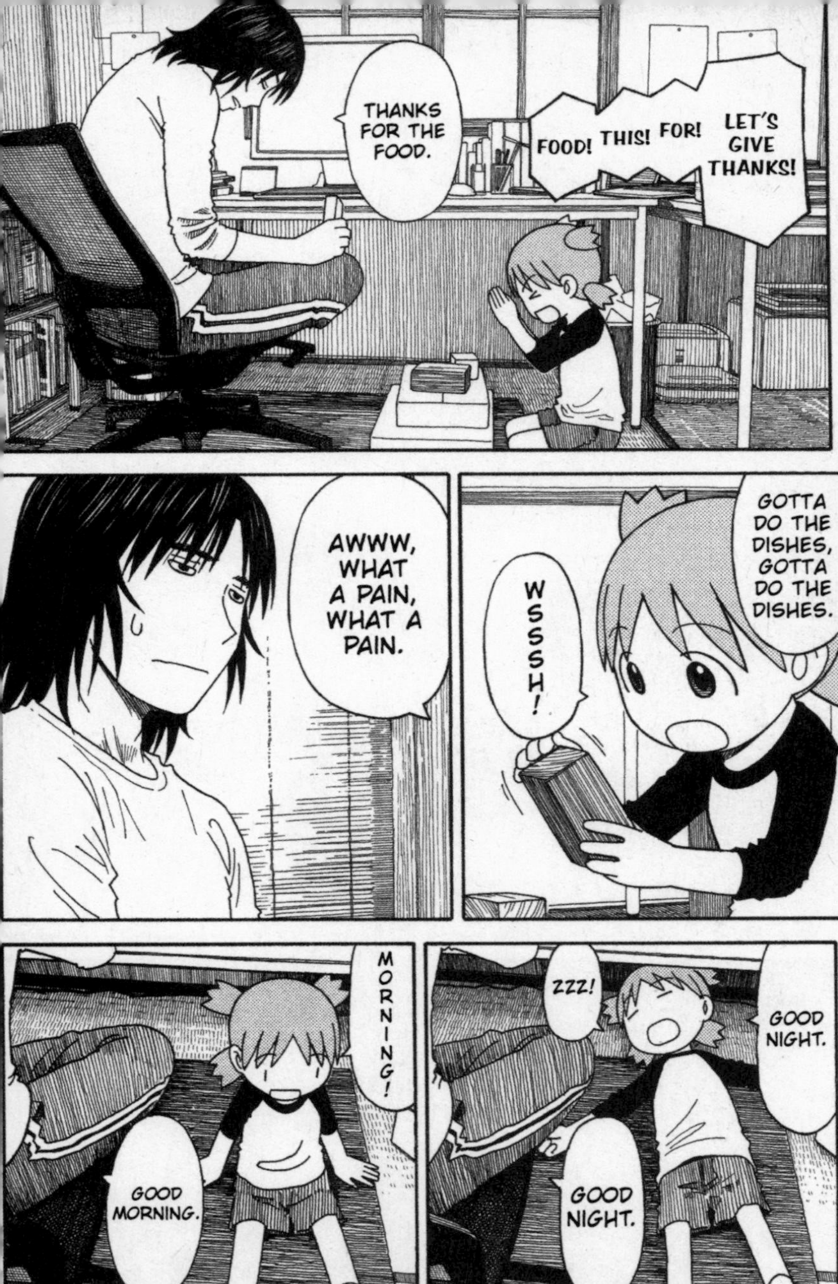
LET'S GIVE THANKS! FOR! THIS! FOOD!
THANKS FOR THE FOOD.
GOTTA DO THE DISHES, GOTTA DO THE DISHES.
WSSSH!
AWWW, WHAT A PAIN, WHAT A PAIN.
GOOD NIGHT.
ZZZ!
GOOD NIGHT.
MORNING!
GOOD MORNING.

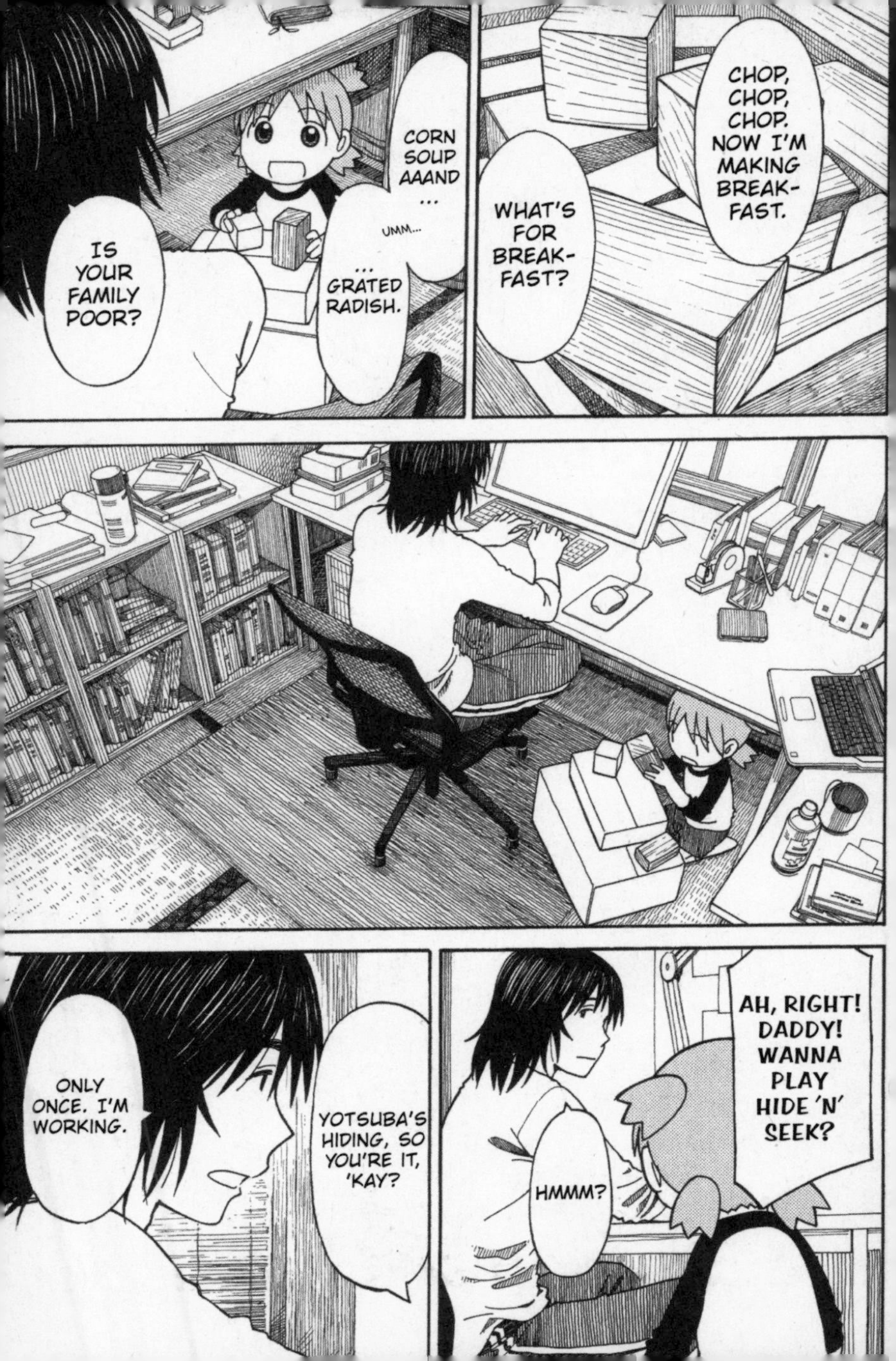
CHOP, CHOP, CHOP. NOW I'M MAKING BREAK-FAST.
WHAT'S FOR BREAK-FAST?
CORN SOUP AAAND ...
UMM...
... GRATED RADISH.
IS YOUR FAMILY POOR?
AH, RIGHT! DADDY! WANNA PLAY HIDE 'N' SEEK?
HMMM?
YOTSUBA'S HIDING, SO YOU'RE IT, 'KAY?
ONLY ONCE. I'M WORKING.

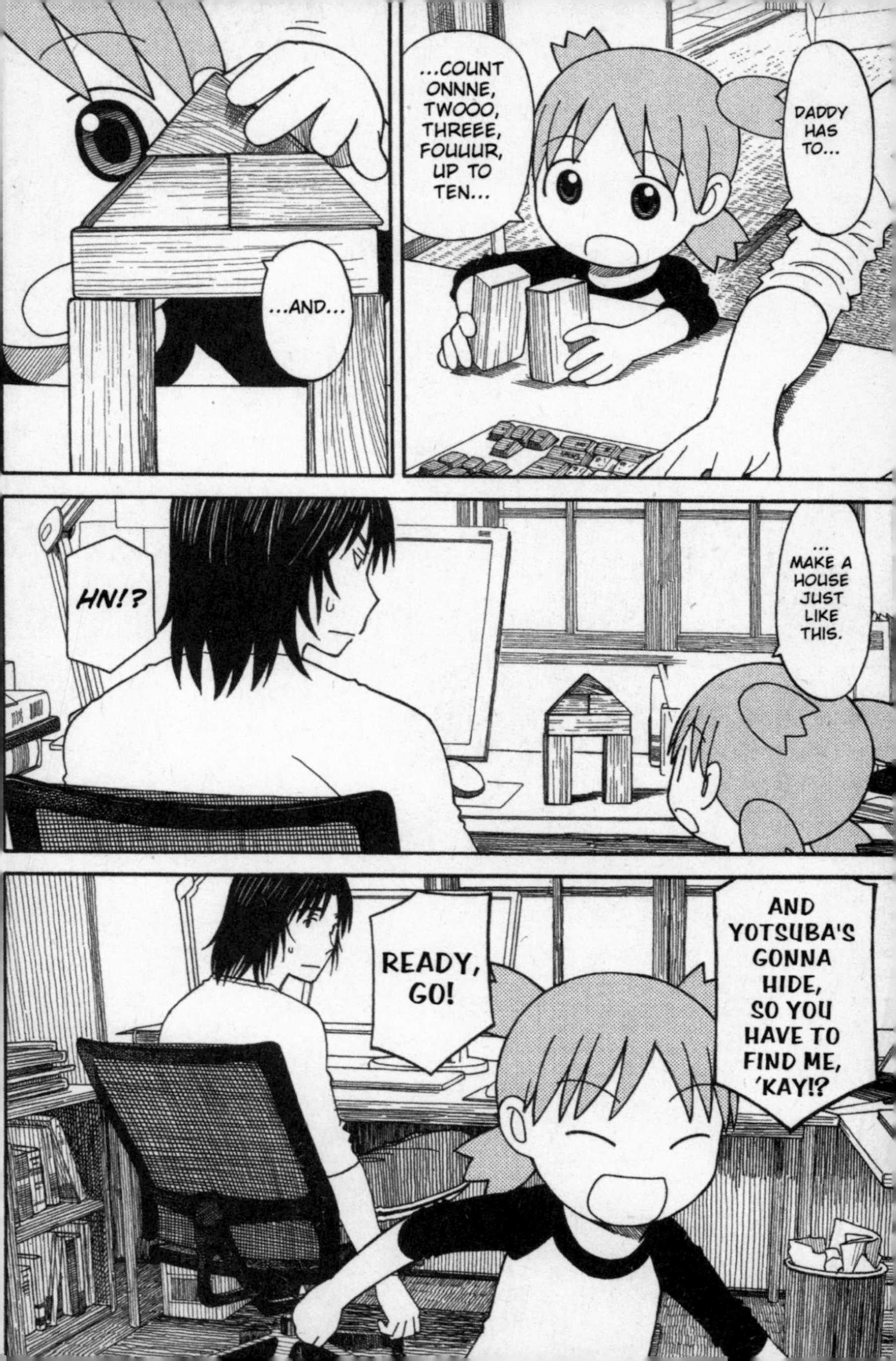
DADDY HAS TO...
...COUNT ONNNE, TWOOO, THREEE, FOUUUR, UP TO TEN...
...AND...
... MAKE A HOUSE JUST LIKE THIS.
HN!?
AND YOTSUBA'S GONNA HIDE, SO YOU HAVE TO FIND ME, 'KAY!?
READY, GO!

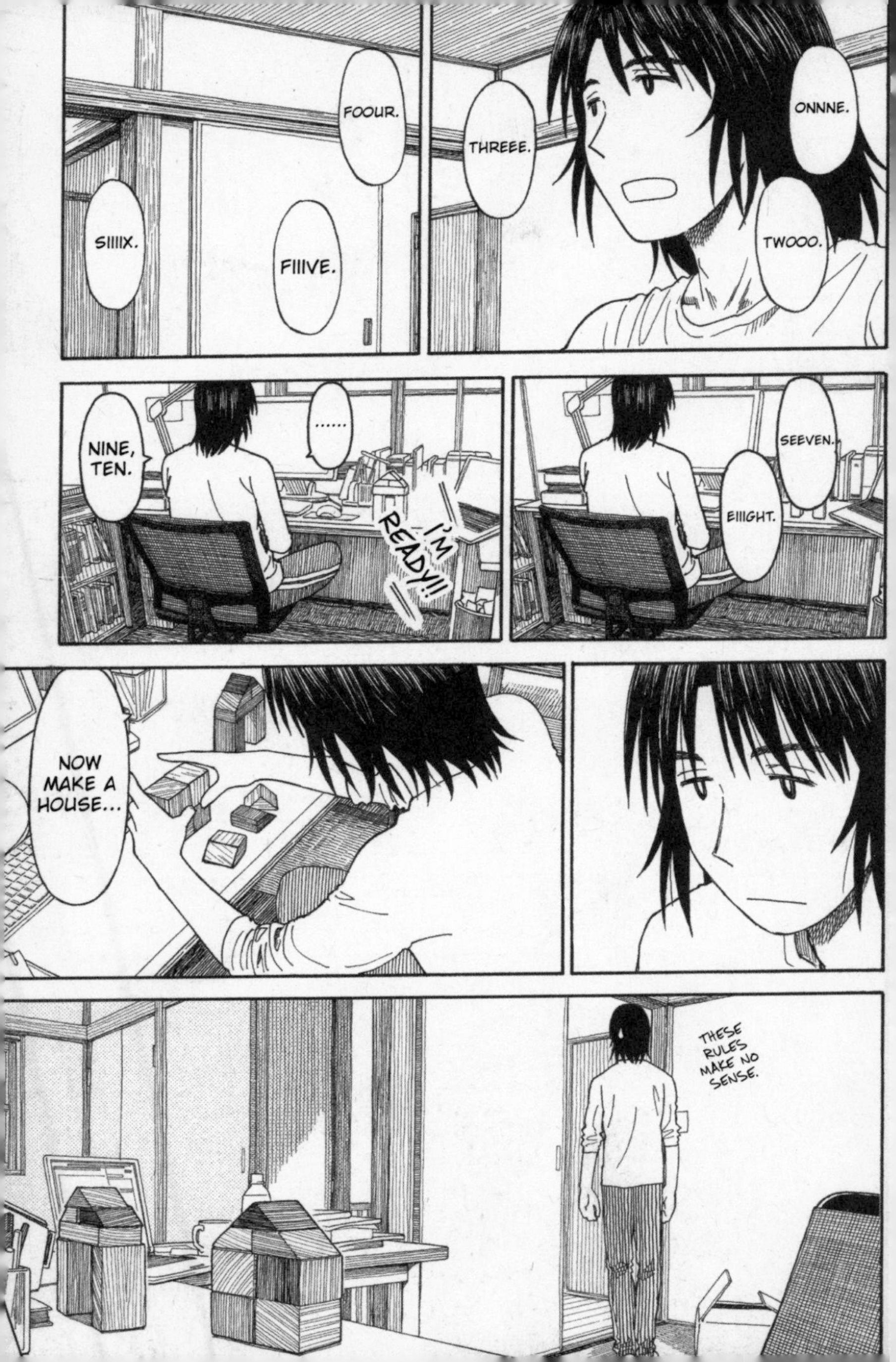

ONNNE.
TWOOO.
THREEE.
FOOUR.
FIIIVE.
SIIIX.
SEEVEN.
EIIIGHT.
......
NINE, TEN.
I'M READY!!!
NOW MAKE A HOUSE...
THESE RULES MAKE NO SENSE.

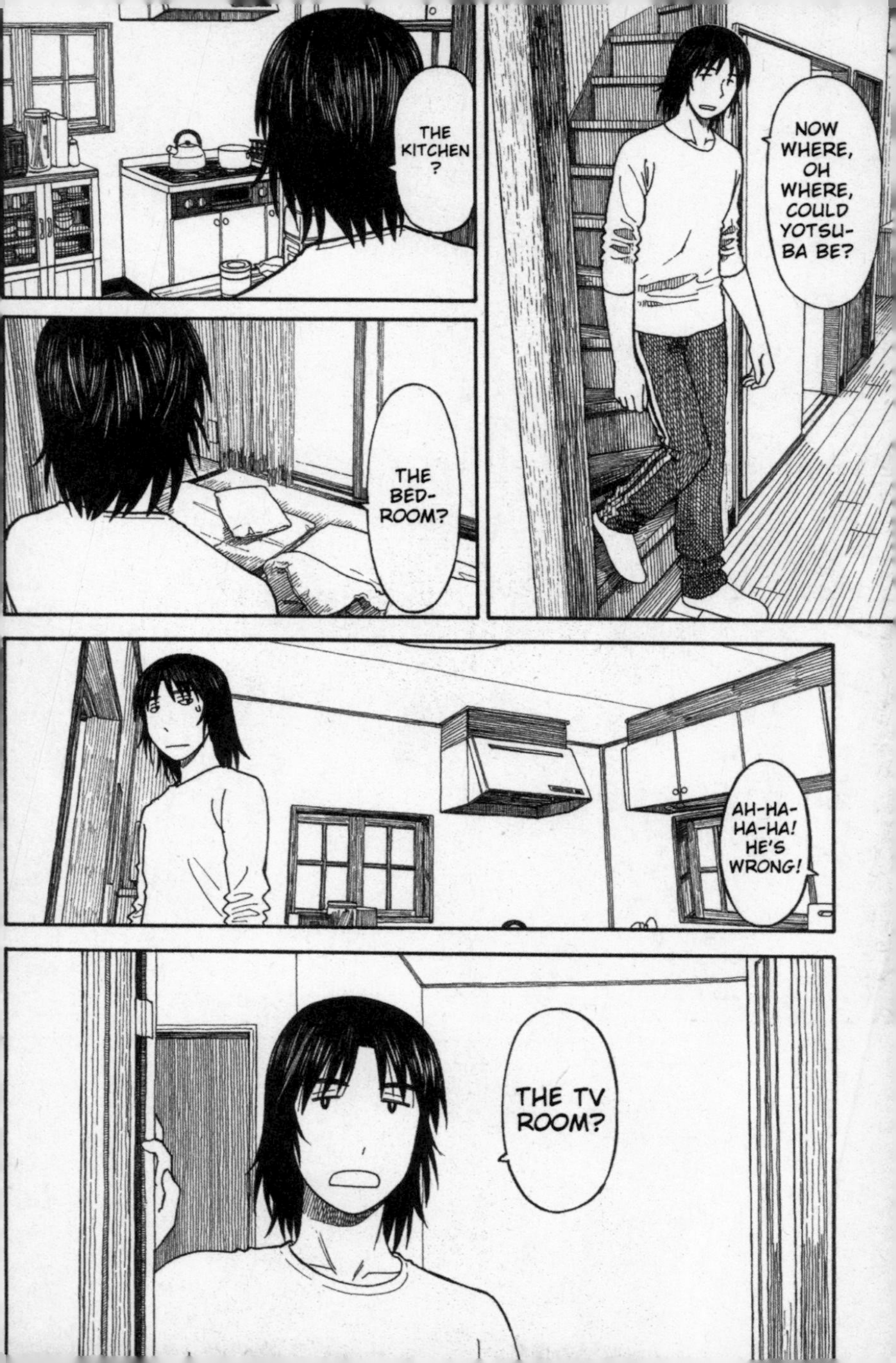
NOW WHERE, OH WHERE, COULD YOTSU-BA BE?
THE KITCHEN ?
THE BED-ROOM?
AH-HA-HA-HA! HE'S WRONG!
THE TV ROOM?

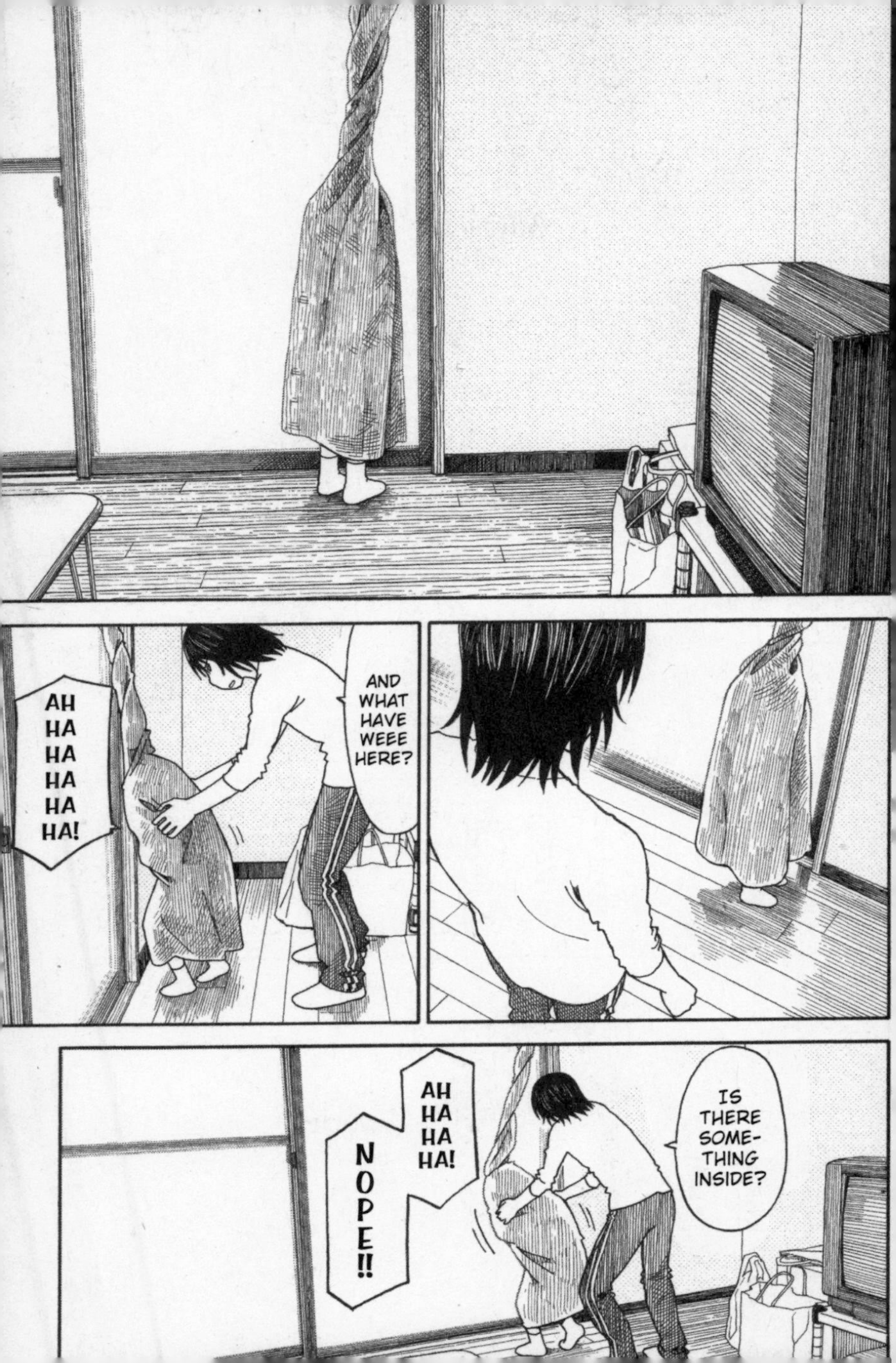
AND WHAT HAVE WEEE HERE?
AH HA HA HA HA HA!
IS THERE SOME-THING INSIDE?
AH HA HA HA!
NOPE!!

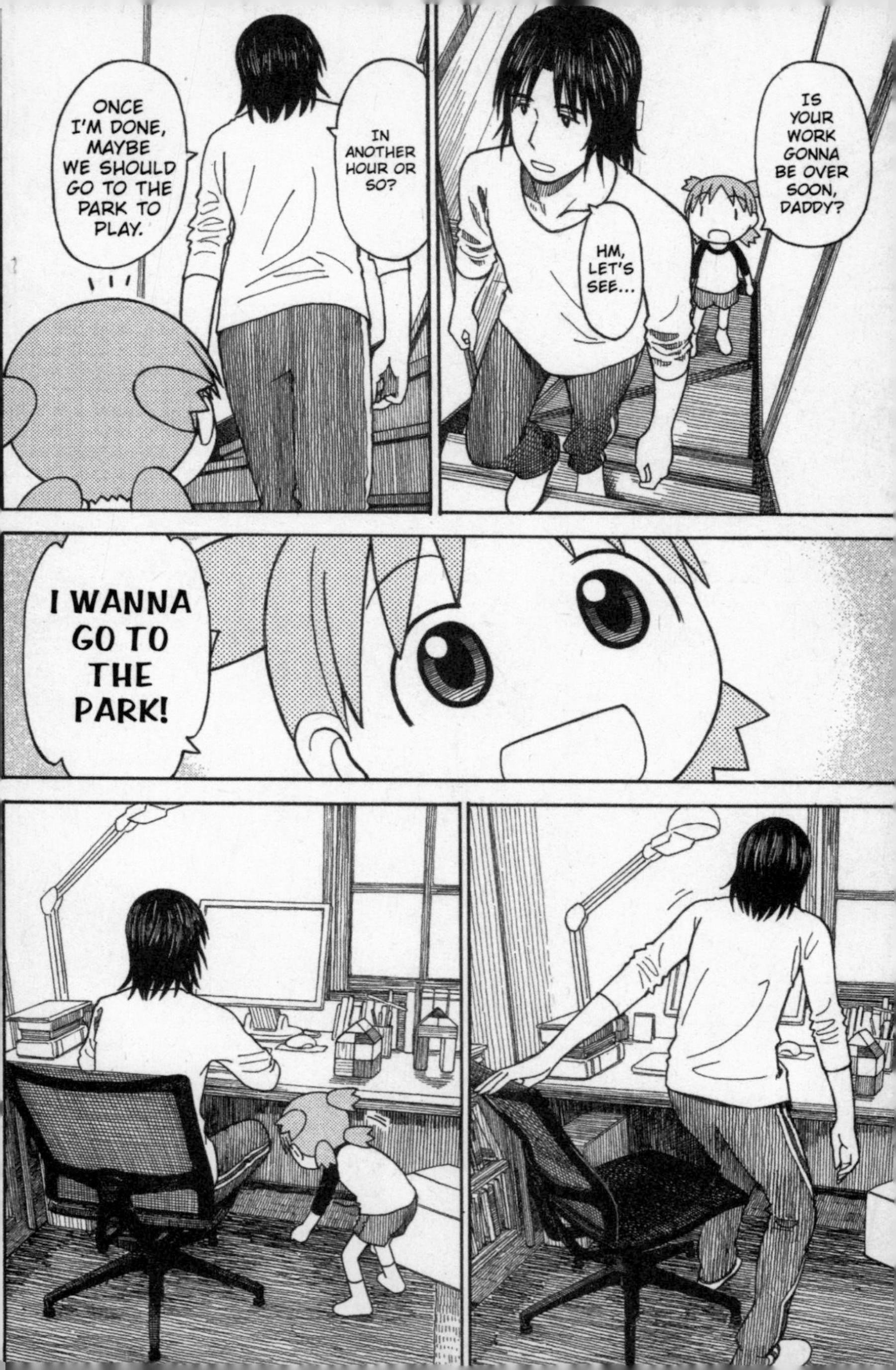
IS YOUR WORK GONNA BE OVER SOON, DADDY?
HM, LET'S SEE...
IN ANOTHER HOUR OR SO?
ONCE I'M DONE, MAYBE WE SHOULD GO TO THE PARK TO PLAY.
I WANNA GO TO THE PARK!

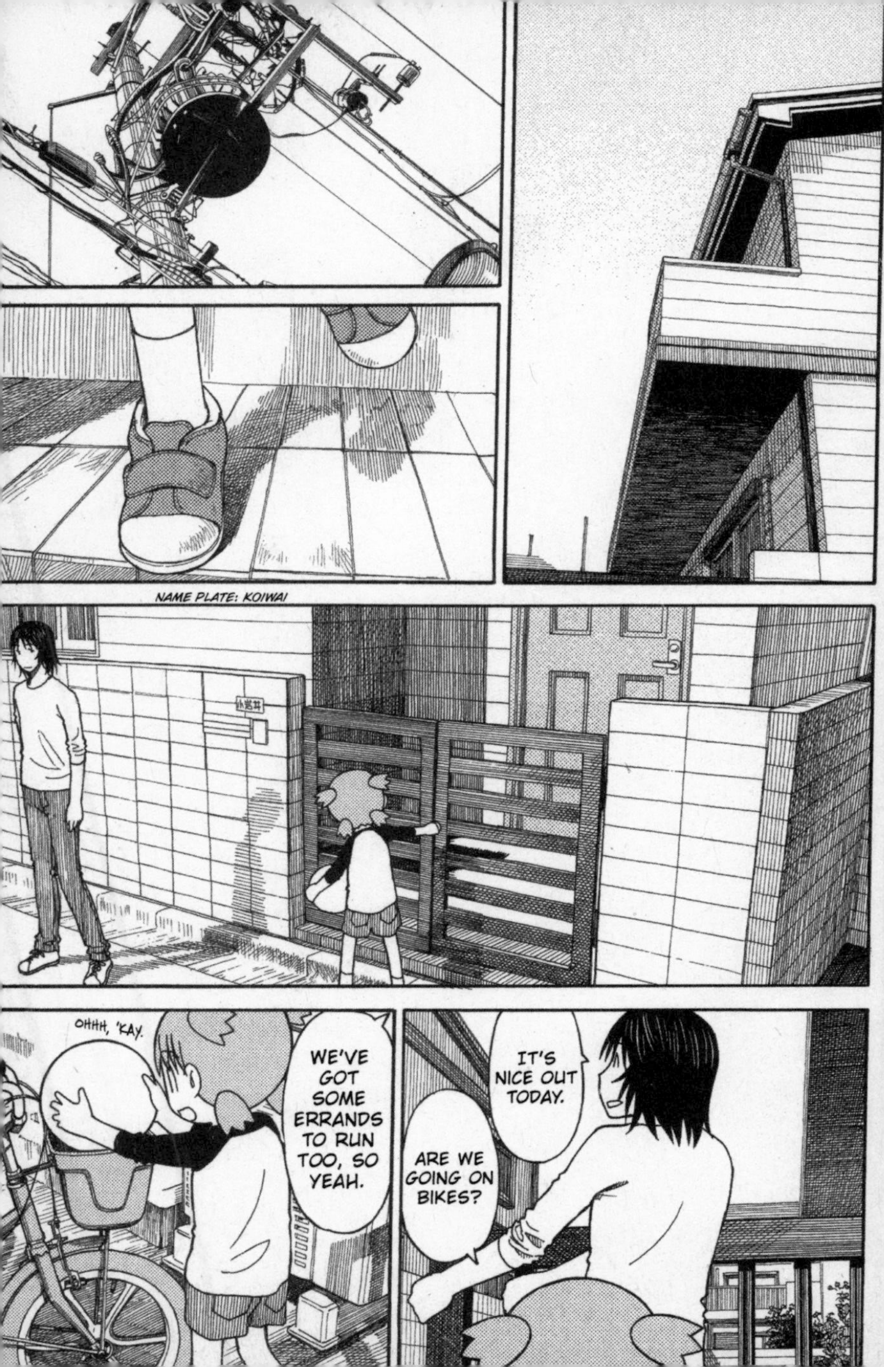
NAME PLATE: KOIWAI
IT'S NICE OUT TODAY.
ARE WE GOING ON BIKES?
WE'VE GOT SOME ERRANDS TO RUN TOO, SO YEAH.
OHHH, 'KAY.

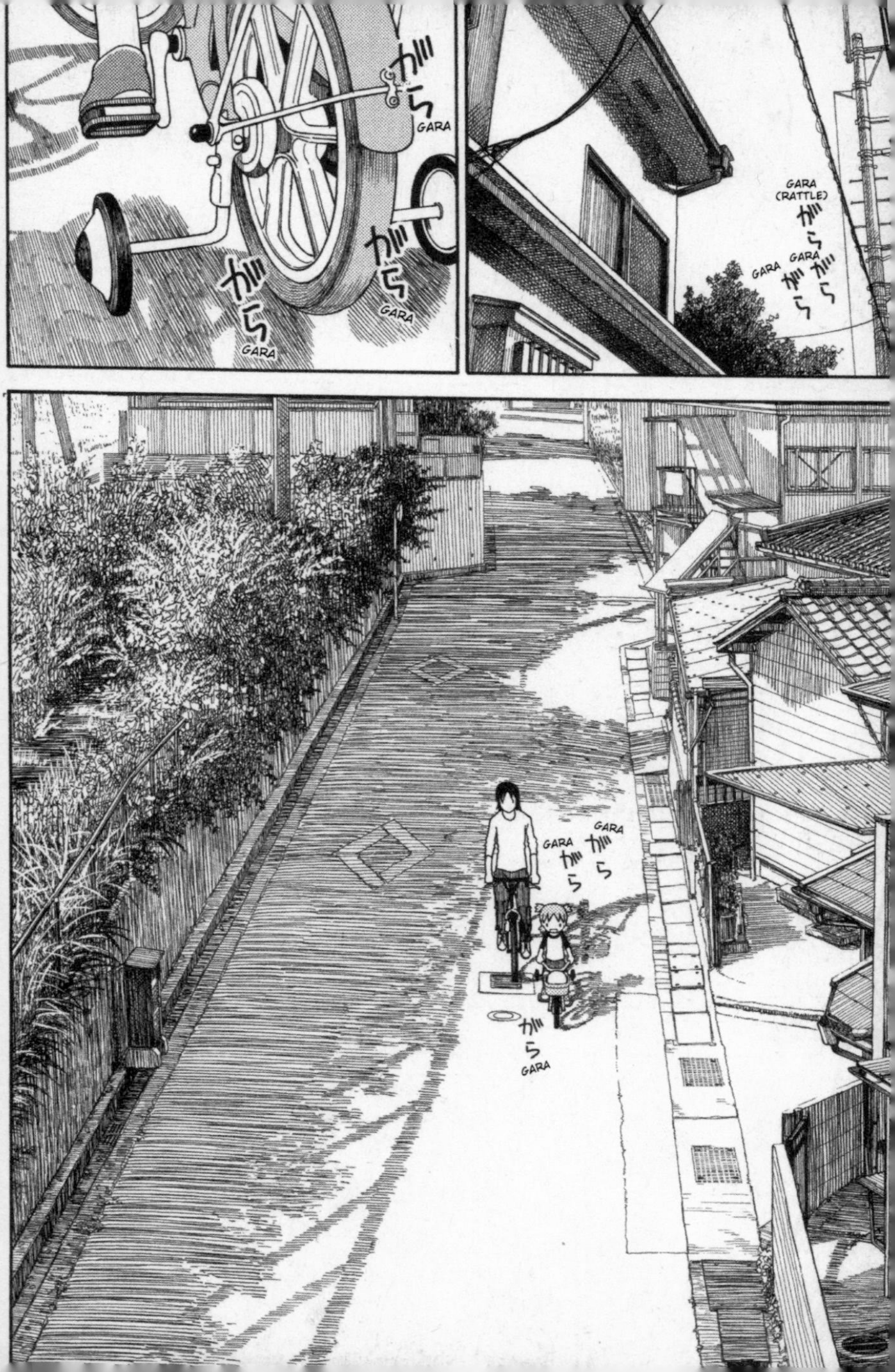
がら
GARA (RATTLE)
がら
GARA
がら
GARA
がら
GARA
がら
GARA
がら
GARA
がら
GARA
がら
GARA
がら
GARA

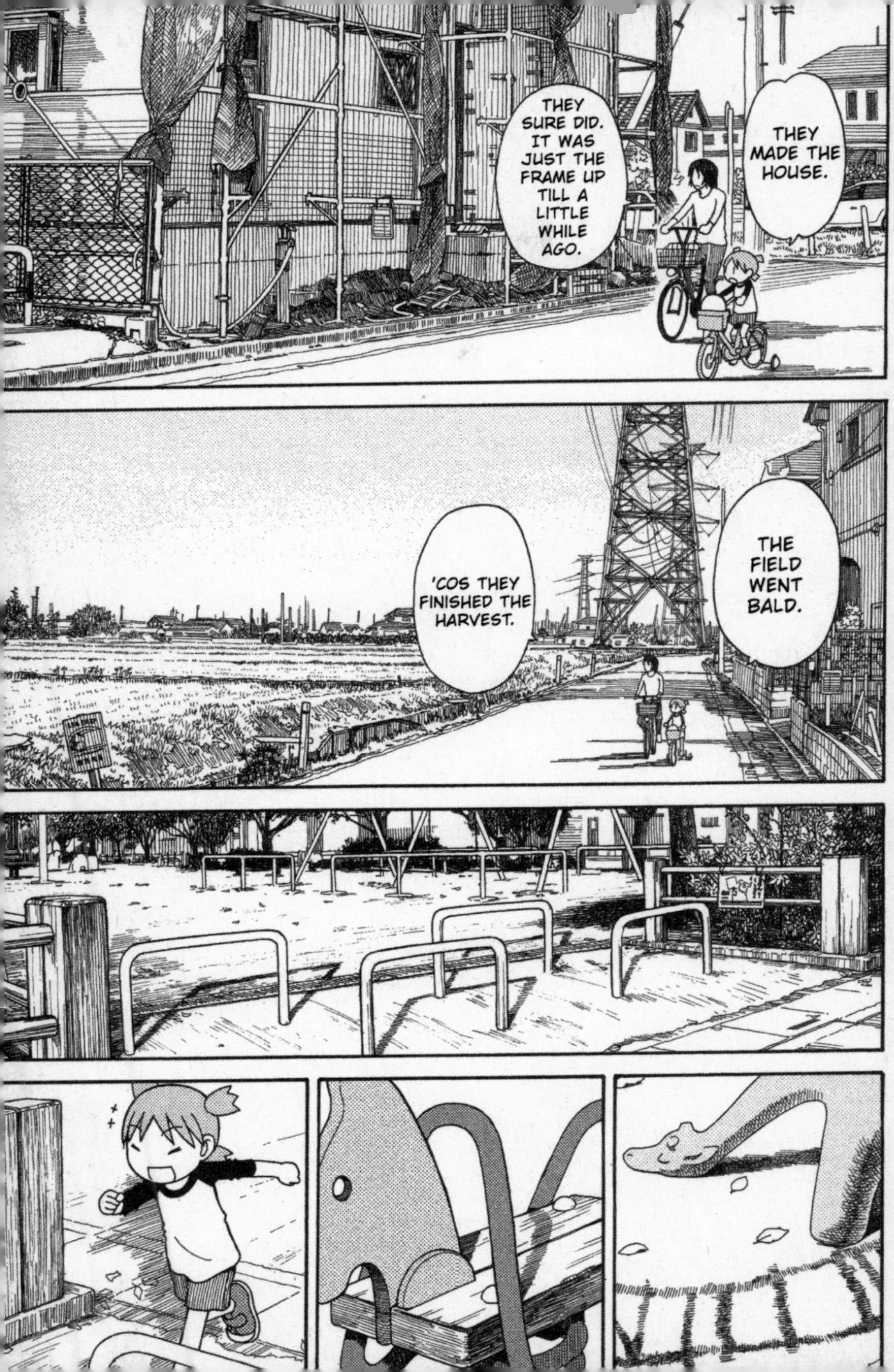
THEY MADE THE HOUSE.
THEY SURE DID. IT WAS JUST THE FRAME UP TILL A LITTLE WHILE AGO.
THE FIELD WENT BALD.
'COS THEY FINISHED THE HARVEST.

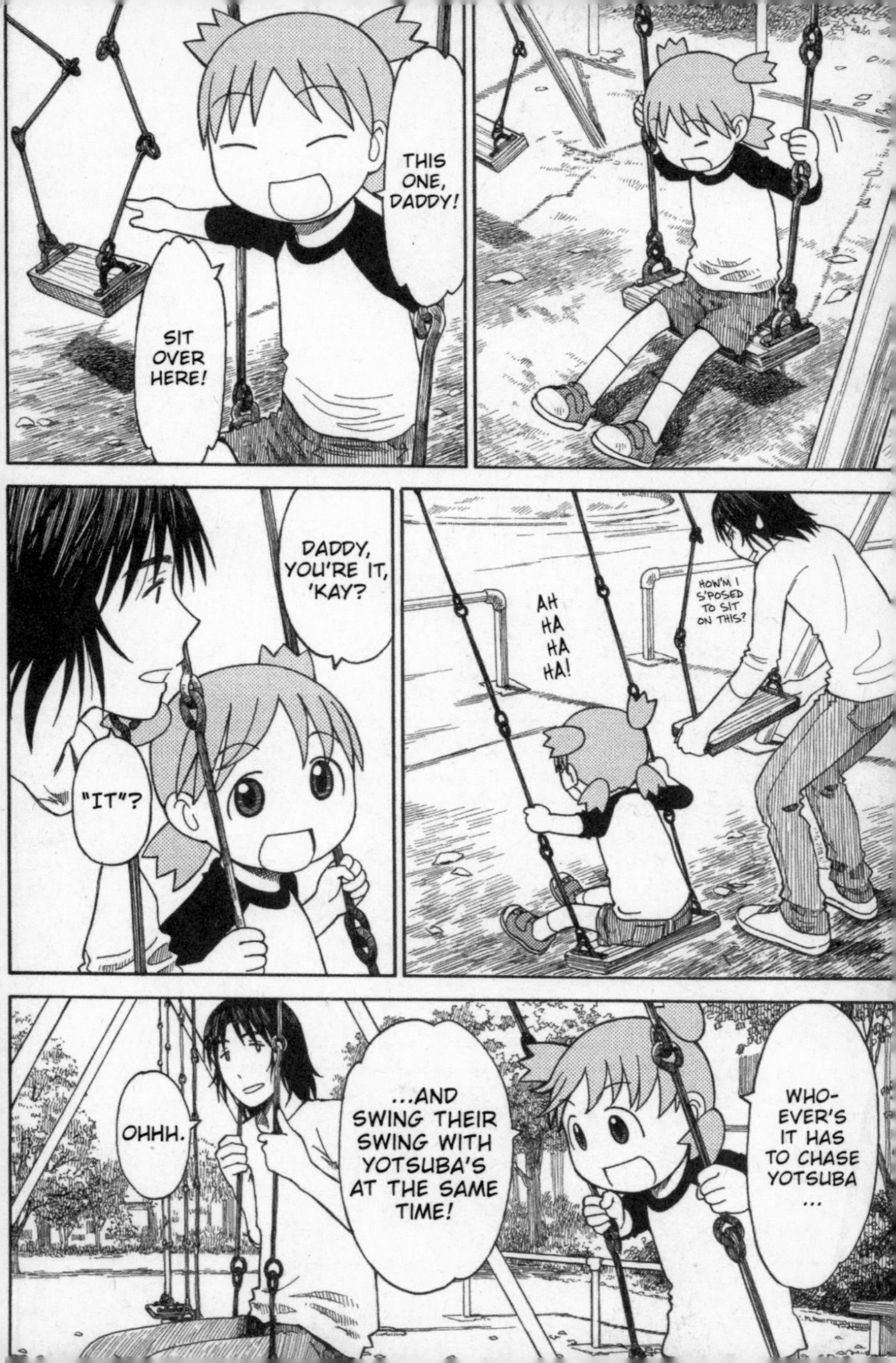
THIS ONE, DADDY!
SIT OVER HERE!
HOW'M I S'POSED TO SIT ON THIS?
AH HA HA HA!
DADDY, YOU'RE IT, 'KAY?
"IT"?
WHO-EVER'S IT HAS TO CHASE YOTSUBA ...
...AND SWING THEIR SWING WITH YOTSUBA'S AT THE SAME TIME!
OHHH.

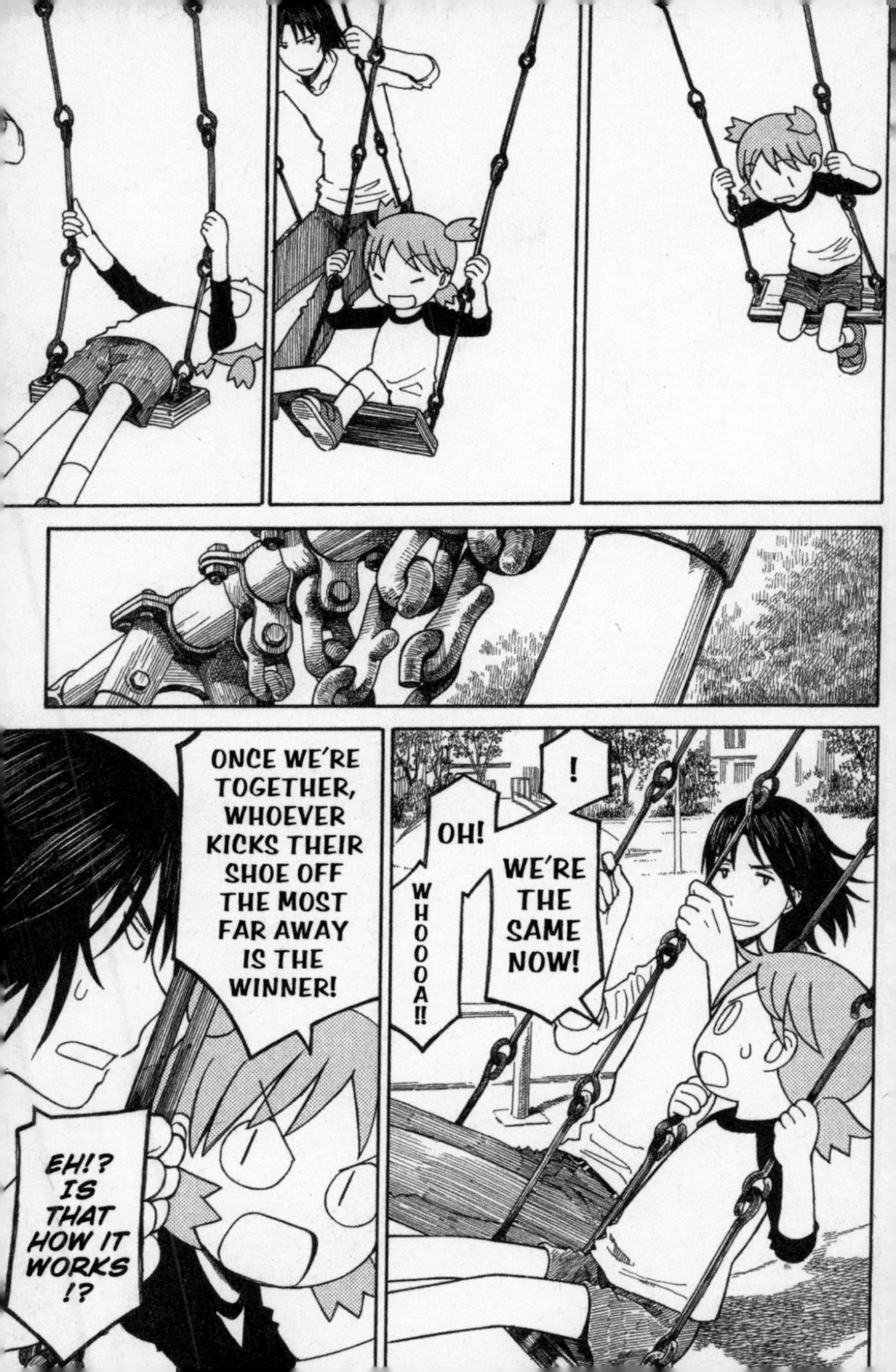
!
OH!
WE'RE THE SAME NOW!
WHOOOOA!!
ONCE WE'RE TOGETHER, WHOEVER KICKS THEIR SHOE OFF THE MOST FAR AWAY IS THE WINNER!
EH!? IS THAT HOW IT WORKS!?

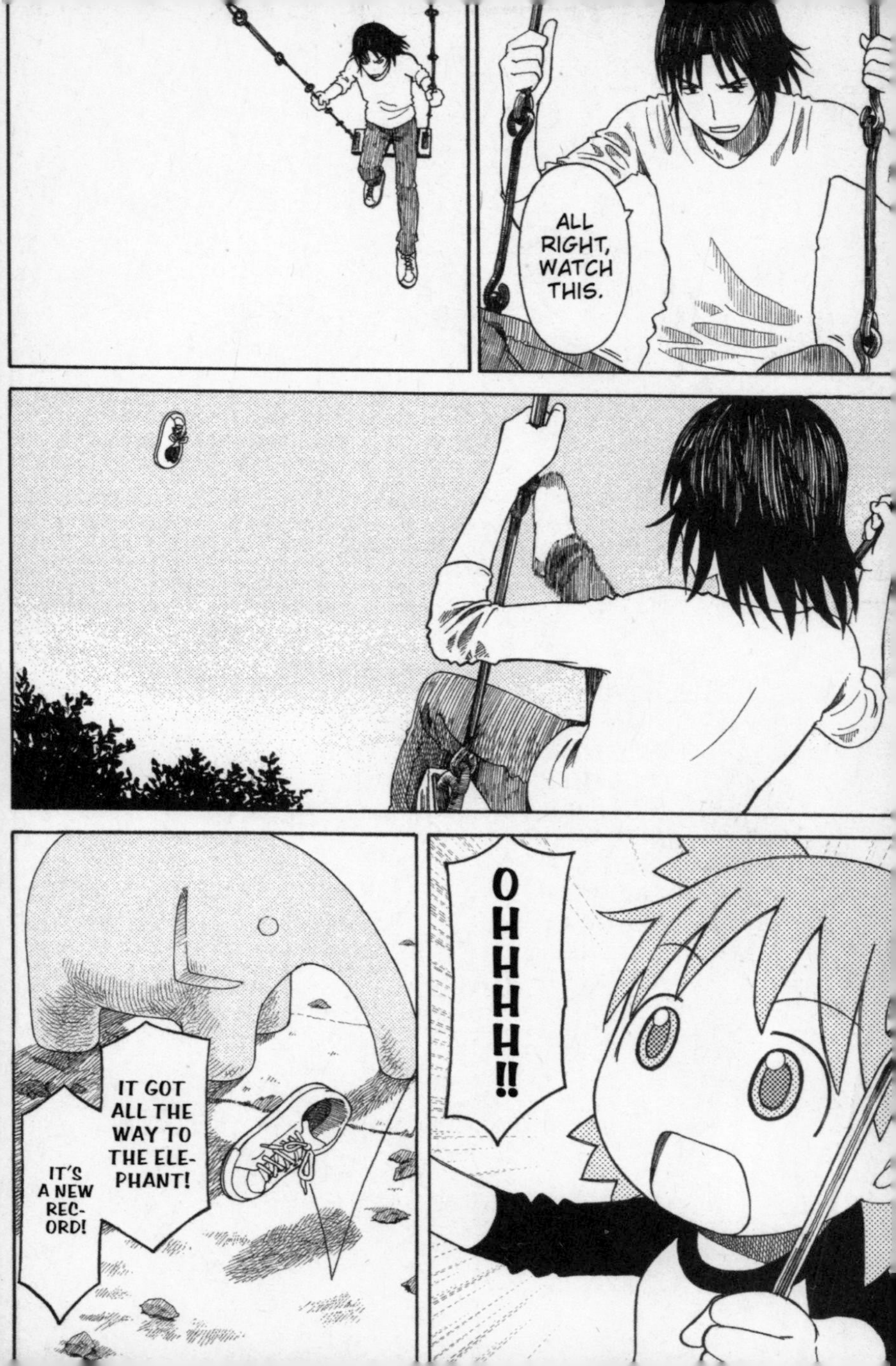
ALL RIGHT, WATCH THIS.
OHHHH!!
IT GOT ALL THE WAY TO THE ELE-PHANT!
IT'S A NEW REC-ORD!

BA
(WHAP)

'KAAY! HERE I GO!

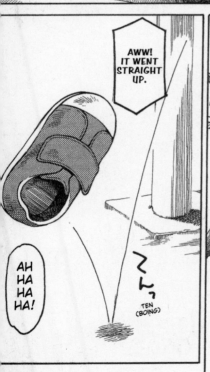

AWW! IT WENT STRAIGHT UP.

AH HA HA HA!

てん
TEN
(BOING)

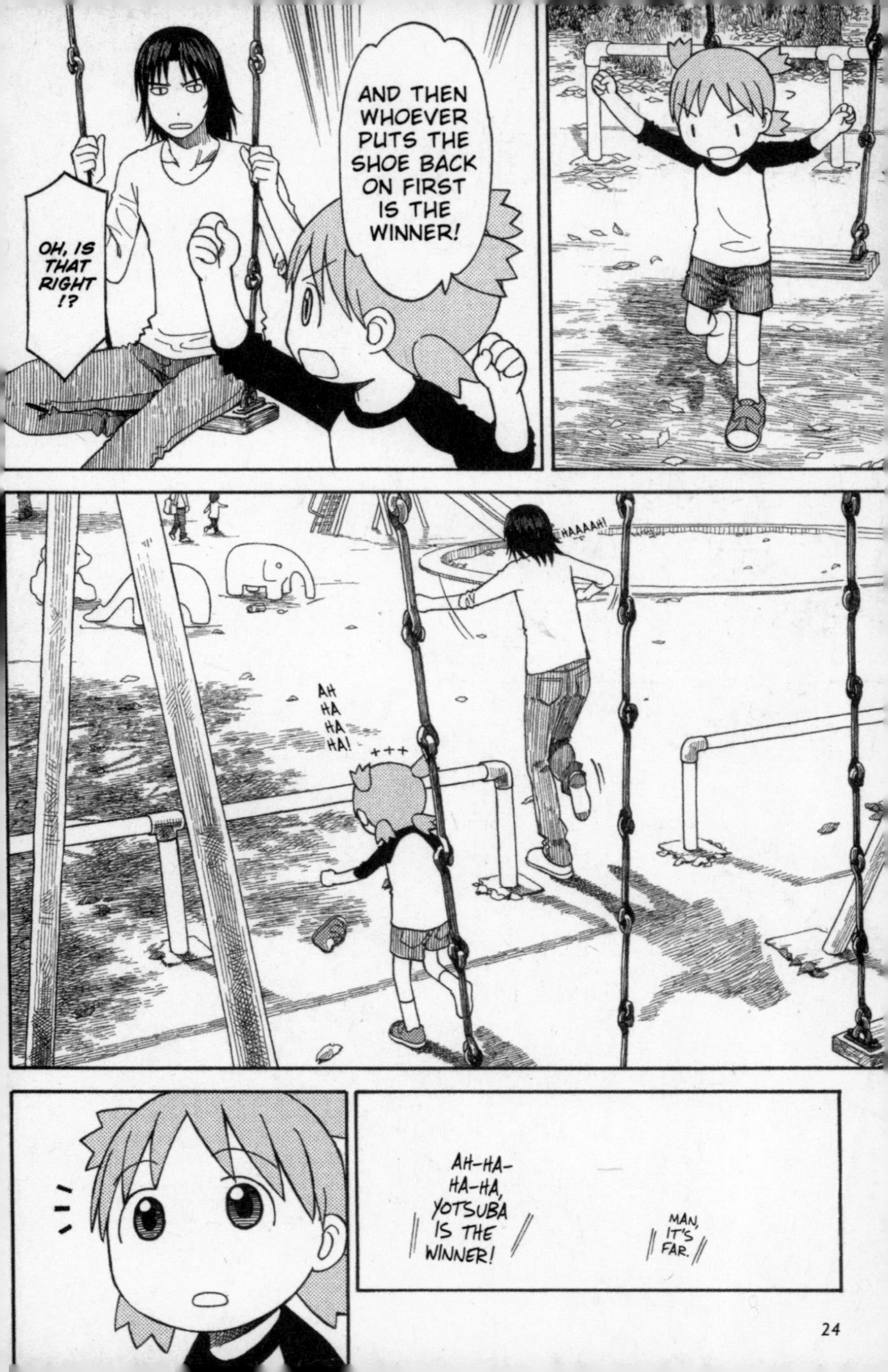
AND THEN WHOEVER PUTS THE SHOE BACK ON FIRST IS THE WINNER!
OH, IS THAT RIGHT!?
HAAAAH!
AH HA HA HA!
+++
AH-HA-HA-HA, YOTSUBA IS THE WINNER!
MAN, IT'S FAR.

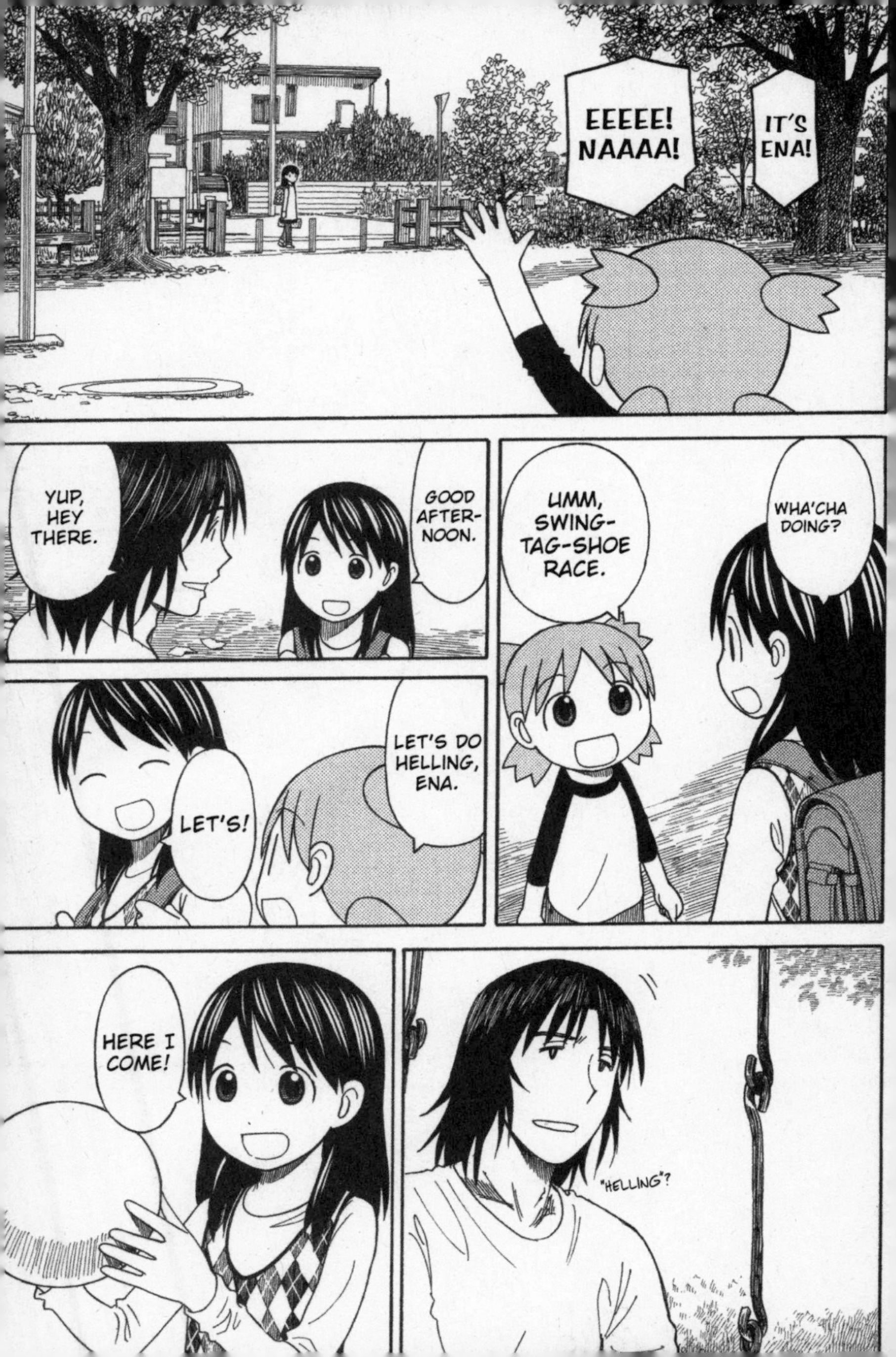
IT'S ENA!
EEEEE! NAAAA!
WHA'CHA DOING?
UMM, SWING-TAG-SHOE RACE.
GOOD AFTERNOON.
YUP, HEY THERE.
LET'S DO HELLING, ENA.
LET'S!
"HELLING"?
HERE I COME!

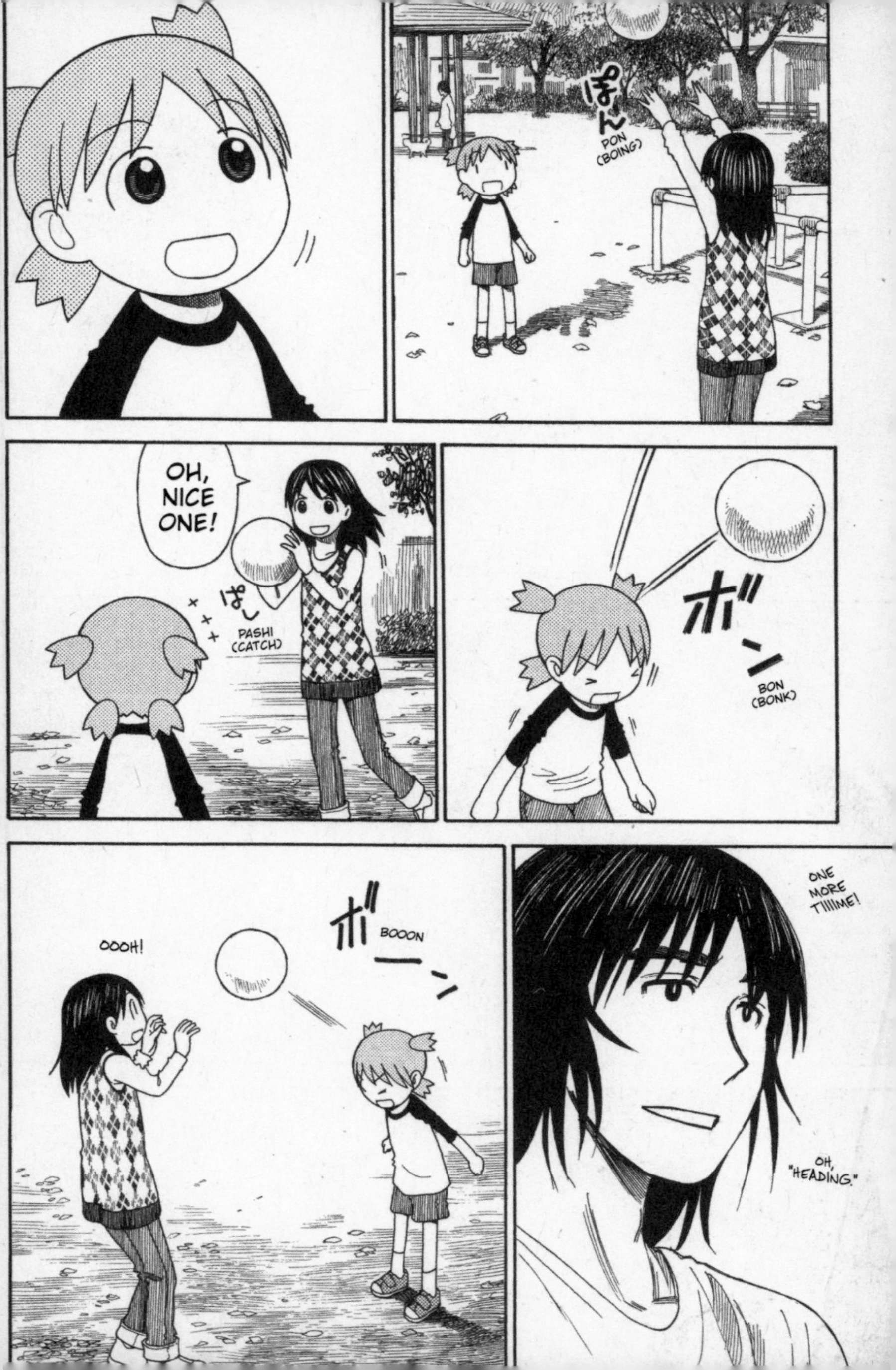
ぽん
PON (BOING)
ボン
BON (BONK)
OH, NICE ONE!
ぱし
PASHI (CATCH)
ONE MORE TIIIIME!
OH, "HEADING."
ボーン
BOOON
OOOH!

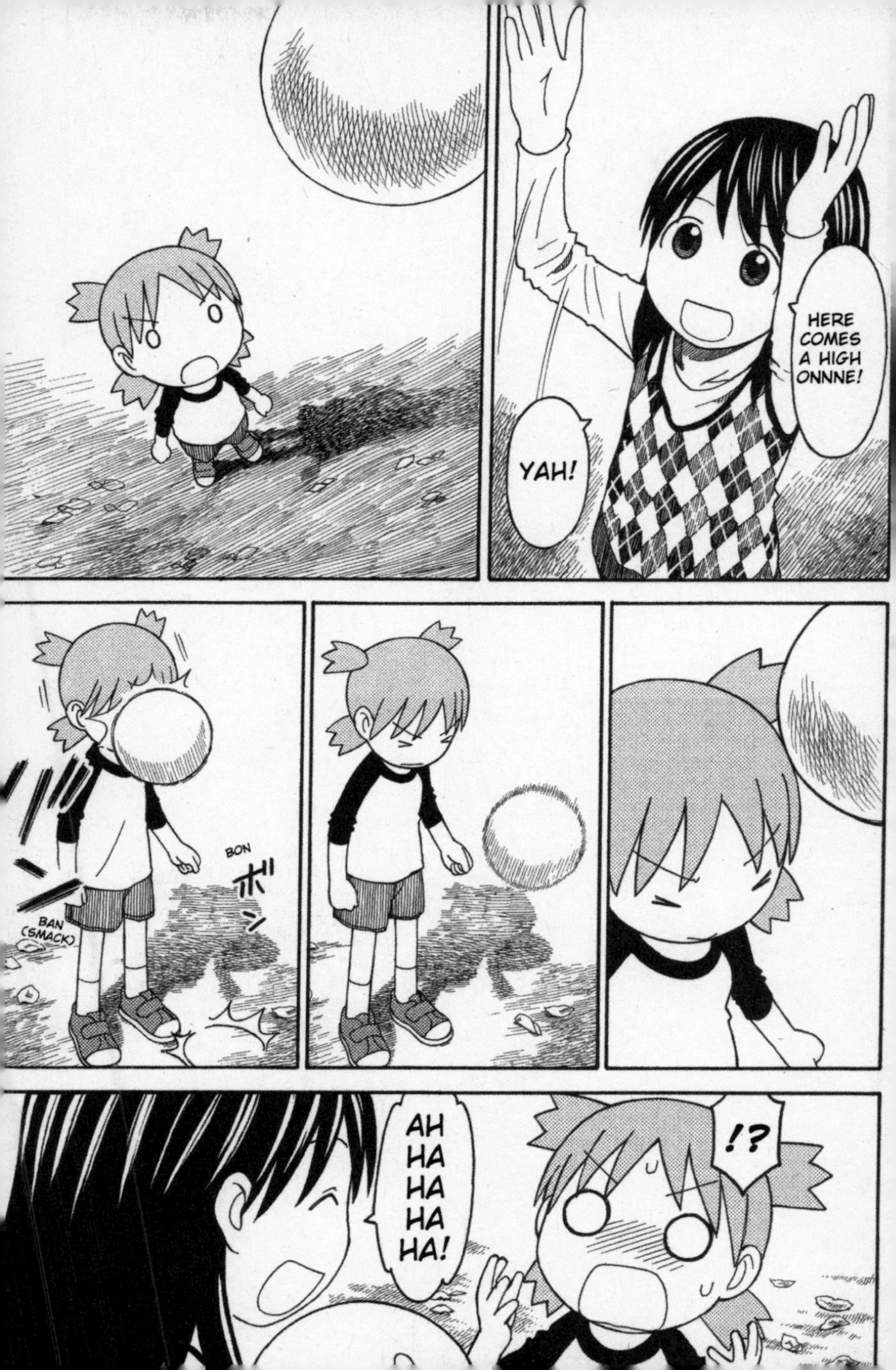
HERE COMES A HIGH ONNNE!
YAH!
BON
ボン
BAN
(SMACK)
!?
AH HA HA HA HA!

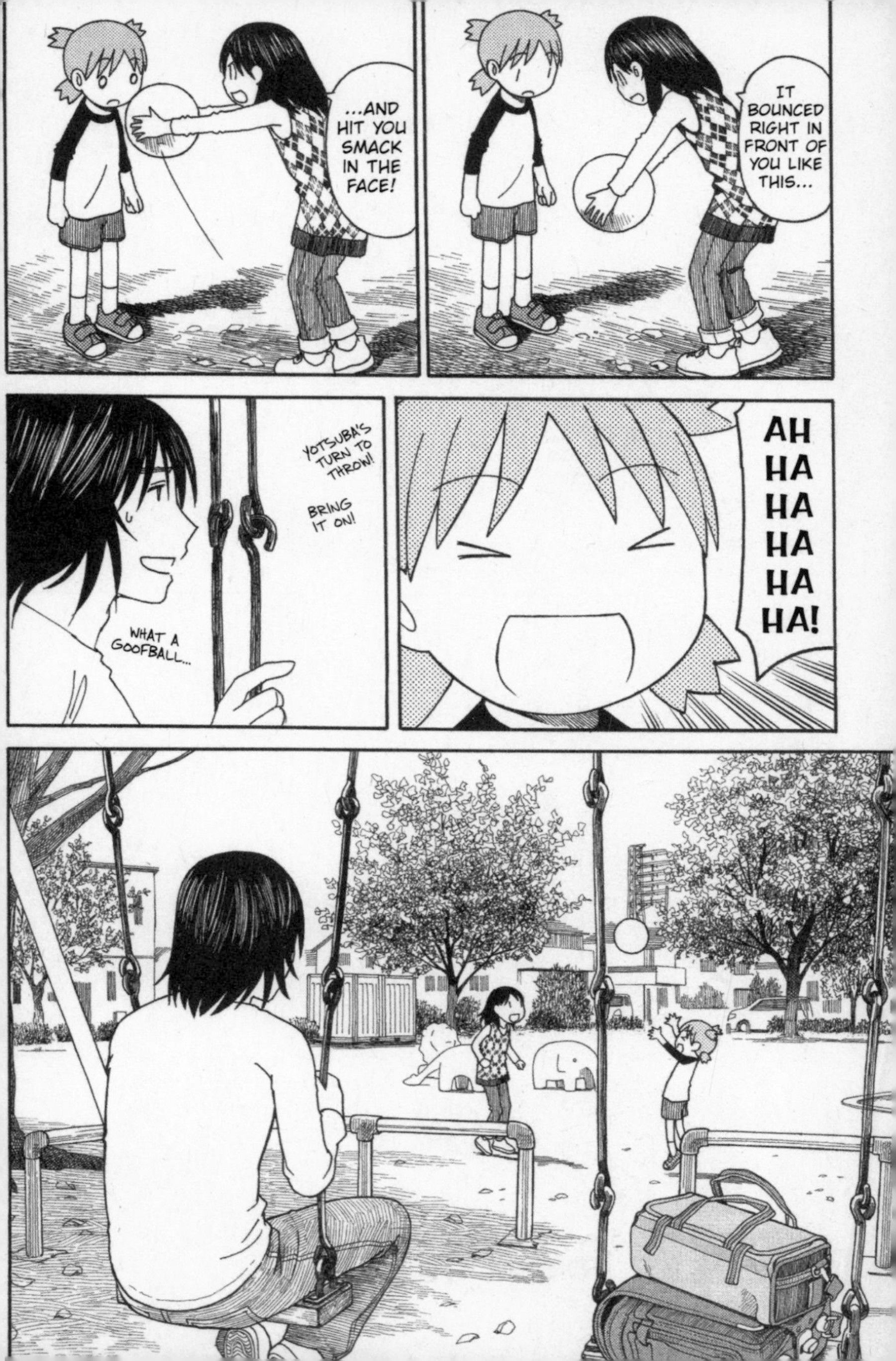
IT BOUNCED RIGHT IN FRONT OF YOU LIKE THIS...
...AND HIT YOU SMACK IN THE FACE!
AH HA HA HA HA HA!
YOTSUBA'S TURN TO THROW!
BRING IT ON!
WHAT A GOOFBALL...

YOTSUBA&!

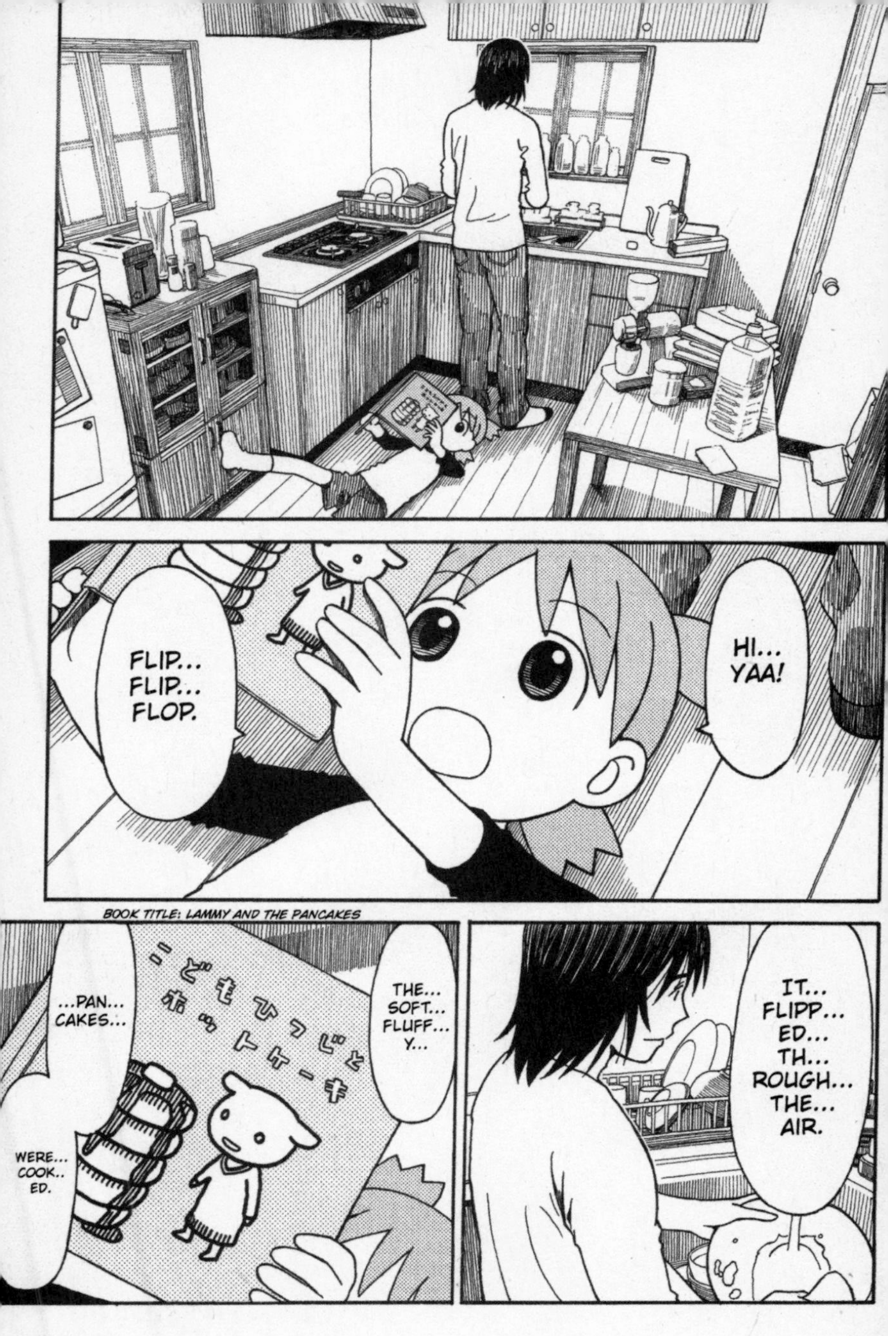
HI... YAA!
FLIP... FLIP... FLOP.
BOOK TITLE: LAMMY AND THE PANCAKES
IT... FLIPP... ED... TH... ROUGH... THE... AIR.
THE... SOFT... FLUFF... Y...
こどもひつじと ホットケーキ
...PAN... CAKES...
WERE... COOK.. ED.

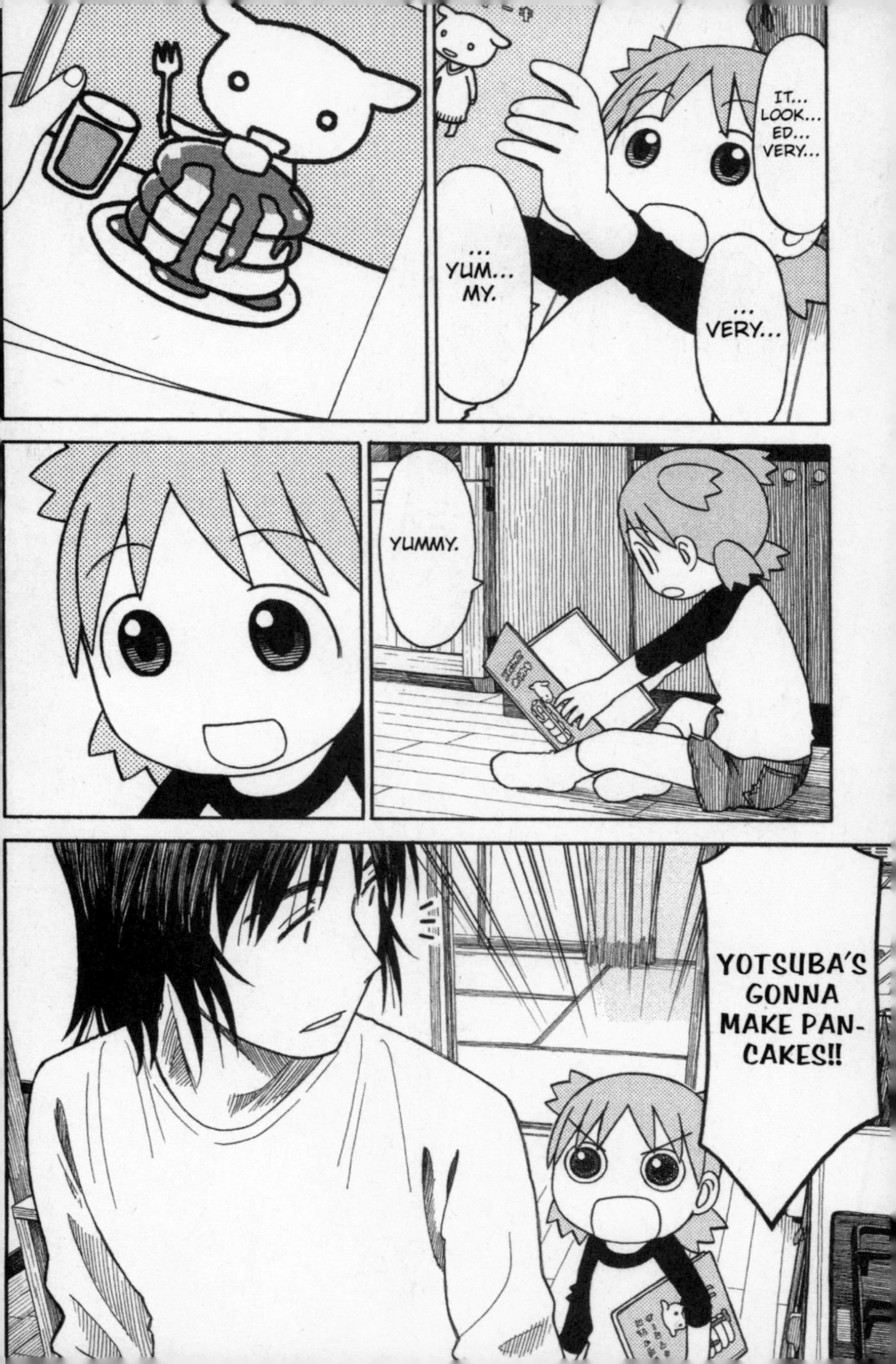
IT... LOOK... ED... VERY...
... VERY...
... YUM... MY.
YUMMY.
YOTSUBA'S GONNA MAKE PAN-CAKES!!

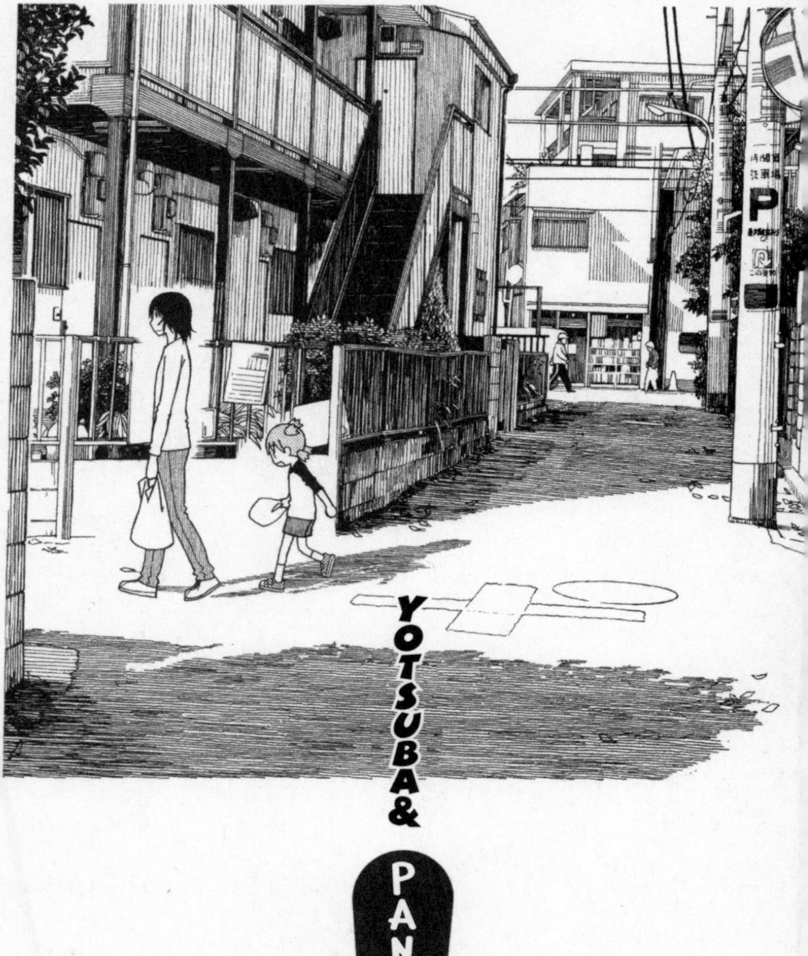

YOTSUBA & PANCAKES!

#64

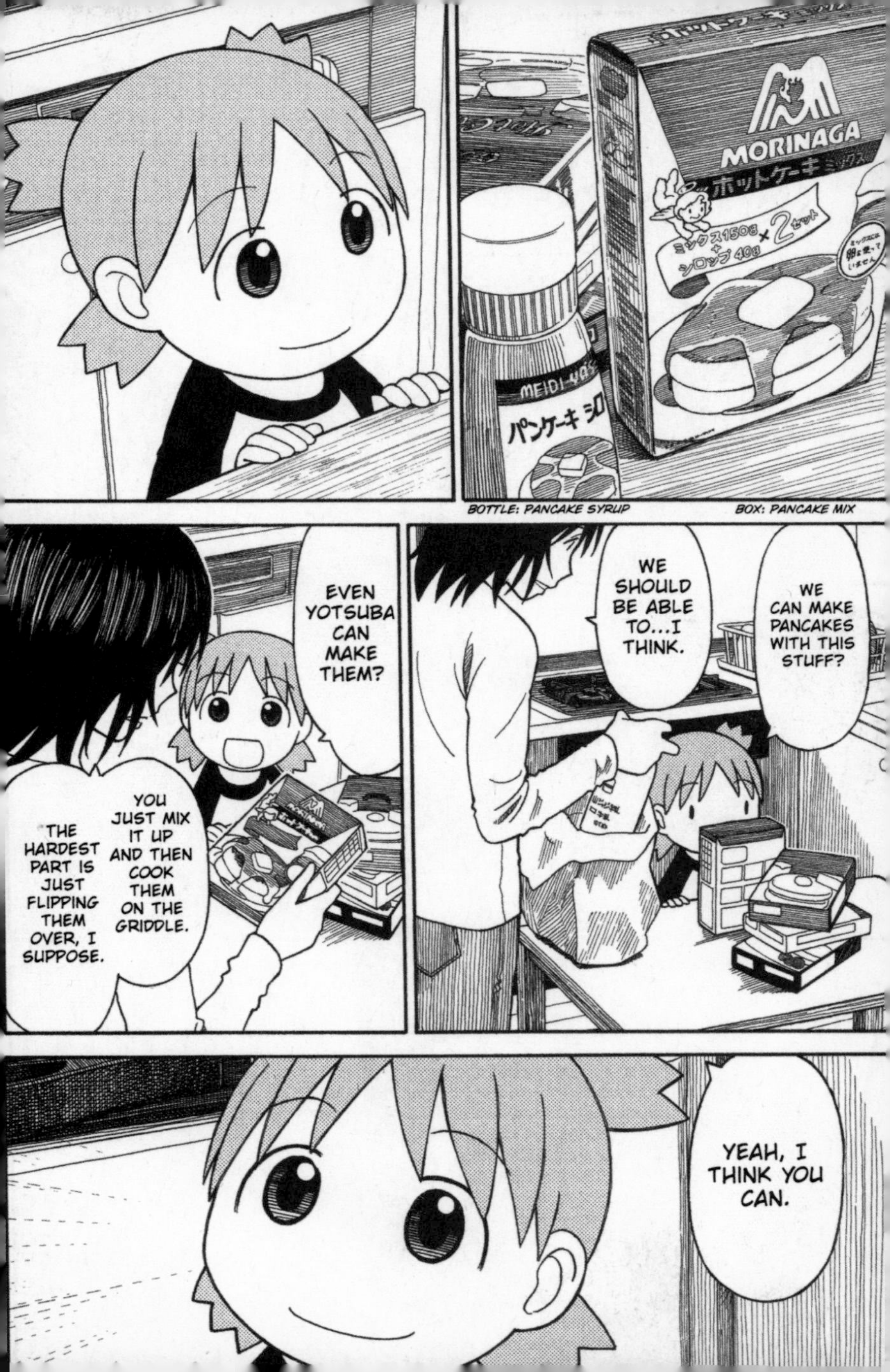
MORINAGA
MEIDI-YA
パンケーキ シロ
BOX: PANCAKE MIX
BOTTLE: PANCAKE SYRUP
WE CAN MAKE PANCAKES WITH THIS STUFF?
WE SHOULD BE ABLE TO...I THINK.
EVEN YOTSUBA CAN MAKE THEM?
YOU JUST MIX IT UP AND THEN COOK THEM ON THE GRIDDLE.
THE HARDEST PART IS JUST FLIPPING THEM OVER, I SUPPOSE.
YEAH, I THINK YOU CAN.

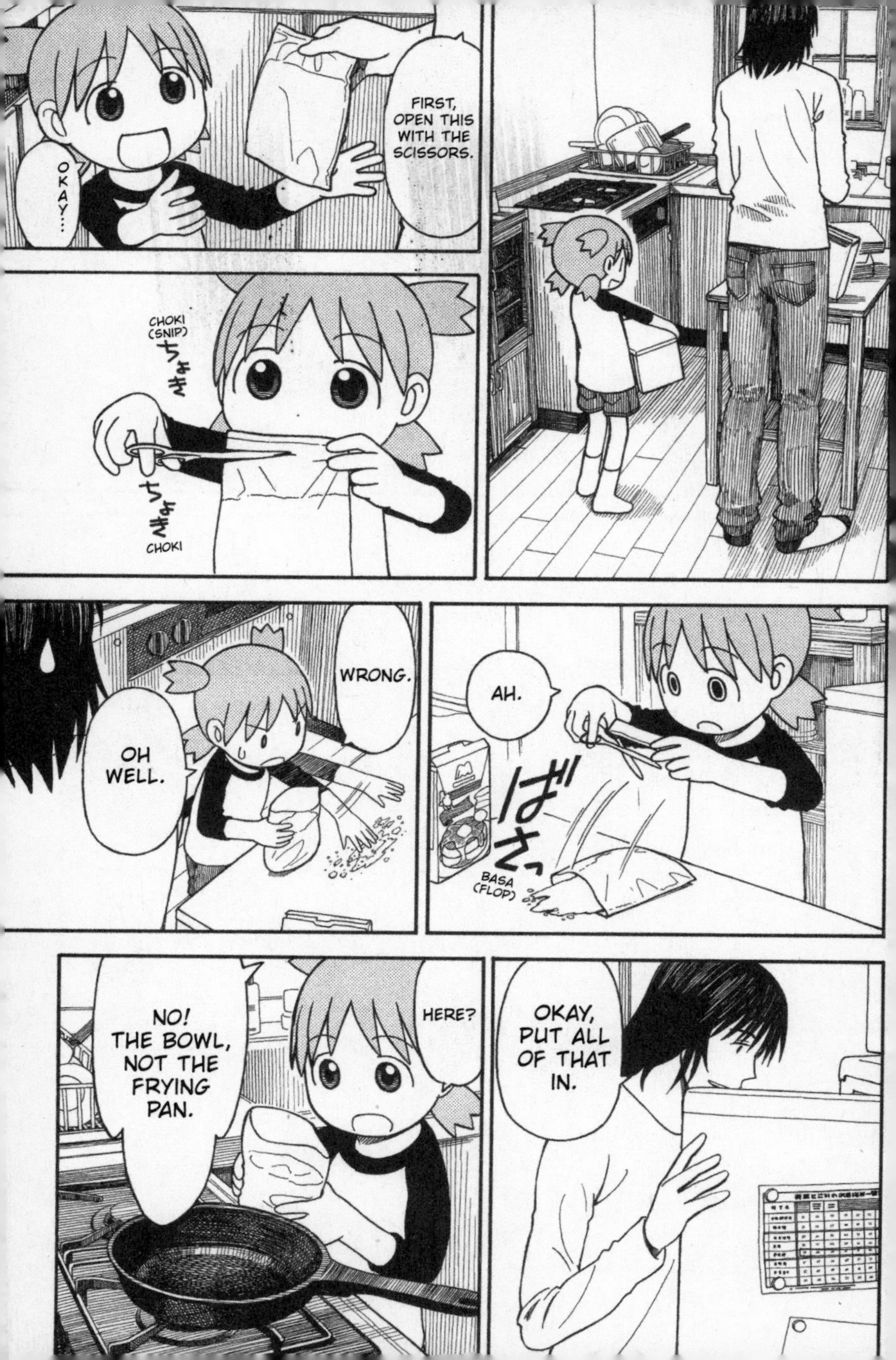
FIRST, OPEN THIS WITH THE SCISSORS.
OKAY...
ちょき
CHOKI (SNIP)
ちょき
CHOKI
AH.
ばさっ
BASA (FLOP)
WRONG.
OH WELL.
OKAY, PUT ALL OF THAT IN.
HERE?
NO! THE BOWL, NOT THE FRYING PAN.

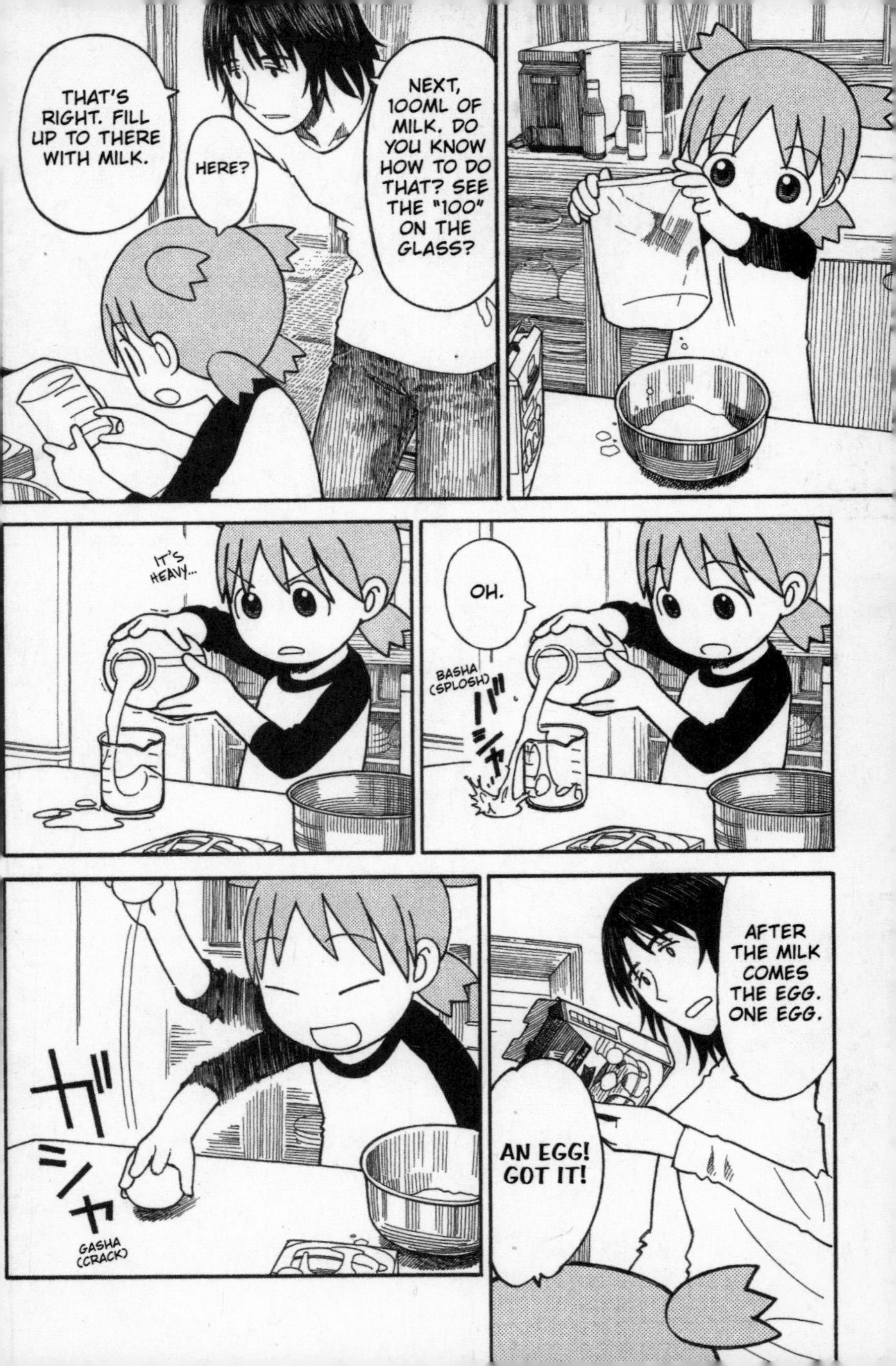
NEXT, 100ML OF MILK. DO YOU KNOW HOW TO DO THAT? SEE THE "100" ON THE GLASS?
HERE?
THAT'S RIGHT. FILL UP TO THERE WITH MILK.
OH.
バシャ
BASHA (SPLOSH)
IT'S HEAVY...
AFTER THE MILK COMES THE EGG. ONE EGG.
AN EGG! GOT IT!
ガシャ
GASHA (CRACK)

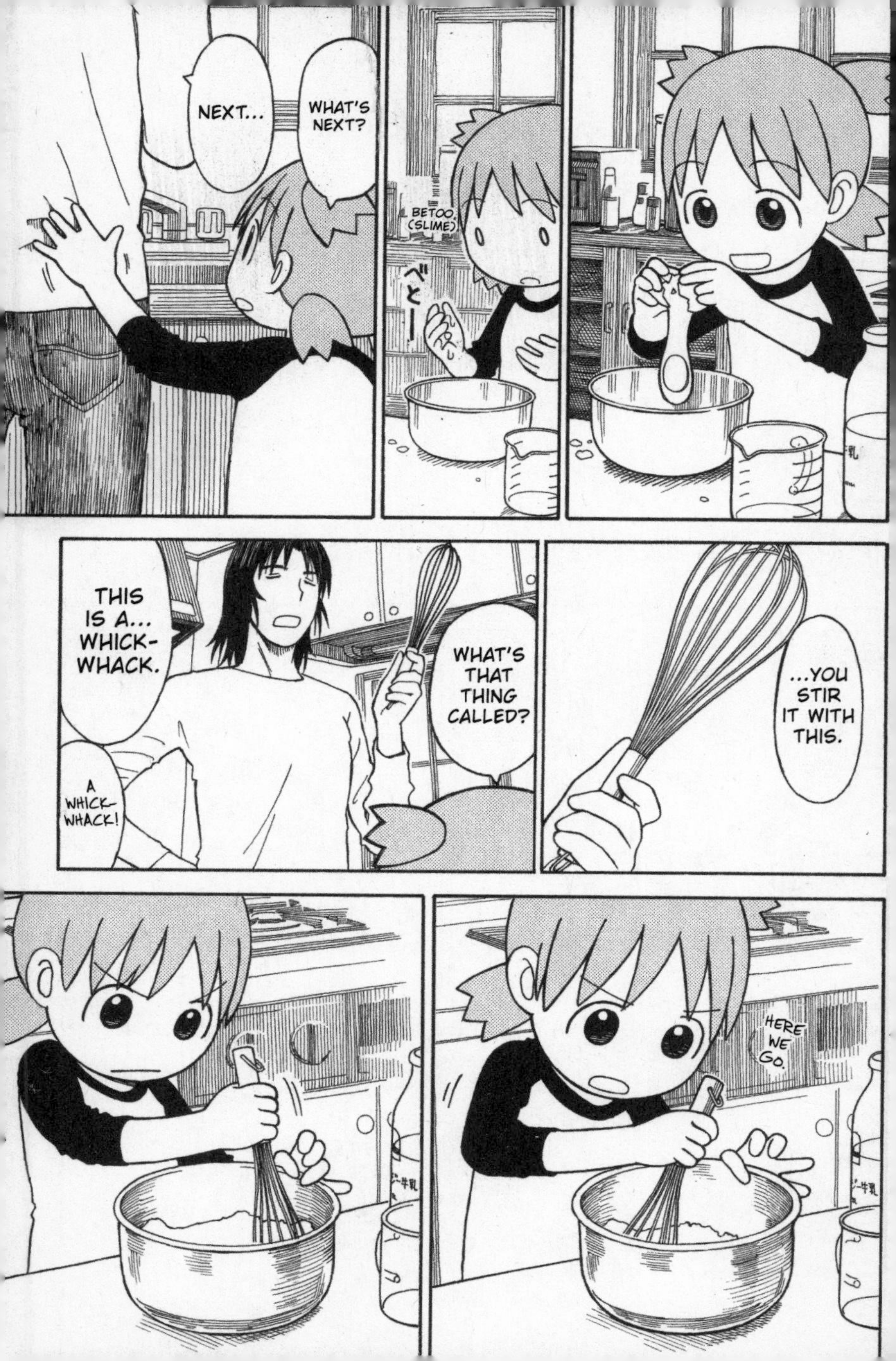
BETOO (SLIME)
べとー
WHAT'S NEXT?
NEXT...
...YOU STIR IT WITH THIS.
WHAT'S THAT THING CALLED?
THIS IS A... WHICK-WHACK.
A WHICK-WHACK!
HERE WE GO.

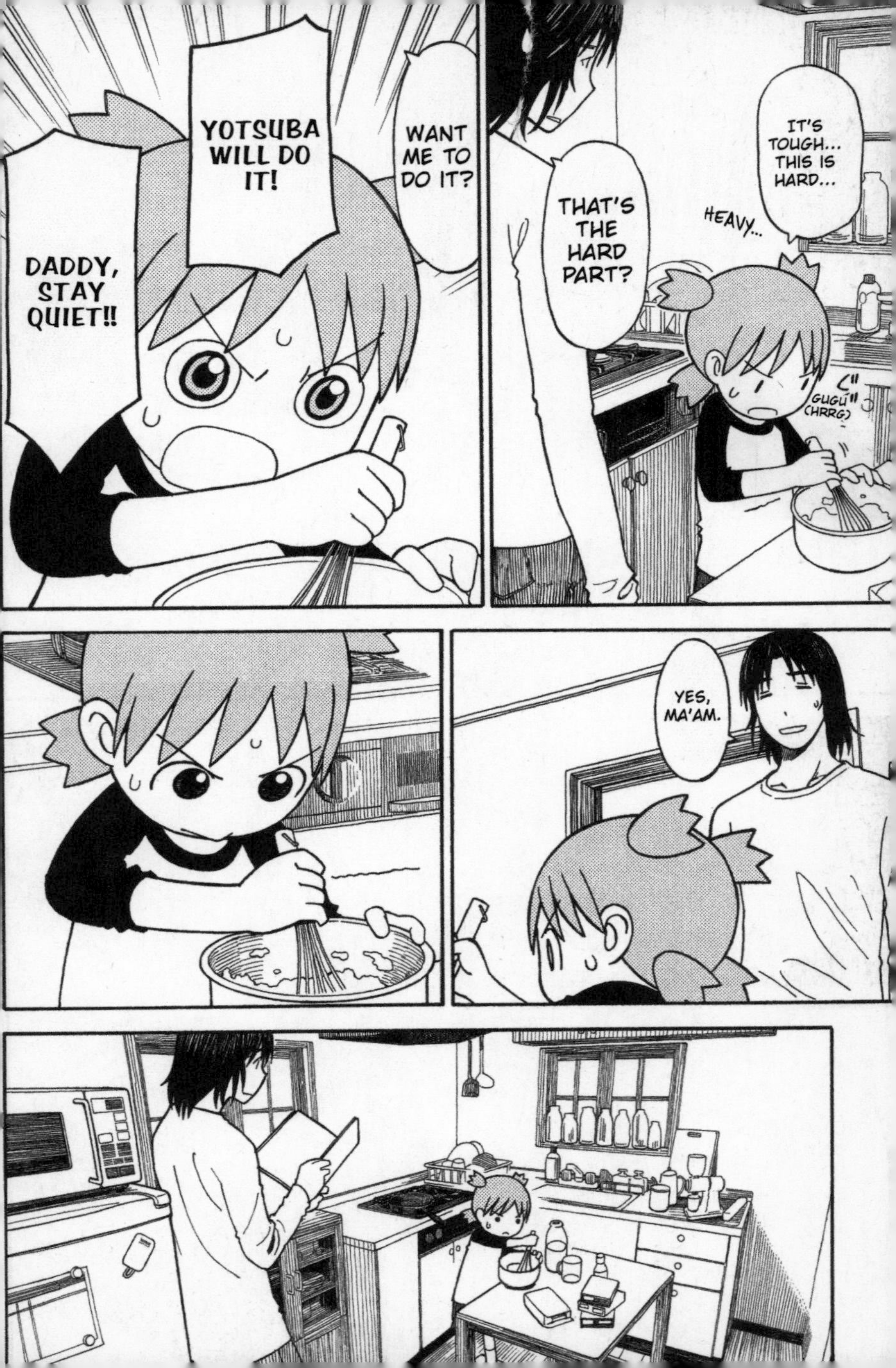
IT'S TOUGH... THIS IS HARD...
HEAVY...
GUGU (HRRG)
THAT'S THE HARD PART?
WANT ME TO DO IT?
YOTSUBA WILL DO IT!
DADDY, STAY QUIET!!
YES, MA'AM.

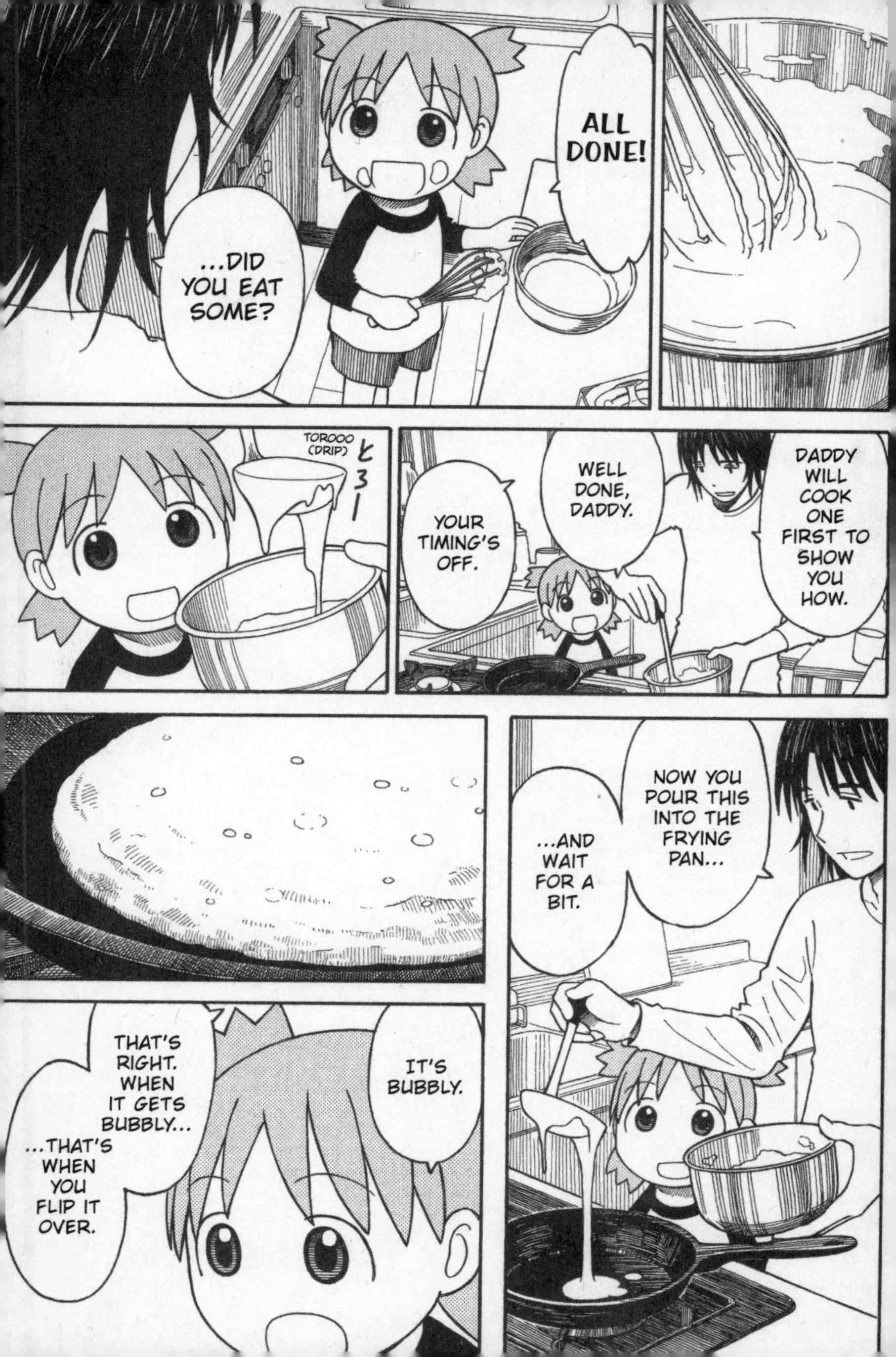
ALL DONE!
...DID YOU EAT SOME?
DADDY WILL COOK ONE FIRST TO SHOW YOU HOW.
WELL DONE, DADDY.
YOUR TIMING'S OFF.
とろー
TOROOO (DRIP)
NOW YOU POUR THIS INTO THE FRYING PAN...
...AND WAIT FOR A BIT.
IT'S BUBBLY.
THAT'S RIGHT. WHEN IT GETS BUBBLY...
...THAT'S WHEN YOU FLIP IT OVER.

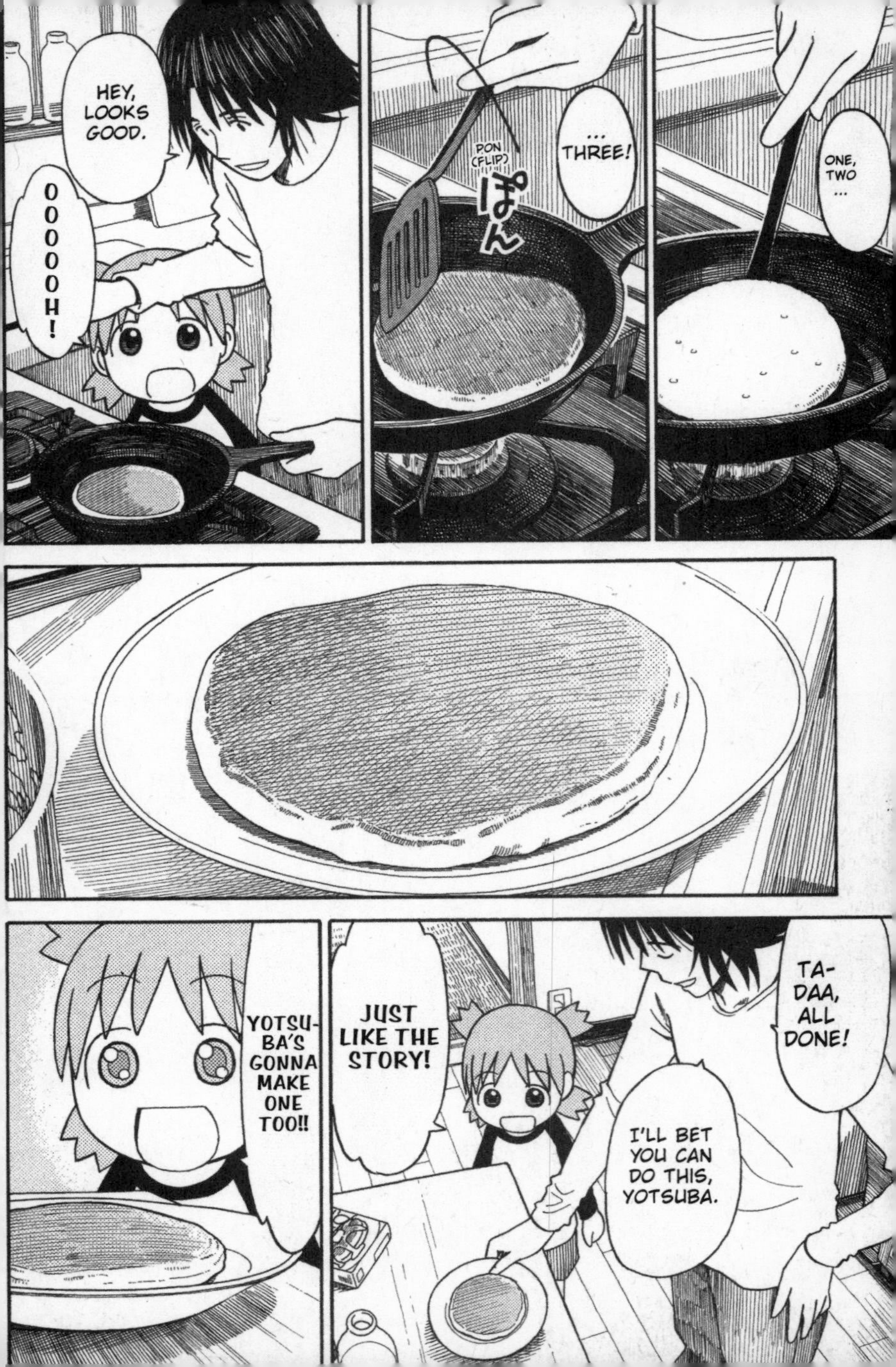
ONE, TWO ...
... THREE!
PON (FLIP)
ぽん
HEY, LOOKS GOOD.
OOOOOOH!
TA-DAA, ALL DONE!
I'LL BET YOU CAN DO THIS, YOTSUBA.
JUST LIKE THE STORY!
YOTSU-BA'S GONNA MAKE ONE TOO!!

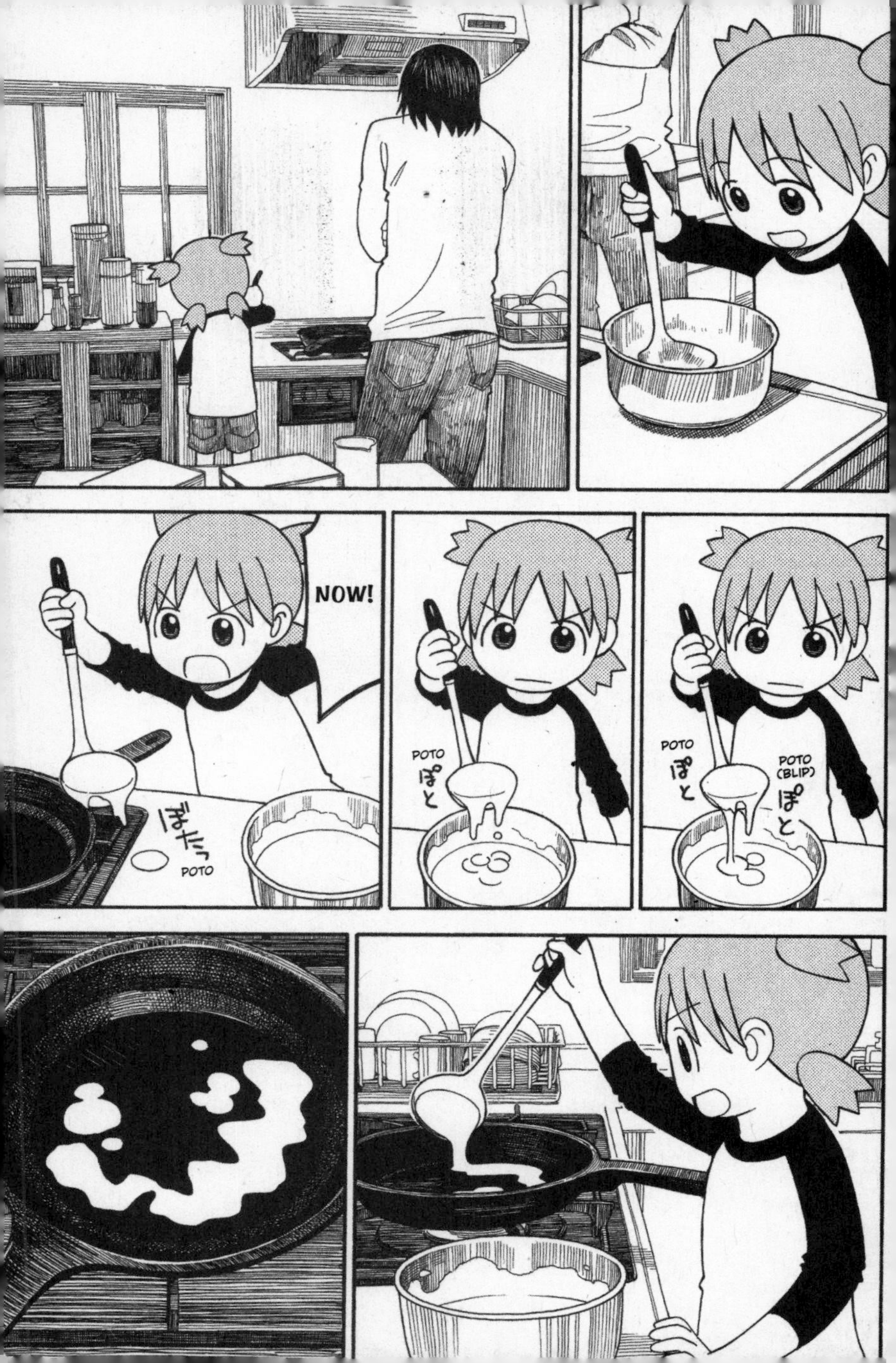

POTO (BLIP)
ぽと
POTO
ぽと
POTO
ぽと
NOW!
ぽたっ
POTO

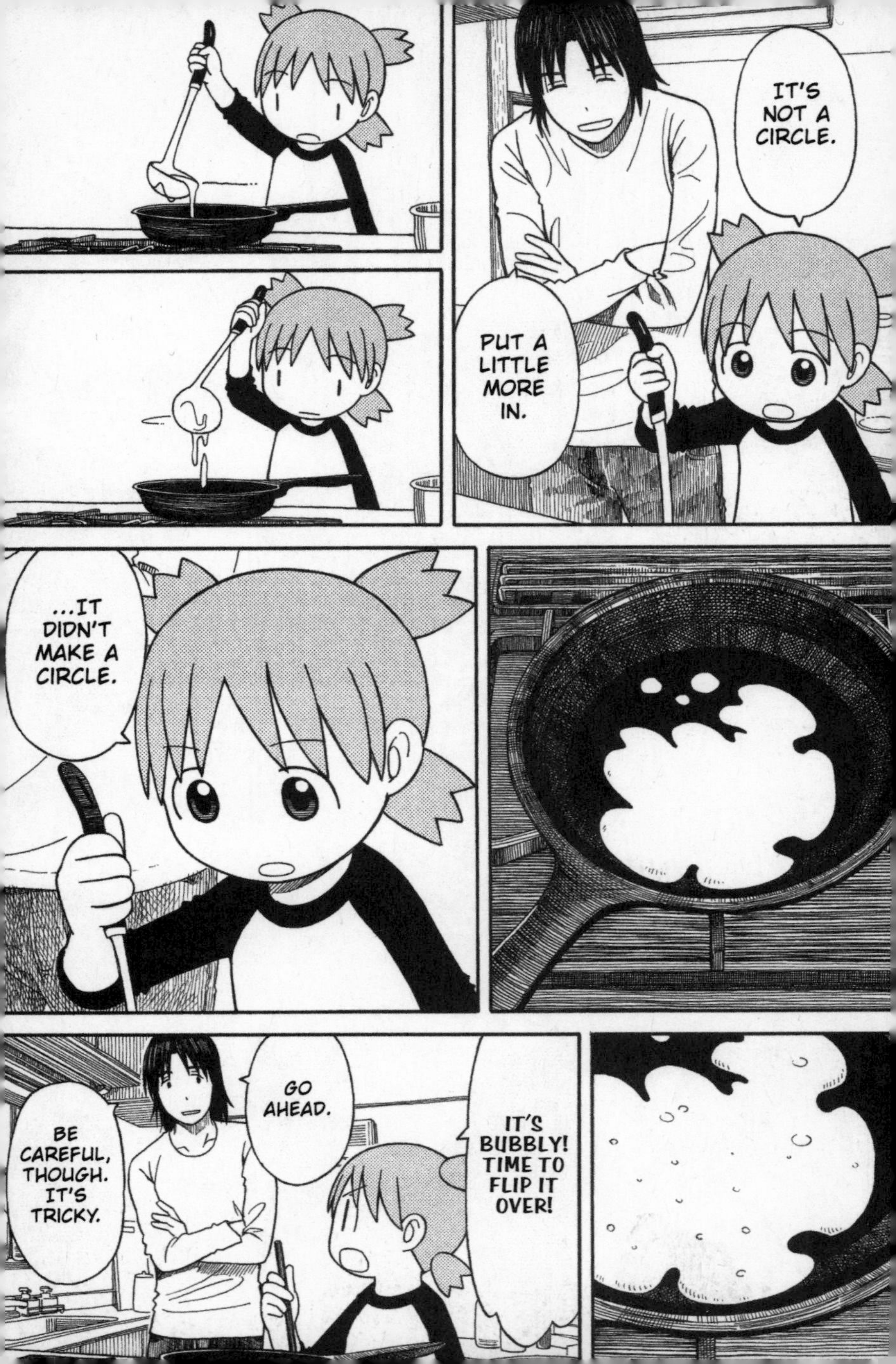
IT'S NOT A CIRCLE.
PUT A LITTLE MORE IN.
...IT DIDN'T MAKE A CIRCLE.
IT'S BUBBLY! TIME TO FLIP IT OVER!
GO AHEAD.
BE CAREFUL, THOUGH. IT'S TRICKY.

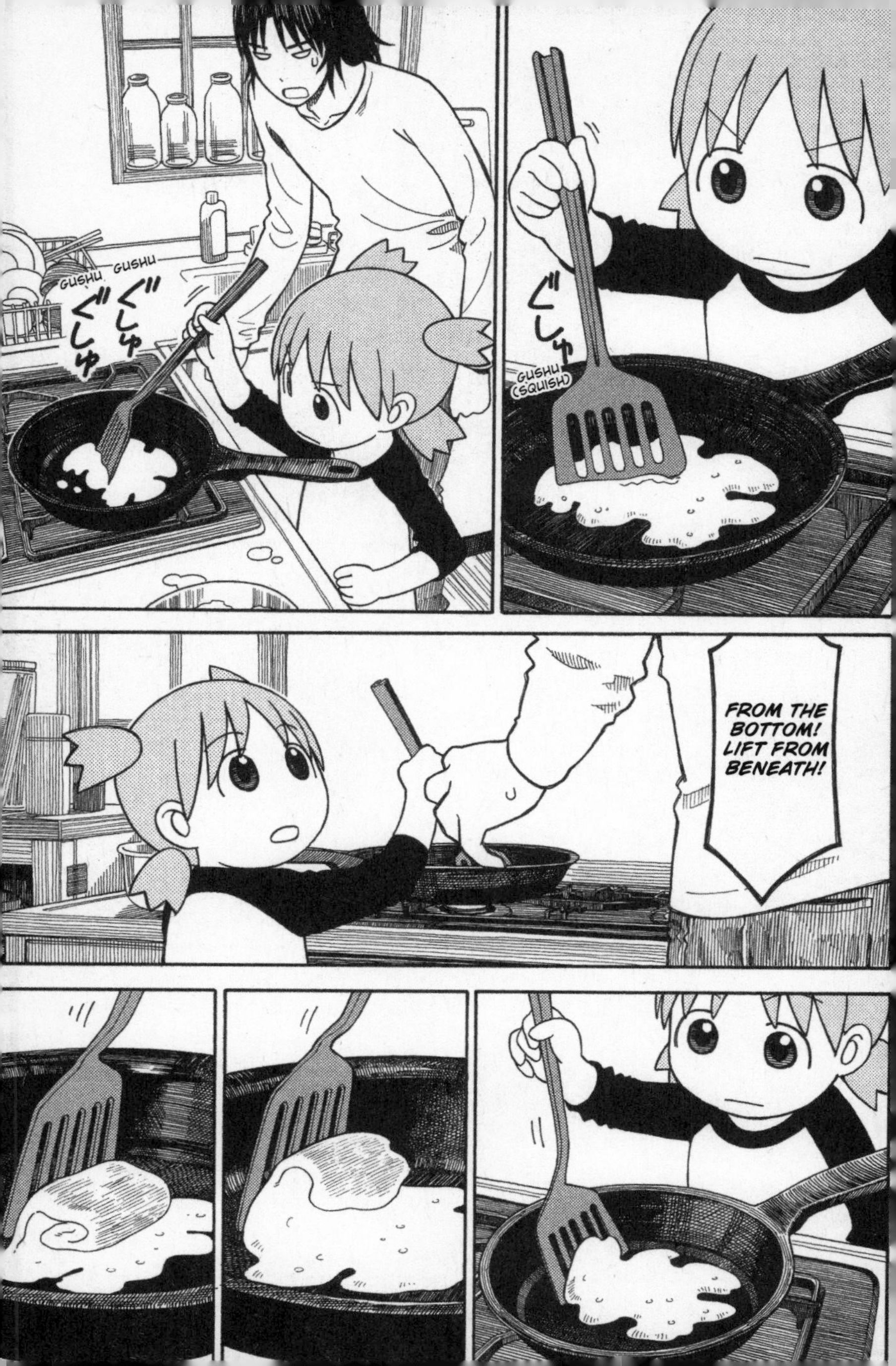
ぐしゅ
GUSHU (SQUISH)
GUSHU GUSHU
ぐしゅぐしゅ
FROM THE BOTTOM! LIFT FROM BENEATH!

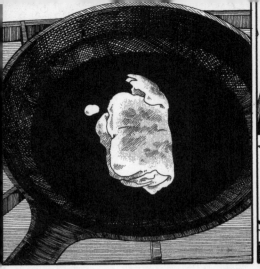

KINDA LOOKS LIKE ROLLED EGGS.

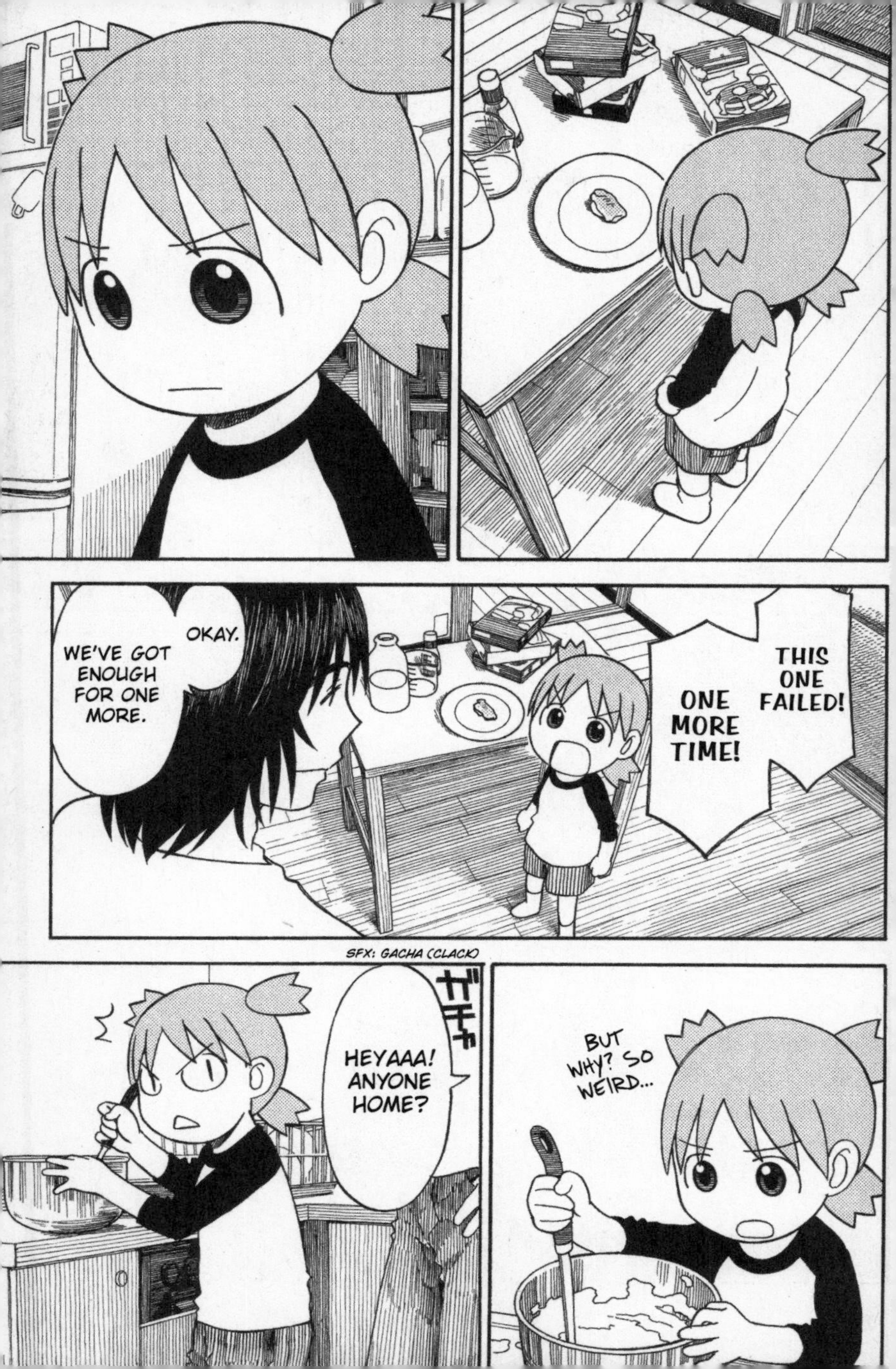
THIS ONE FAILED!
ONE MORE TIME!
OKAY.
WE'VE GOT ENOUGH FOR ONE MORE.
SFX: GACHA (CLACK)
BUT WHY? SO WEIRD...
ガチャ
HEYAAA! ANYONE HOME?

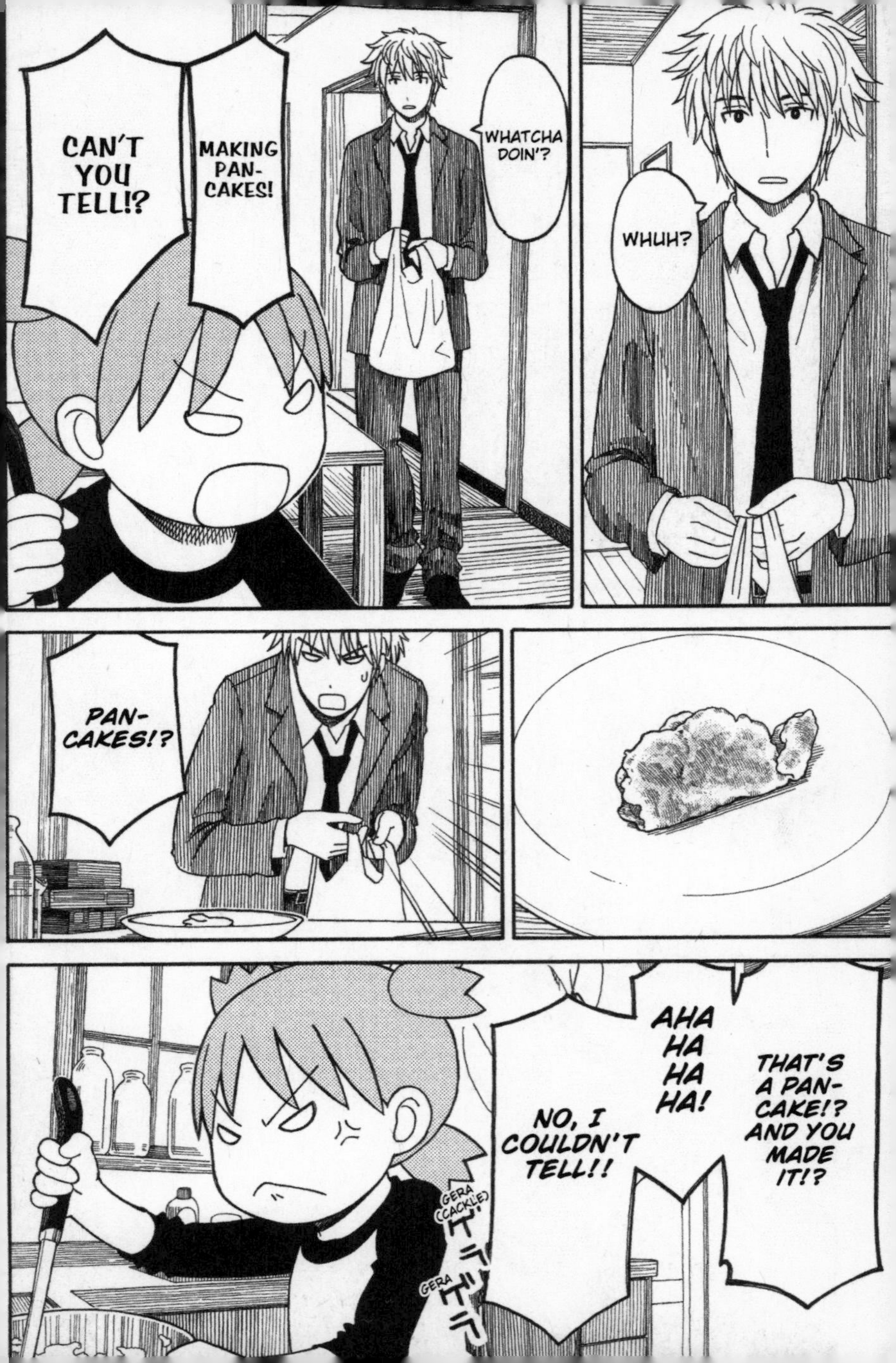
WHUH?
WHATCHA DOIN'?
MAKING PAN-CAKES!
CAN'T YOU TELL!?
PAN-CAKES!?
THAT'S A PAN-CAKE!? AND YOU MADE IT!?
AHA HA HA HA!
NO, I COULDN'T TELL!!
GERA (CACKLE)
GERA

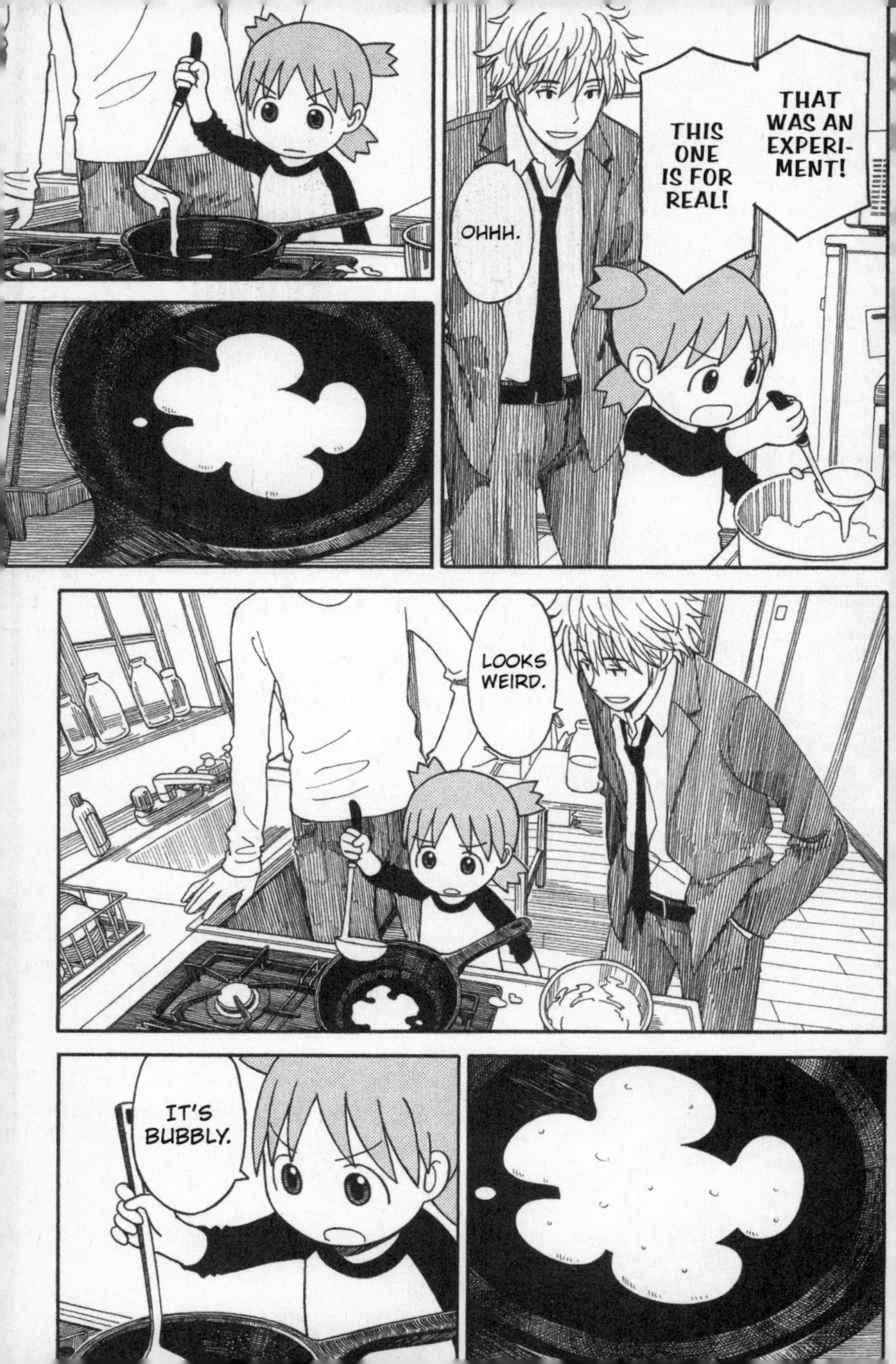
THAT WAS AN EXPERIMENT!
THIS ONE IS FOR REAL!
OHHH.
LOOKS WEIRD.
IT'S BUBBLY.

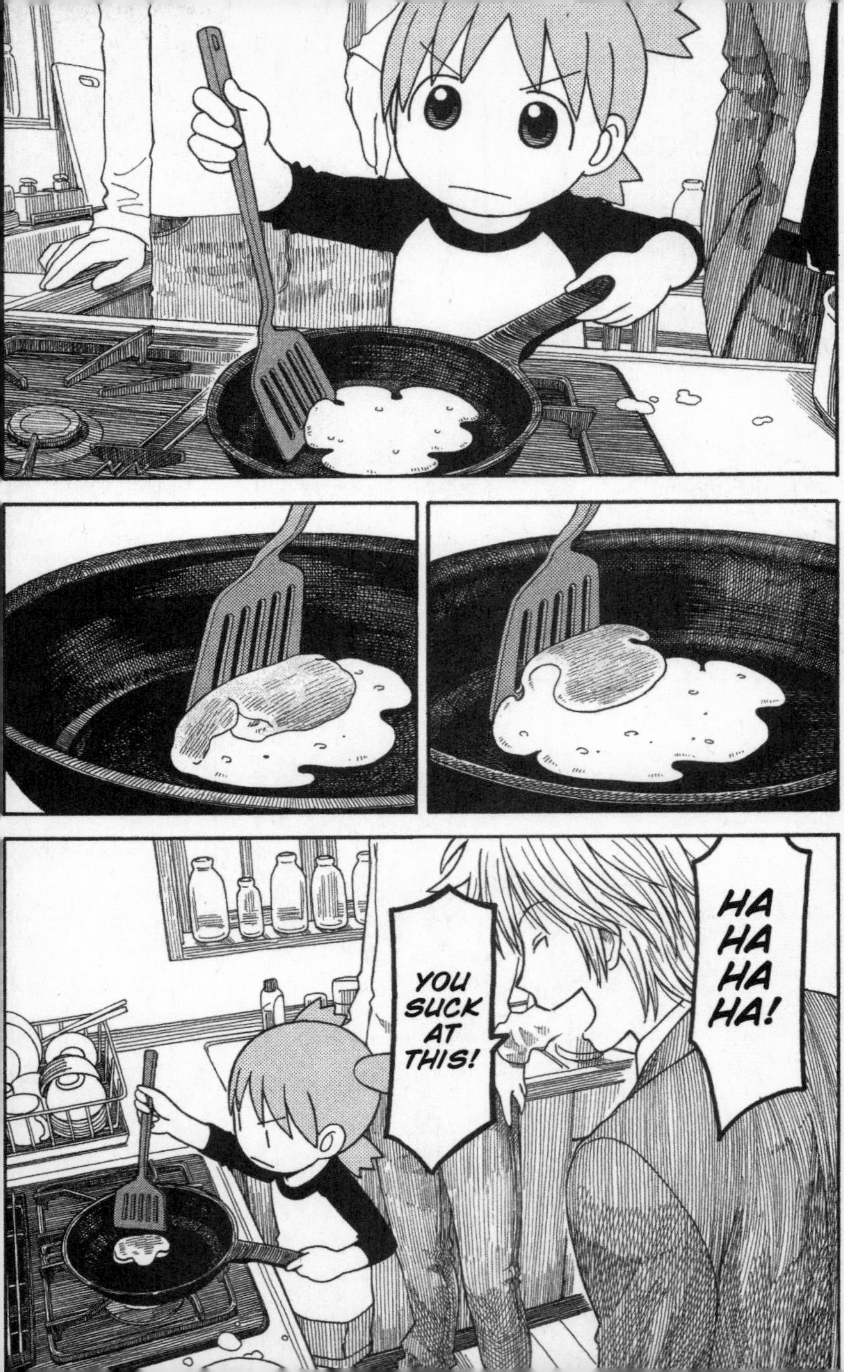
HA HA HA HA!
YOU SUCK AT THIS!

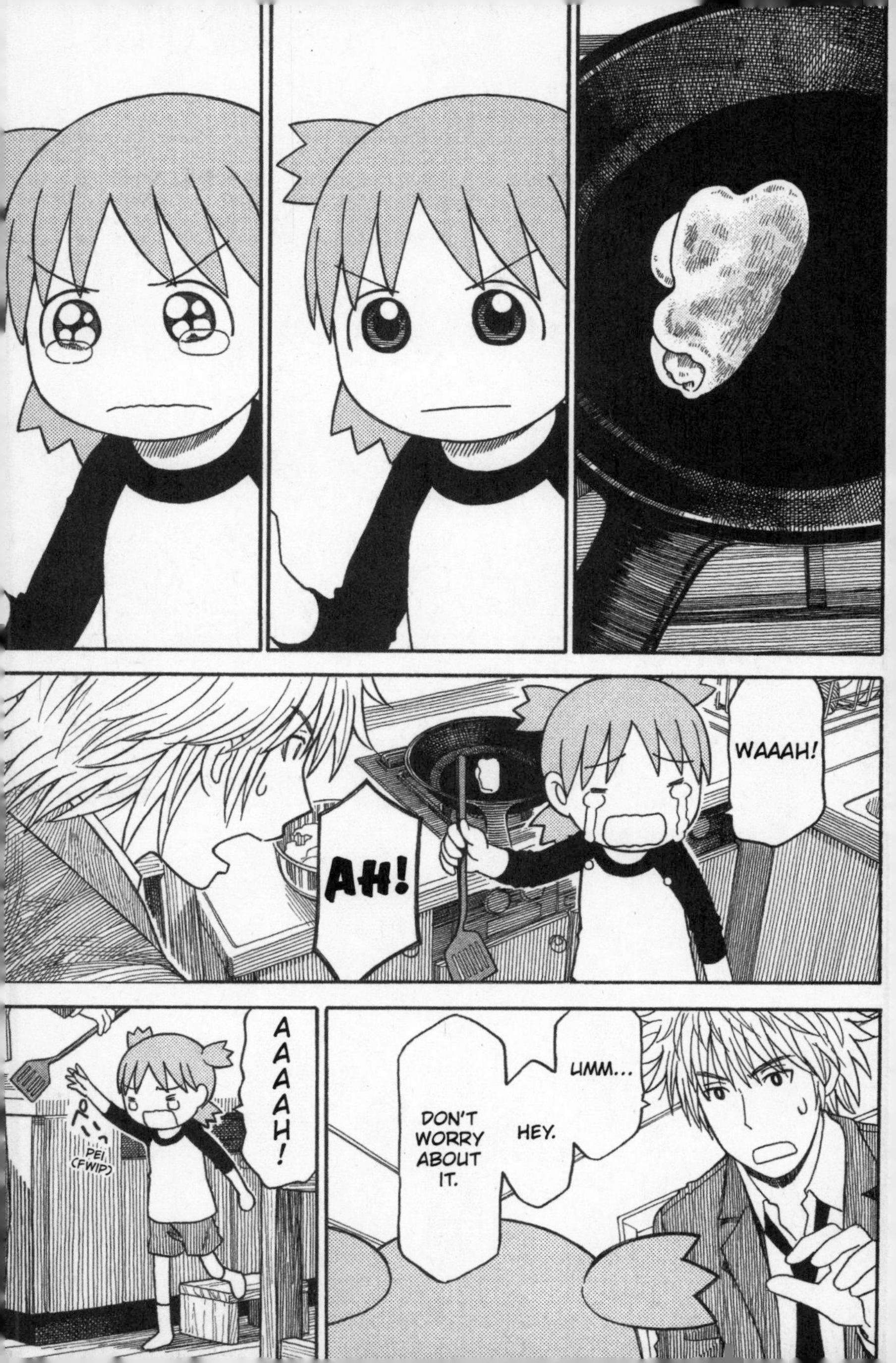
WAAAH!
AH!
UMM...
HEY.
DON'T WORRY ABOUT IT.
AAAAAH!
PEI (FWIP)

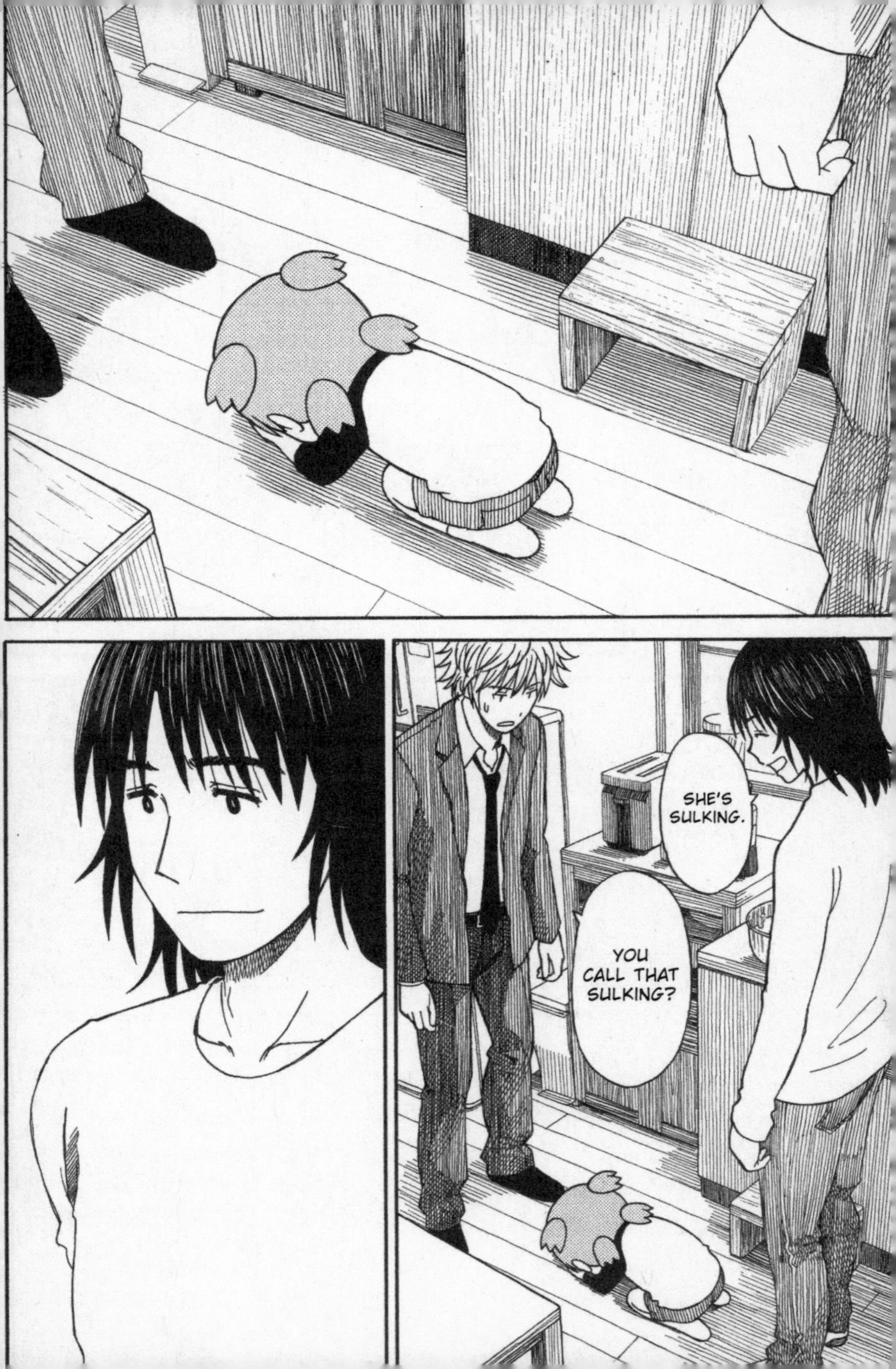
SHE'S SULKING.
YOU CALL THAT SULKING?

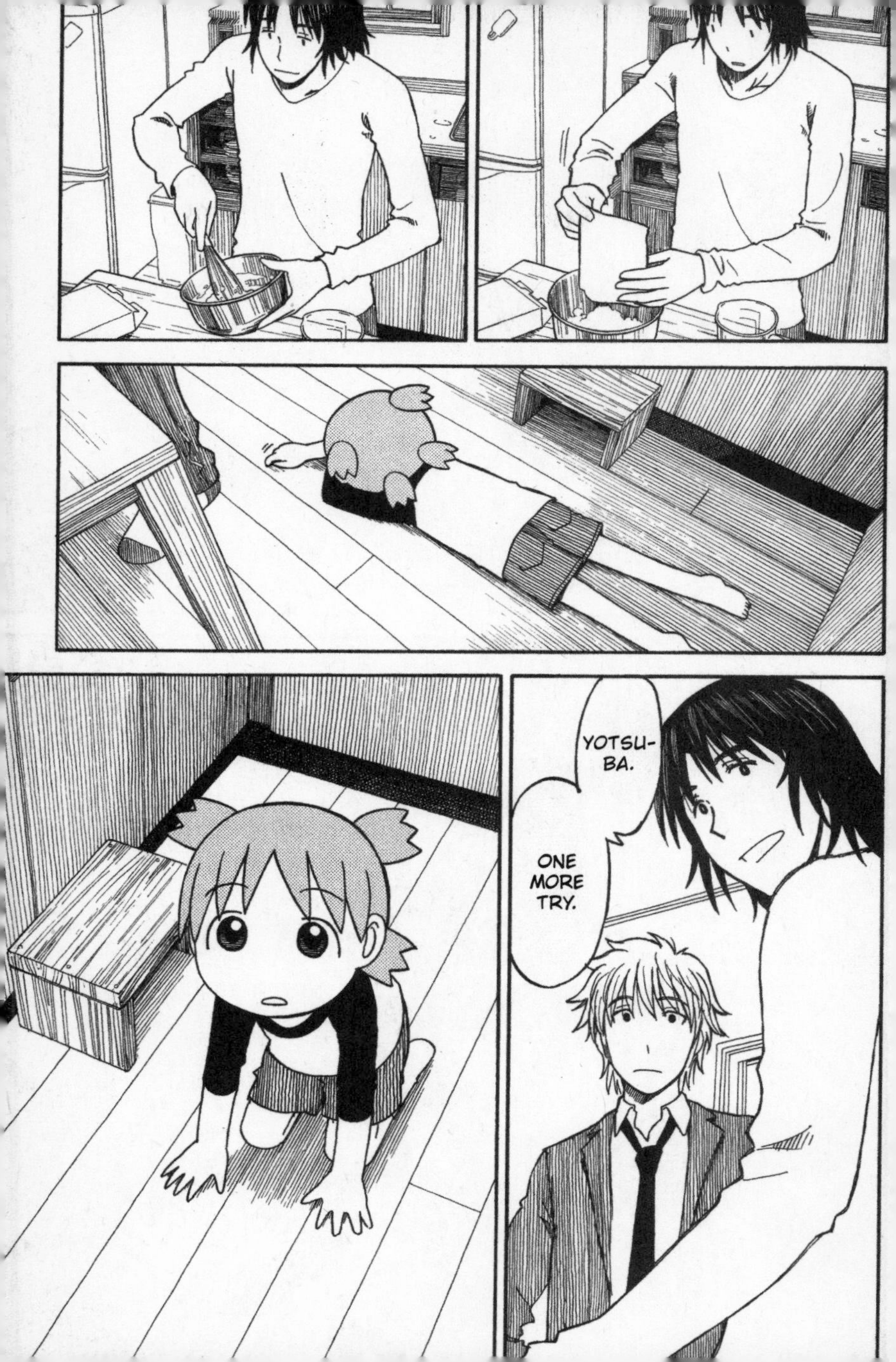
YOTSU-BA.
ONE MORE TRY.

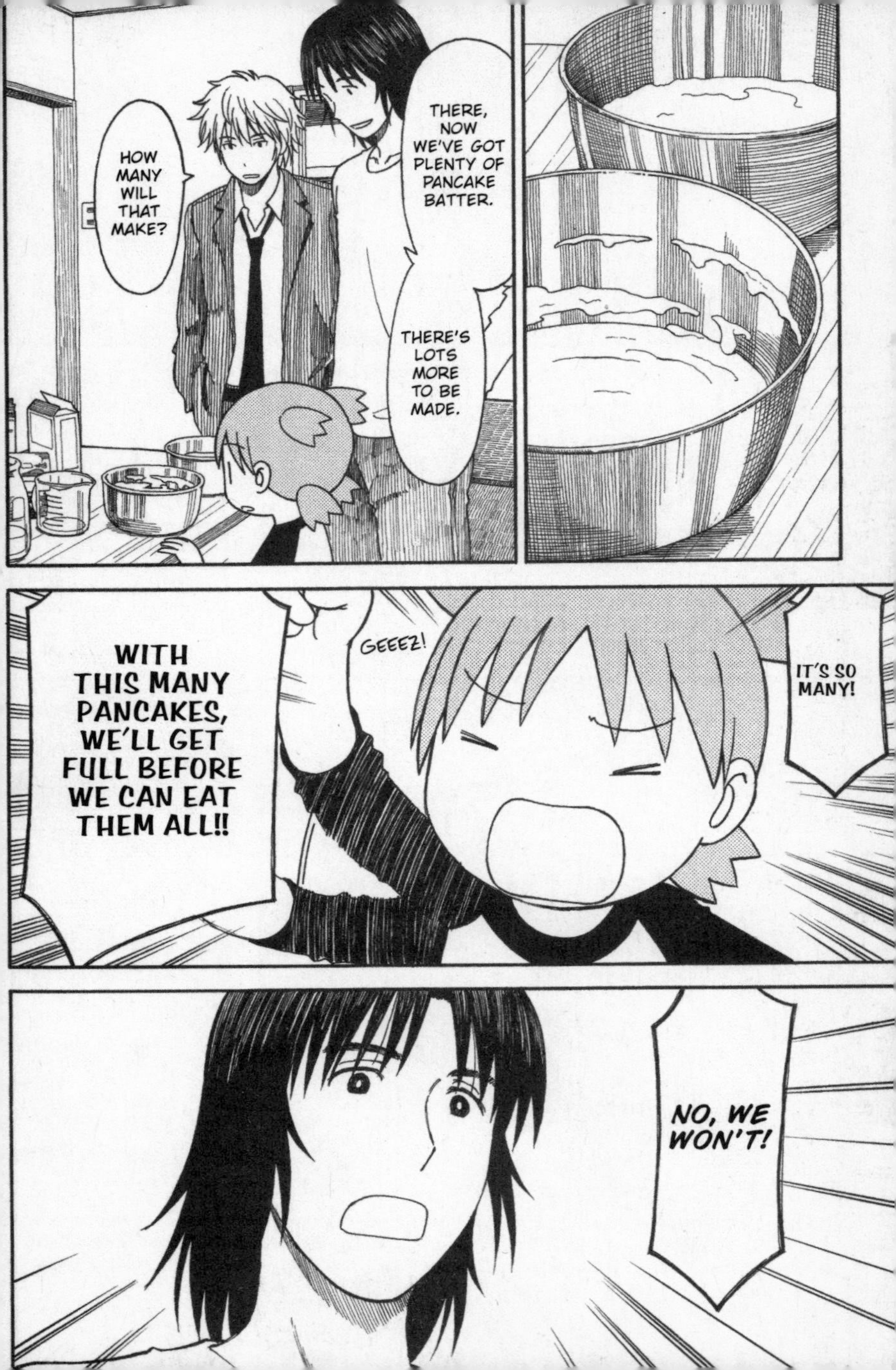
THERE, NOW WE'VE GOT PLENTY OF PANCAKE BATTER.
HOW MANY WILL THAT MAKE?
THERE'S LOTS MORE TO BE MADE.
IT'S SO MANY!
GEEEZ!
WITH THIS MANY PANCAKES, WE'LL GET FULL BEFORE WE CAN EAT THEM ALL!!
NO, WE WON'T!

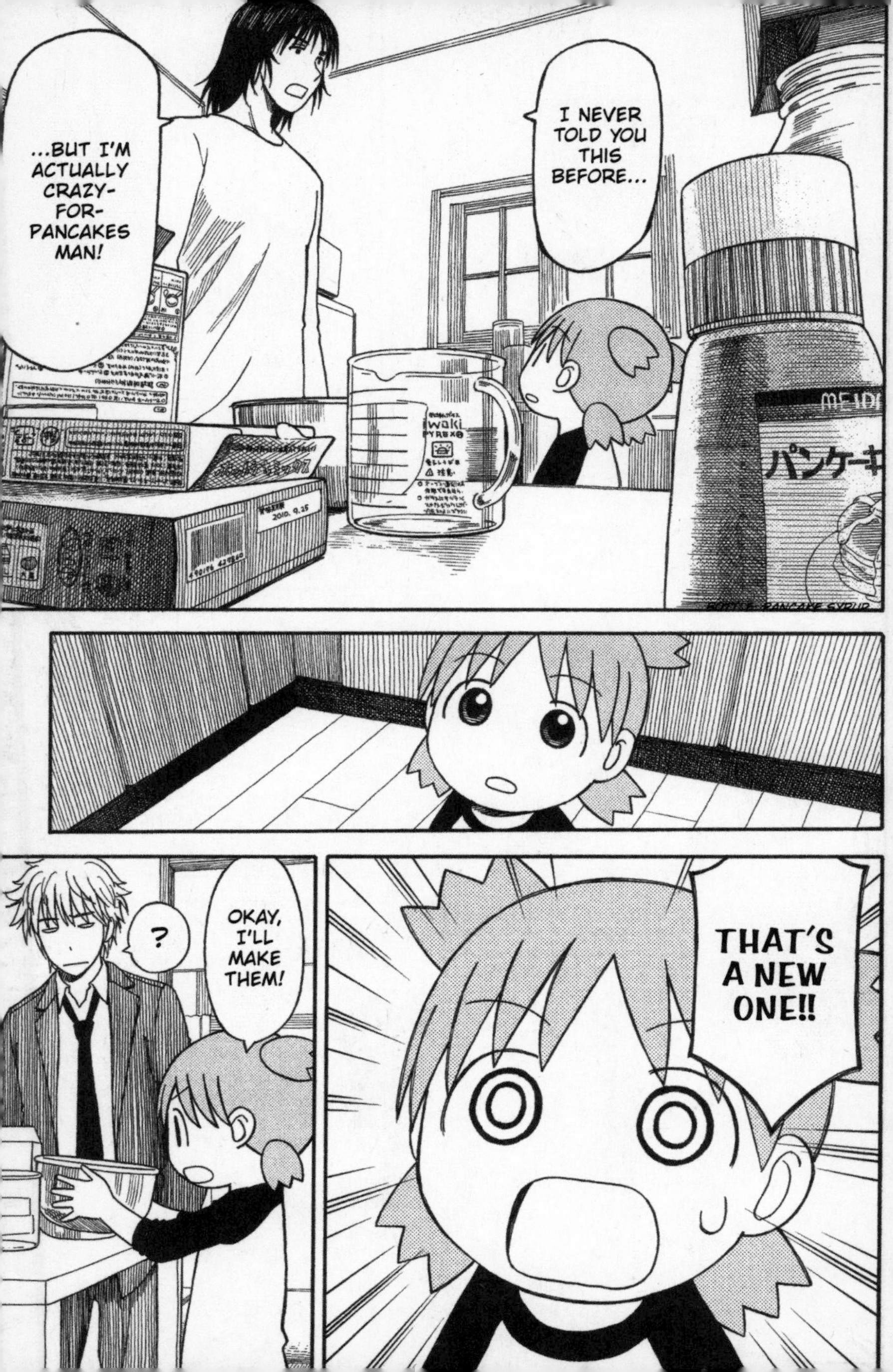

I NEVER TOLD YOU THIS BEFORE...
...BUT I'M ACTUALLY CRAZY-FOR-PANCAKES MAN!
iwaki
PYREX
BOTTLE: PANCAKE SYRUP
THAT'S A NEW ONE!!
OKAY, I'LL MAKE THEM!
?

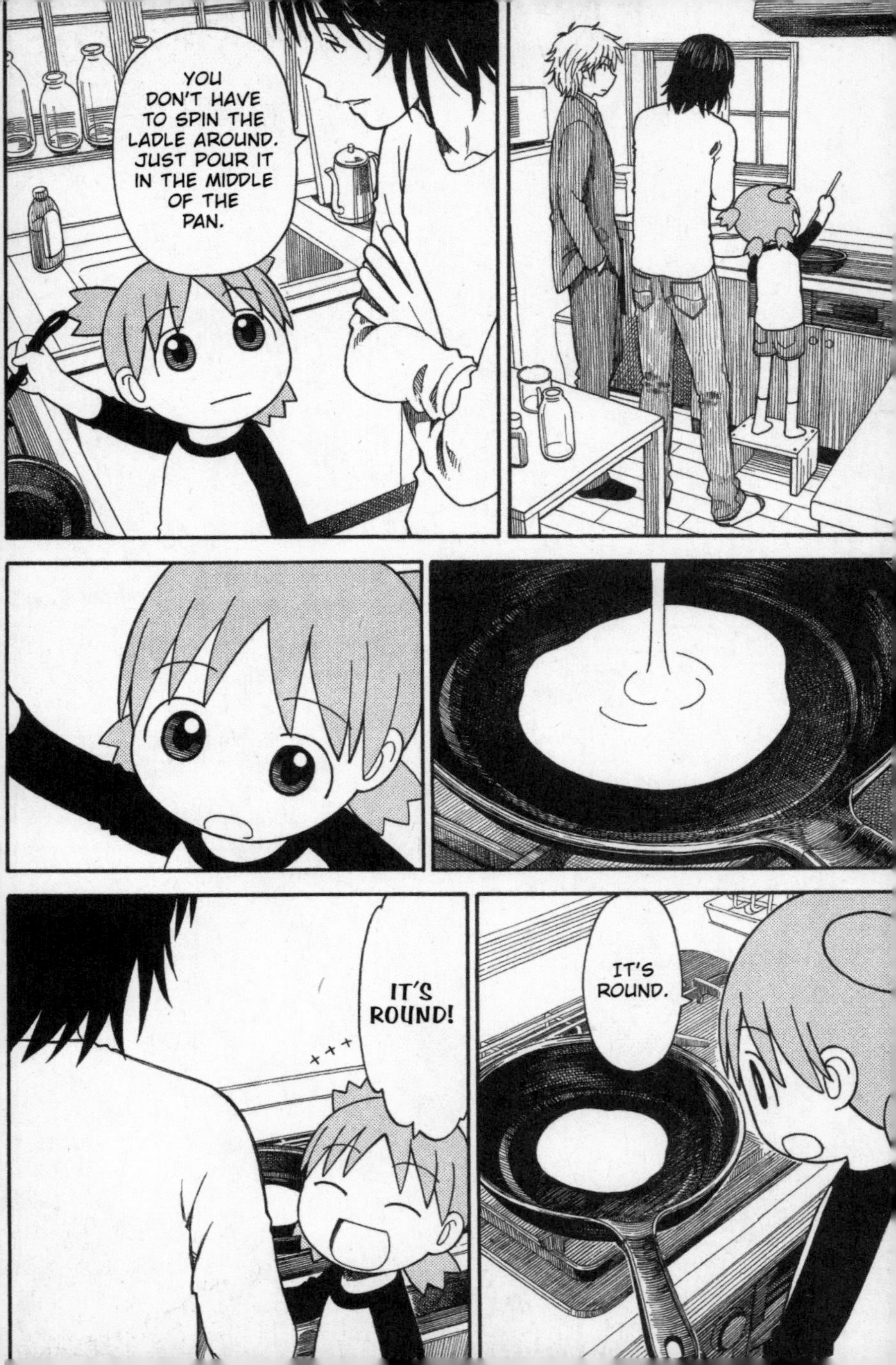
YOU DON'T HAVE TO SPIN THE LADLE AROUND. JUST POUR IT IN THE MIDDLE OF THE PAN.
IT'S ROUND.
IT'S ROUND!

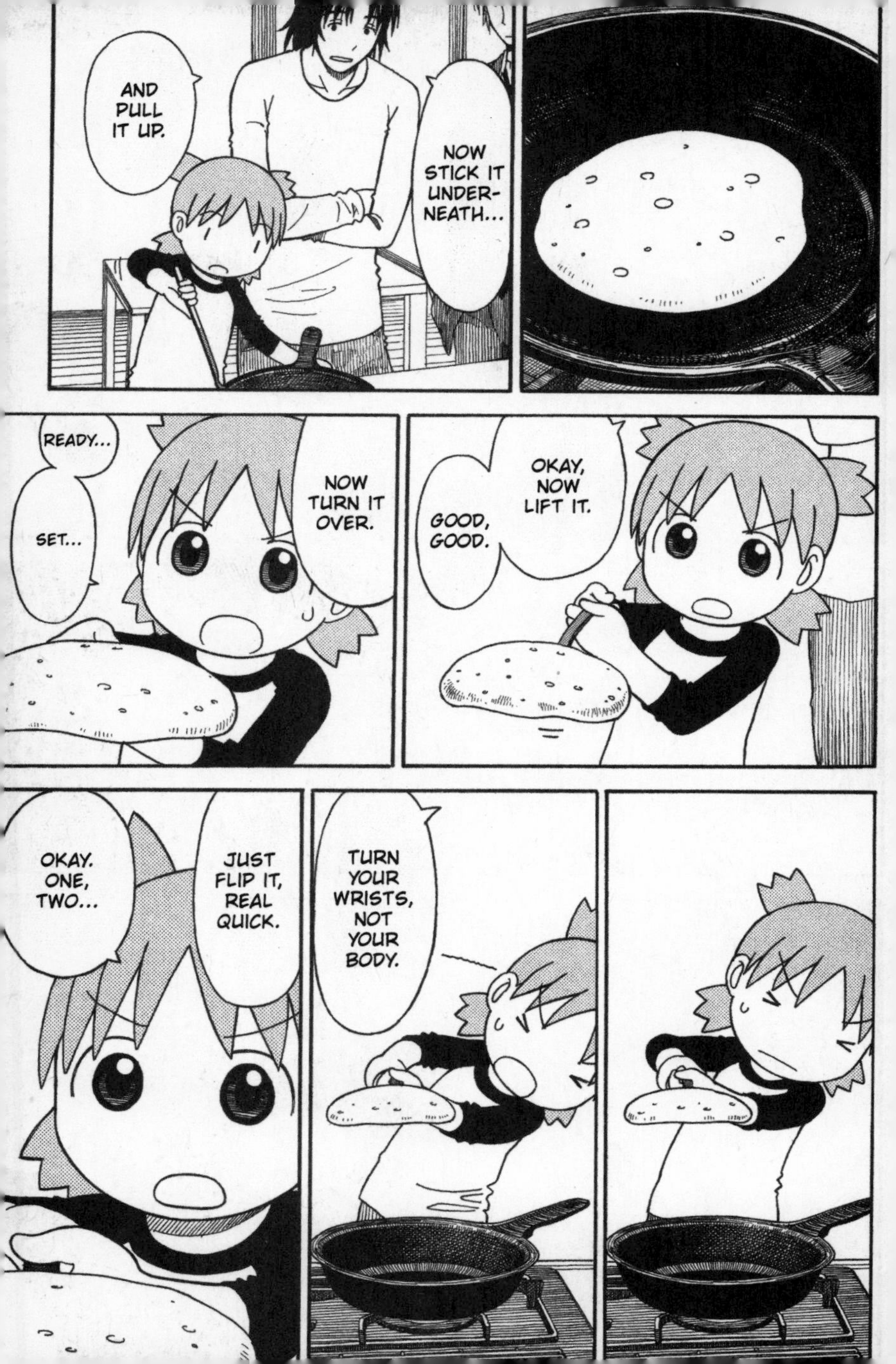
NOW STICK IT UNDERNEATH...
AND PULL IT UP.
OKAY, NOW LIFT IT.
GOOD, GOOD.
NOW TURN IT OVER.
READY...
SET...
TURN YOUR WRISTS, NOT YOUR BODY.
JUST FLIP IT, REAL QUICK.
OKAY. ONE, TWO...

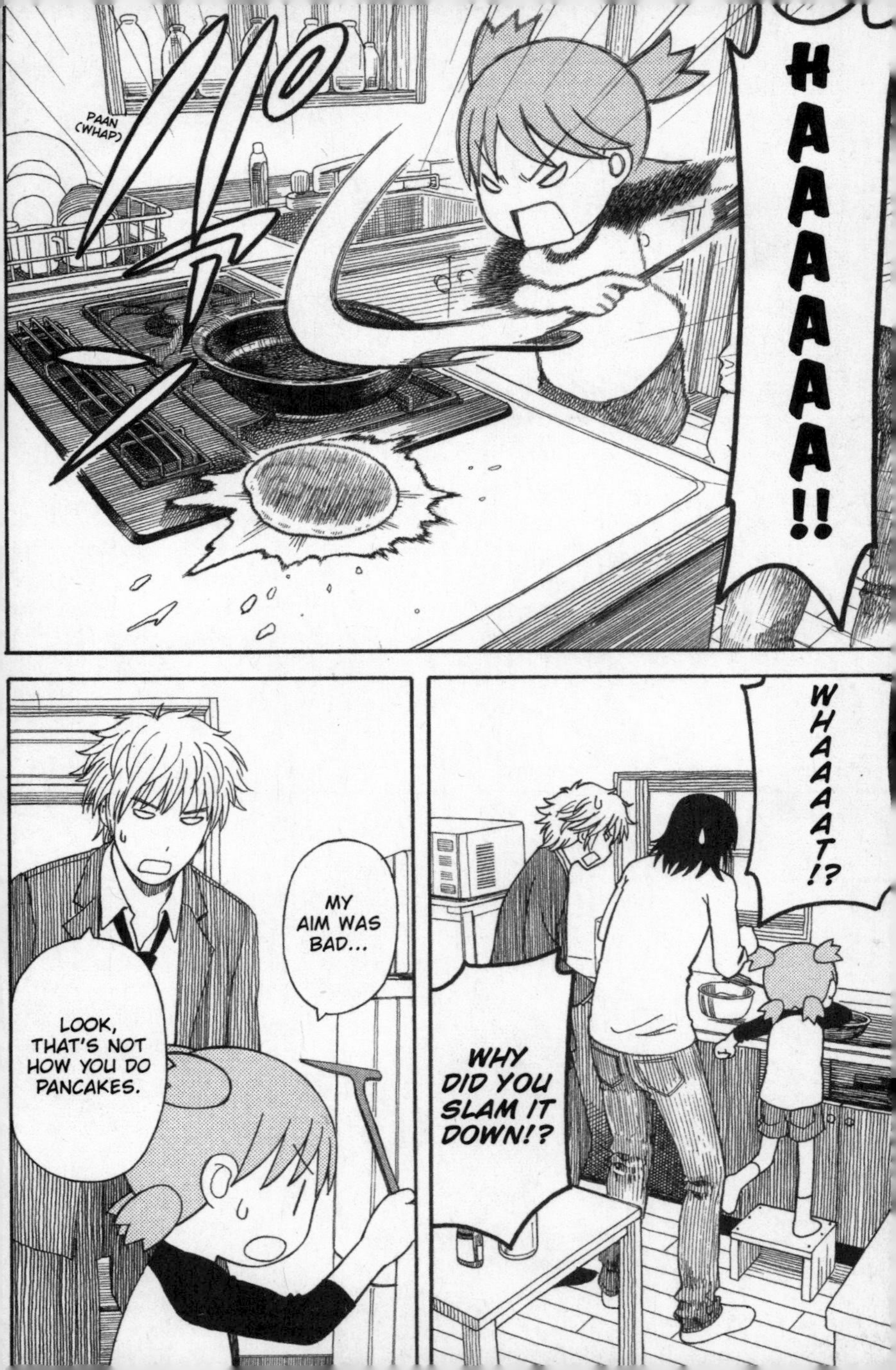
HAAAAA!!
PAAN (WHAP)
WHAAAAT!?
WHY DID YOU SLAM IT DOWN!?
MY AIM WAS BAD...
LOOK, THAT'S NOT HOW YOU DO PANCAKES.

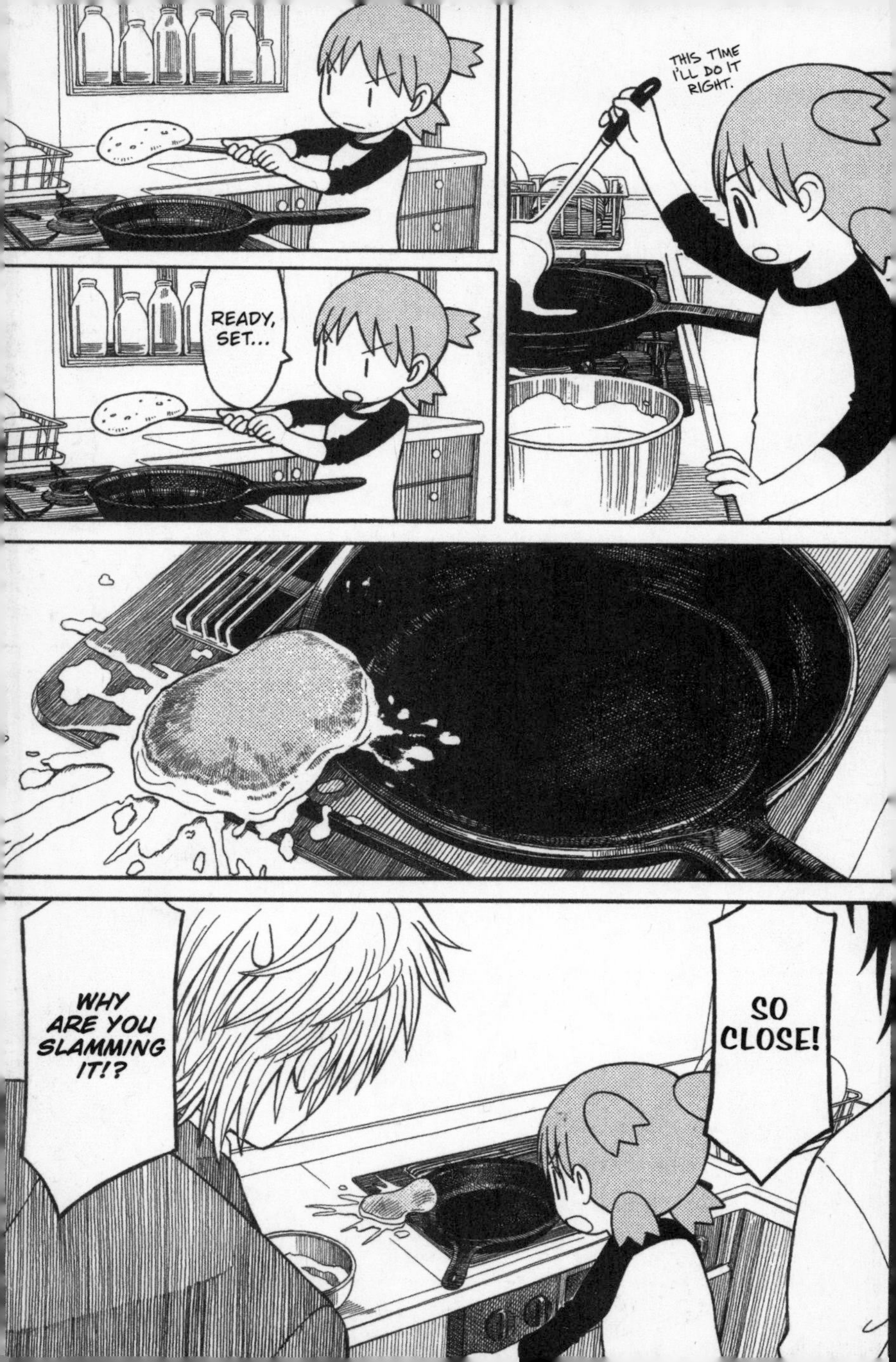
THIS TIME I'LL DO IT RIGHT.
READY, SET...
SO CLOSE!
WHY ARE YOU SLAMMING IT!?

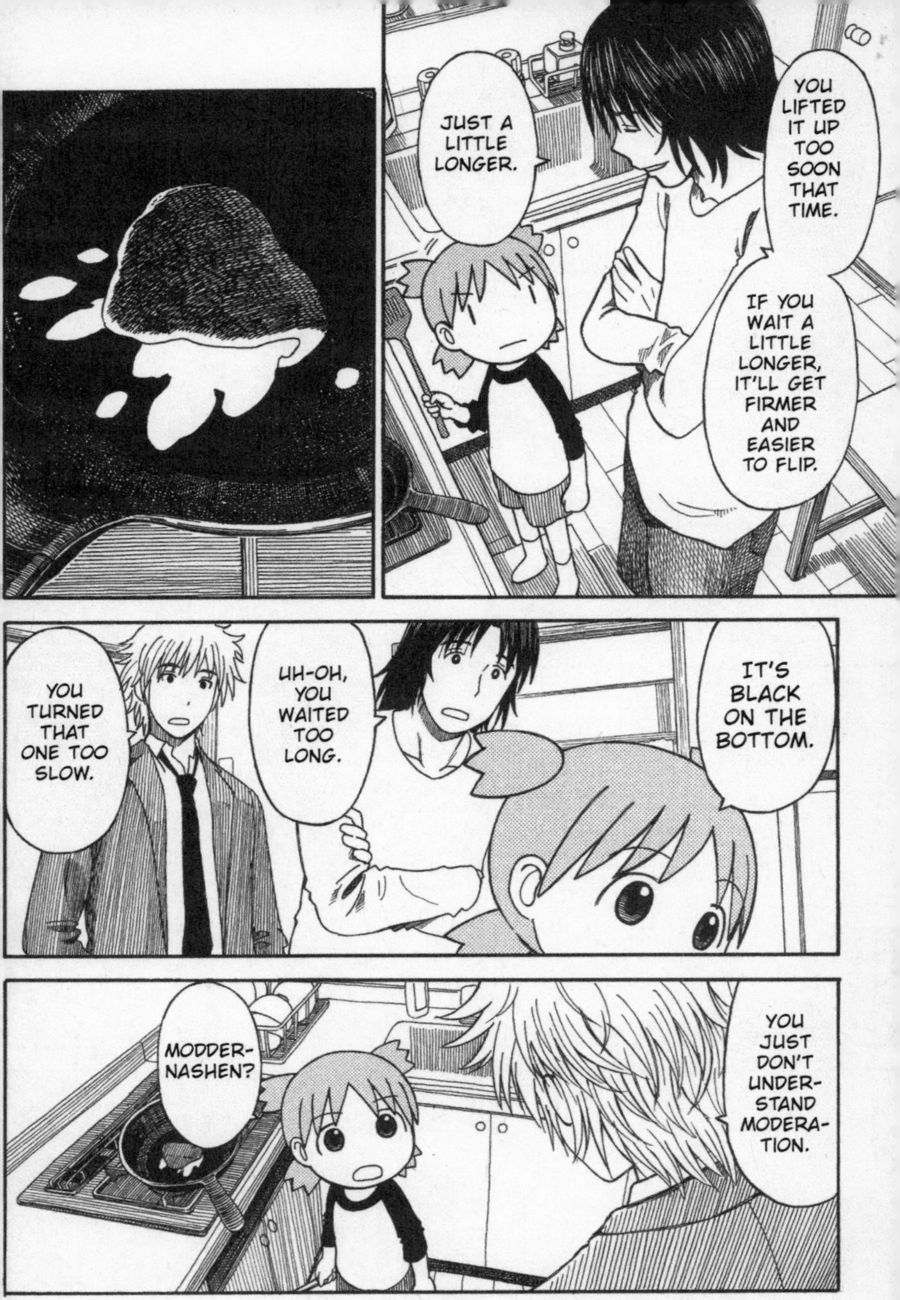
YOU LIFTED IT UP TOO SOON THAT TIME.
JUST A LITTLE LONGER.
IF YOU WAIT A LITTLE LONGER, IT'LL GET FIRMER AND EASIER TO FLIP.
IT'S BLACK ON THE BOTTOM.
UH-OH, YOU WAITED TOO LONG.
YOU TURNED THAT ONE TOO SLOW.
YOU JUST DON'T UNDER-STAND MODERA-TION.
MODDER-NASHEN?

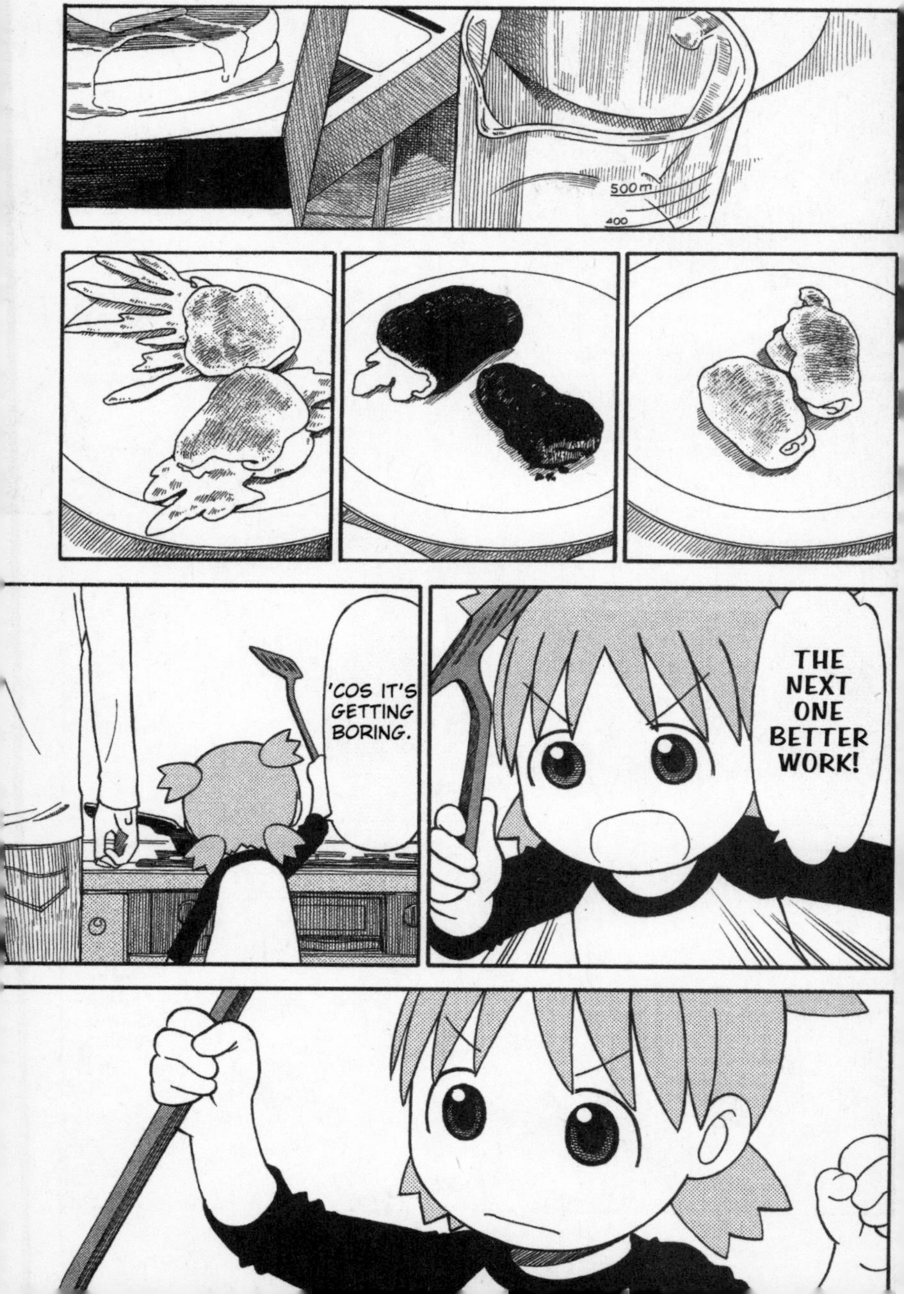
500m
400
THE NEXT ONE BETTER WORK!
'COS IT'S GETTING BORING.

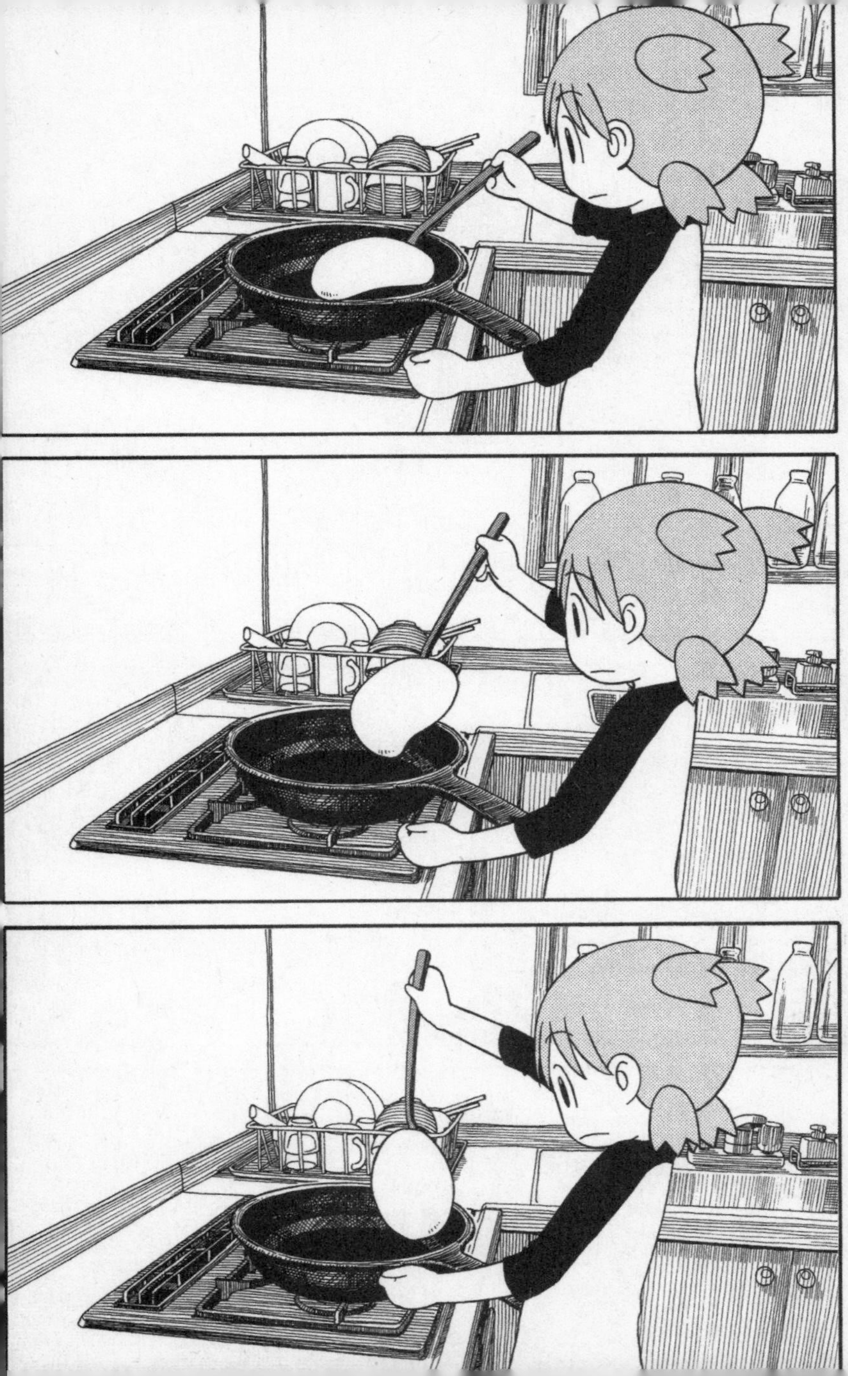

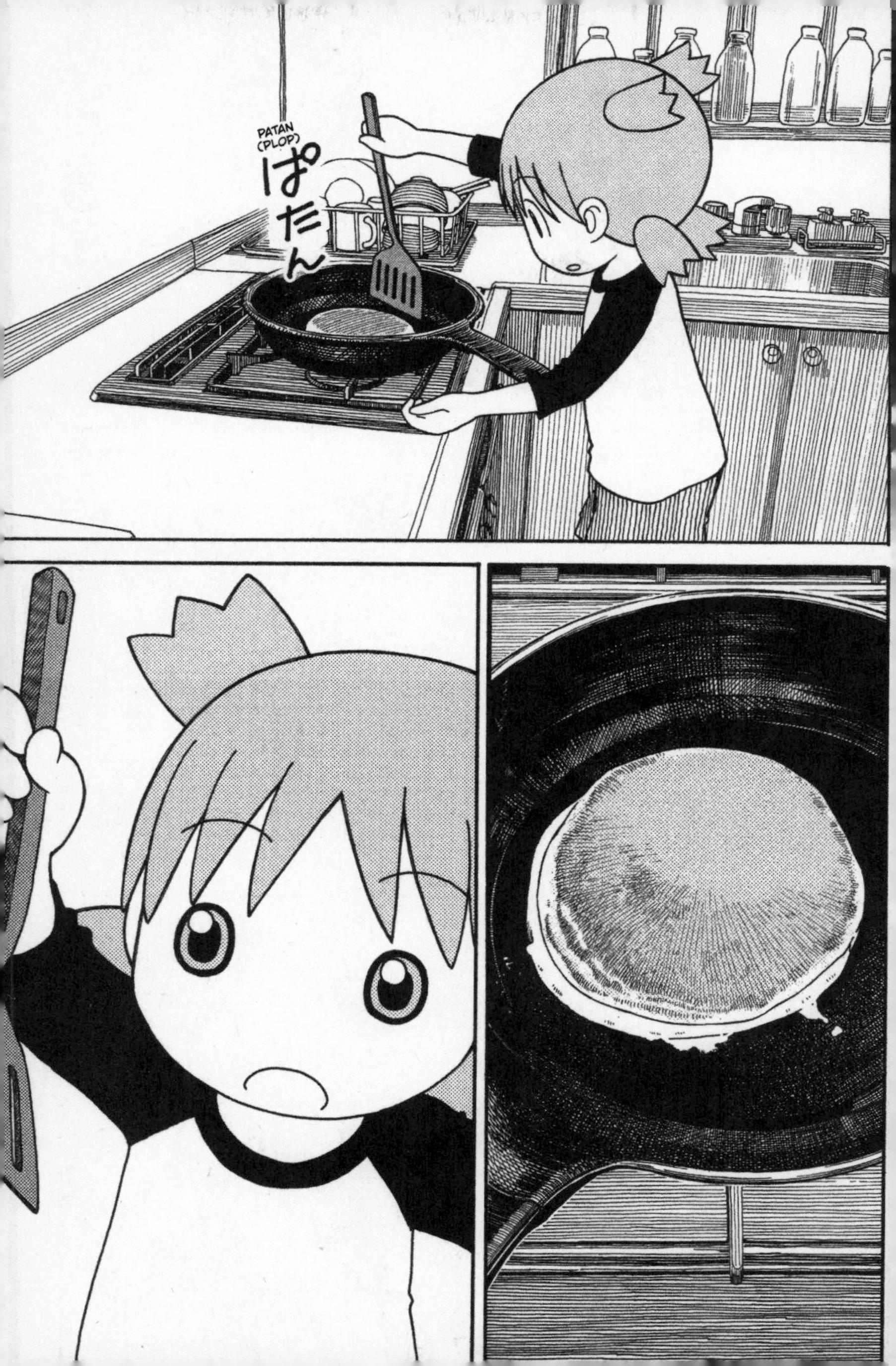
PATAN (PLOP)
ぱたん

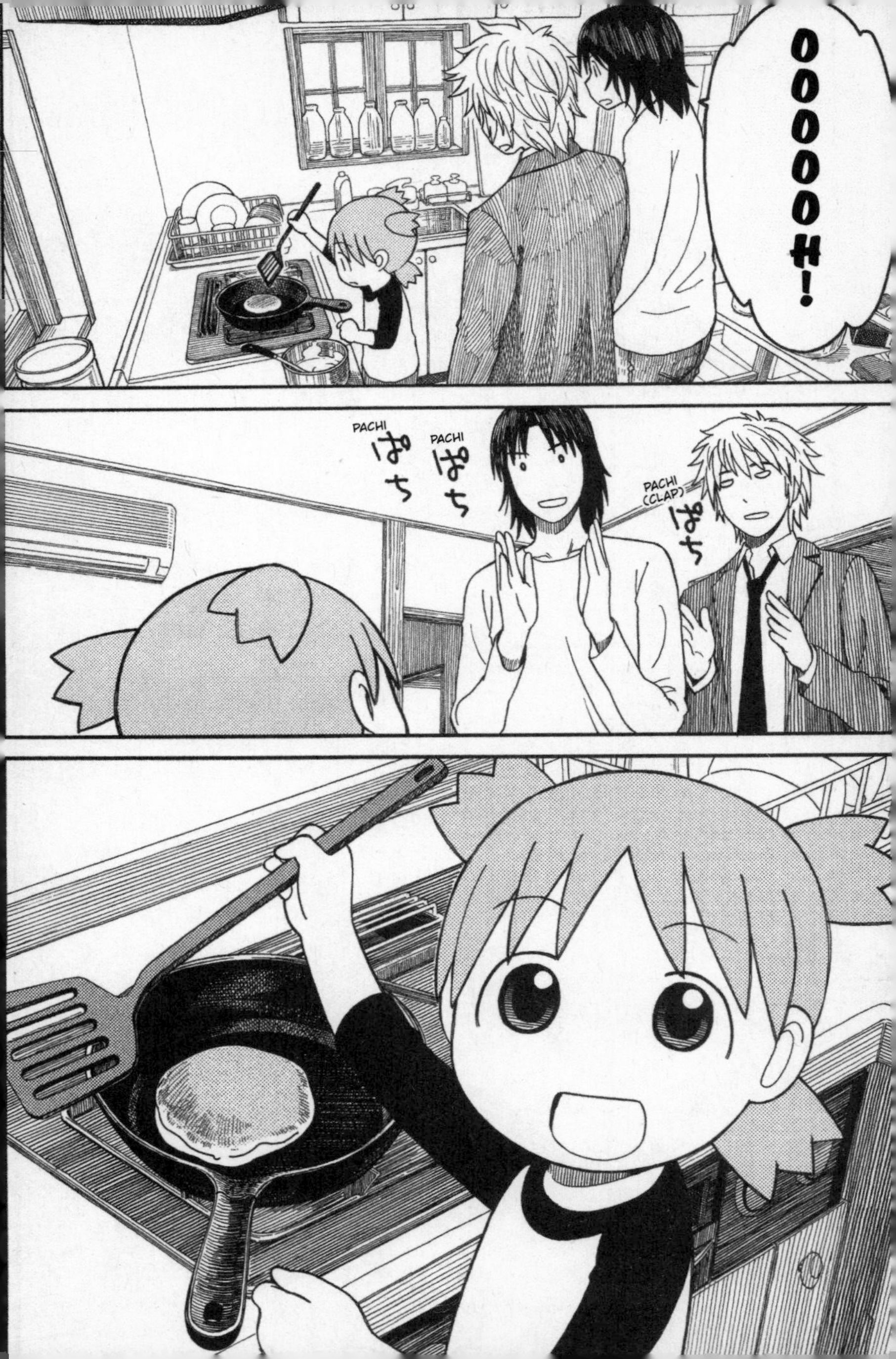
OOOOOOH!
PACHI
ぱち
PACHI
ぱち
PACHI (CLAP)
ぱち

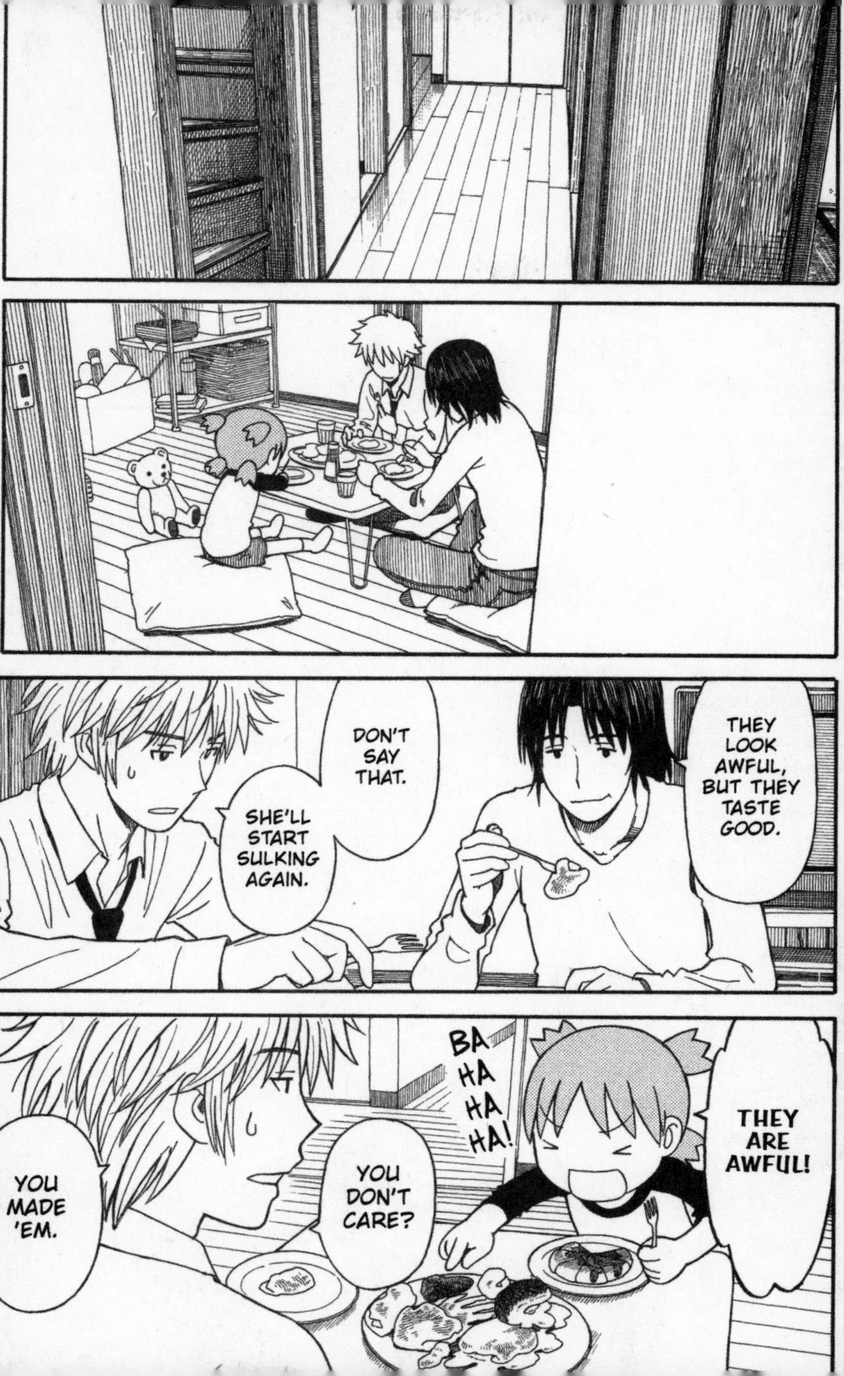
THEY LOOK AWFUL, BUT THEY TASTE GOOD.
DON'T SAY THAT.
SHE'LL START SULKING AGAIN.
THEY ARE AWFUL!
BAHAHAHA!
YOU DON'T CARE?
YOU MADE 'EM.

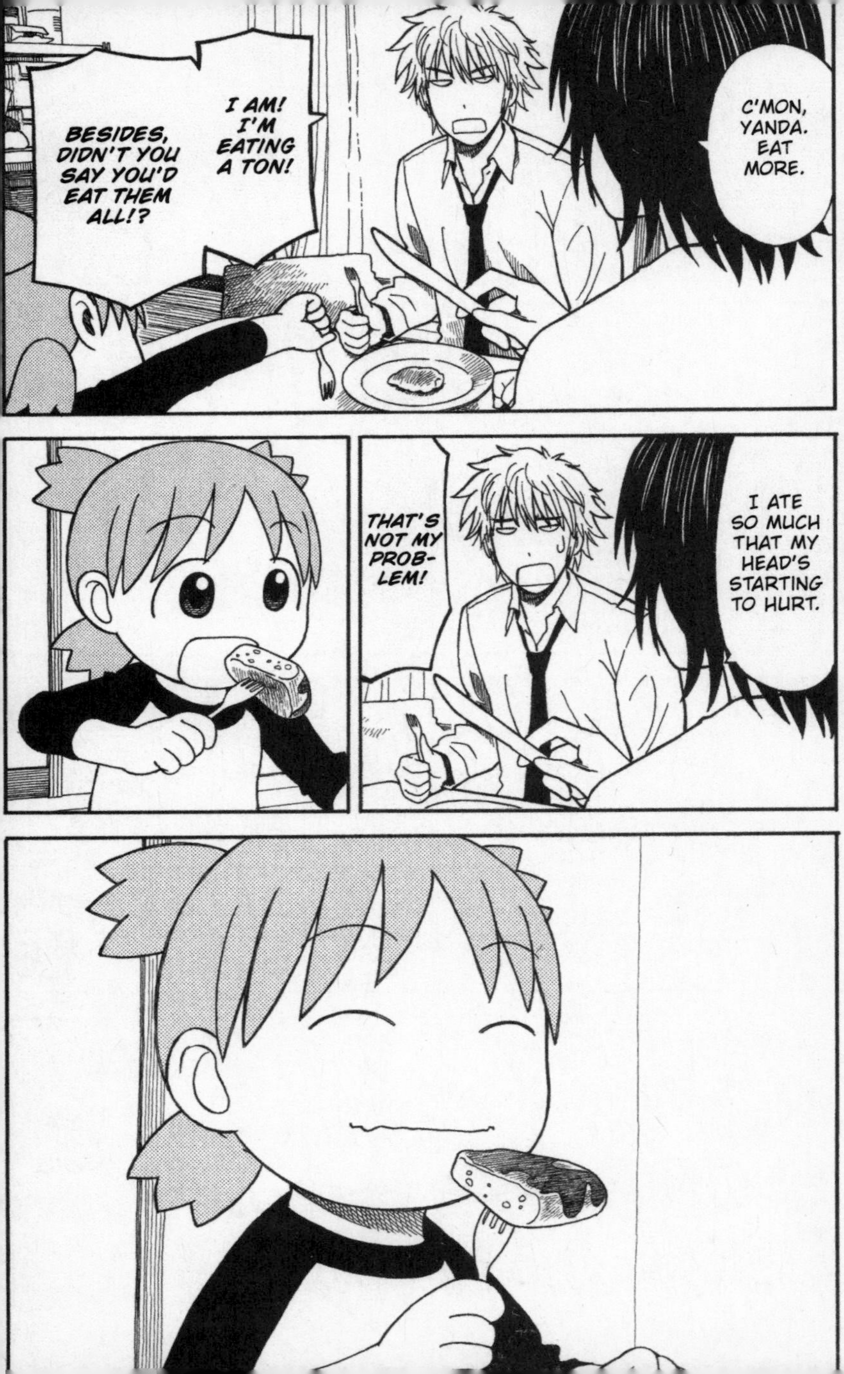
C'MON, YANDA. EAT MORE.
I AM! I'M EATING A TON!
BESIDES, DIDN'T YOU SAY YOU'D EAT THEM ALL!?
I ATE SO MUCH THAT MY HEAD'S STARTING TO HURT.
THAT'S NOT MY PROB-LEM!

YOTSUBA&!

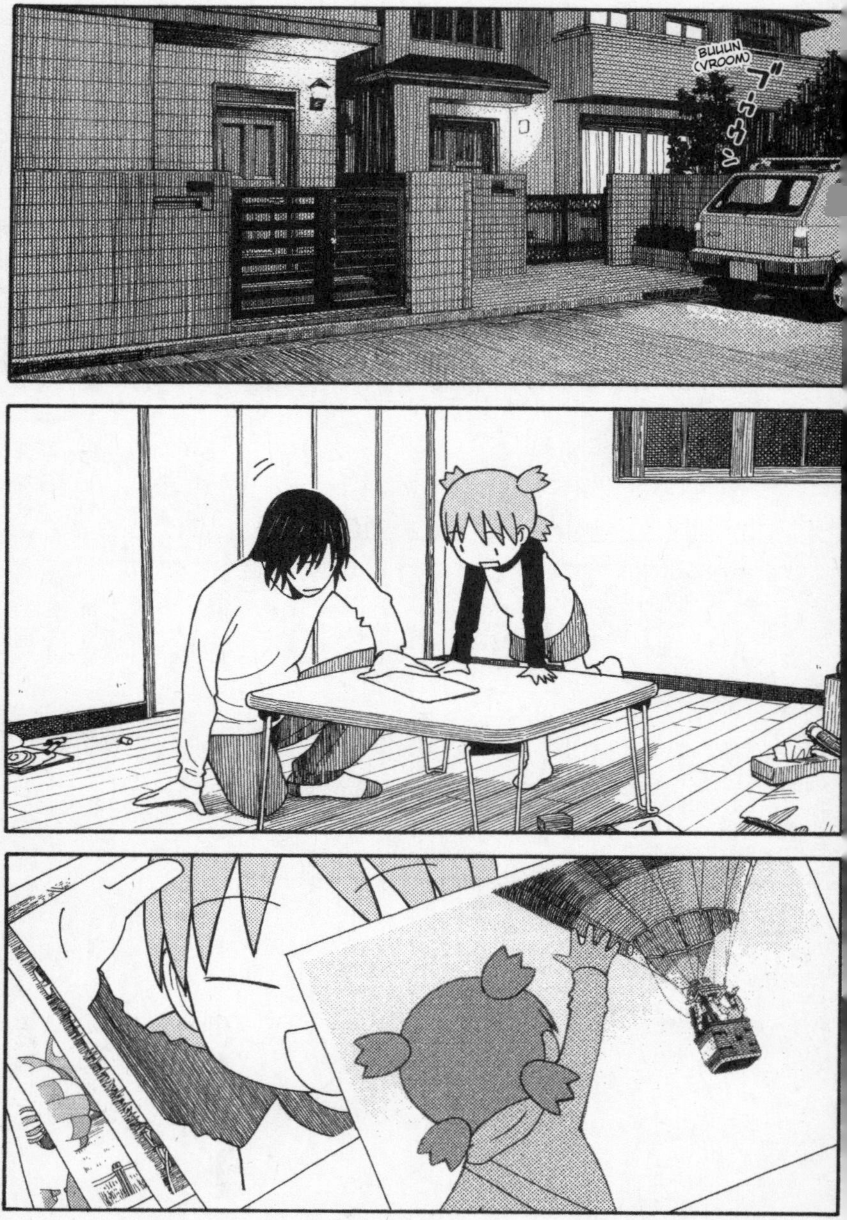
BUUUN (VROOM)
ブゥゥン

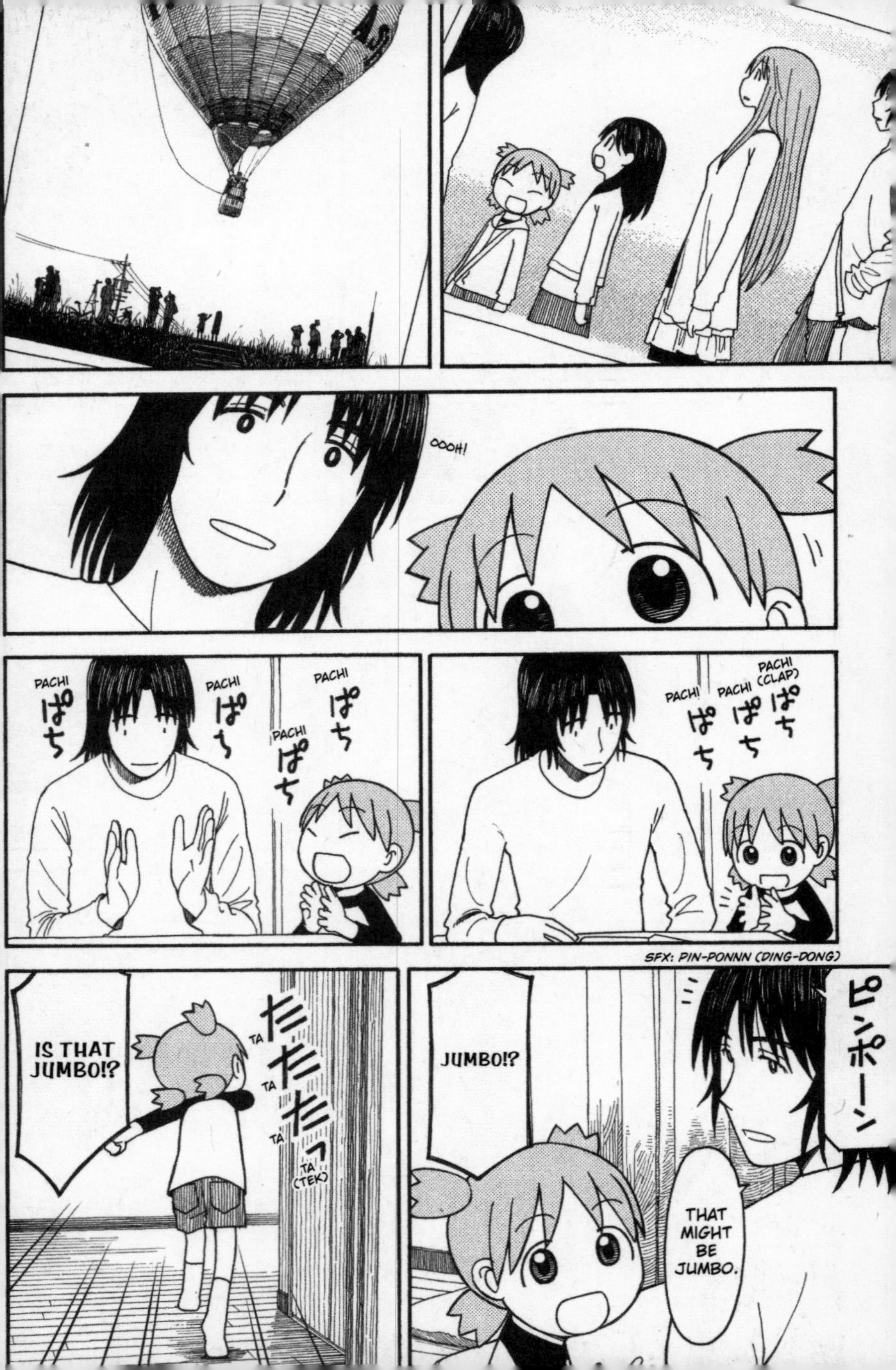
OOOH!
PACHI (CLAP)
ぱち
PACHI
ぱち
PACHI!
ぱち
PACHI
ぱち
PACHI
ぱち
PACHI
ぱち
PACHI
ぱち
SFX: PIN-PONNN (DING-DONG)
ピンポーン
THAT MIGHT BE JUMBO.
JUMBO!?
TA
TA
TA
TA (TEK)
たたたっ
IS THAT JUMBO!?

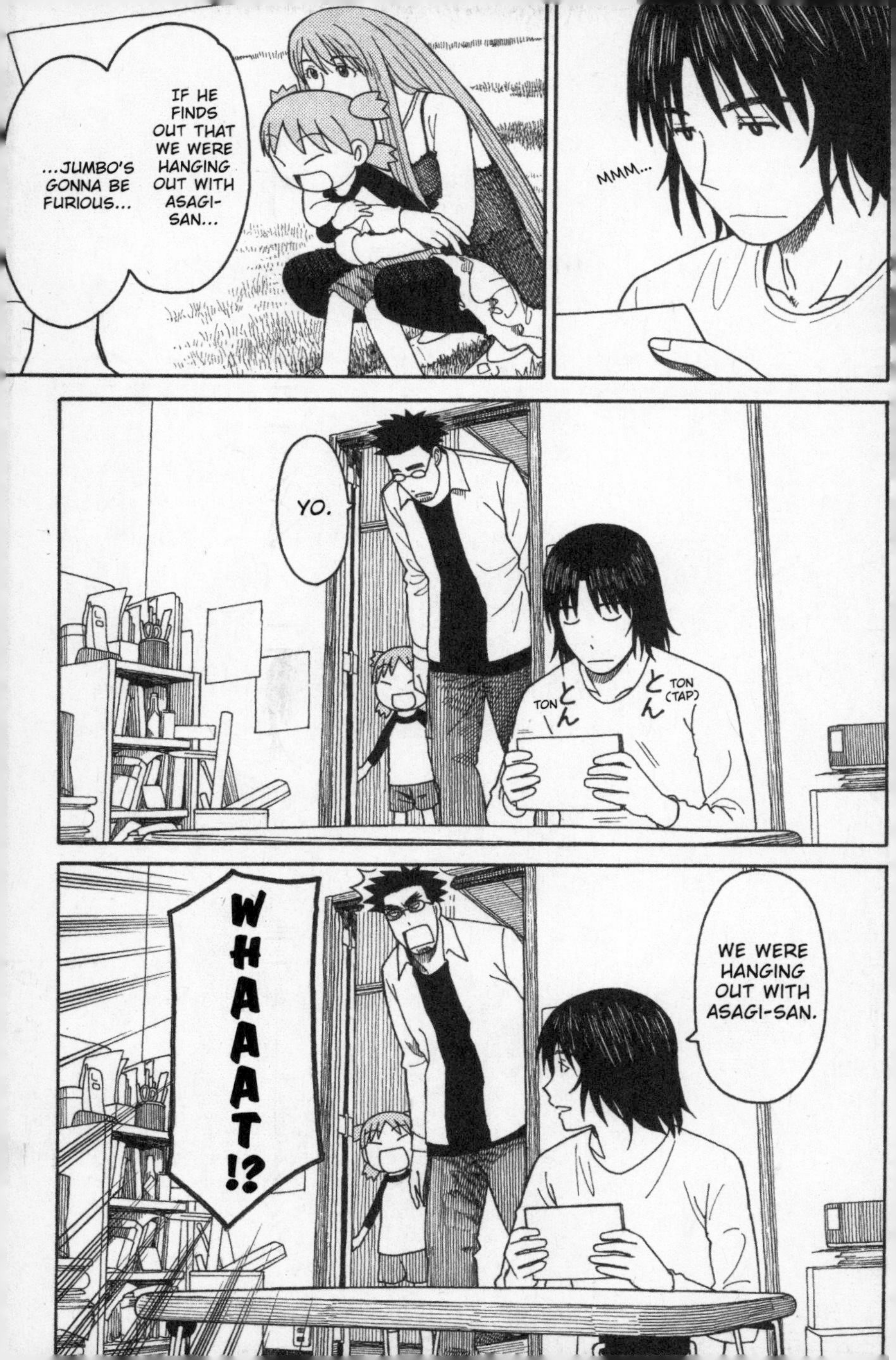
MMM...
IF HE FINDS OUT THAT WE WERE HANGING OUT WITH ASAGI-SAN...
...JUMBO'S GONNA BE FURIOUS...
YO.
とん TON (TAP)
とん TON
WE WERE HANGING OUT WITH ASAGI-SAN.
WHAAAT!?

YOTSUBA& JUMBO

#65

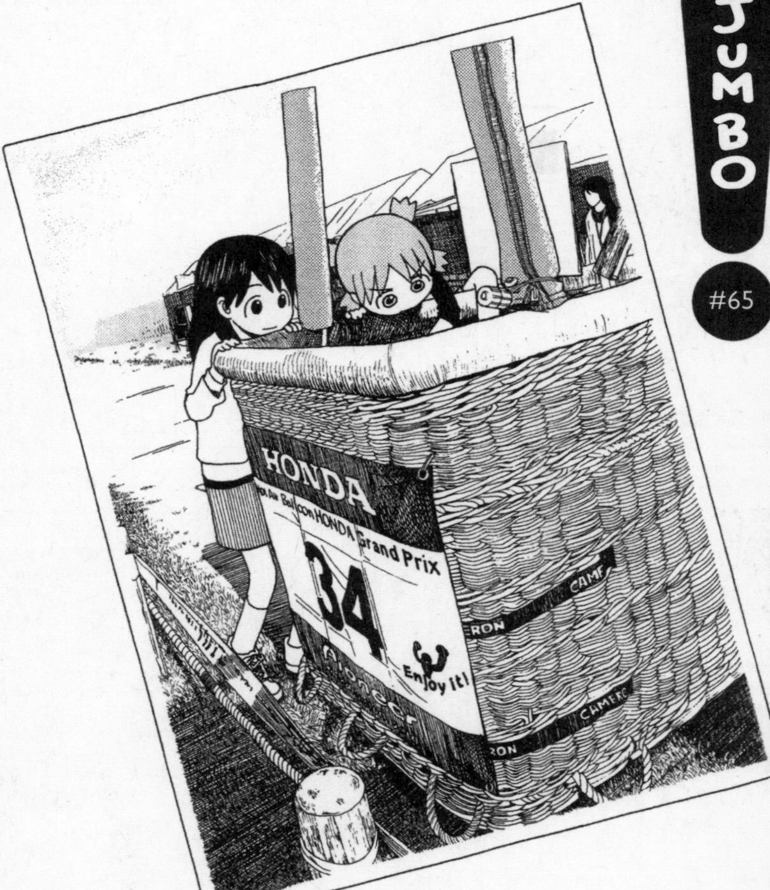
HONDA
Grand Prix
34
Enjoy it!

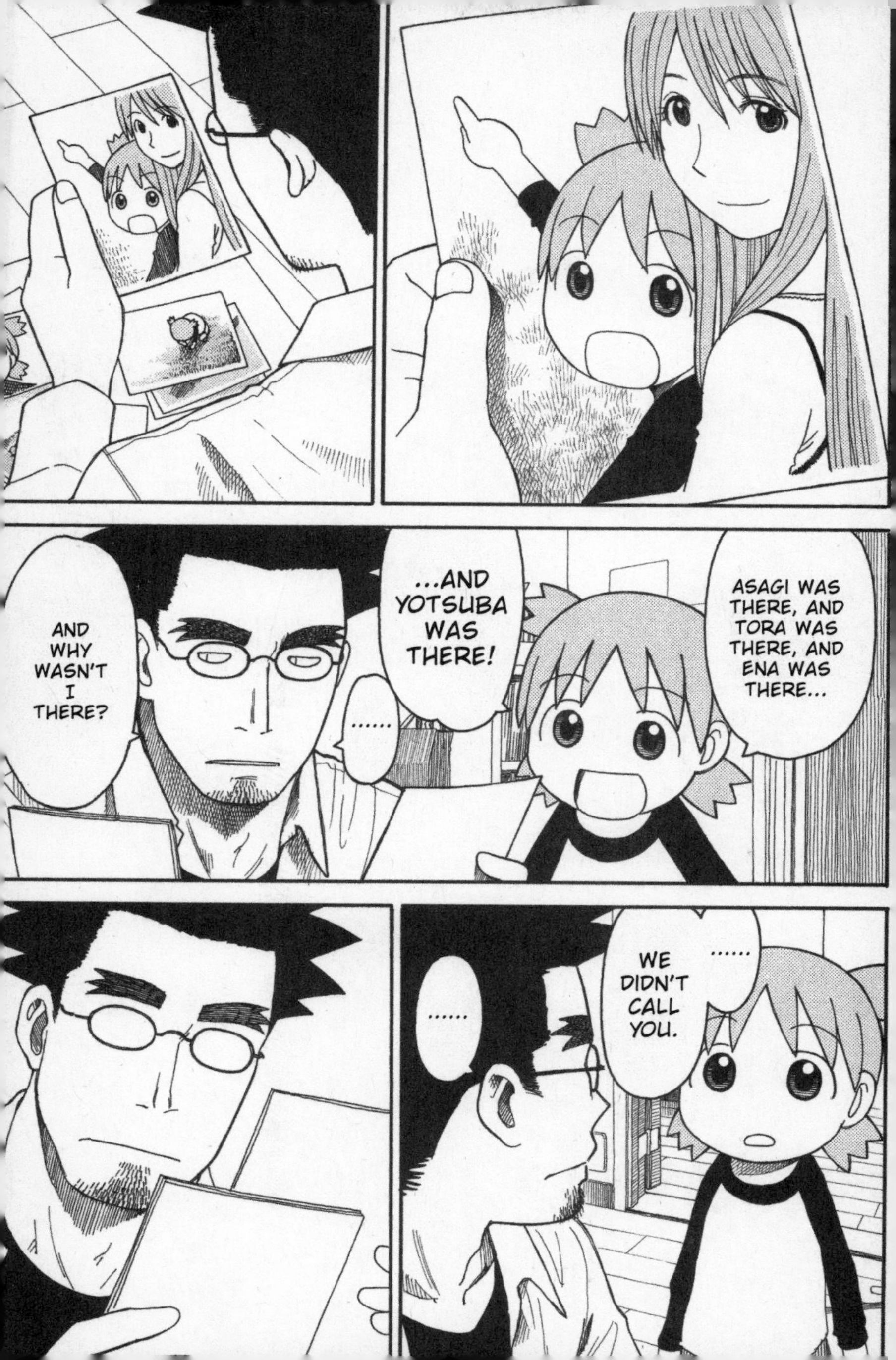
ASAGI WAS THERE, AND TORA WAS THERE, AND ENA WAS THERE...
...AND YOTSUBA WAS THERE!
......
AND WHY WASN'T I THERE?
......
WE DIDN'T CALL YOU.
......

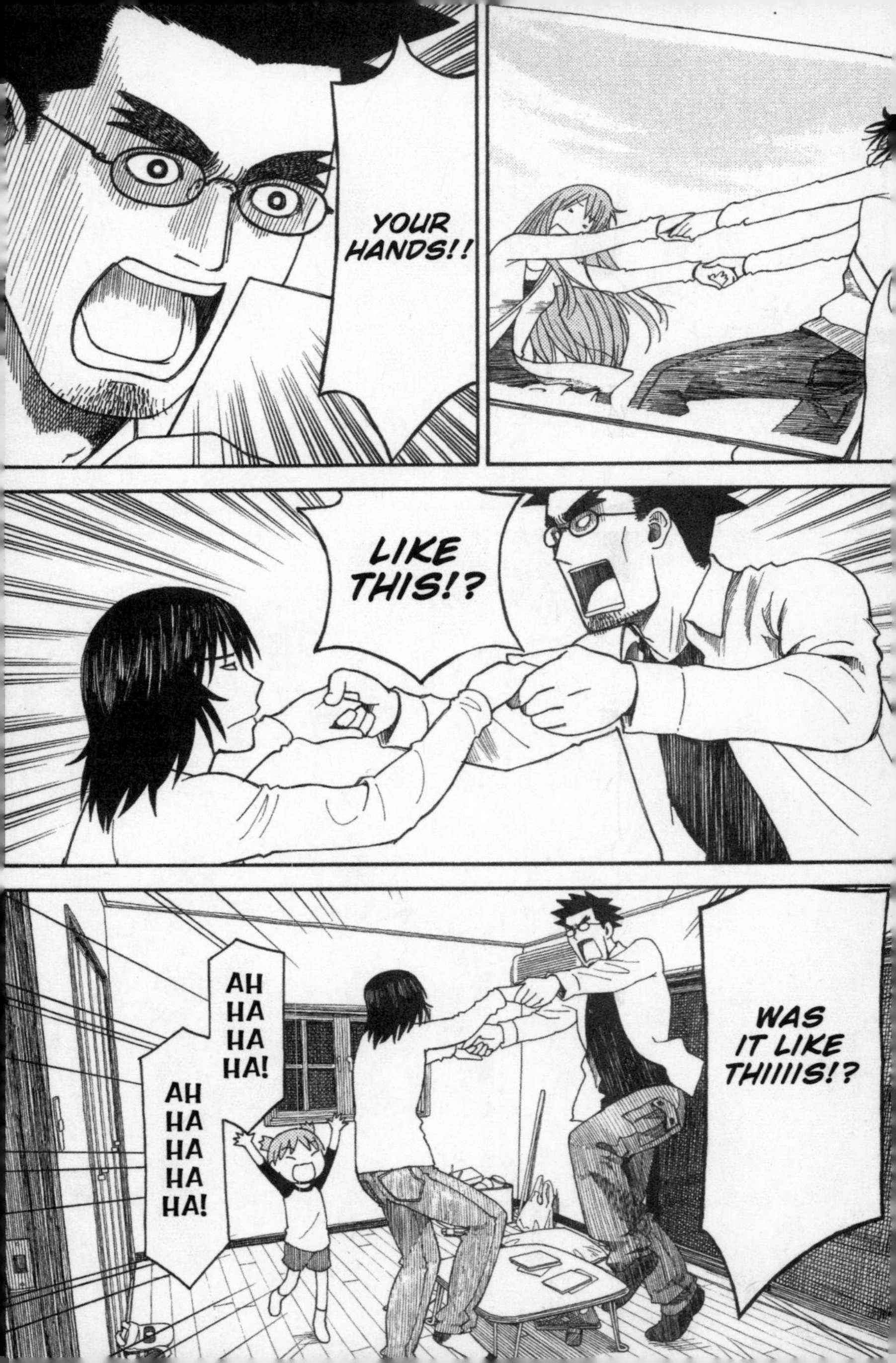
YOUR HANDS!!
LIKE THIS!?
WAS IT LIKE THIIIIS!?
AH HA HA HA!
AH HA HA HA HA HA!

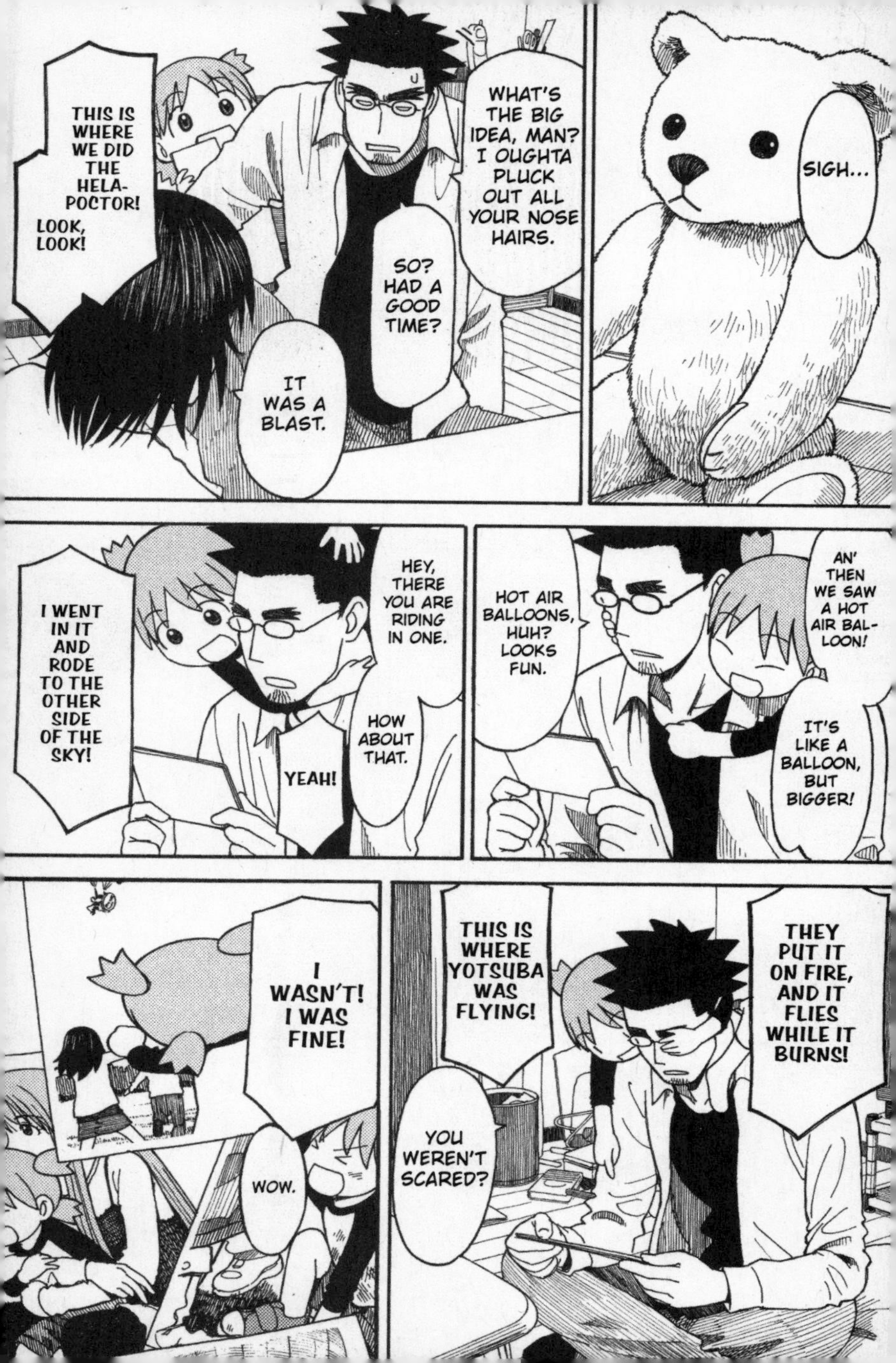
SIGH...
WHAT'S THE BIG IDEA, MAN? I OUGHTA PLUCK OUT ALL YOUR NOSE HAIRS.
THIS IS WHERE WE DID THE HELA-POCTOR!
LOOK, LOOK!
SO? HAD A GOOD TIME?
IT WAS A BLAST.
AN' THEN WE SAW A HOT AIR BAL-LOON!
HOT AIR BALLOONS, HUH? LOOKS FUN.
IT'S LIKE A BALLOON, BUT BIGGER!
HEY, THERE YOU ARE RIDING IN ONE.
I WENT IN IT AND RODE TO THE OTHER SIDE OF THE SKY!
HOW ABOUT THAT.
YEAH!
THEY PUT IT ON FIRE, AND IT FLIES WHILE IT BURNS!
THIS IS WHERE YOTSUBA WAS FLYING!
YOU WEREN'T SCARED?
I WASN'T! I WAS FINE!
WOW.

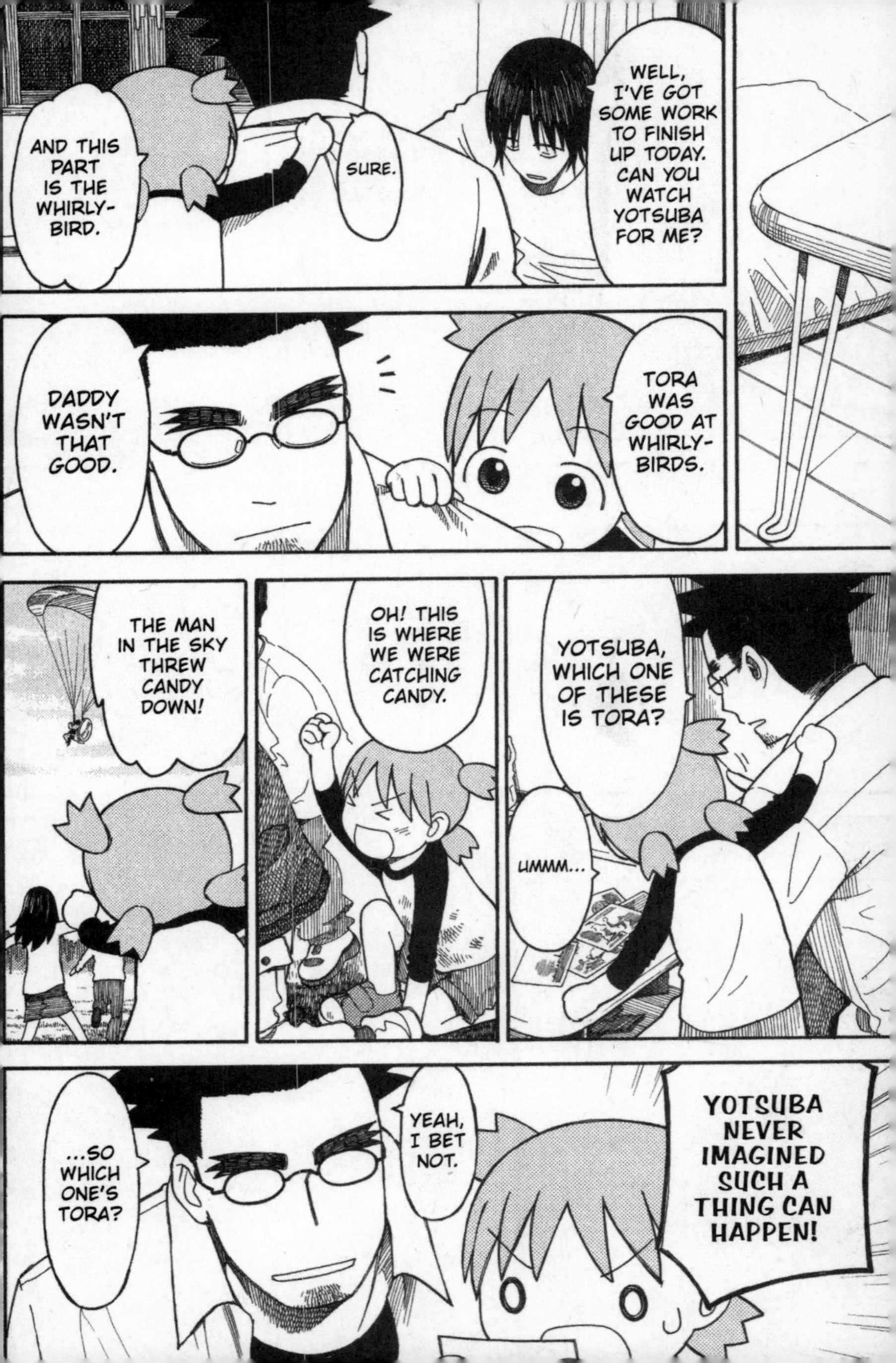
WELL, I'VE GOT SOME WORK TO FINISH UP TODAY. CAN YOU WATCH YOTSUBA FOR ME?
SURE.
AND THIS PART IS THE WHIRLY-BIRD.
TORA WAS GOOD AT WHIRLY-BIRDS.
DADDY WASN'T THAT GOOD.
YOTSUBA, WHICH ONE OF THESE IS TORA?
UMMM...
OH! THIS IS WHERE WE WERE CATCHING CANDY.
THE MAN IN THE SKY THREW CANDY DOWN!
YOTSUBA NEVER IMAGINED SUCH A THING CAN HAPPEN!
YEAH, I BET NOT.
...SO WHICH ONE'S TORA?

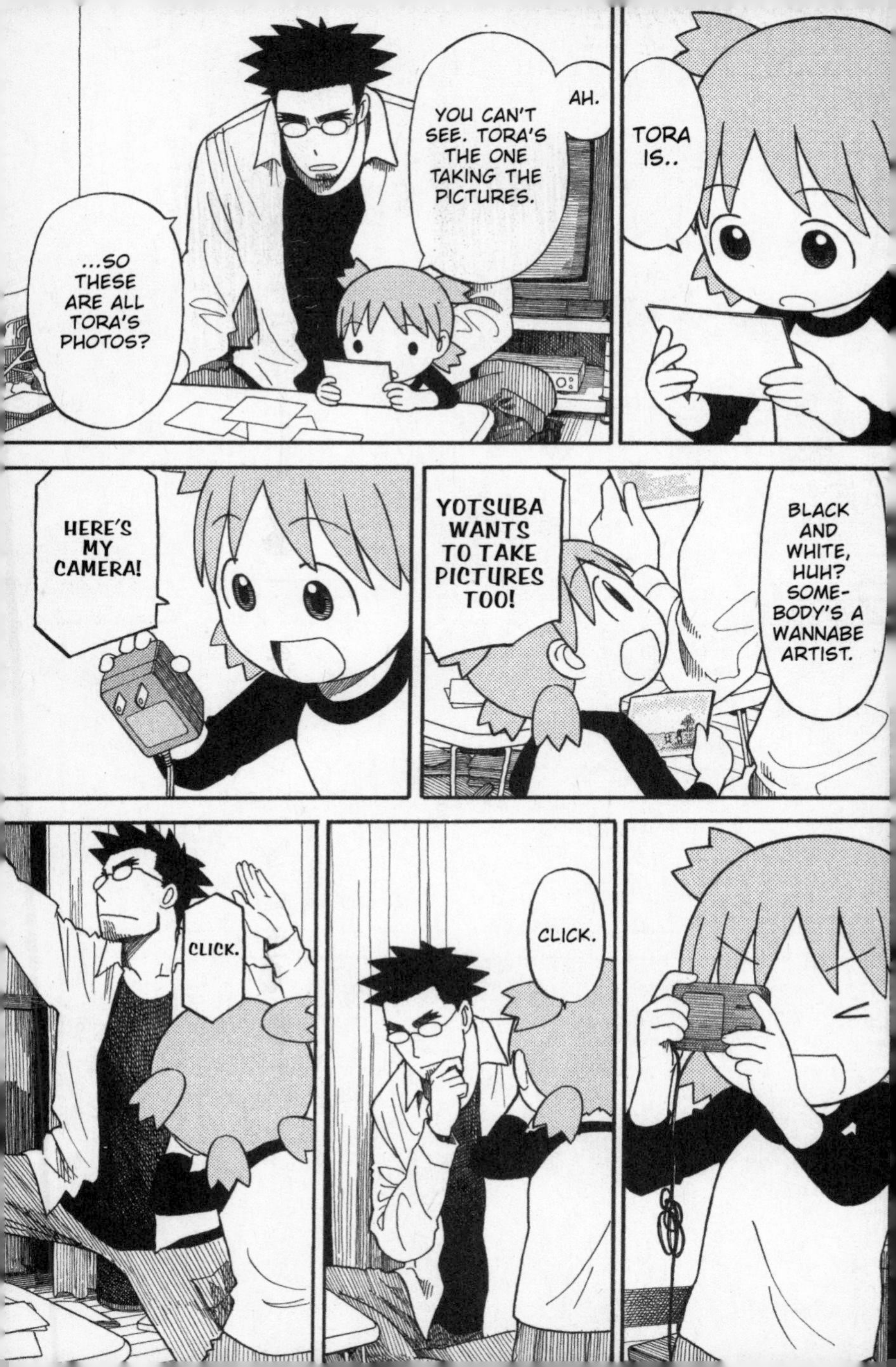
TORA IS..
AH.
YOU CAN'T SEE. TORA'S THE ONE TAKING THE PICTURES.
...SO THESE ARE ALL TORA'S PHOTOS?
BLACK AND WHITE, HUH? SOME-BODY'S A WANNABE ARTIST.
YOTSUBA WANTS TO TAKE PICTURES TOO!
HERE'S MY CAMERA!
CLICK.
CLICK.

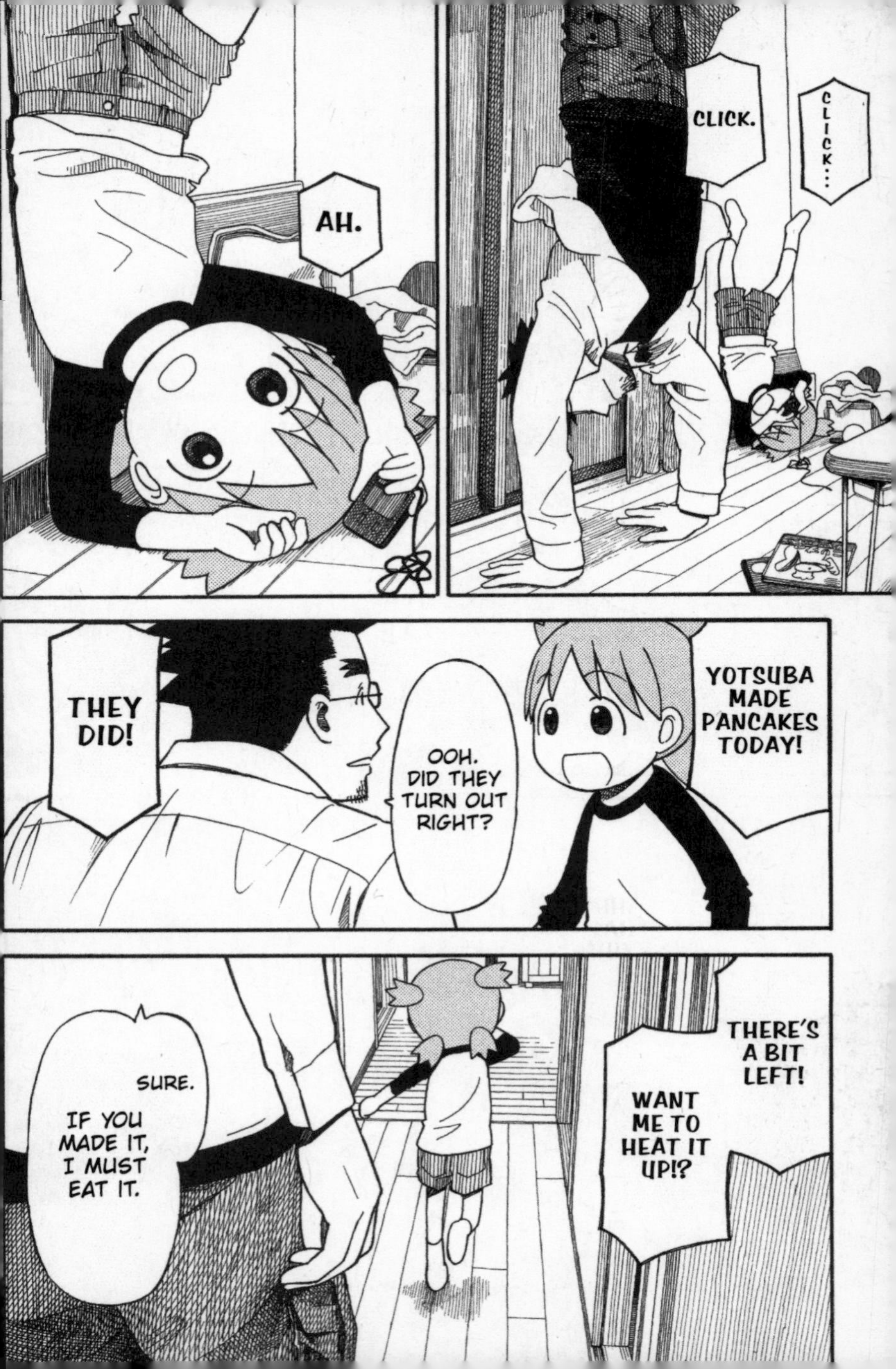
CLICK...
CLICK.
AH.
YOTSUBA MADE PANCAKES TODAY!
OOH. DID THEY TURN OUT RIGHT?
THEY DID!
THERE'S A BIT LEFT!
WANT ME TO HEAT IT UP!?
SURE.
IF YOU MADE IT, I MUST EAT IT.

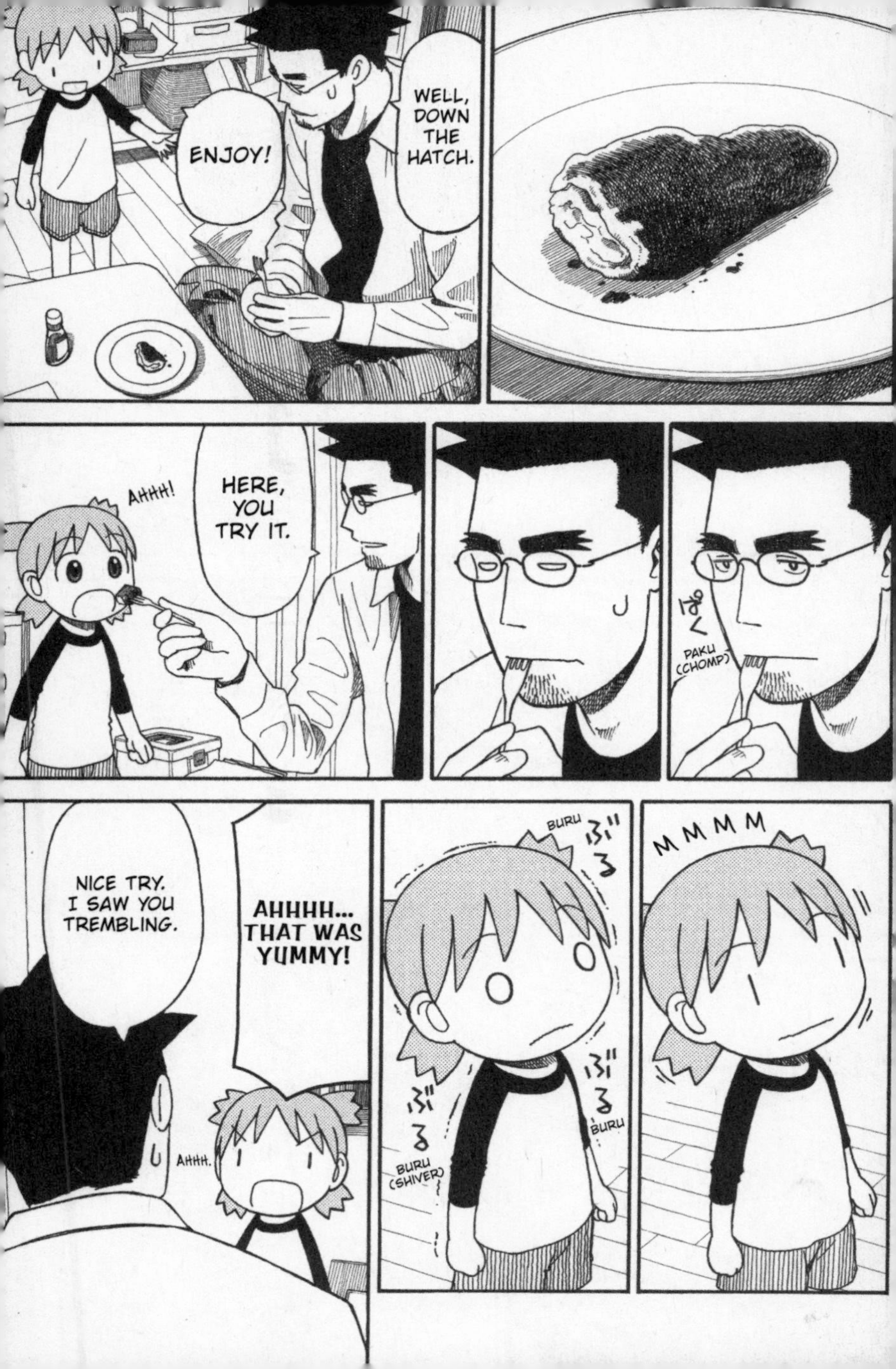
WELL, DOWN THE HATCH.
ENJOY!
ぱく
PAKU (CHOMP)
HERE, YOU TRY IT.
AHHH!
M M M M
BURU
ぶる
ぶる
BURU
ぶる
BURU (SHIVER)
AHHHH... THAT WAS YUMMY!
NICE TRY. I SAW YOU TREMBLING.
AHHH.

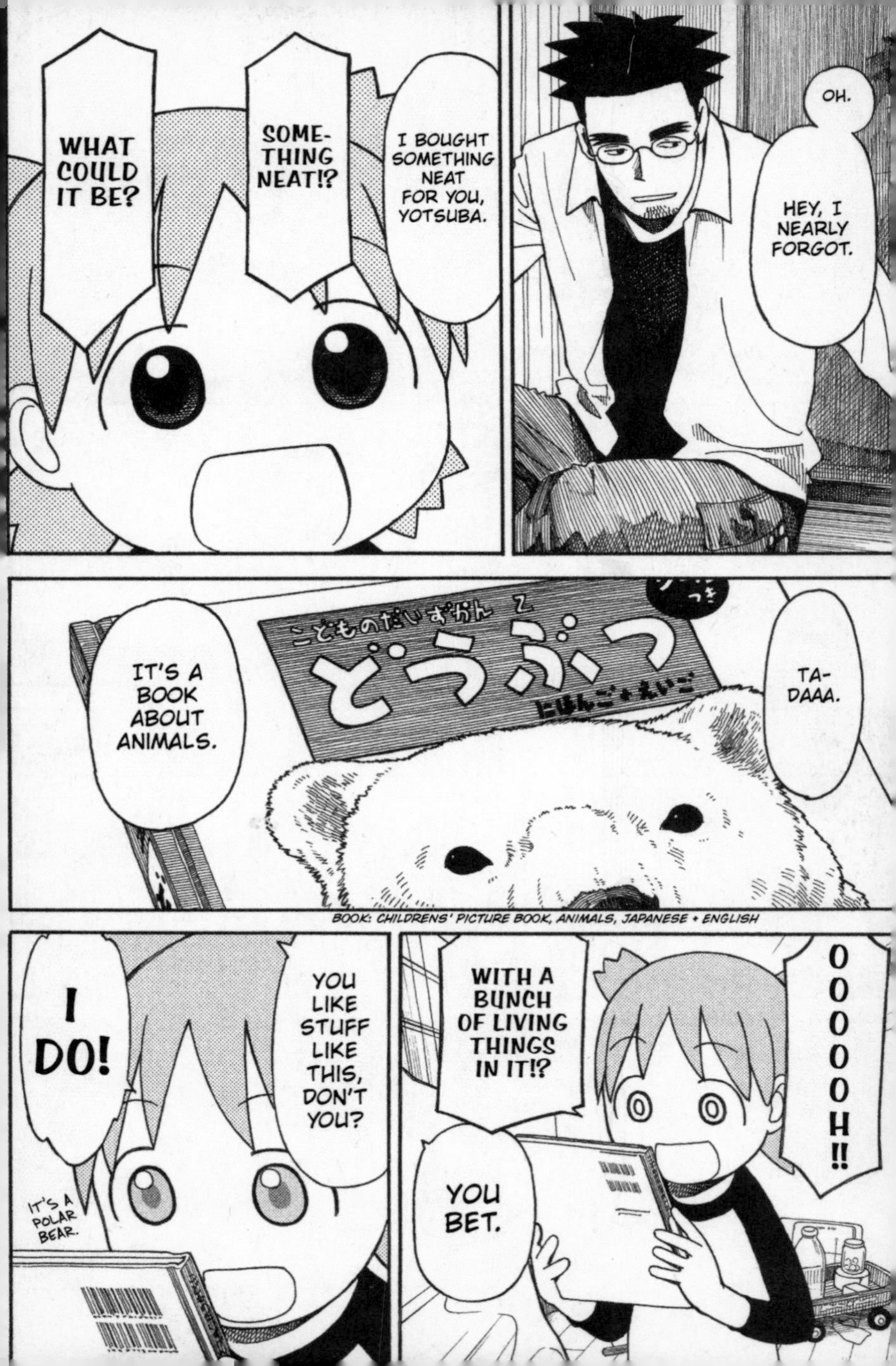
OH.
HEY, I NEARLY FORGOT.
I BOUGHT SOMETHING NEAT FOR YOU, YOTSUBA.
SOME-THING NEAT!?
WHAT COULD IT BE?
TA-DAAA.
こどものだいずかん 2
どうぶつ
にほんご+えいご
IT'S A BOOK ABOUT ANIMALS.
BOOK: CHILDRENS' PICTURE BOOK, ANIMALS, JAPANESE + ENGLISH
OOOOOOH!!
WITH A BUNCH OF LIVING THINGS IN IT!?
YOU BET.
YOU LIKE STUFF LIKE THIS, DON'T YOU?
I DO!
IT'S A POLAR BEAR.

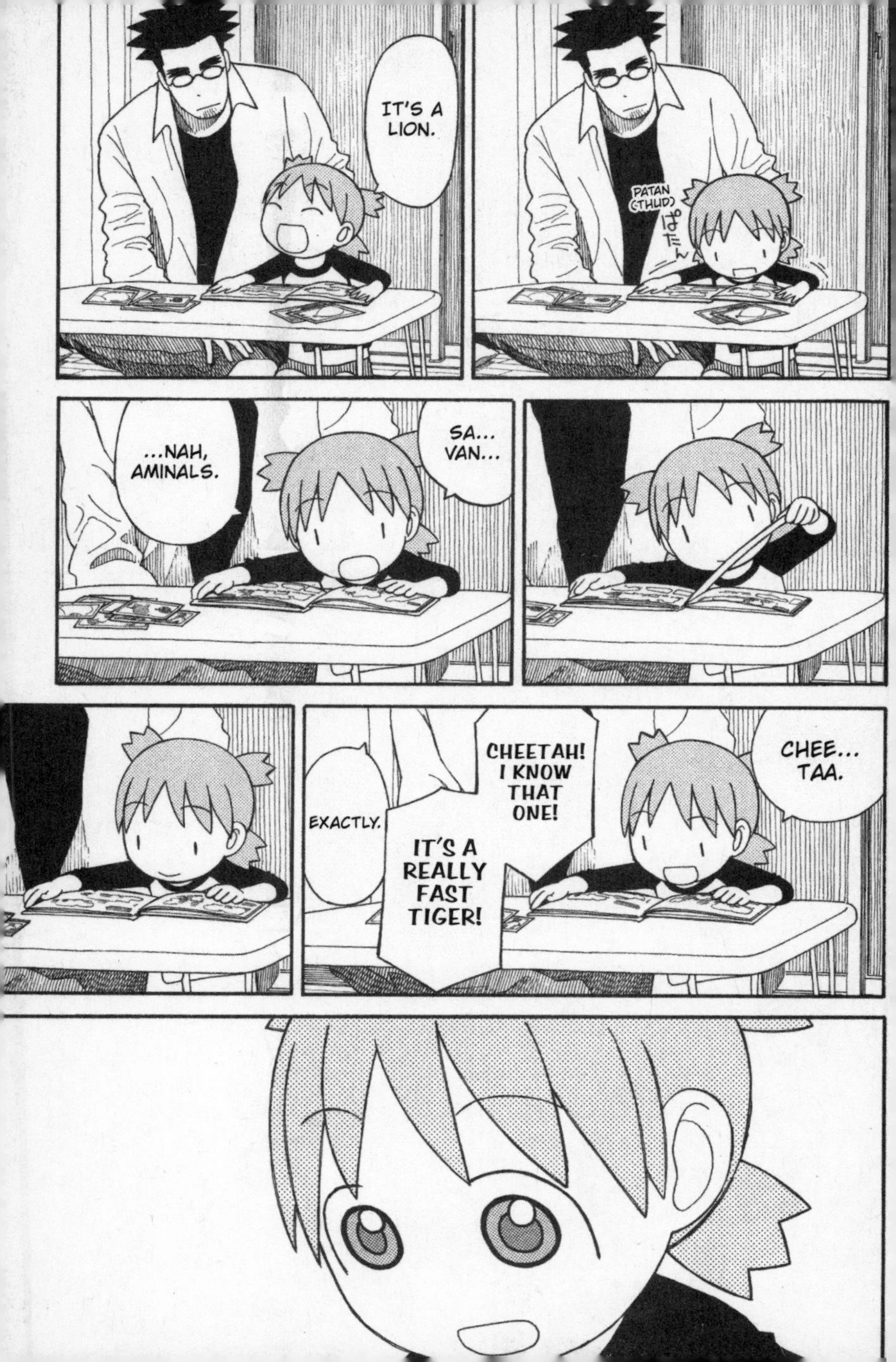
PATAN (THUD)
ぱたん
IT'S A LION.
SA... VAN...
...NAH, AMINALS.
CHEE... TAA.
CHEETAH! I KNOW THAT ONE!
IT'S A REALLY FAST TIGER!
EXACTLY.

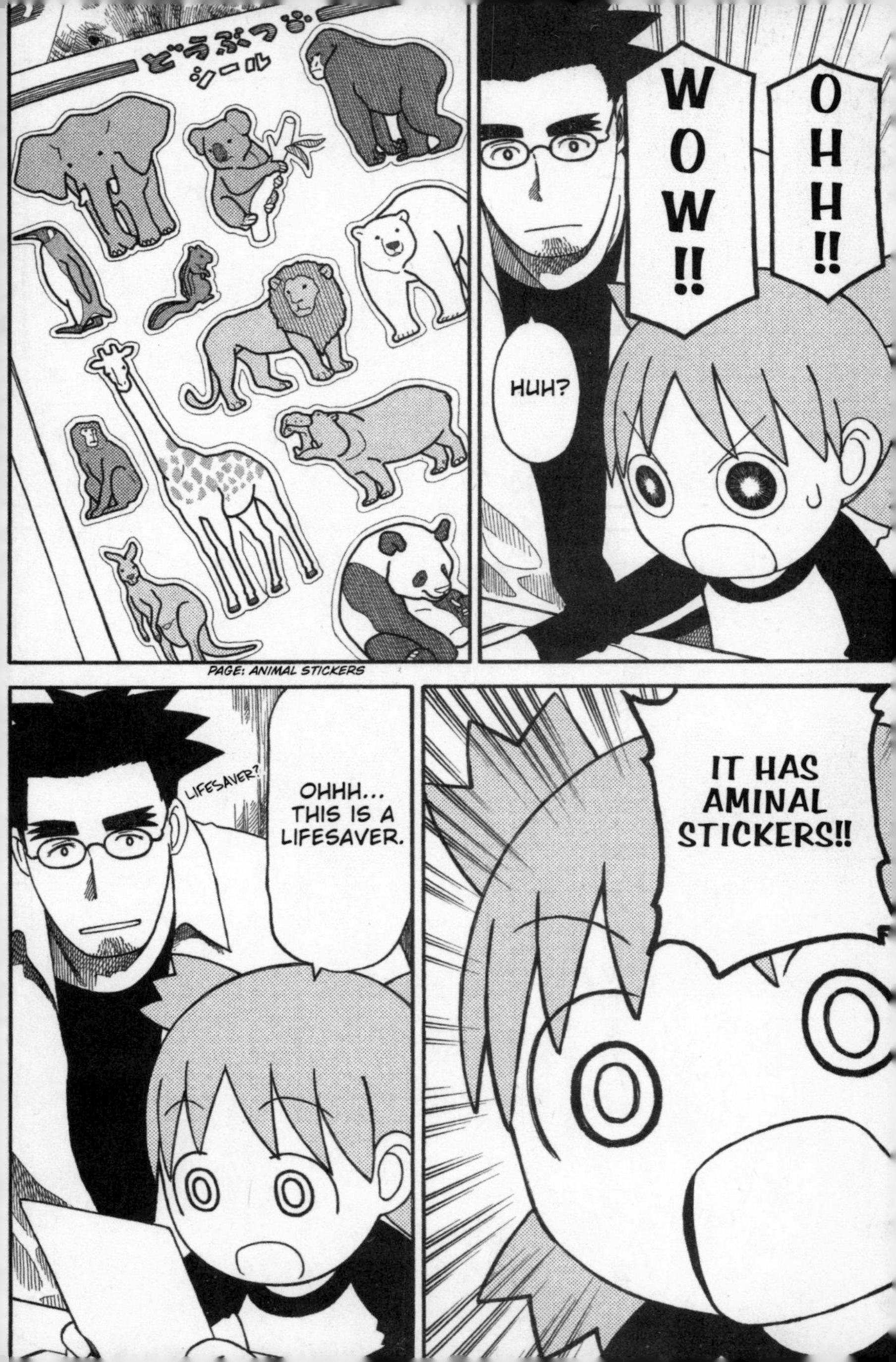

OHH!!
WOW!!
HUH?
どうぶつシール
PAGE: ANIMAL STICKERS
IT HAS AMINAL STICKERS!!
OHHH... THIS IS A LIFESAVER.
LIFESAVER?

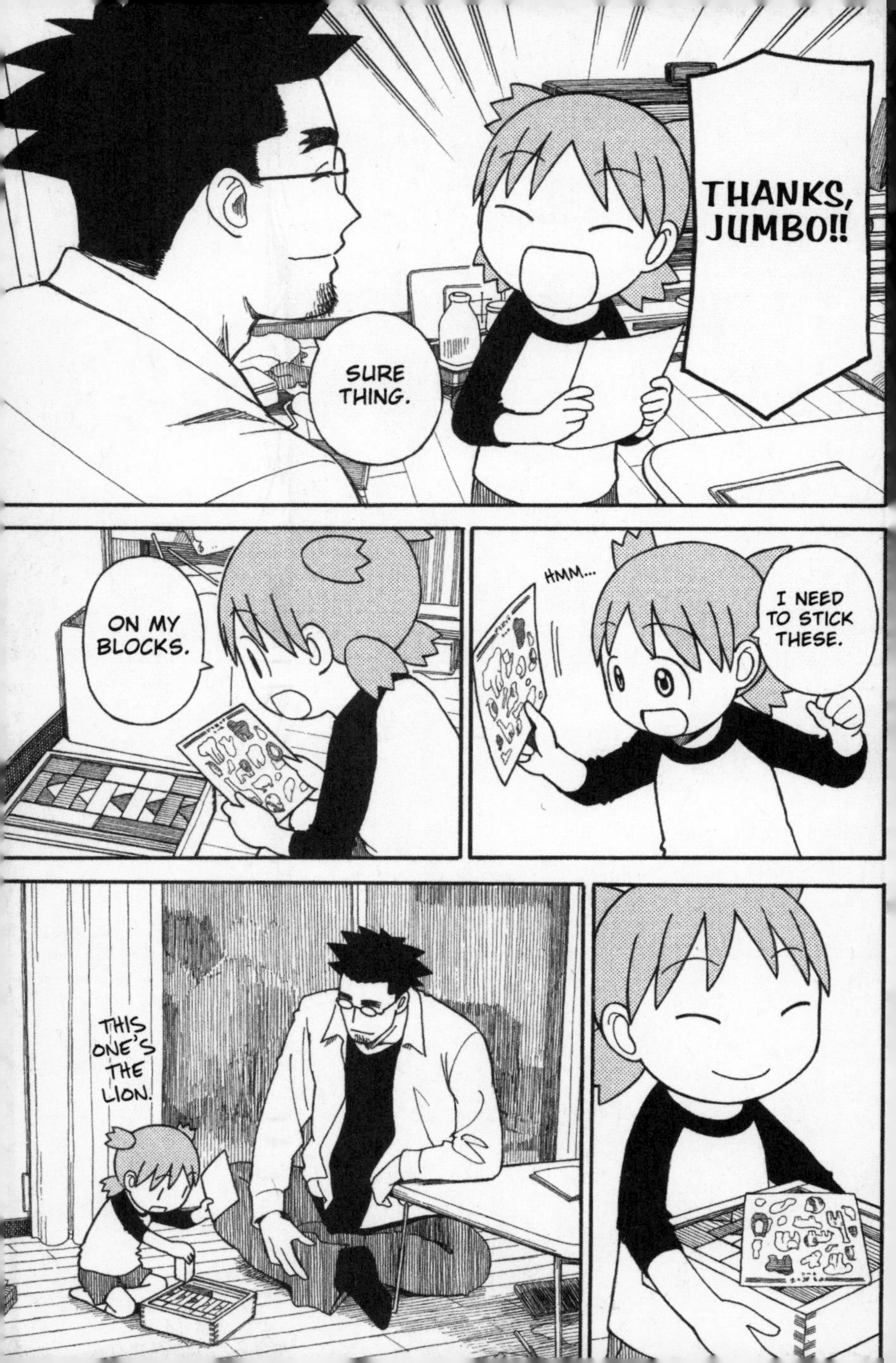
THANKS, JUMBO!!
SURE THING.
HMM...
I NEED TO STICK THESE.
ON MY BLOCKS.
THIS ONE'S THE LION.

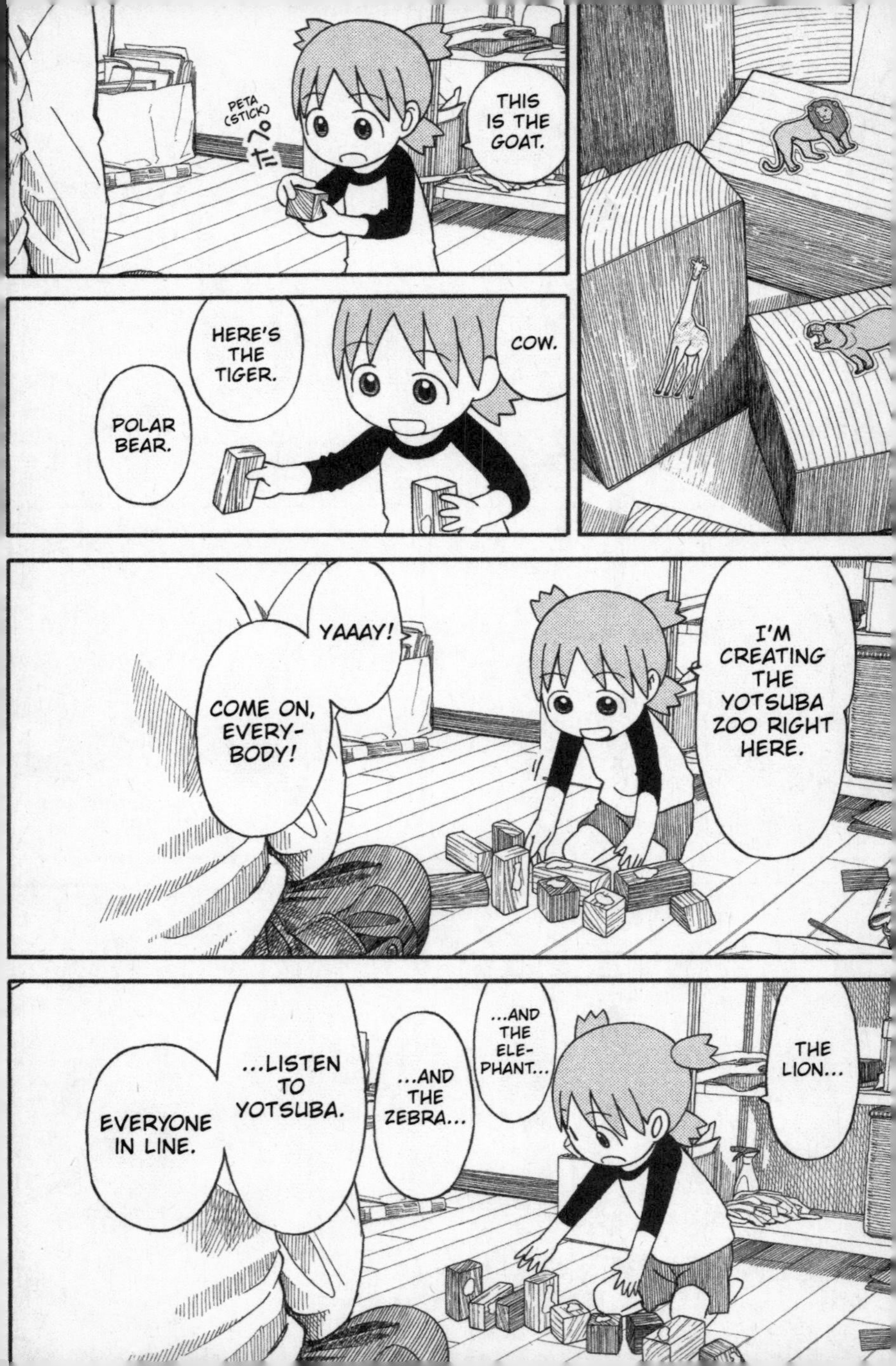

ぺた
PETA (STICK)
THIS IS THE GOAT.
COW.
HERE'S THE TIGER.
POLAR BEAR.
I'M CREATING THE YOTSUBA ZOO RIGHT HERE.
YAAAY!
COME ON, EVERY-BODY!
THE LION...
...AND THE ELE-PHANT...
...AND THE ZEBRA...
...LISTEN TO YOTSUBA.
EVERYONE IN LINE.

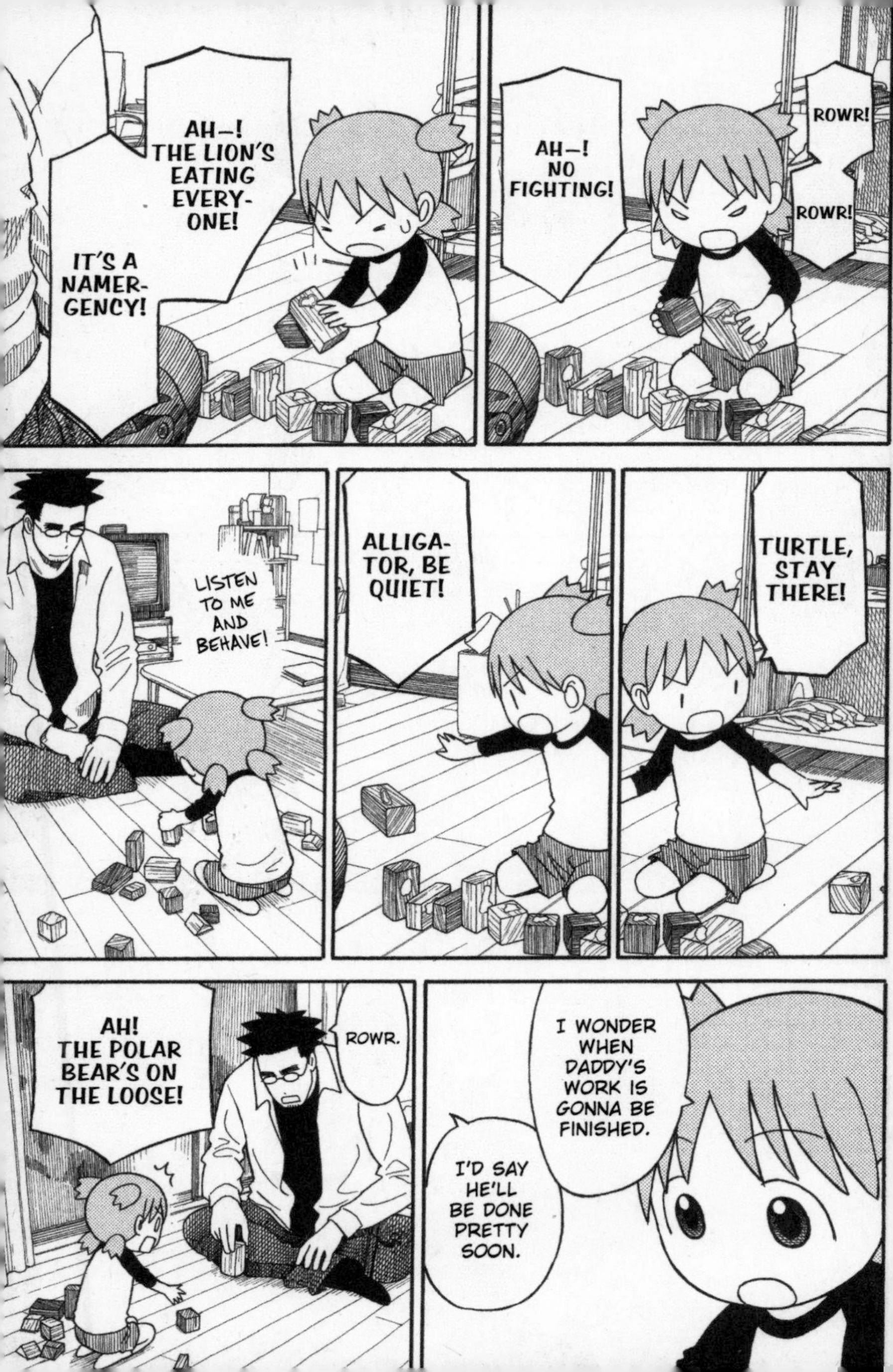
ROWR!
ROWR!
AH—! NO FIGHTING!
AH—! THE LION'S EATING EVERY-ONE!
IT'S A NAMER-GENCY!
TURTLE, STAY THERE!
ALLIGA-TOR, BE QUIET!
LISTEN TO ME AND BEHAVE!
I WONDER WHEN DADDY'S WORK IS GONNA BE FINISHED.
I'D SAY HE'LL BE DONE PRETTY SOON.
ROWR.
AH! THE POLAR BEAR'S ON THE LOOSE!

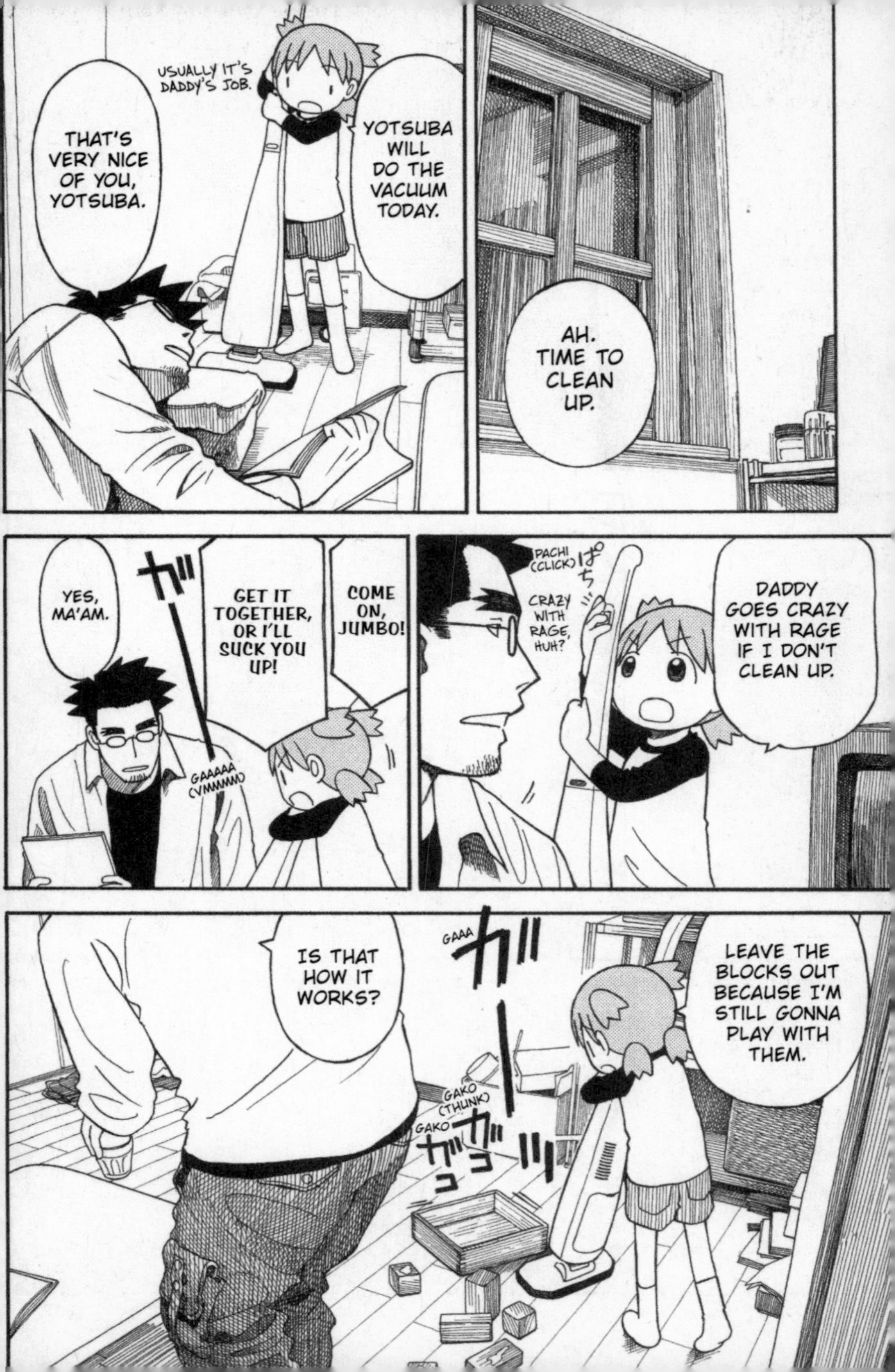
AH. TIME TO CLEAN UP.
YOTSUBA WILL DO THE VACUUM TODAY.
USUALLY IT'S DADDY'S JOB.
THAT'S VERY NICE OF YOU, YOTSUBA.
DADDY GOES CRAZY WITH RAGE IF I DON'T CLEAN UP.
PACHI (CLICK)
ぱち
CRAZY WITH RAGE, HUH?
COME ON, JUMBO!
GET IT TOGETHER, OR I'LL SUCK YOU UP!
ガー
GAAAAA (VMMMM)
YES, MA'AM.
LEAVE THE BLOCKS OUT BECAUSE I'M STILL GONNA PLAY WITH THEM.
GAAA
ガー
GAKO (THUNK)
GAKO
ガコ ガコッ
IS THAT HOW IT WORKS?

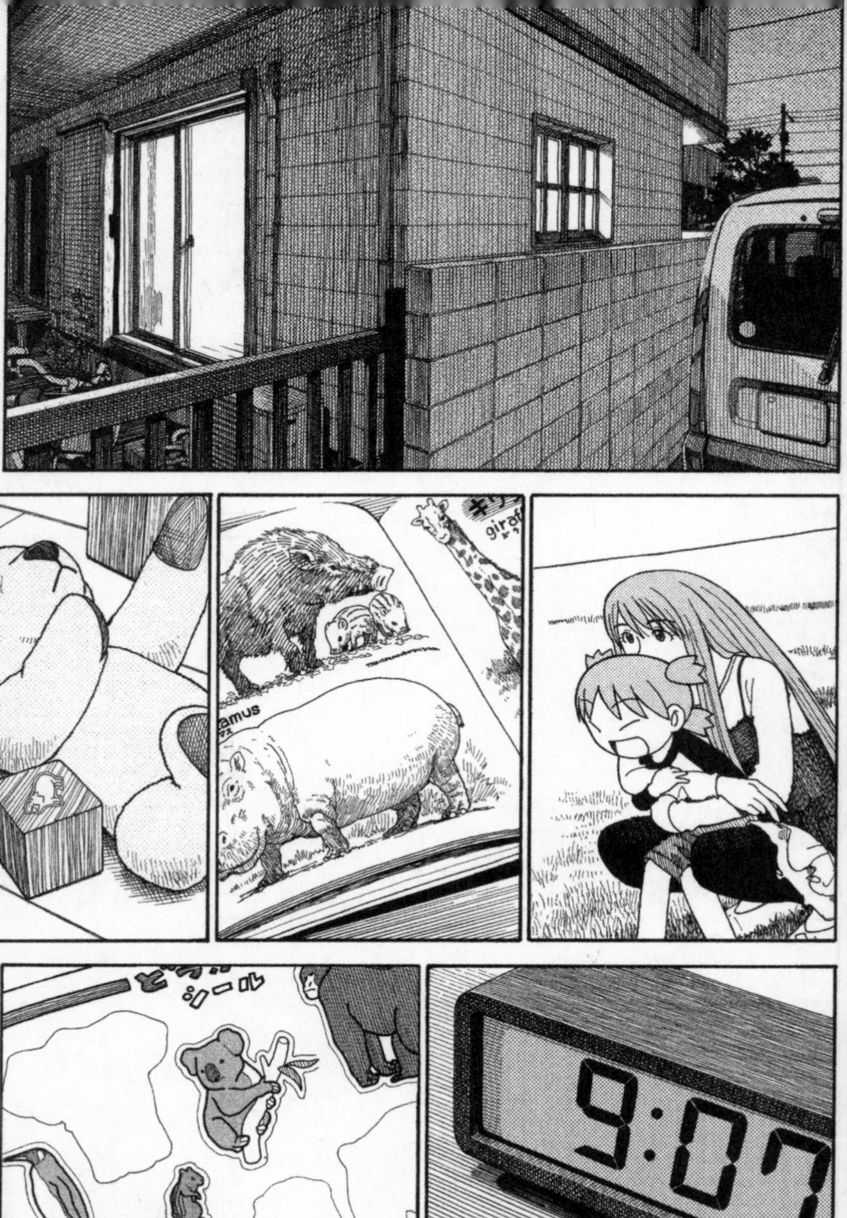
giraf
amus
9:07
シール

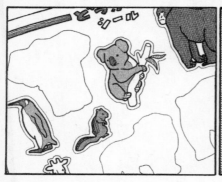

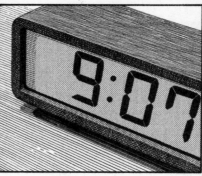

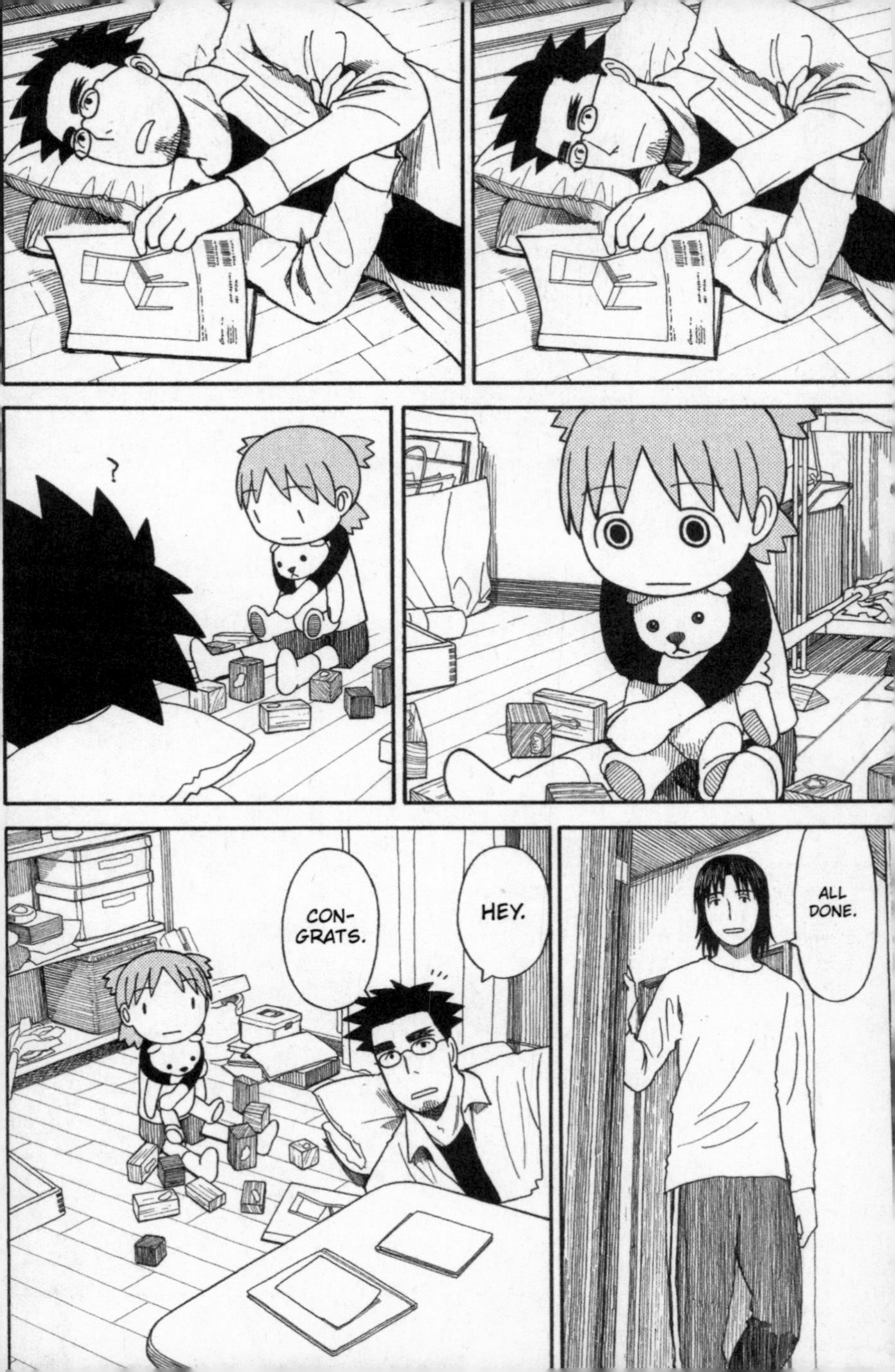
?
ALL DONE.
HEY.
CON-GRATS.

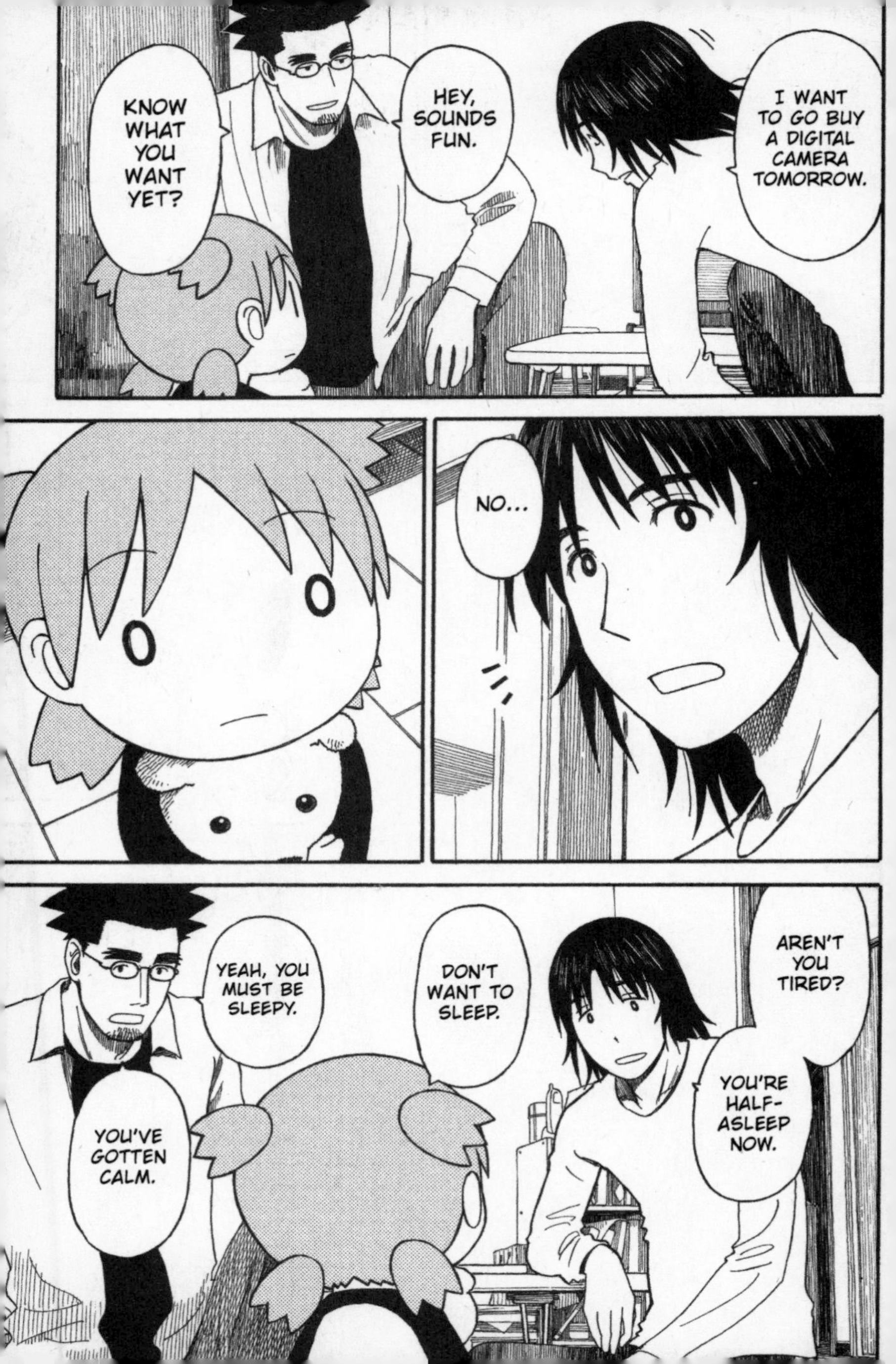
I WANT TO GO BUY A DIGITAL CAMERA TOMORROW.
HEY, SOUNDS FUN.
KNOW WHAT YOU WANT YET?
NO...
AREN'T YOU TIRED?
YOU'RE HALF-ASLEEP NOW.
DON'T WANT TO SLEEP.
YEAH, YOU MUST BE SLEEPY.
YOU'VE GOTTEN CALM.

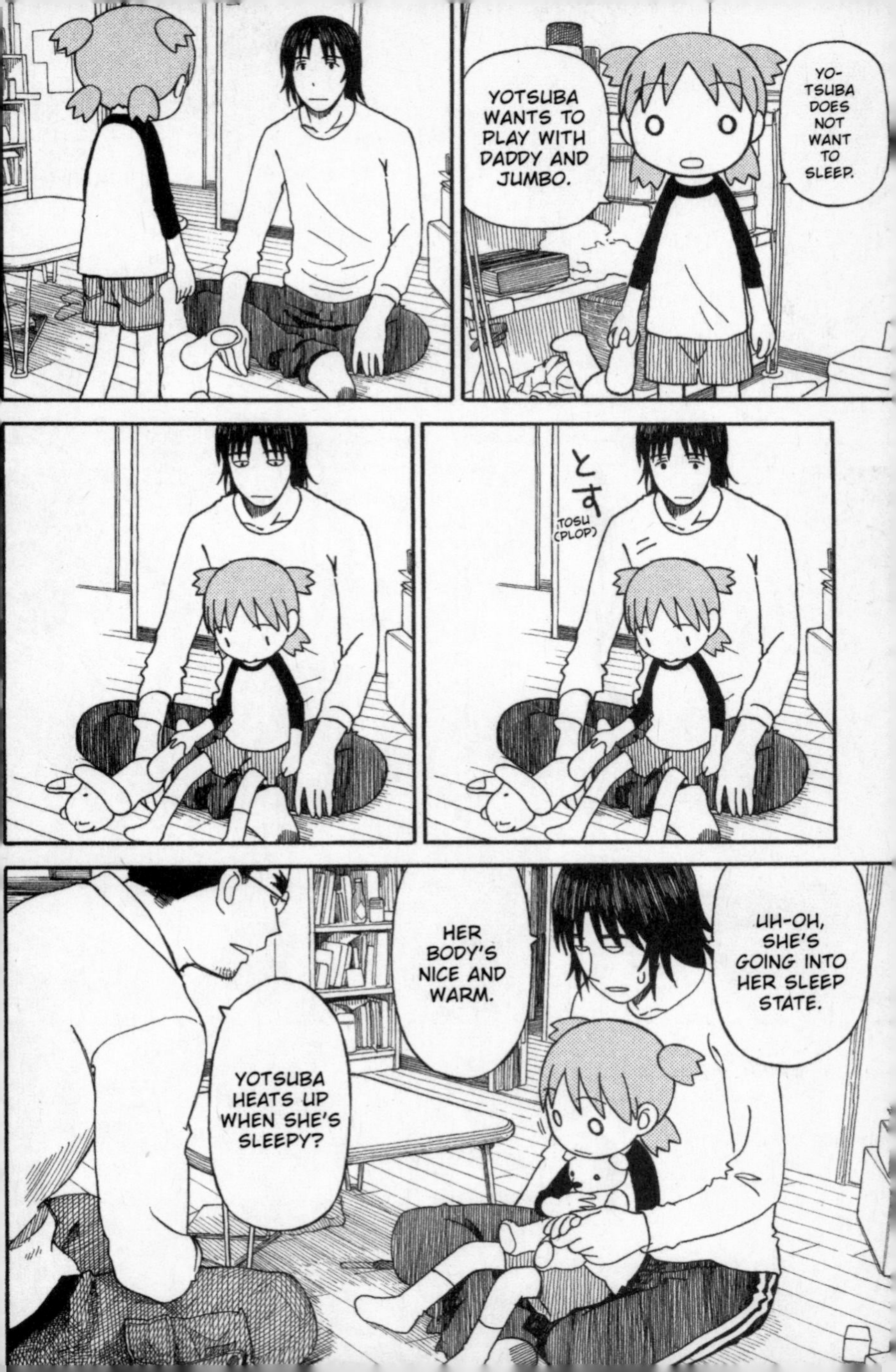

YO-TSUBA DOES NOT WANT TO SLEEP.
YOTSUBA WANTS TO PLAY WITH DADDY AND JUMBO.
とす
TOSU (PLOP)
UH-OH, SHE'S GOING INTO HER SLEEP STATE.
HER BODY'S NICE AND WARM.
YOTSUBA HEATS UP WHEN SHE'S SLEEPY?

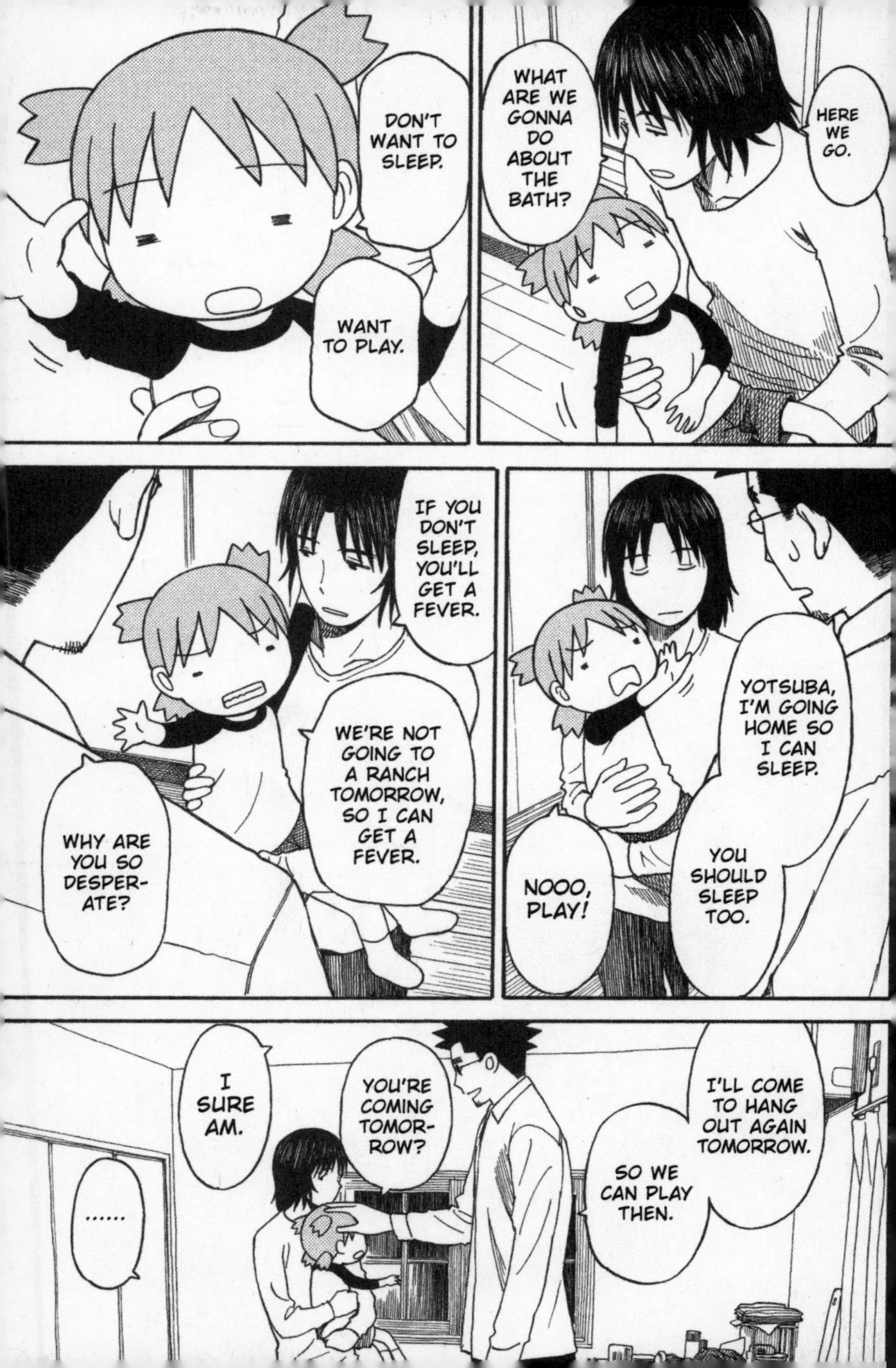
HERE WE GO.
WHAT ARE WE GONNA DO ABOUT THE BATH?
DON'T WANT TO SLEEP.
WANT TO PLAY.
YOTSUBA, I'M GOING HOME SO I CAN SLEEP.
YOU SHOULD SLEEP TOO.
NOOO, PLAY!
IF YOU DON'T SLEEP, YOU'LL GET A FEVER.
WE'RE NOT GOING TO A RANCH TOMORROW, SO I CAN GET A FEVER.
WHY ARE YOU SO DESPER-ATE?
I'LL COME TO HANG OUT AGAIN TOMORROW.
SO WE CAN PLAY THEN.
YOU'RE COMING TOMOR-ROW?
I SURE AM.
......

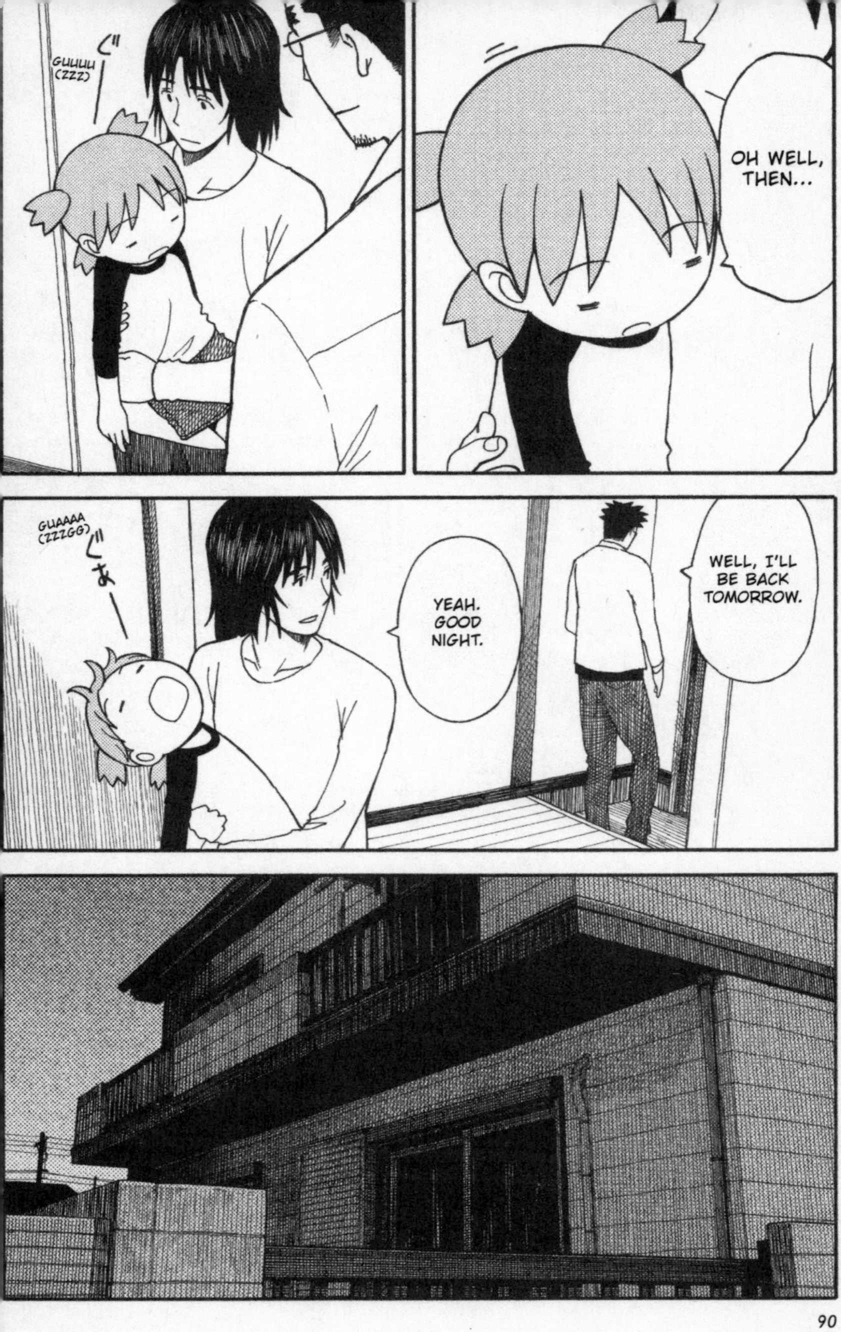
OH WELL, THEN...
ぐー
GUUUU (ZZZ)
WELL, I'LL BE BACK TOMORROW.
YEAH. GOOD NIGHT.
ぐあー
GUAAAA (ZZZGG)

YOTSUBA&!

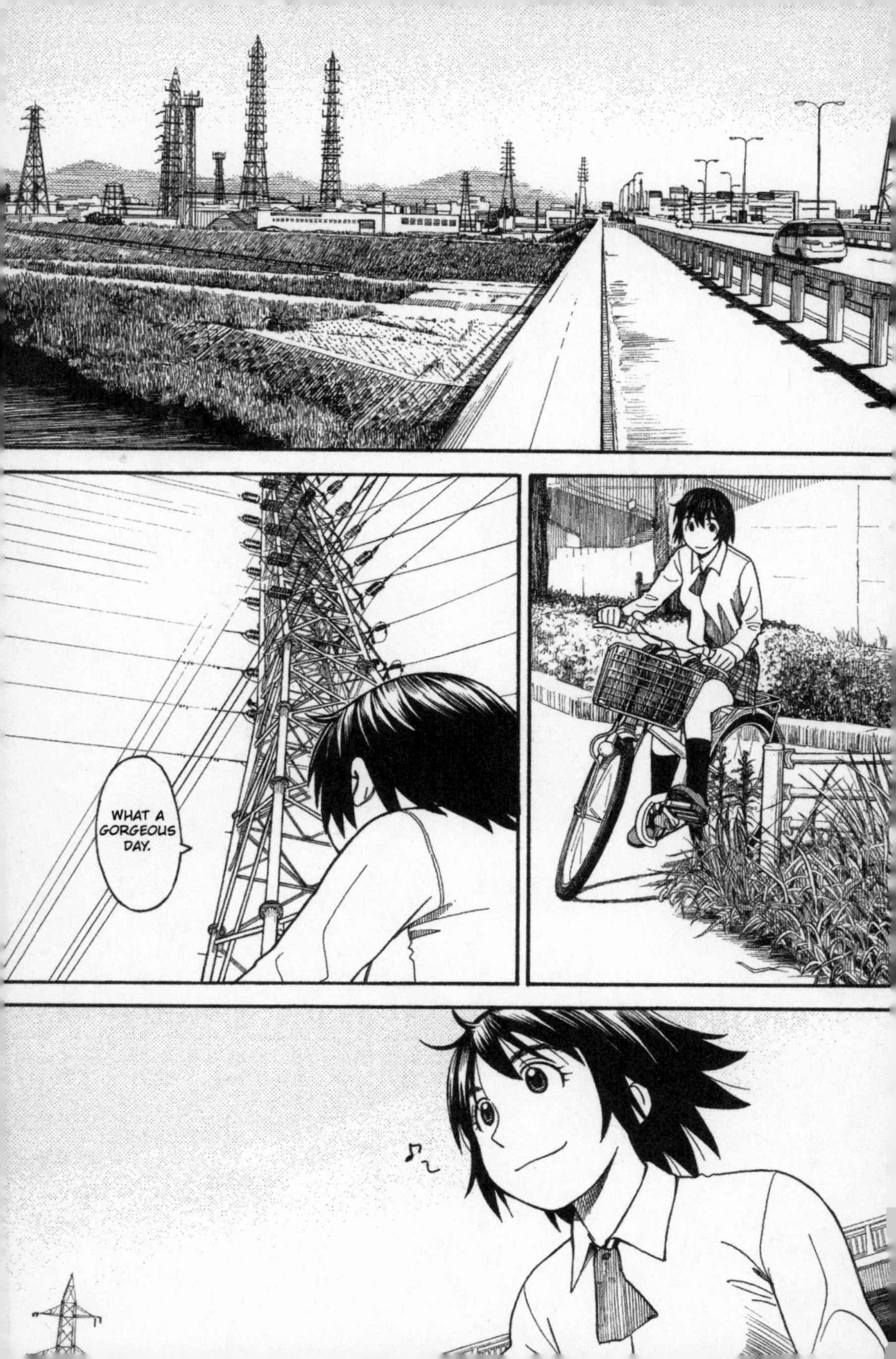
WHAT A GORGEOUS DAY.

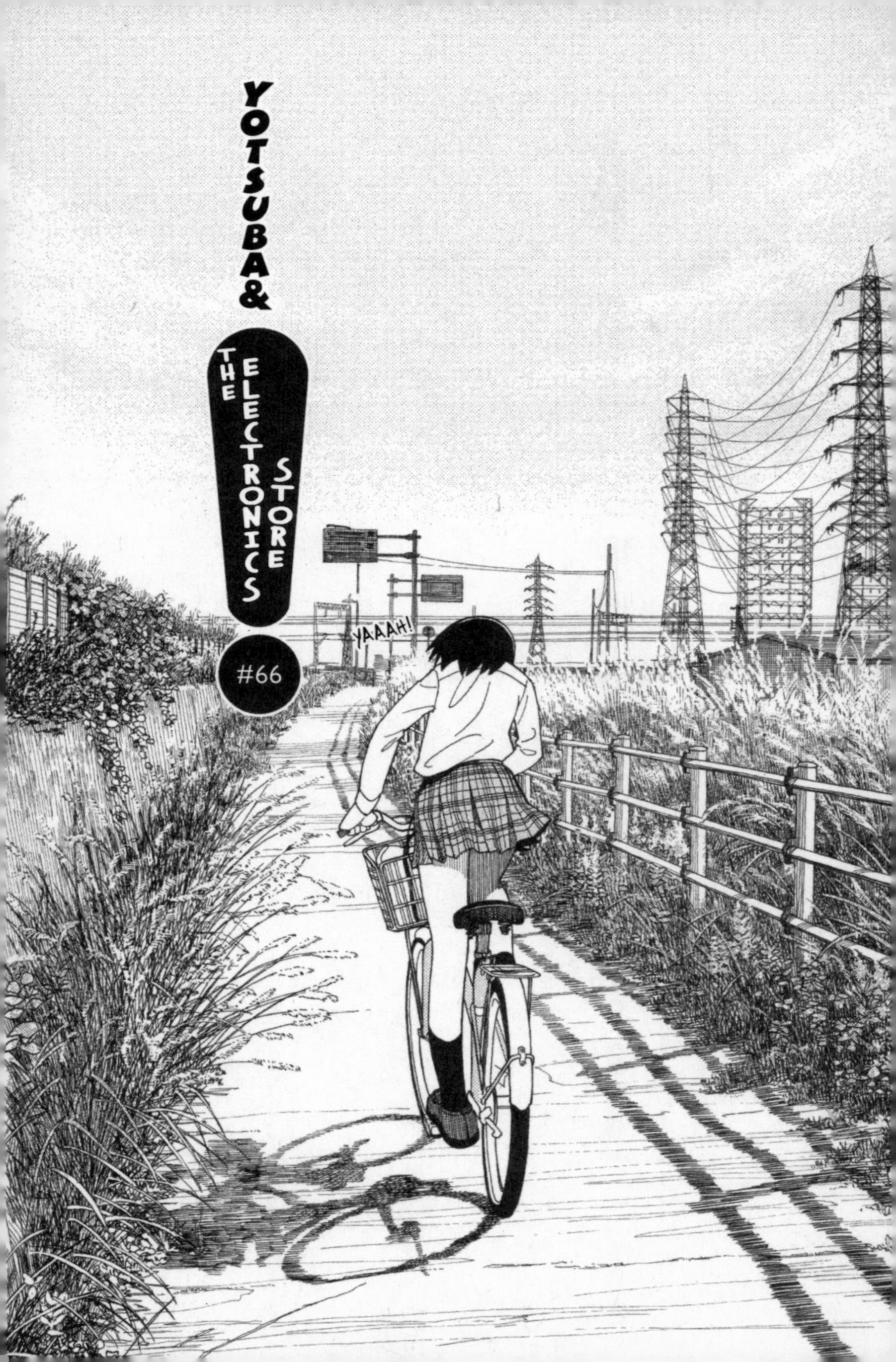
YOTSUBA&
THE ELECTRONICS STORE
#66
YAAAH!

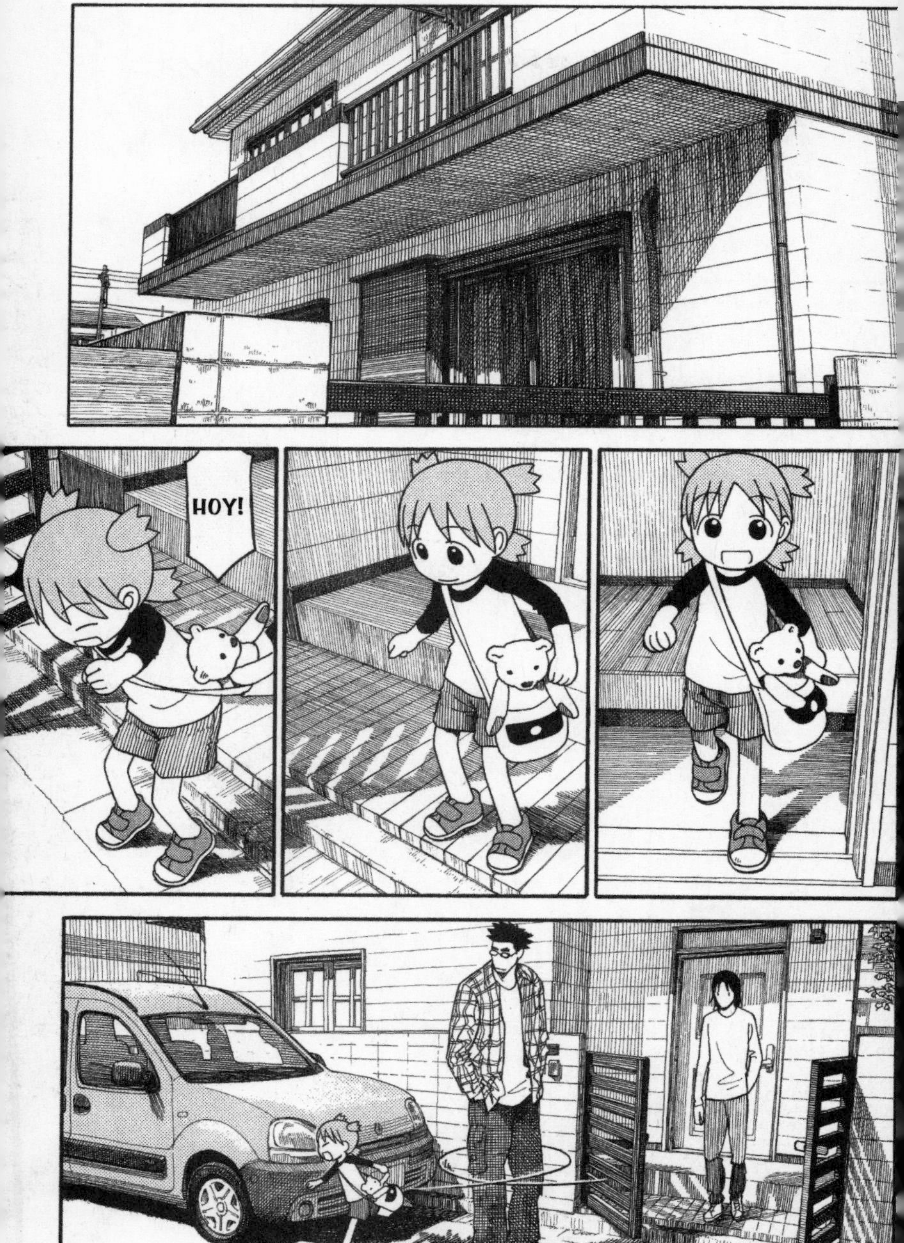
HOY!

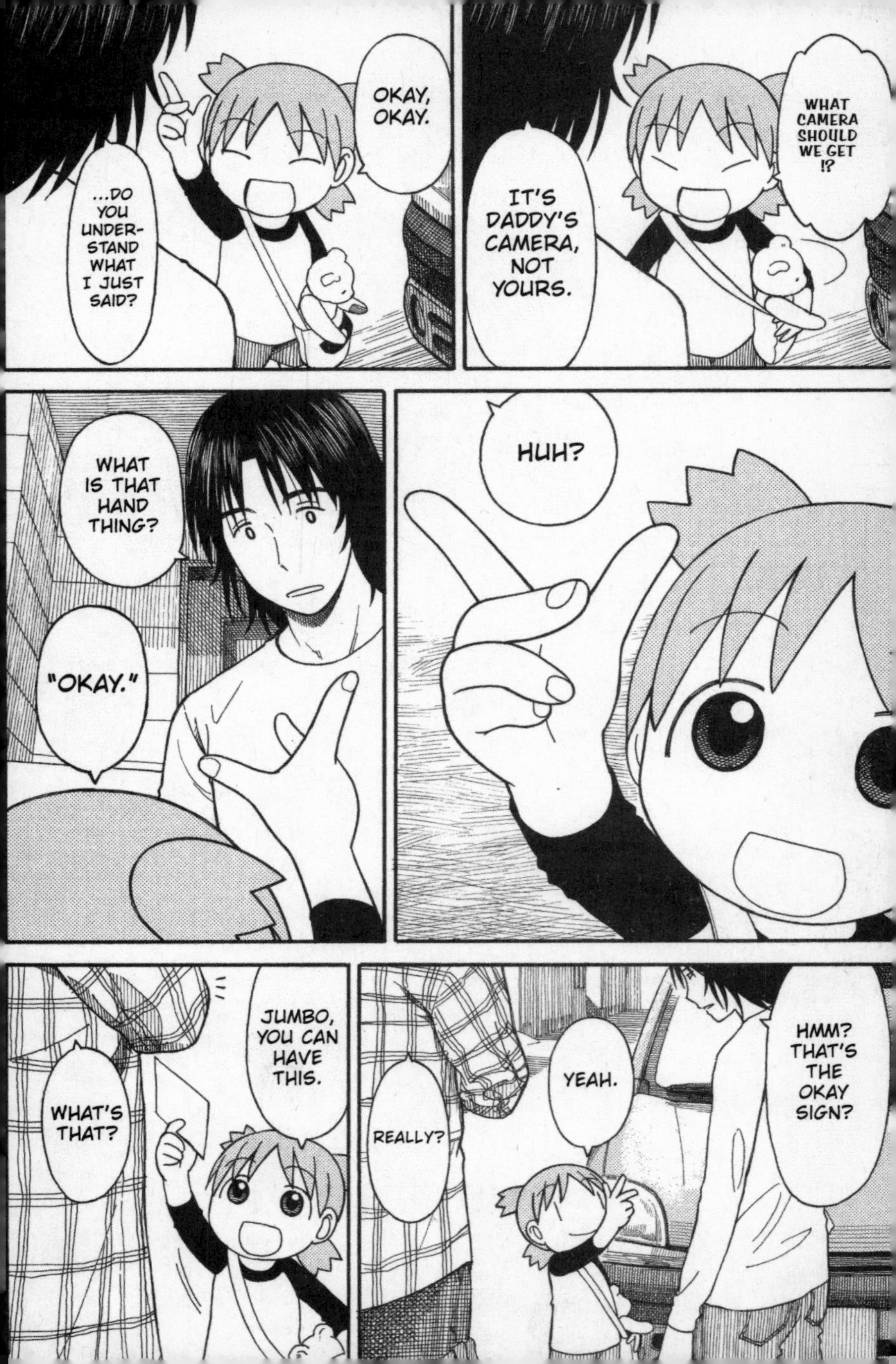
WHAT CAMERA SHOULD WE GET!?
IT'S DADDY'S CAMERA, NOT YOURS.
OKAY, OKAY.
...DO YOU UNDER-STAND WHAT I JUST SAID?
HUH?
WHAT IS THAT HAND THING?
"OKAY."
HMM? THAT'S THE OKAY SIGN?
YEAH.
REALLY?
JUMBO, YOU CAN HAVE THIS.
WHAT'S THAT?

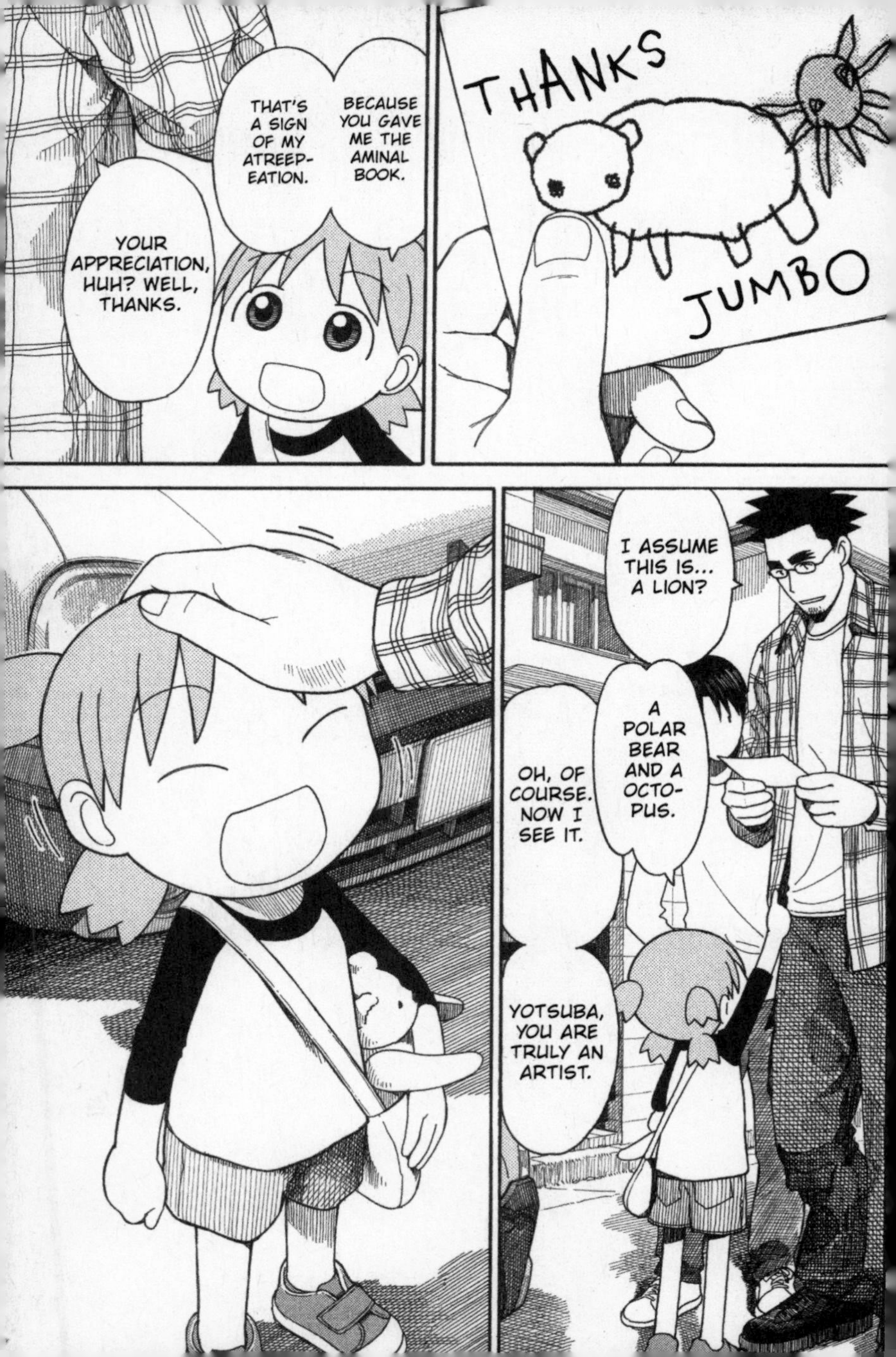
THANKS
JUMBO
BECAUSE YOU GAVE ME THE AMINAL BOOK.
THAT'S A SIGN OF MY ATREEP-EATION.
YOUR APPRECIATION, HUH? WELL, THANKS.
I ASSUME THIS IS... A LION?
A POLAR BEAR AND A OCTO-PUS.
OH, OF COURSE. NOW I SEE IT.
YOTSUBA, YOU ARE TRULY AN ARTIST.

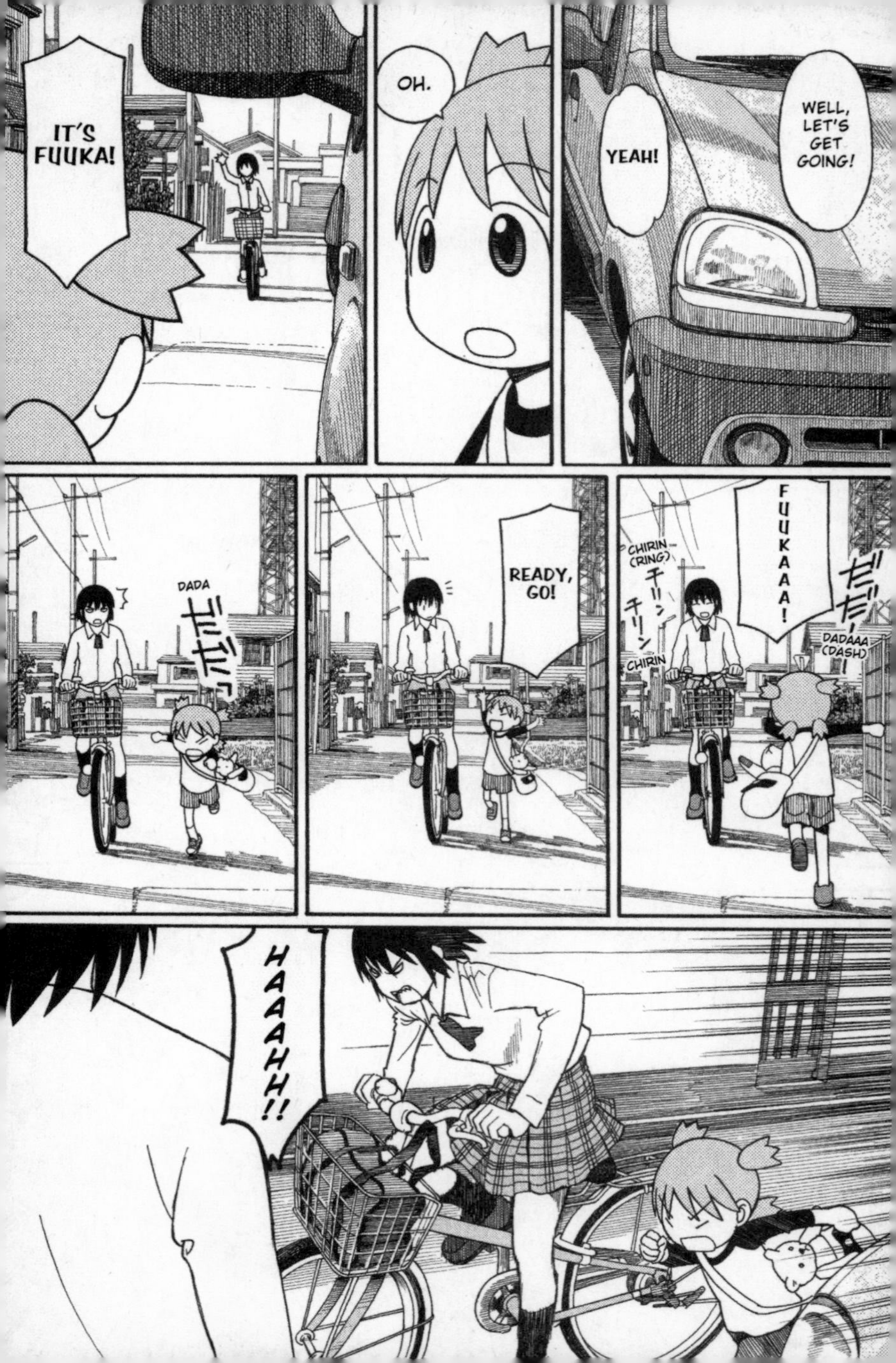
WELL, LET'S GET GOING!
YEAH!
OH.
IT'S FUUKA!
FUUKAAA!
CHIRIN (RING)
チリン
チリン
CHIRIN
DADAAA (DASH)!
READY, GO!
DADA
HAAAAHH!!

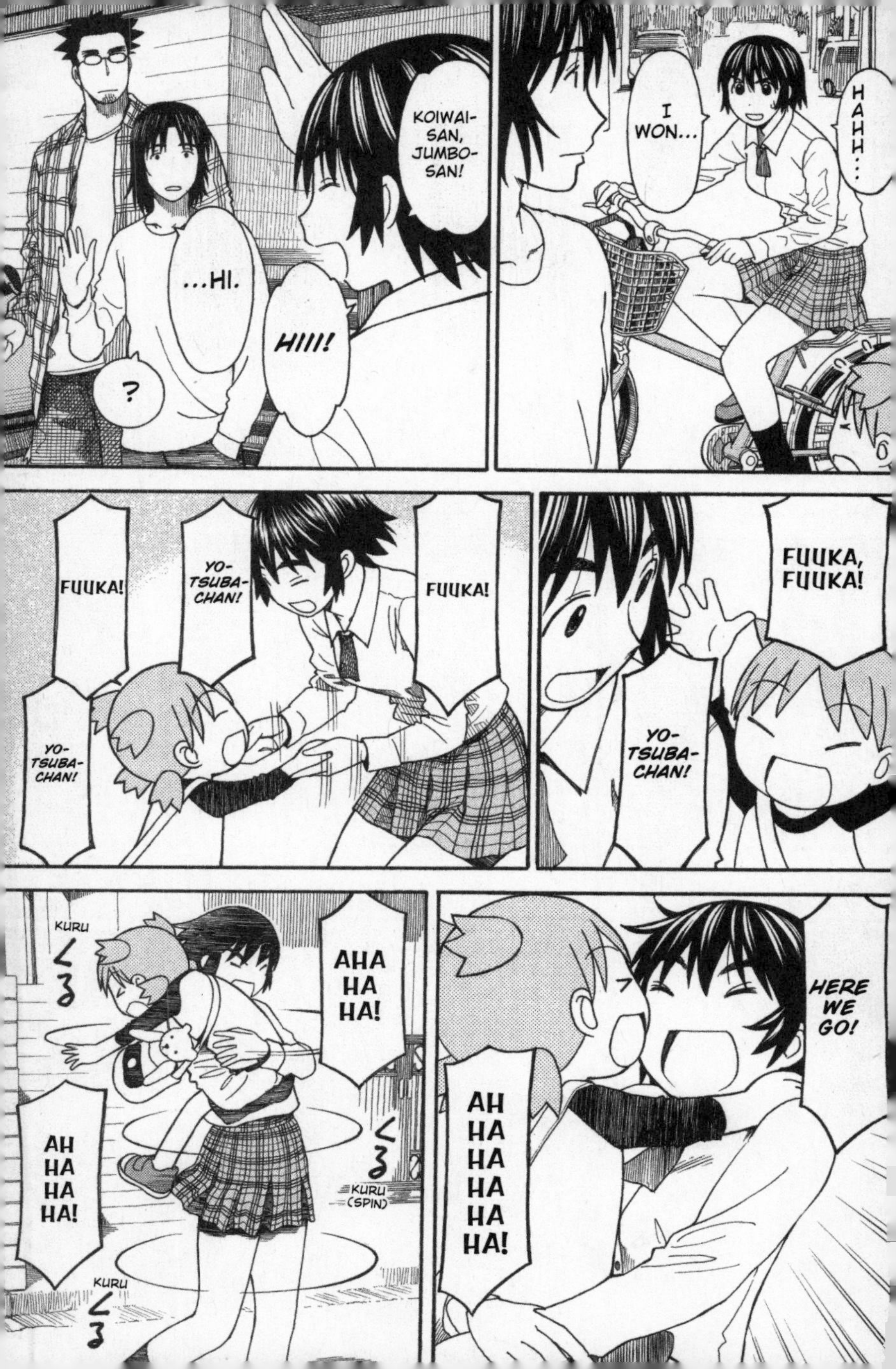
HAHH...
I WON...
KOIWAI-SAN, JUMBO-SAN!
HIII!
...HI.
?
FUUKA, FUUKA!
YO-TSUBA-CHAN!
FUUKA!
YO-TSUBA-CHAN!
FUUKA!
YO-TSUBA-CHAN!
HERE WE GO!
AH HA HA HA HA HA HA!
AHA HA HA!
KURU
くる
くる
KURU (SPIN)
AH HA HA HA!
KURU
くる

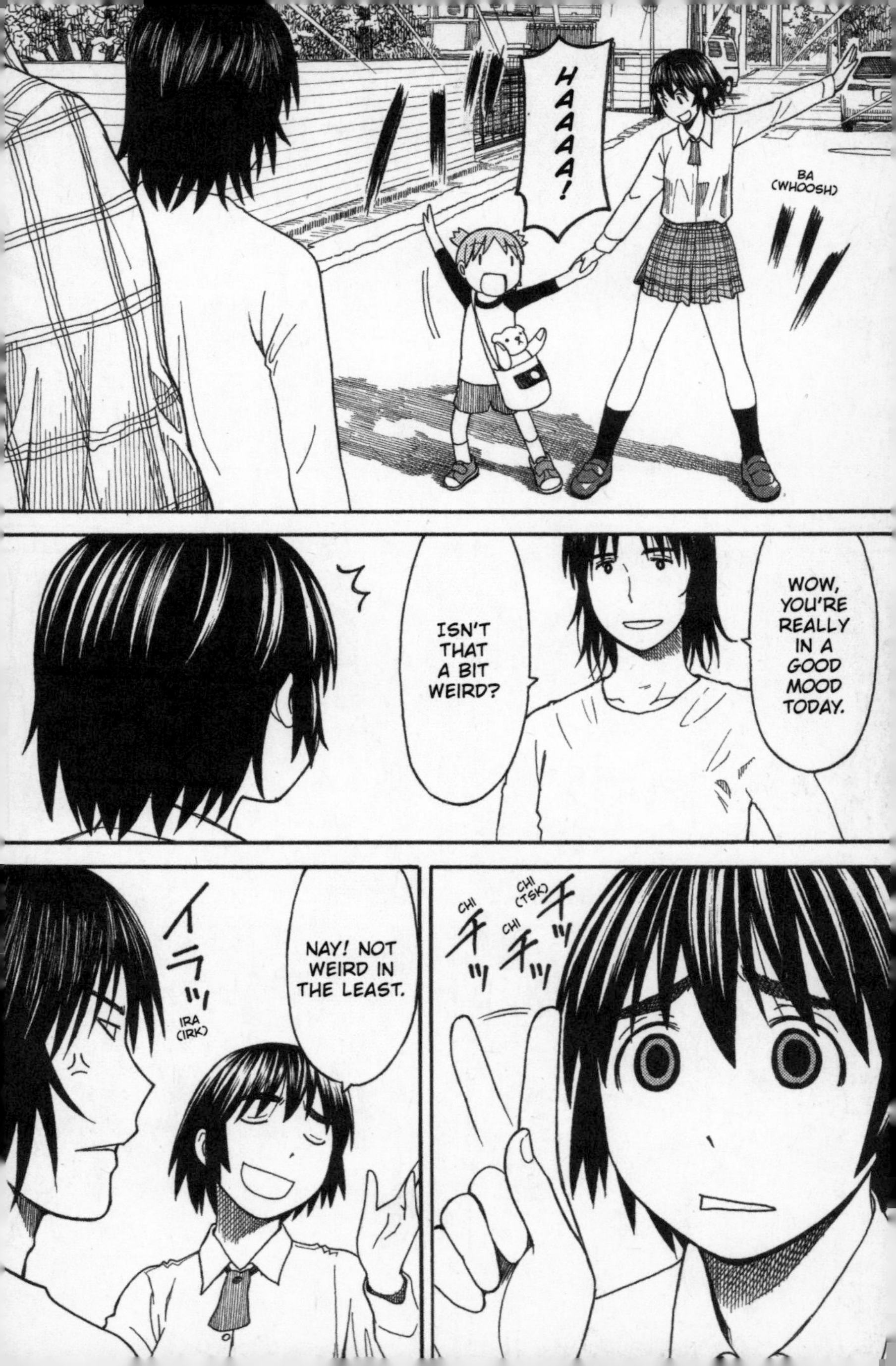
HAAAAA!
BA (WHOOSH)
WOW, YOU'RE REALLY IN A GOOD MOOD TODAY.
ISN'T THAT A BIT WEIRD?
チッ
CHI (TSK)
チッ
CHI
チッ
CHI
NAY! NOT WEIRD IN THE LEAST.
イラッ
IRA (IRK)

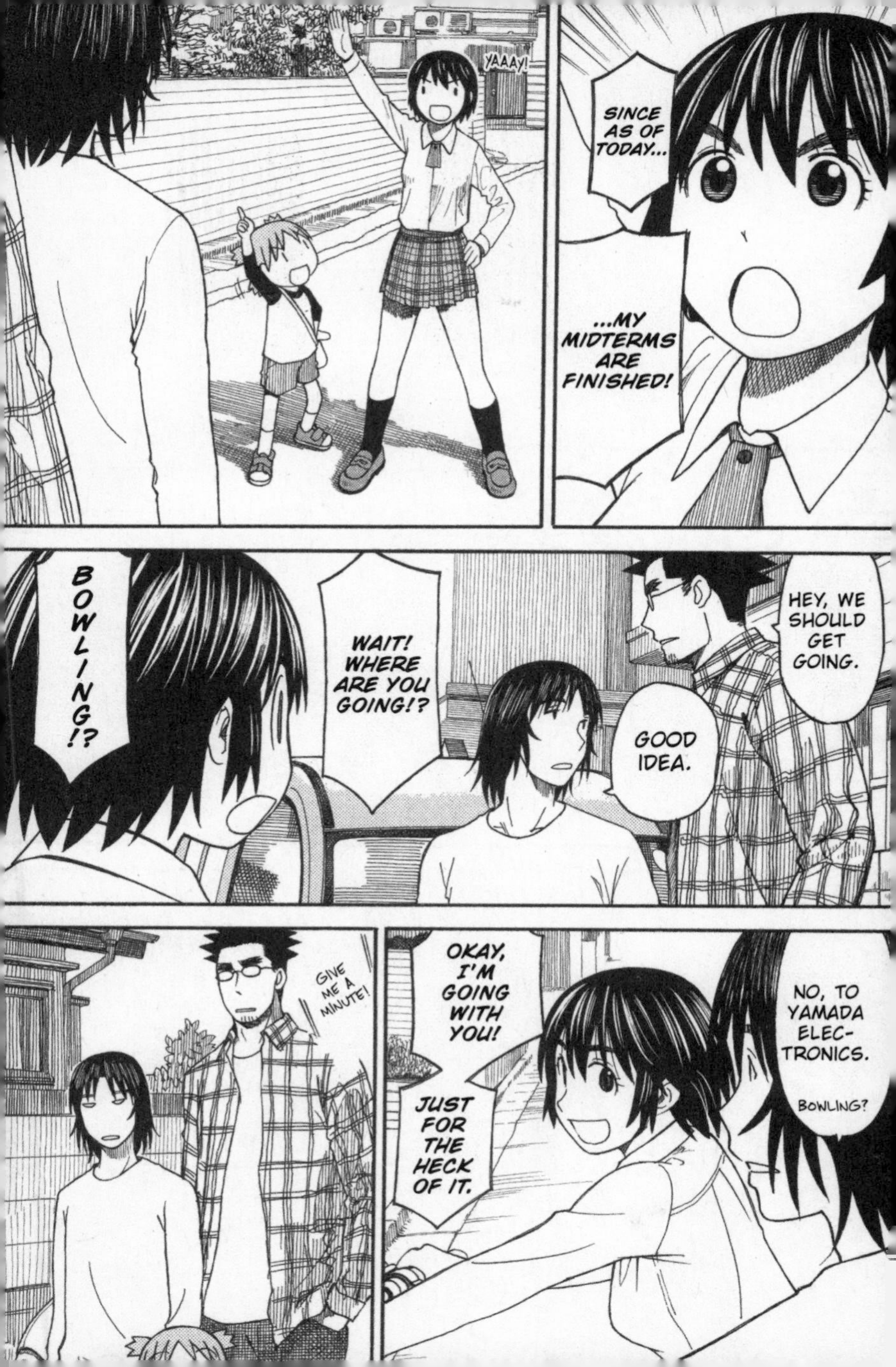
SINCE AS OF TODAY...
...MY MIDTERMS ARE FINISHED!
YAAAY!
HEY, WE SHOULD GET GOING.
GOOD IDEA.
WAIT! WHERE ARE YOU GOING!?
BOWLING!?
NO, TO YAMADA ELECTRONICS.
BOWLING?
OKAY, I'M GOING WITH YOU!
JUST FOR THE HECK OF IT.
GIVE ME A MINUTE!

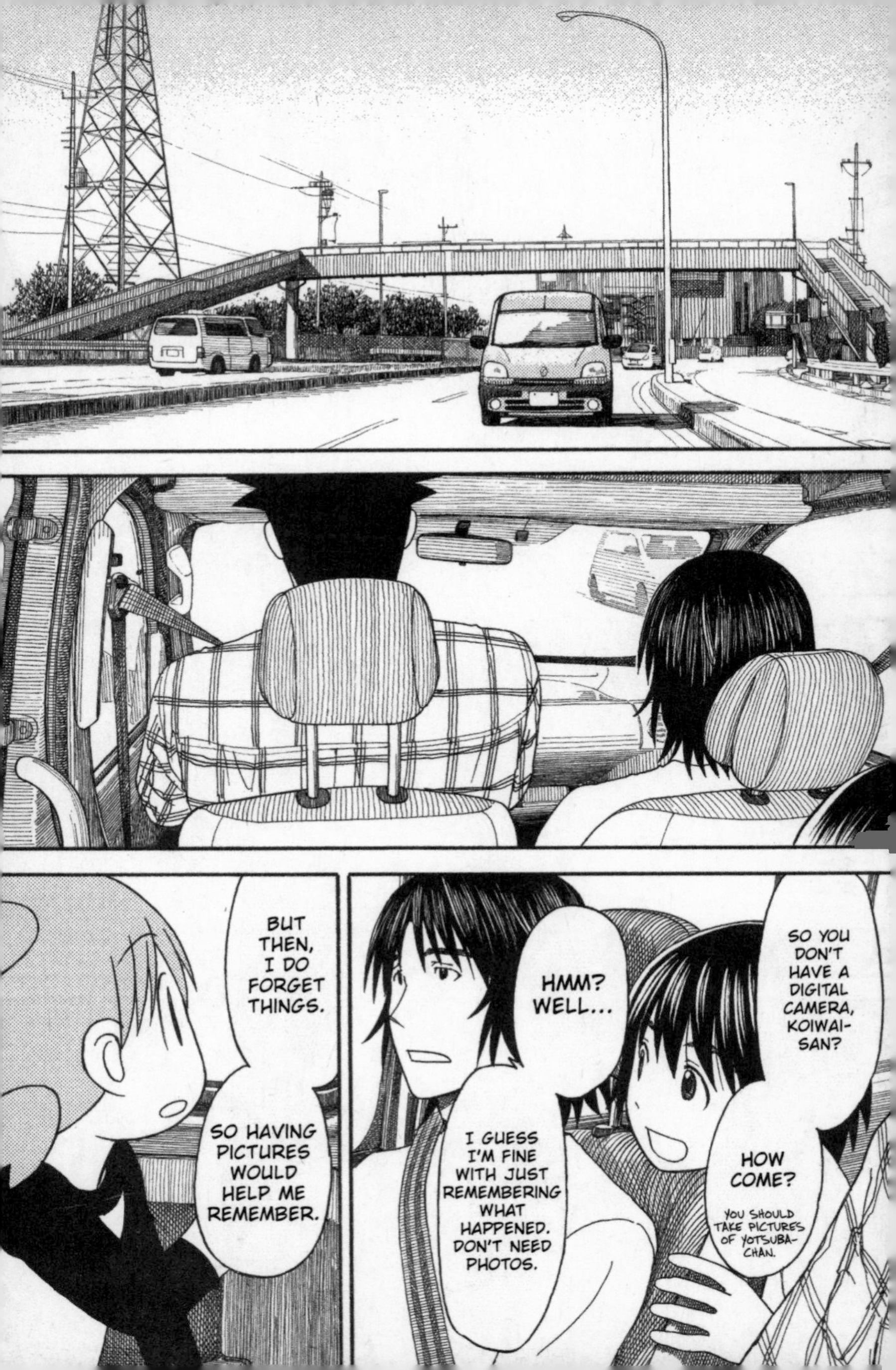
SO YOU DON'T HAVE A DIGITAL CAMERA, KOIWAI-SAN?
HMM? WELL...
HOW COME?
YOU SHOULD TAKE PICTURES OF YOTSUBA-CHAN.
I GUESS I'M FINE WITH JUST REMEMBERING WHAT HAPPENED. DON'T NEED PHOTOS.
BUT THEN, I DO FORGET THINGS.
SO HAVING PICTURES WOULD HELP ME REMEMBER.

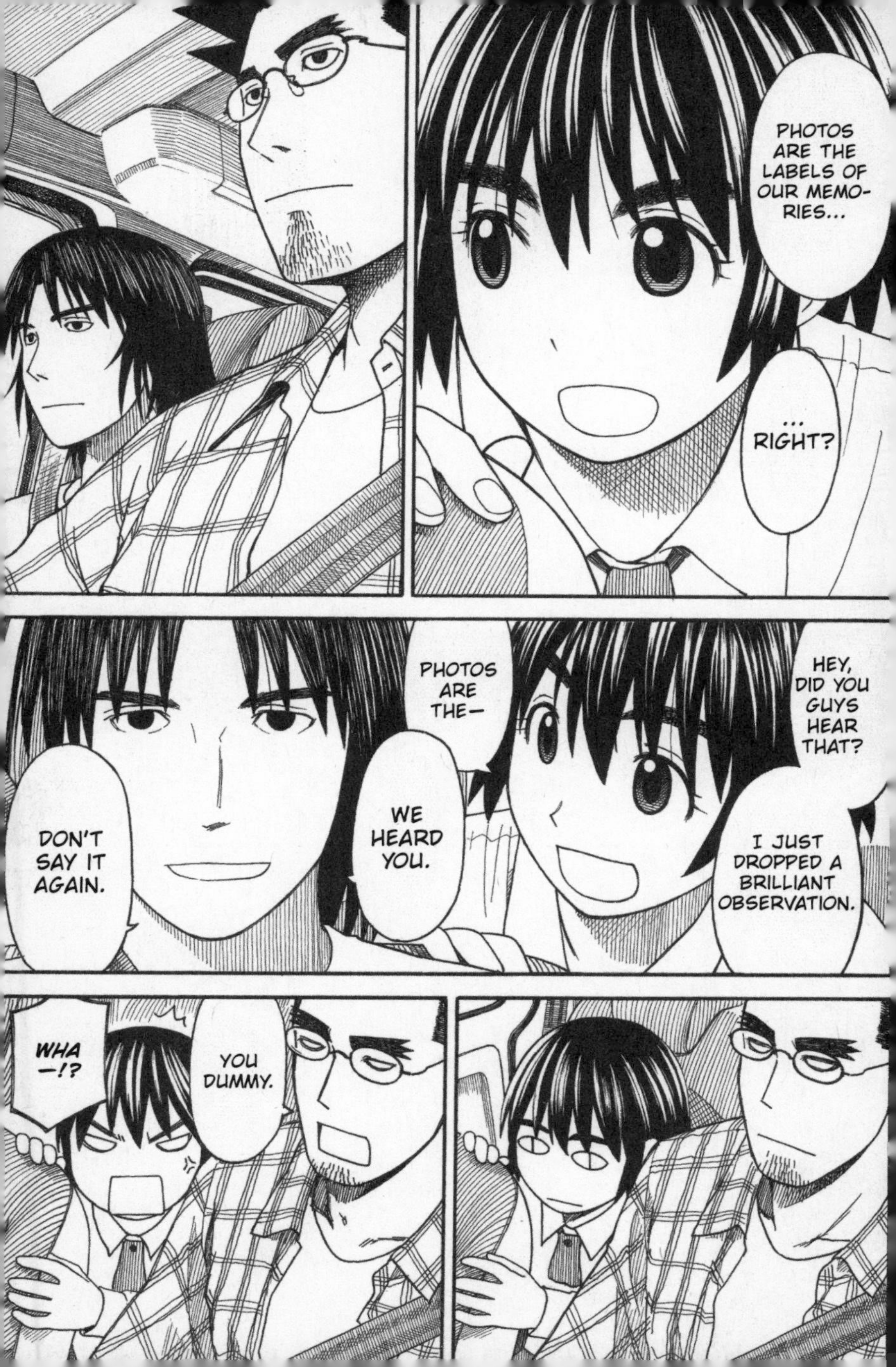
PHOTOS ARE THE LABELS OF OUR MEMORIES...
...RIGHT?
HEY, DID YOU GUYS HEAR THAT?
I JUST DROPPED A BRILLIANT OBSERVATION.
PHOTOS ARE THE—
WE HEARD YOU.
DON'T SAY IT AGAIN.
YOU DUMMY.
WHA—!?

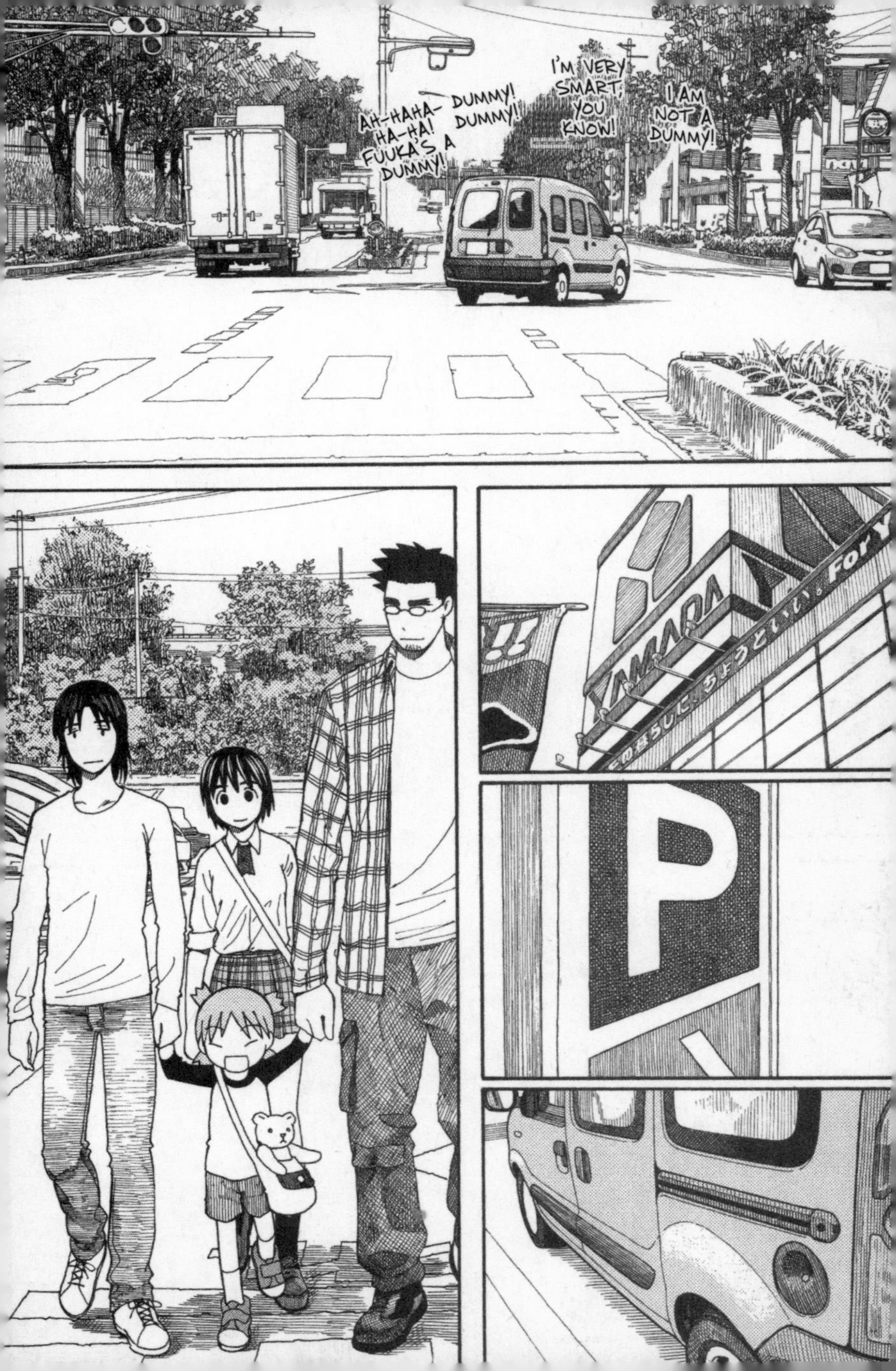

I AM NOT A DUMMY!
I'M VERY SMART, YOU KNOW!
DUMMY! DUMMY!
AH-HAHA-HA-HA! FUUKA'S A DUMMY!
YAMADA

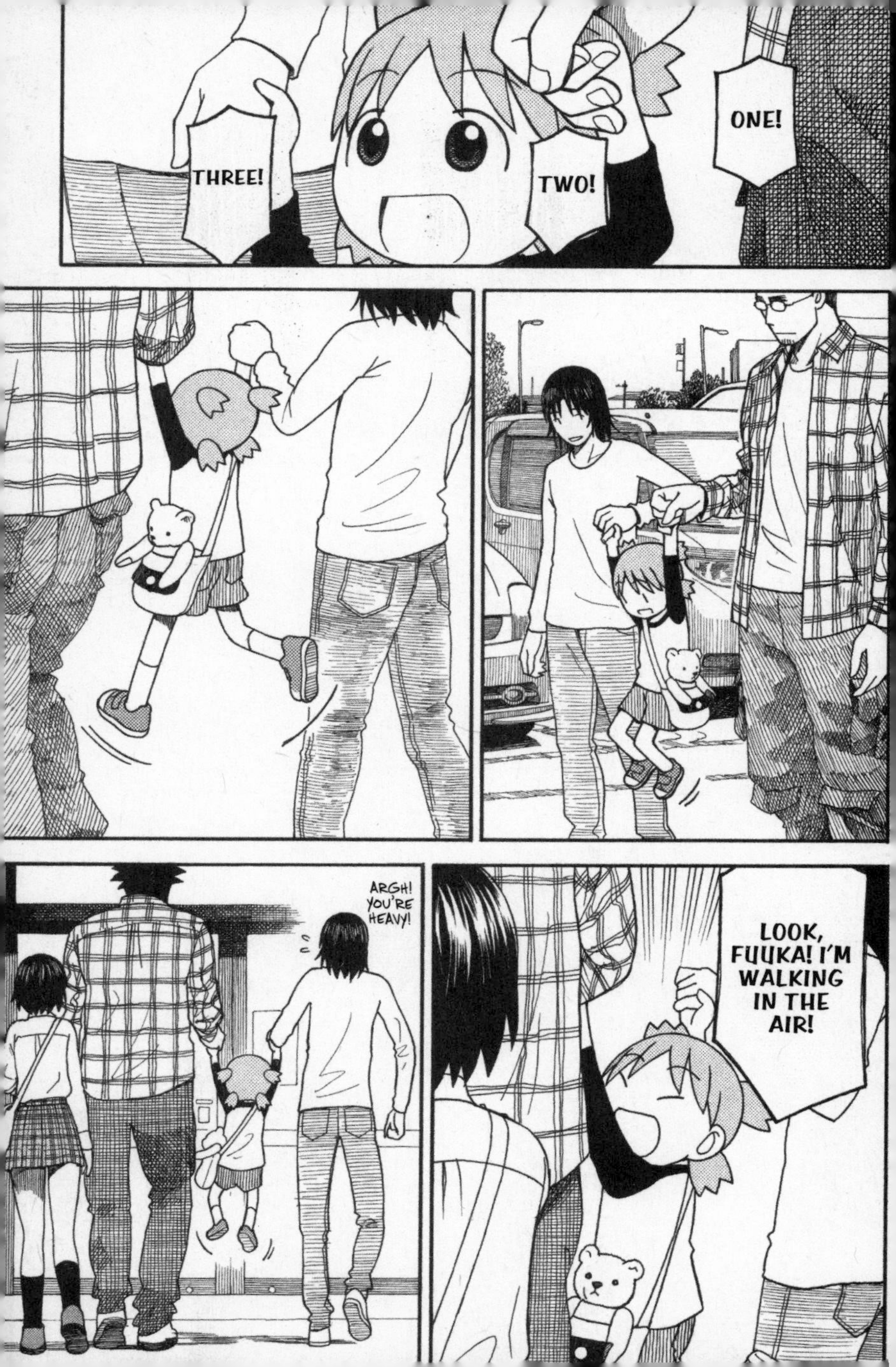
ONE!
TWO!
THREE!
LOOK, FUUKA! I'M WALKING IN THE AIR!
ARGH! YOU'RE HEAVY!

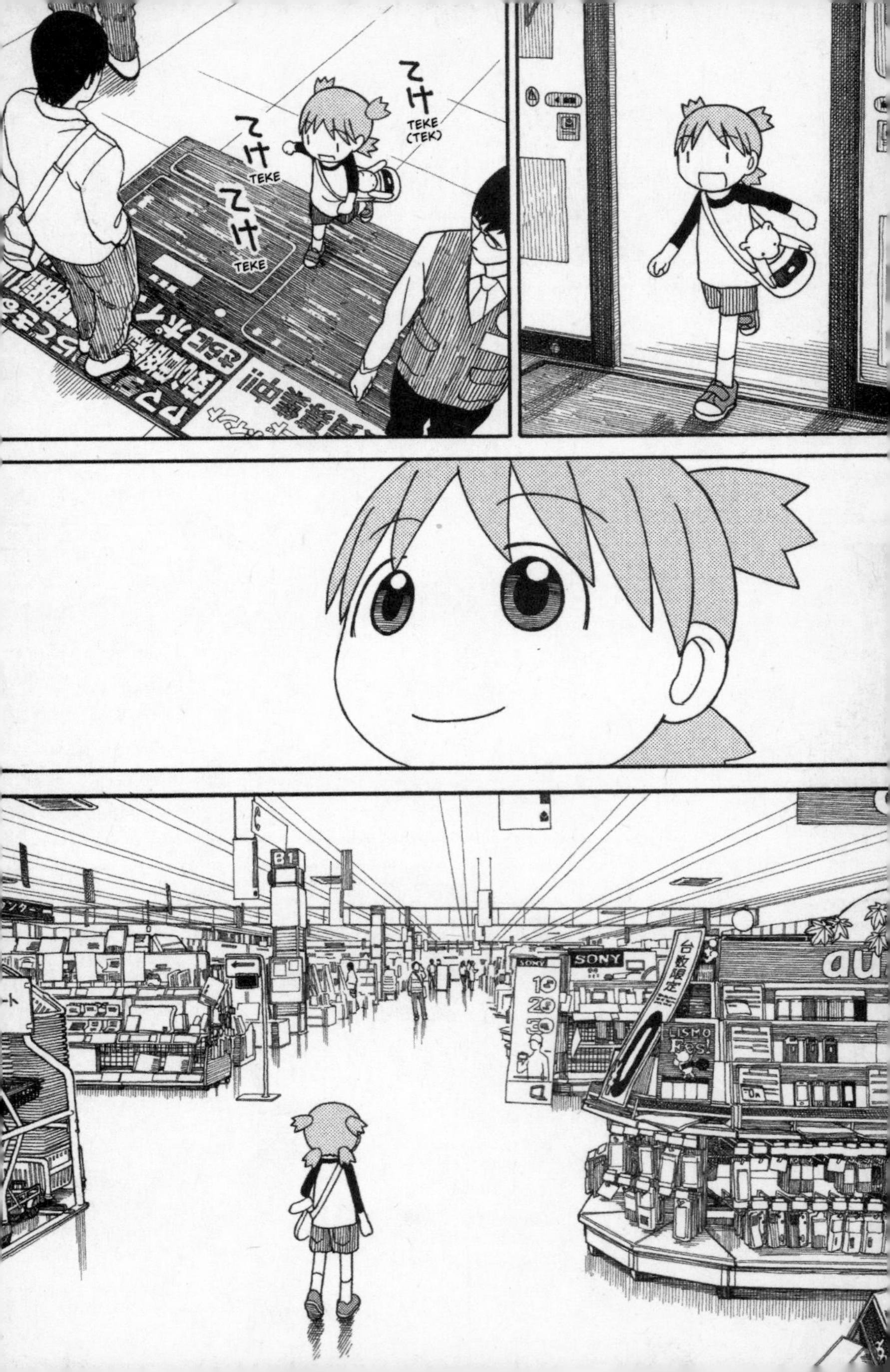

てけ
TEKE (TEK)
てけ
TEKE
てけ
TEKE
B1
SONY
台数限定
LISMO Fes!
au

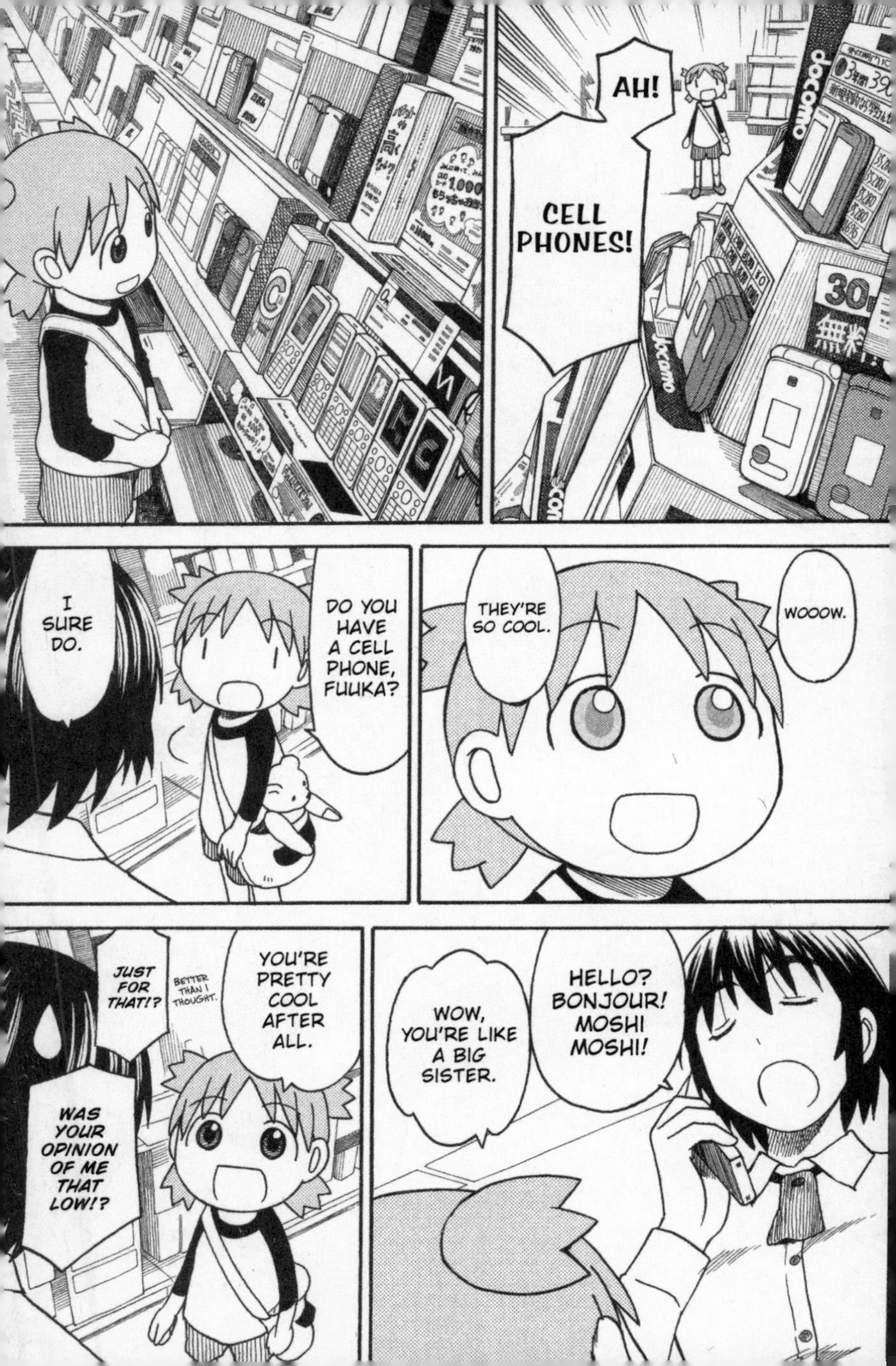
AH!
CELL PHONES!
docomo
WOOOW.
THEY'RE SO COOL.
DO YOU HAVE A CELL PHONE, FUUKA?
I SURE DO.
HELLO? BONJOUR! MOSHI MOSHI!
WOW, YOU'RE LIKE A BIG SISTER.
YOU'RE PRETTY COOL AFTER ALL.
BETTER THAN I THOUGHT.
JUST FOR THAT!?
WAS YOUR OPINION OF ME THAT LOW!?

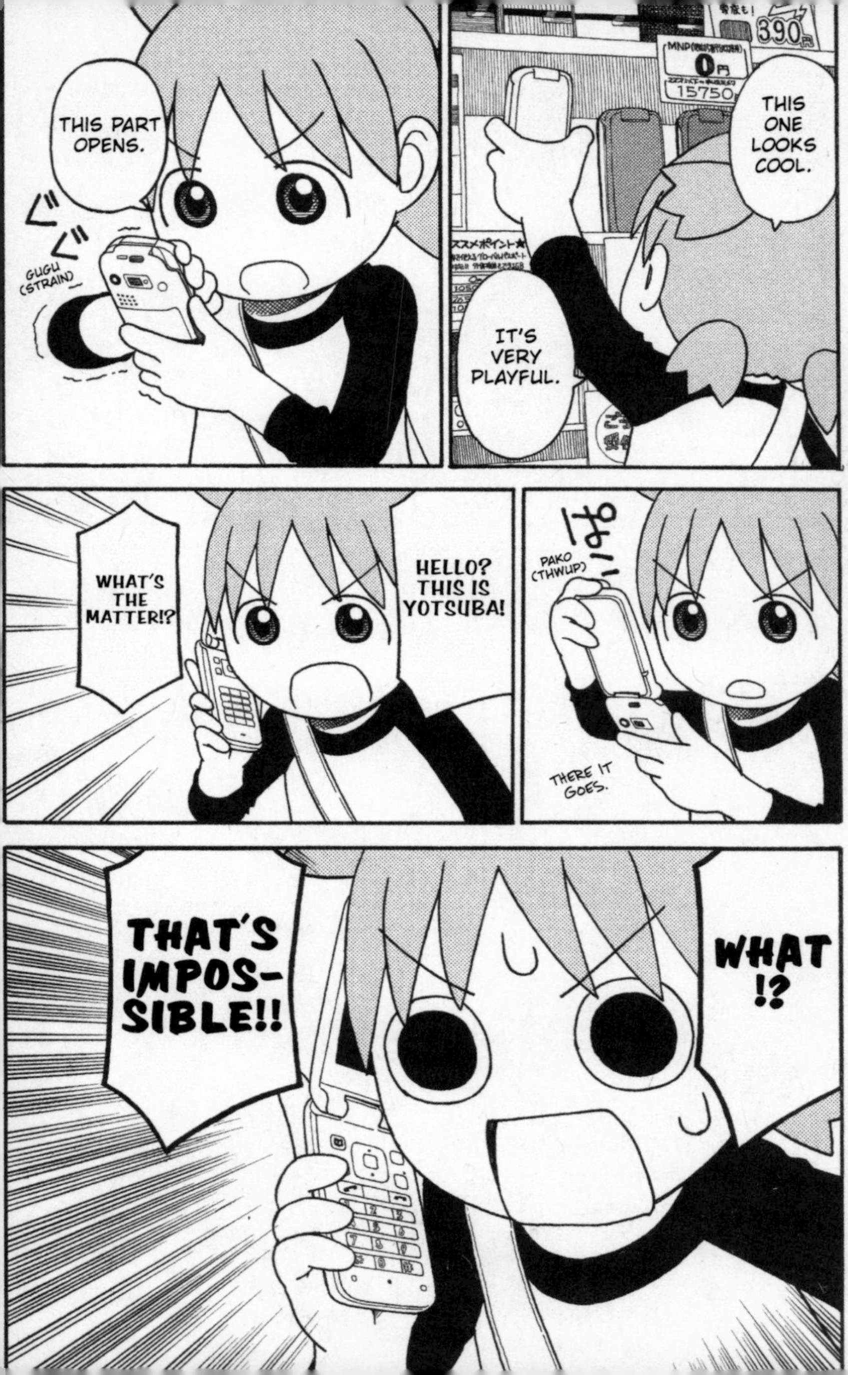

390
0円
15750
ススメポイント★
THIS ONE LOOKS COOL.
IT'S VERY PLAYFUL.
THIS PART OPENS.
ぐぐ
GUGU (STRAIN)
ぱこっ
PAKO (THWUP)
THERE IT GOES.
HELLO? THIS IS YOTSUBA!
WHAT'S THE MATTER!?
WHAT !?
THAT'S IMPOS-SIBLE!!

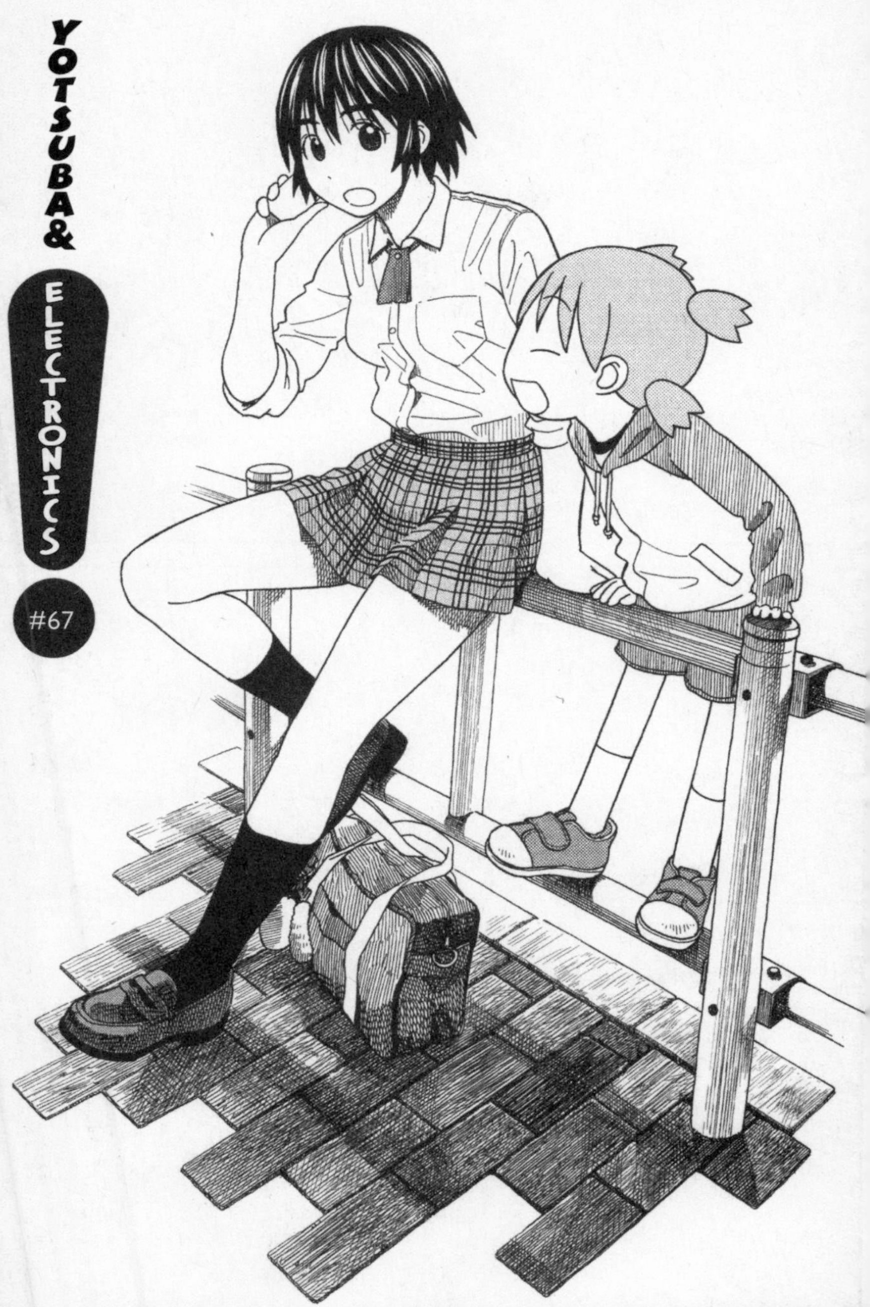
YOTSUBA&
ELECTRONICS
#67

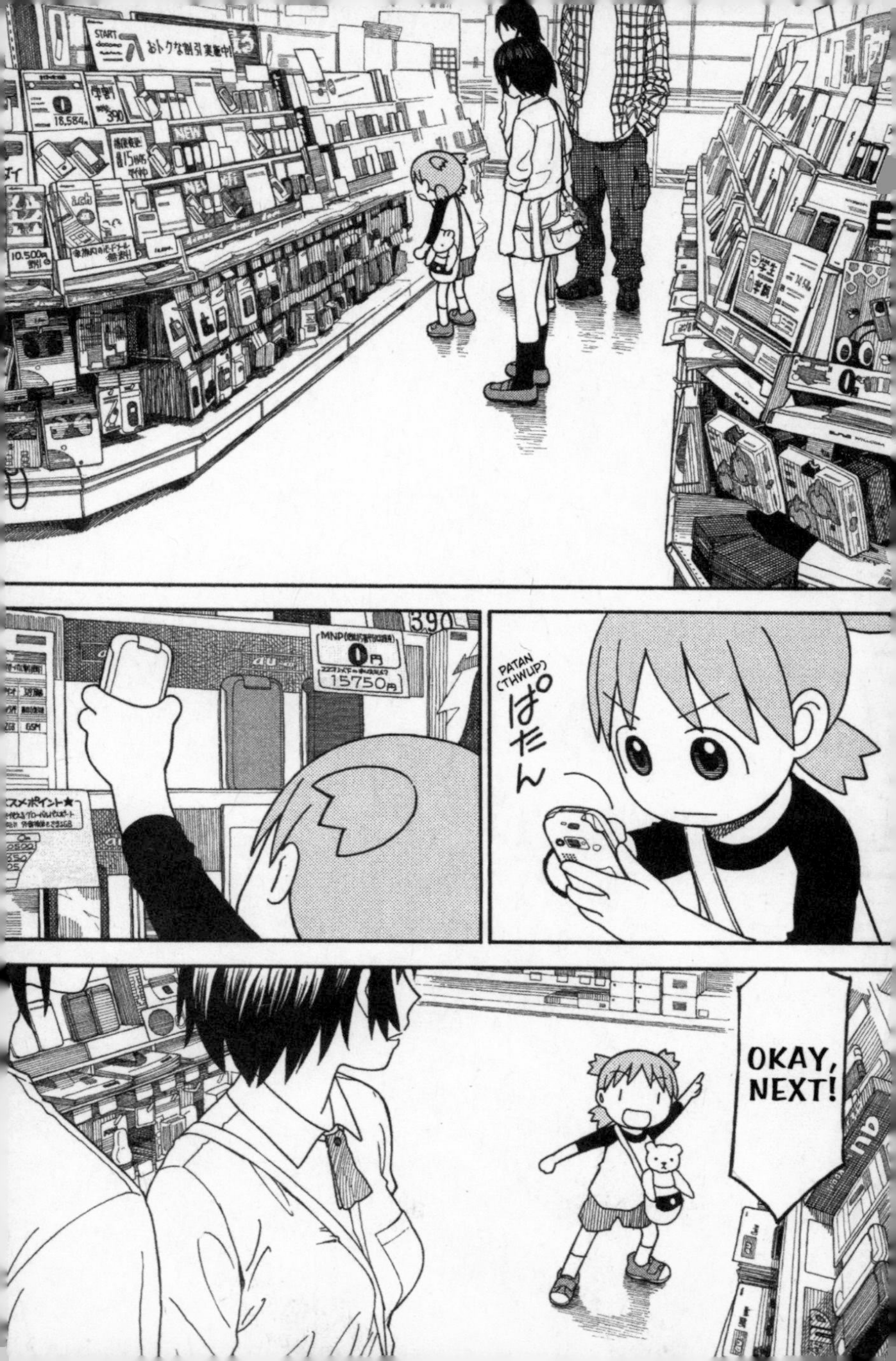
START
おトクな割引実施中!
18,584
390
NEW
10,500
PATAN (THWUP)
ぱたん
390
MNP
0円
15750円
OKAY, NEXT!

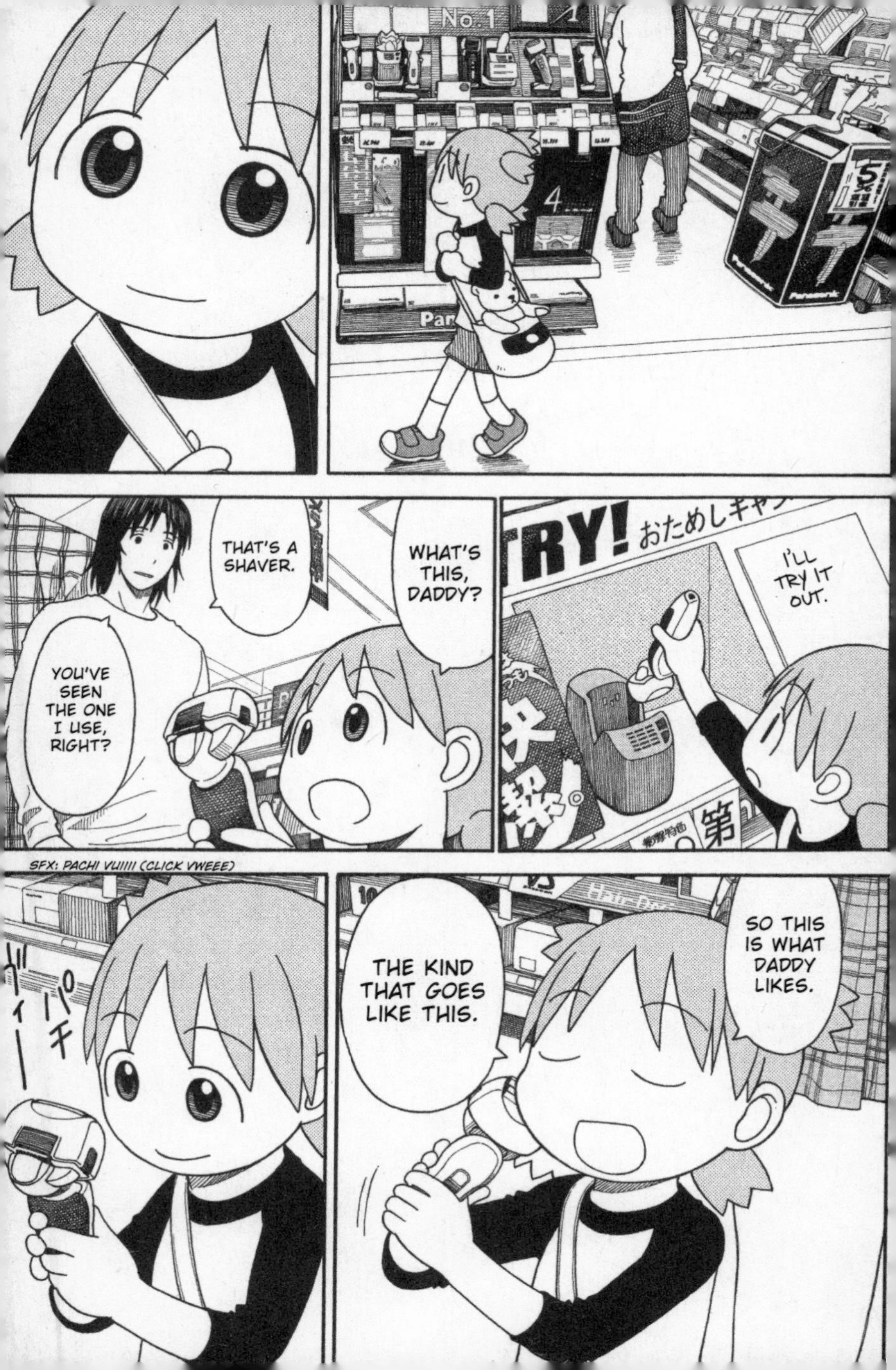
TRY!
I'LL TRY IT OUT.
WHAT'S THIS, DADDY?
THAT'S A SHAVER.
YOU'VE SEEN THE ONE I USE, RIGHT?
SFX: PACHI VUIIII (CLICK VWEEE)
SO THIS IS WHAT DADDY LIKES.
THE KIND THAT GOES LIKE THIS.
パチ
ヴィーー

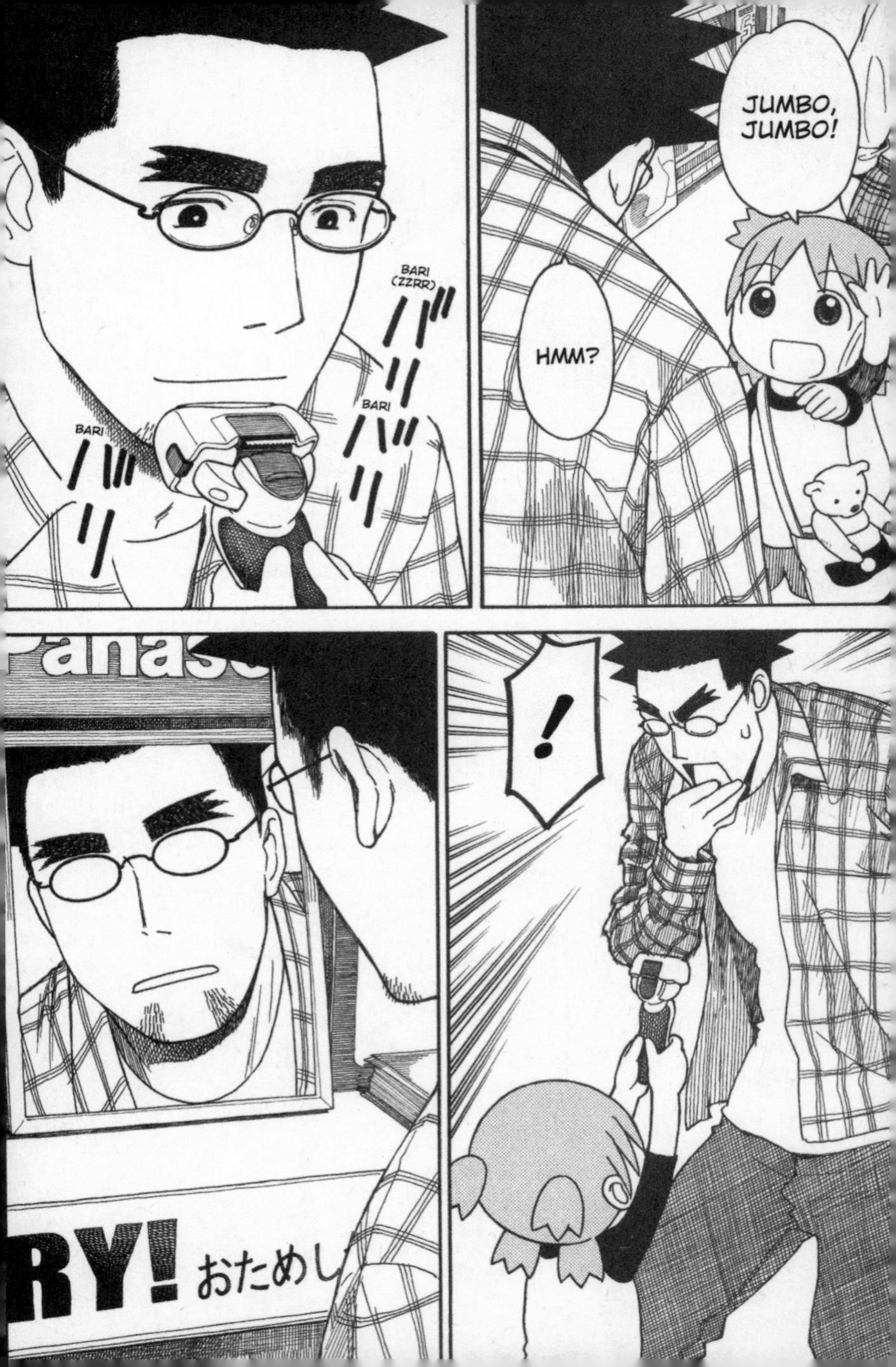
JUMBO, JUMBO!
HMM?
BARI (ZZRR)
バリ
BARI
バリ
BARI
バリ
!
Panas
RY! おためし

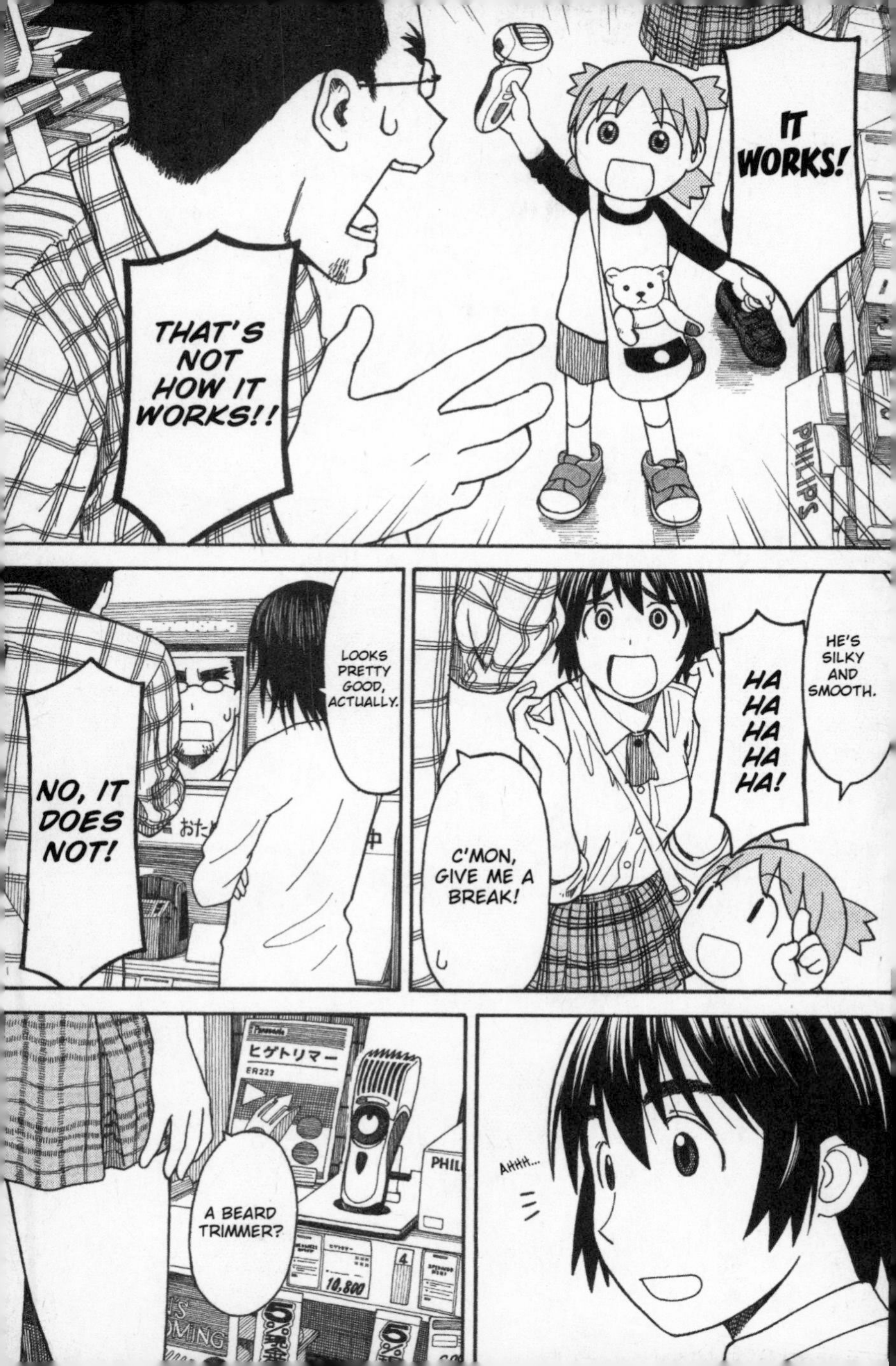

IT WORKS!
THAT'S NOT HOW IT WORKS!!
HE'S SILKY AND SMOOTH.
HA HA HA HA HA!
C'MON, GIVE ME A BREAK!
LOOKS PRETTY GOOD, ACTUALLY.
NO, IT DOES NOT!
AHHH...
ヒゲトリマー
10,800
A BEARD TRIMMER?
PHILIPS

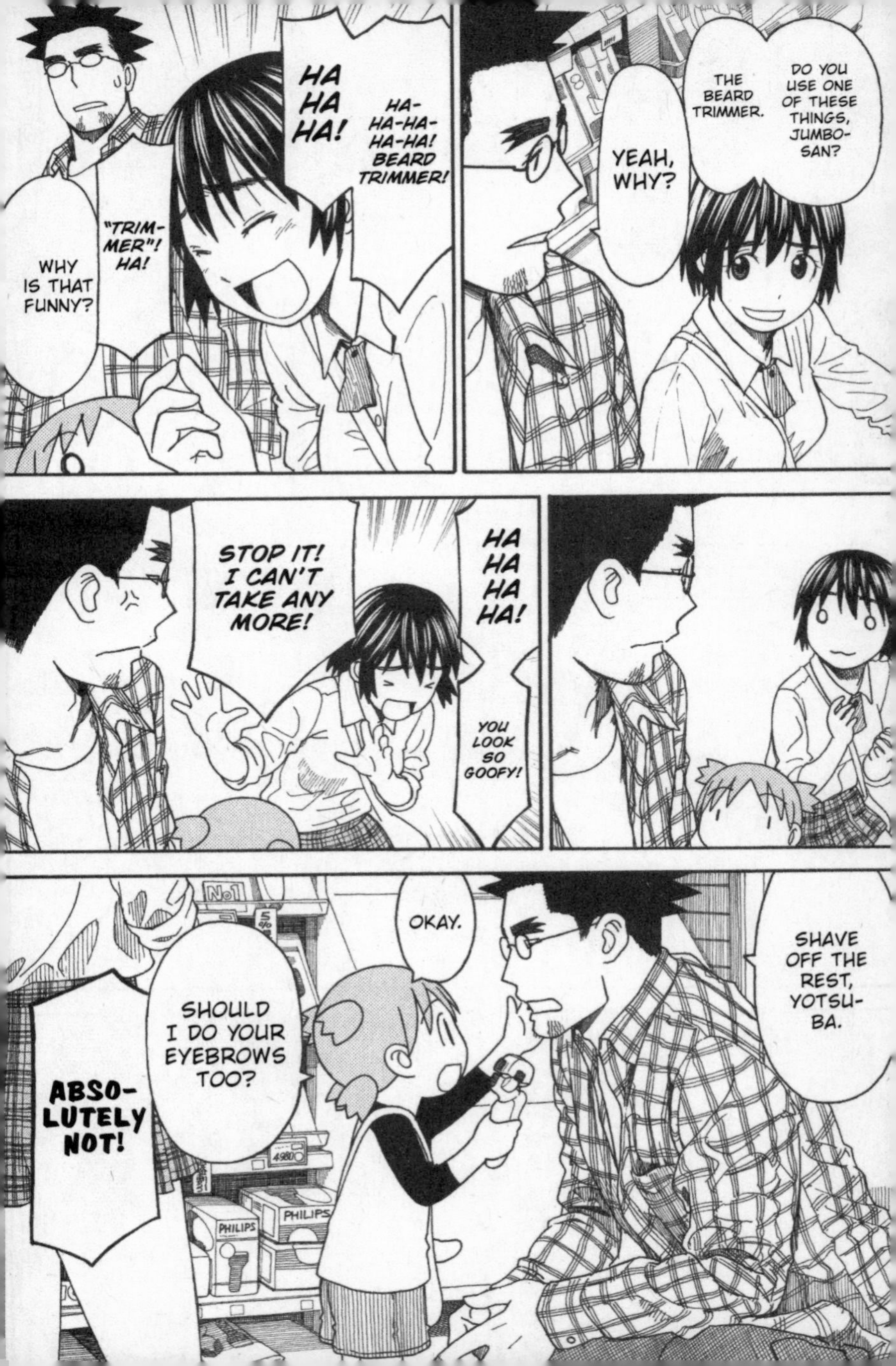

DO YOU USE ONE OF THESE THINGS, JUMBO-SAN?
THE BEARD TRIMMER.
YEAH, WHY?
HA HA HA!
HA-HA-HA-HA-HA! BEARD TRIMMER!
"TRIM-MER"! HA!
WHY IS THAT FUNNY?
HA HA HA HA!
YOU LOOK SO GOOFY!
STOP IT! I CAN'T TAKE ANY MORE!
SHAVE OFF THE REST, YOTSUBA.
OKAY.
SHOULD I DO YOUR EYEBROWS TOO?
ABSOLUTELY NOT!
No1
4980
PHILIPS
PHILIPS

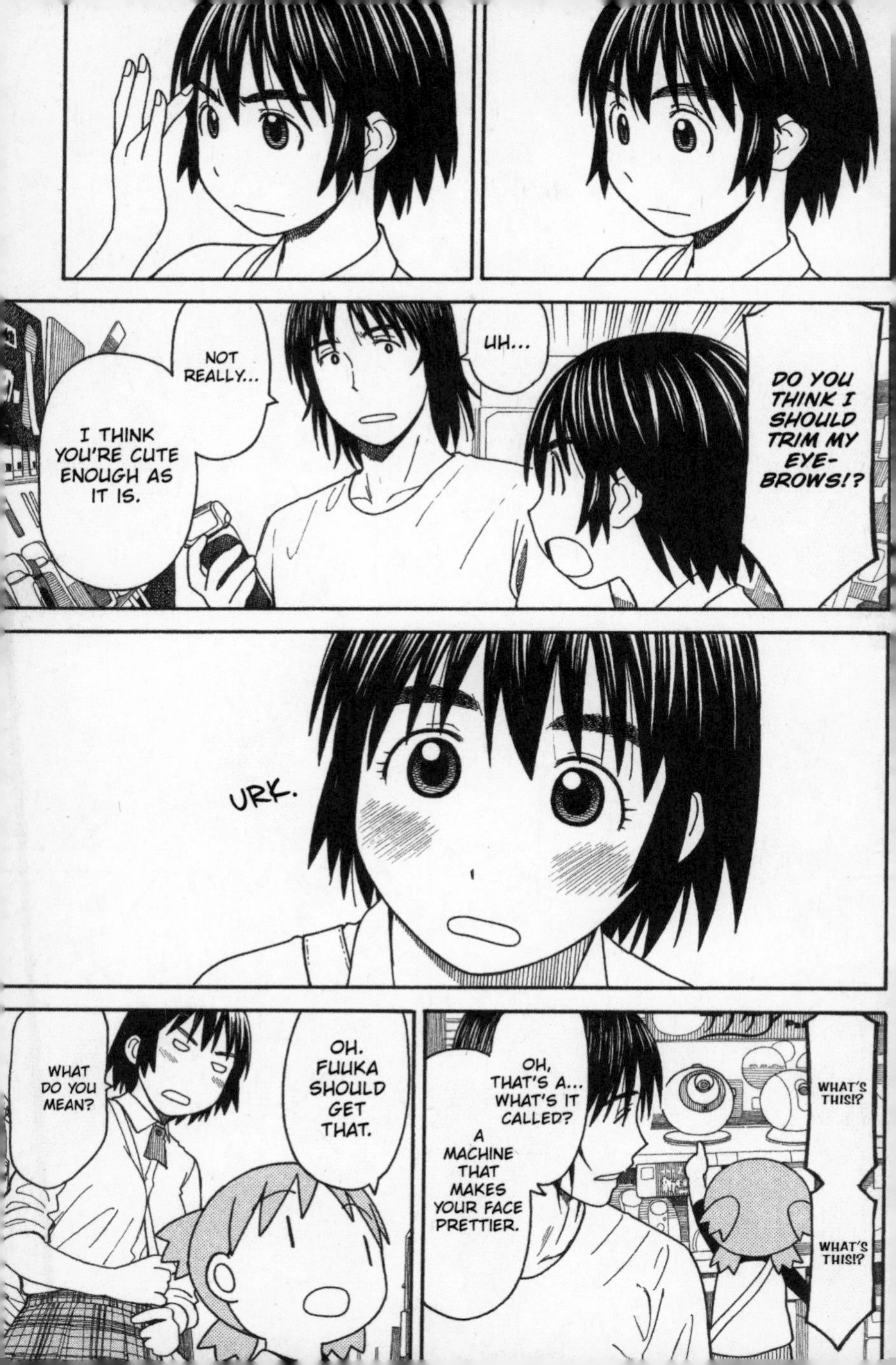
DO YOU THINK I SHOULD TRIM MY EYE-BROWS!?
UH...
NOT REALLY...
I THINK YOU'RE CUTE ENOUGH AS IT IS.
URK.
WHAT'S THIS!?
WHAT'S THIS!?
OH, THAT'S A... WHAT'S IT CALLED?
A MACHINE THAT MAKES YOUR FACE PRETTIER.
OH. FUUKA SHOULD GET THAT.
WHAT DO YOU MEAN?

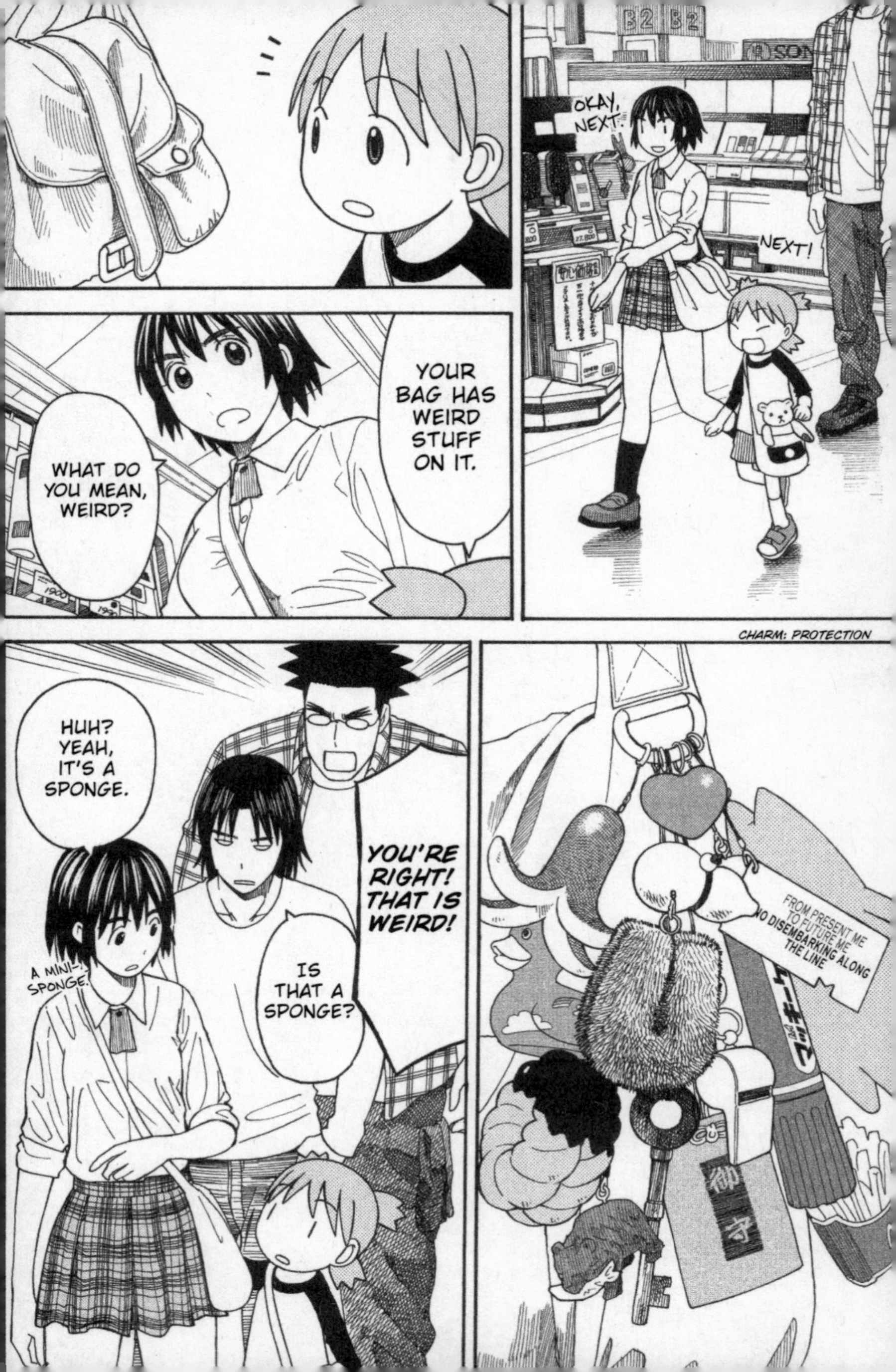
OKAY, NEXT.
NEXT!
YOUR BAG HAS WEIRD STUFF ON IT.
WHAT DO YOU MEAN, WEIRD?
CHARM: PROTECTION
FROM PRESENT ME TO FUTURE ME NO DISEMBARKING ALONG THE LINE
御守
YOU'RE RIGHT! THAT IS WEIRD!
IS THAT A SPONGE?
HUH? YEAH, IT'S A SPONGE.
A MINI-SPONGE.

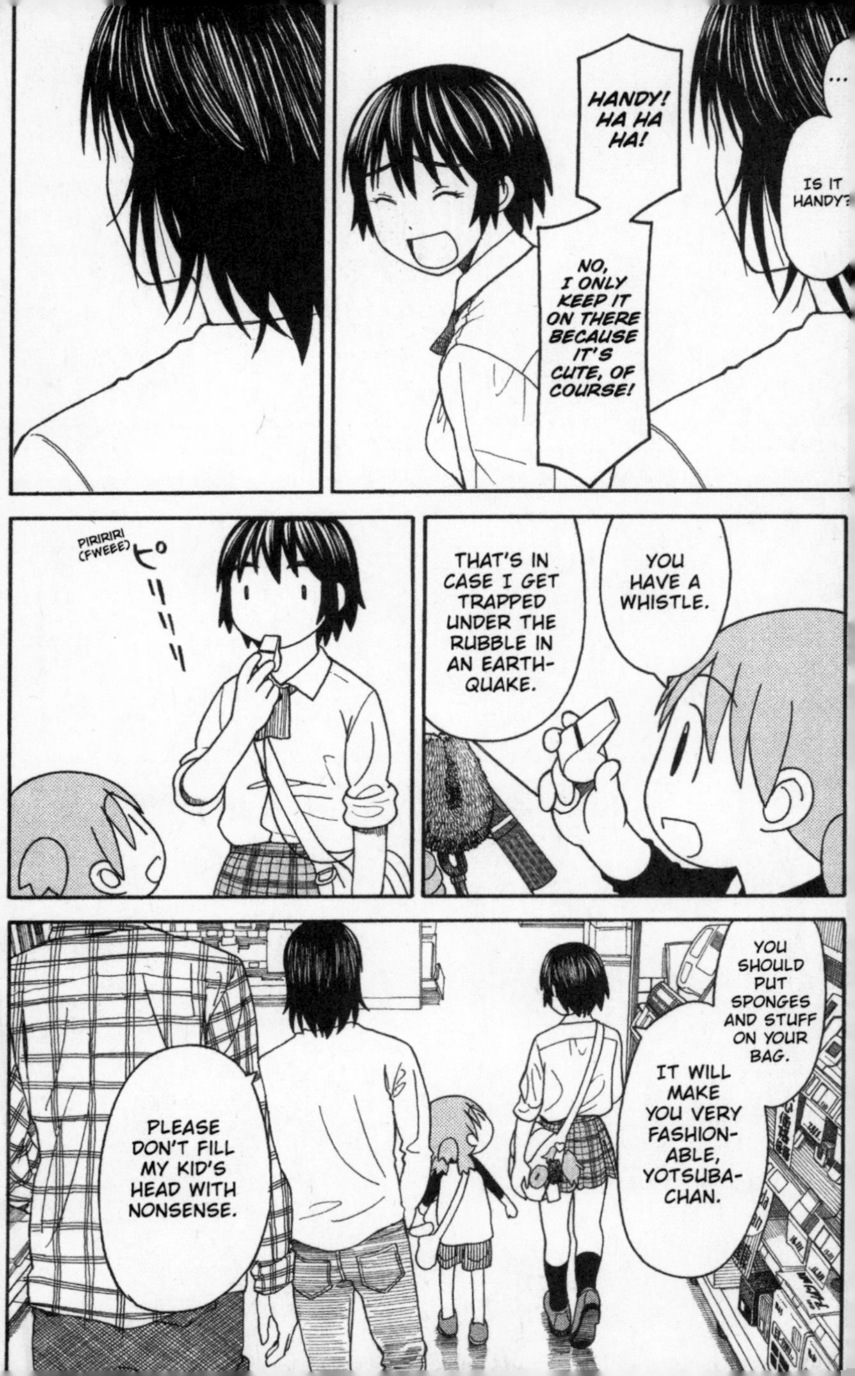
...
IS IT HANDY?
HANDY! HA HA HA!
NO, I ONLY KEEP IT ON THERE BECAUSE IT'S CUTE, OF COURSE!
YOU HAVE A WHISTLE.
THAT'S IN CASE I GET TRAPPED UNDER THE RUBBLE IN AN EARTH-QUAKE.
PIRIRIRI (FWEEE)
YOU SHOULD PUT SPONGES AND STUFF ON YOUR BAG.
IT WILL MAKE YOU VERY FASHION-ABLE, YOTSUBA-CHAN.
PLEASE DON'T FILL MY KID'S HEAD WITH NONSENSE.

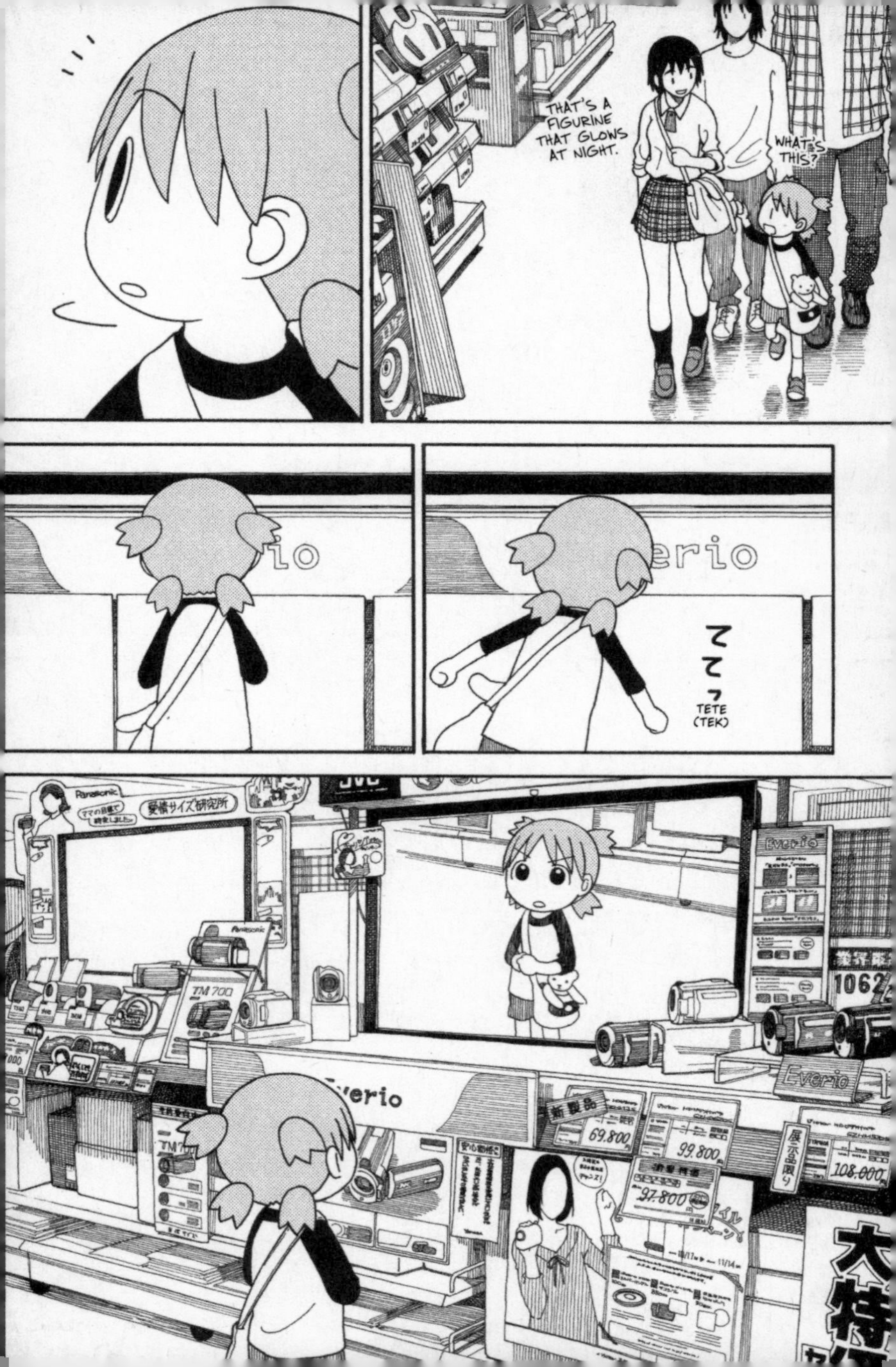
WHAT'S THIS?
THAT'S A FIGURINE THAT GLOWS AT NIGHT.
rio
erio
てて
TETE (TEK)
Panasonic
愛情サイズ研究所
JVC
Everio
TM 700
1062
Everio
Everio
新製品
69,800
99,800
展示品限り
108,000
97,800
大特

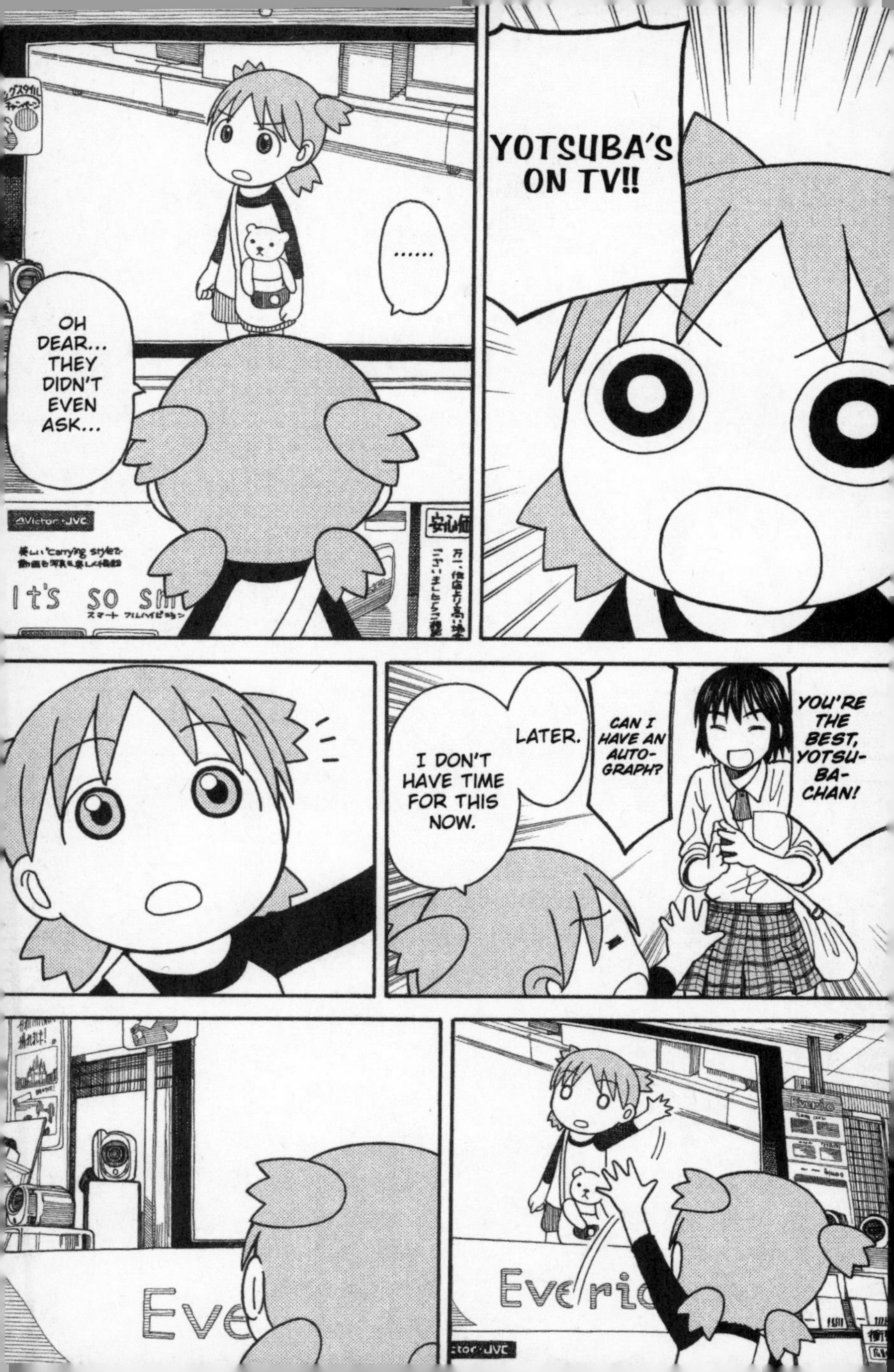
YOTSUBA'S ON TV!!
……
OH DEAR… THEY DIDN'T EVEN ASK…
Victor·JVC
安心価
It's so sm
YOU'RE THE BEST, YOTSUBA-CHAN!
CAN I HAVE AN AUTOGRAPH?
LATER.
I DON'T HAVE TIME FOR THIS NOW.
Everio
Eve rio
Eve
ctor·JVC

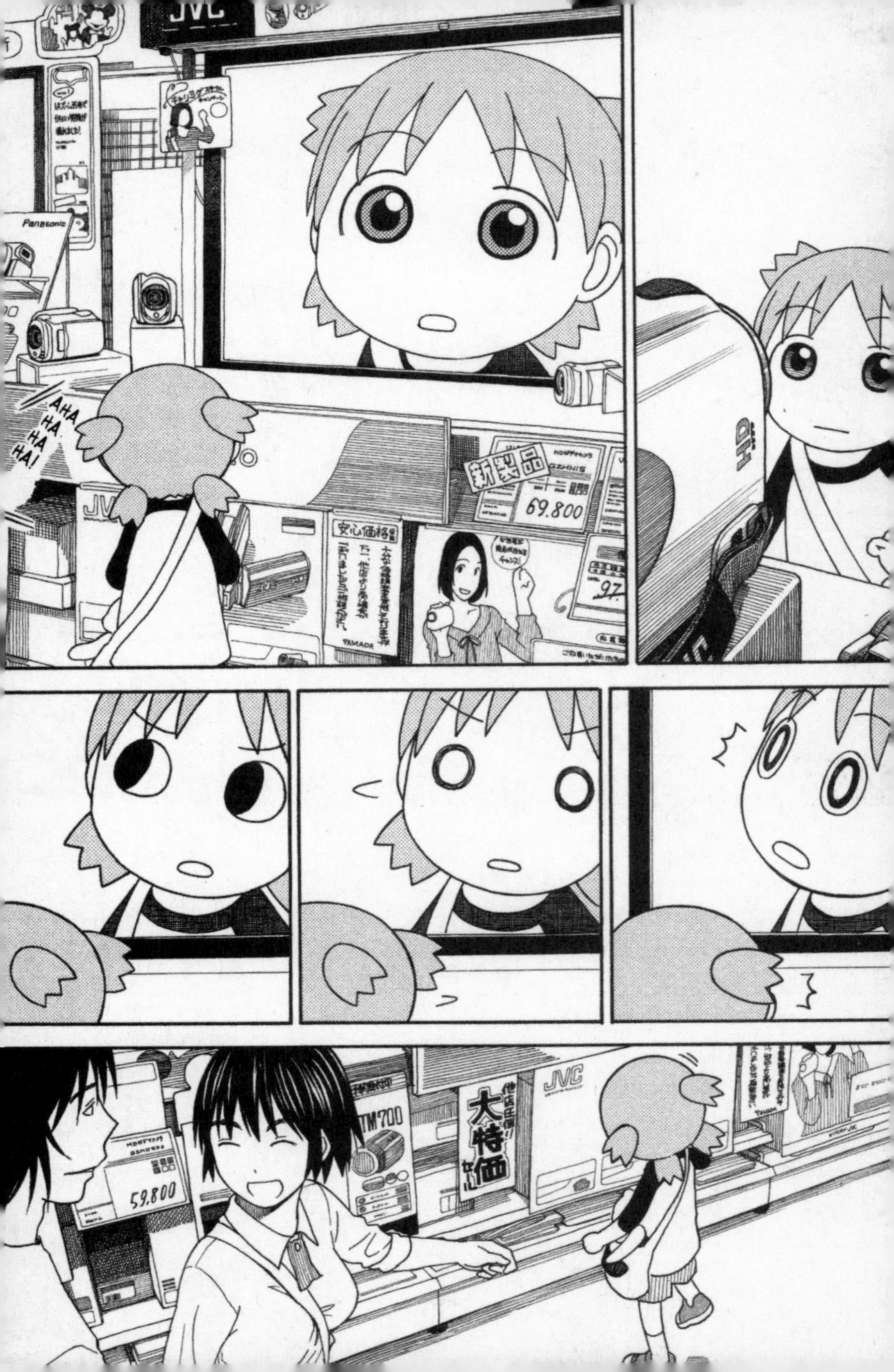
HD
JVC
Panasonic
AHA HA HA HA!
JVC
新製品
69.800
安心価格
YAMADA
JVC
大特価
他店圧倒!!
TM700
59,800

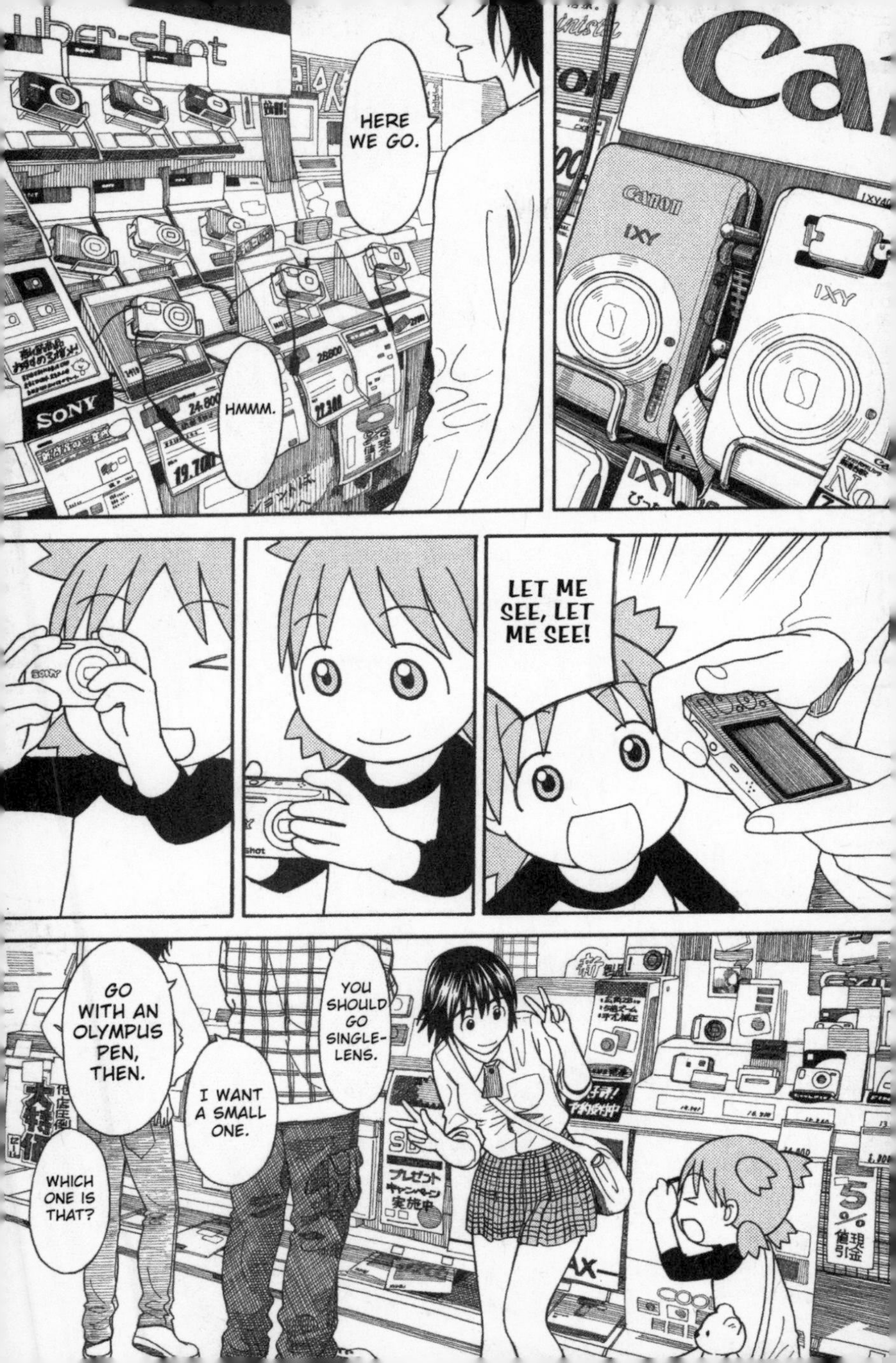
HERE WE GO.
HMMM.
SONY
IXY
LET ME SEE, LET ME SEE!
YOU SHOULD GO SINGLE-LENS.
I WANT A SMALL ONE.
GO WITH AN OLYMPUS PEN, THEN.
WHICH ONE IS THAT?

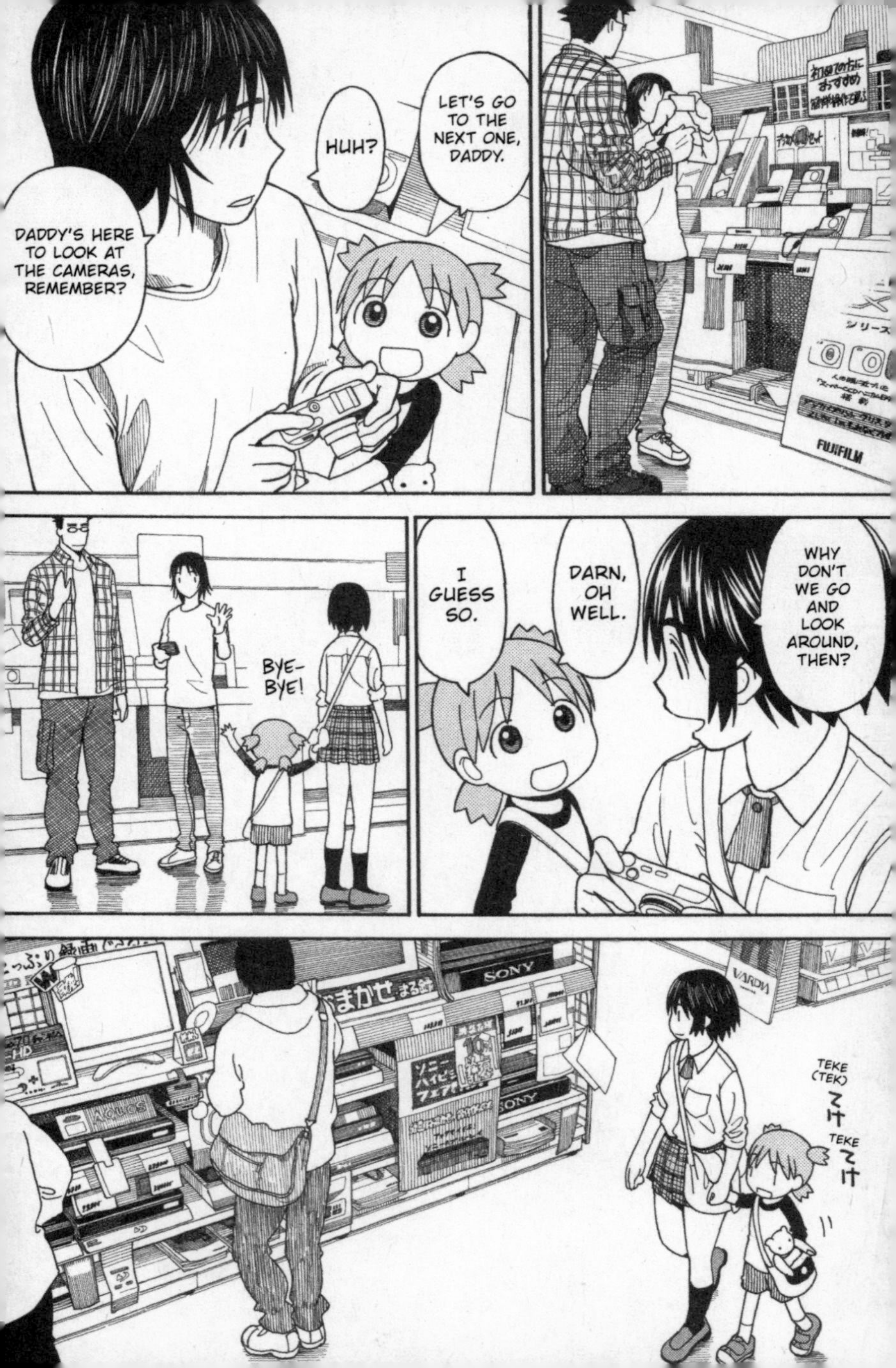
LET'S GO TO THE NEXT ONE, DADDY.
HUH?
DADDY'S HERE TO LOOK AT THE CAMERAS, REMEMBER?
FUJIFILM
WHY DON'T WE GO AND LOOK AROUND, THEN?
DARN, OH WELL.
I GUESS SO.
BYE-BYE!
TEKE (TEK)
てけ
TEKE
てけ
SONY
SONY

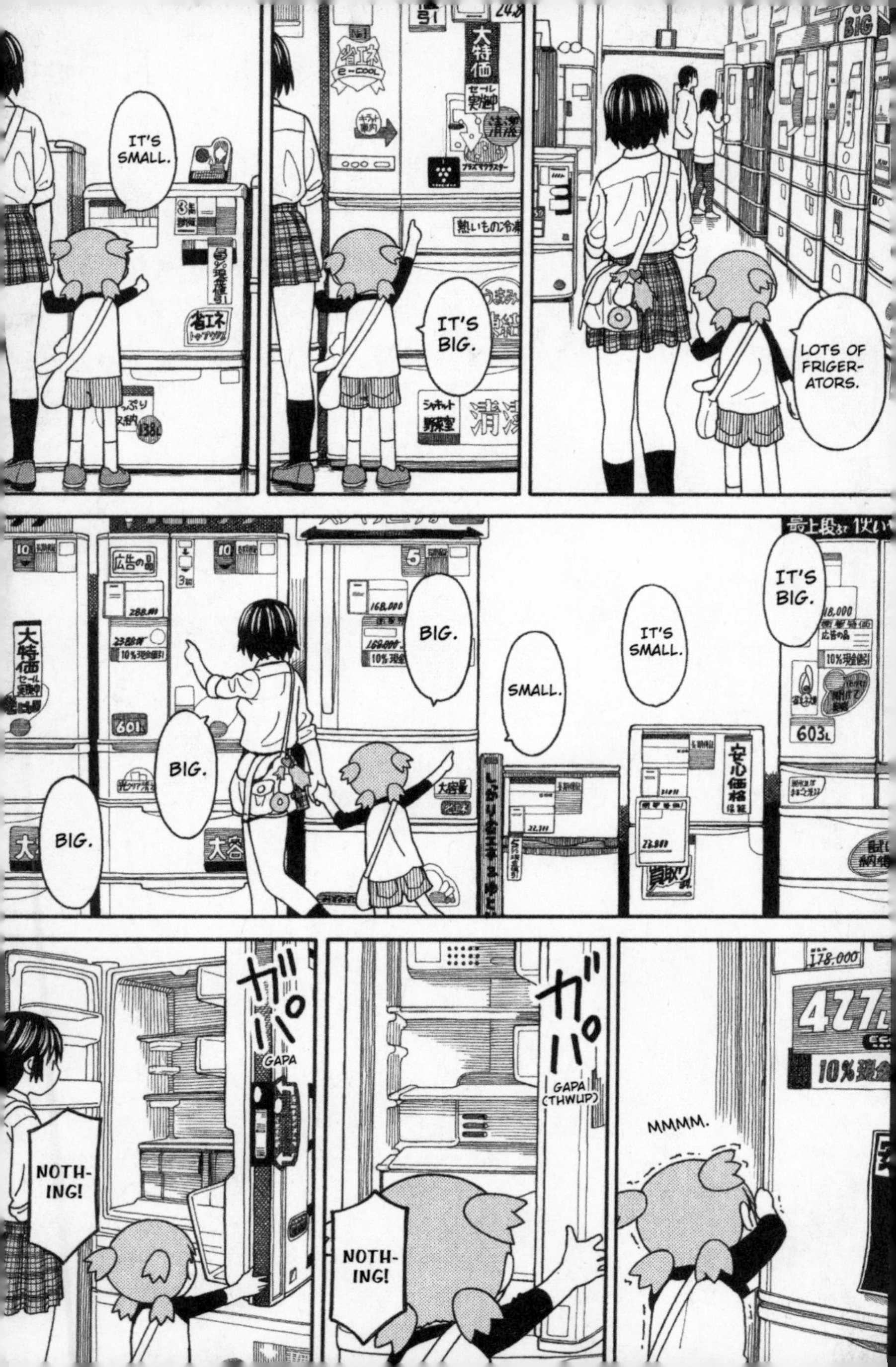
LOTS OF FRIGER-ATORS.
IT'S BIG.
IT'S SMALL.
IT'S BIG.
IT'S SMALL.
SMALL.
BIG.
BIG.
BIG.
MMMM.
ガパ
GAPA (THWUP)
NOTH-ING!
ガパ
GAPA
NOTH-ING!

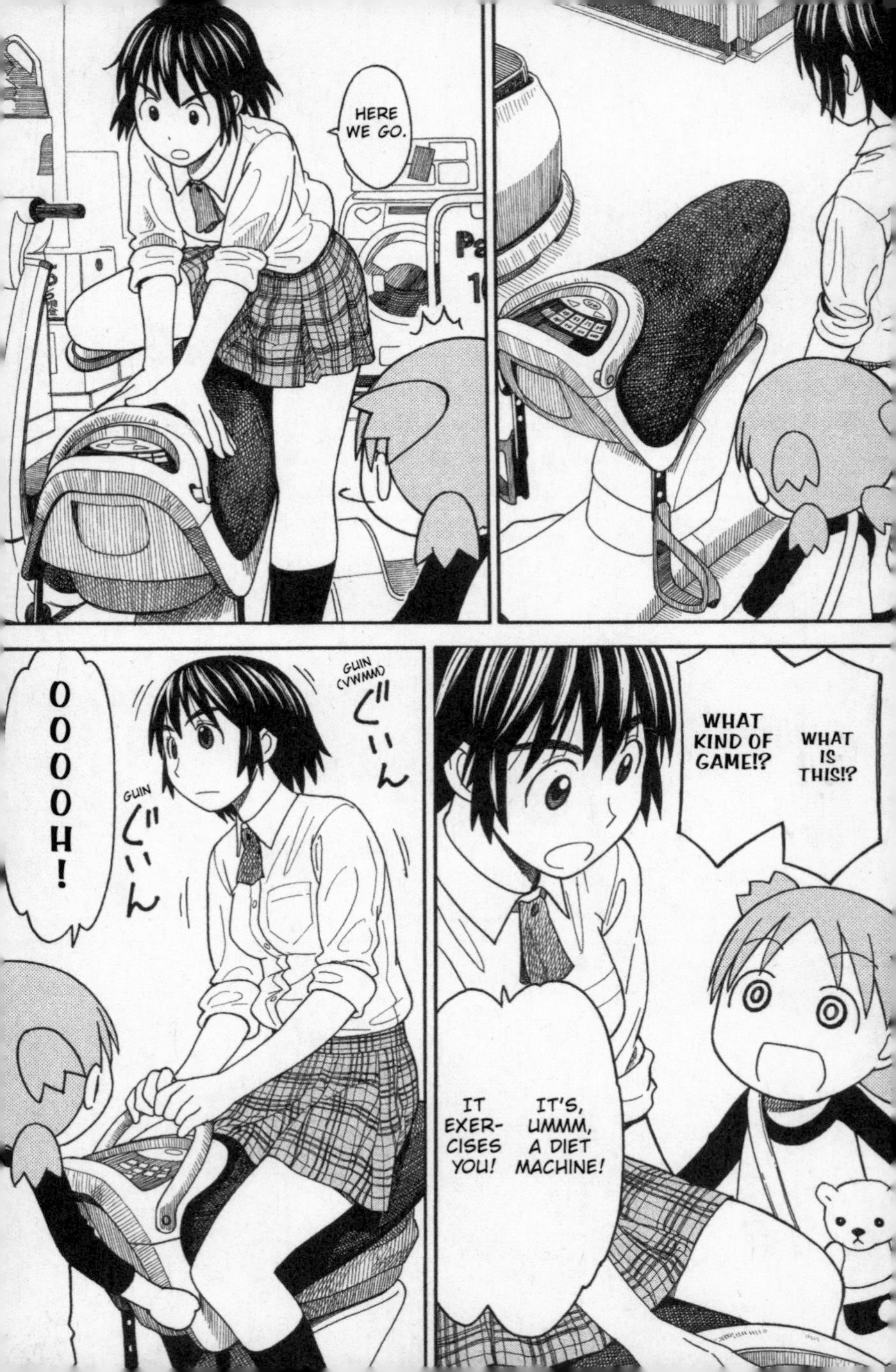
HERE WE GO.
WHAT IS THIS!?
WHAT KIND OF GAME!?
IT'S, UMMM, A DIET MACHINE!
IT EXER-CISES YOU!
GUIN (VWMM)
ぐいん
GUIN
ぐいん
OOOOOH!

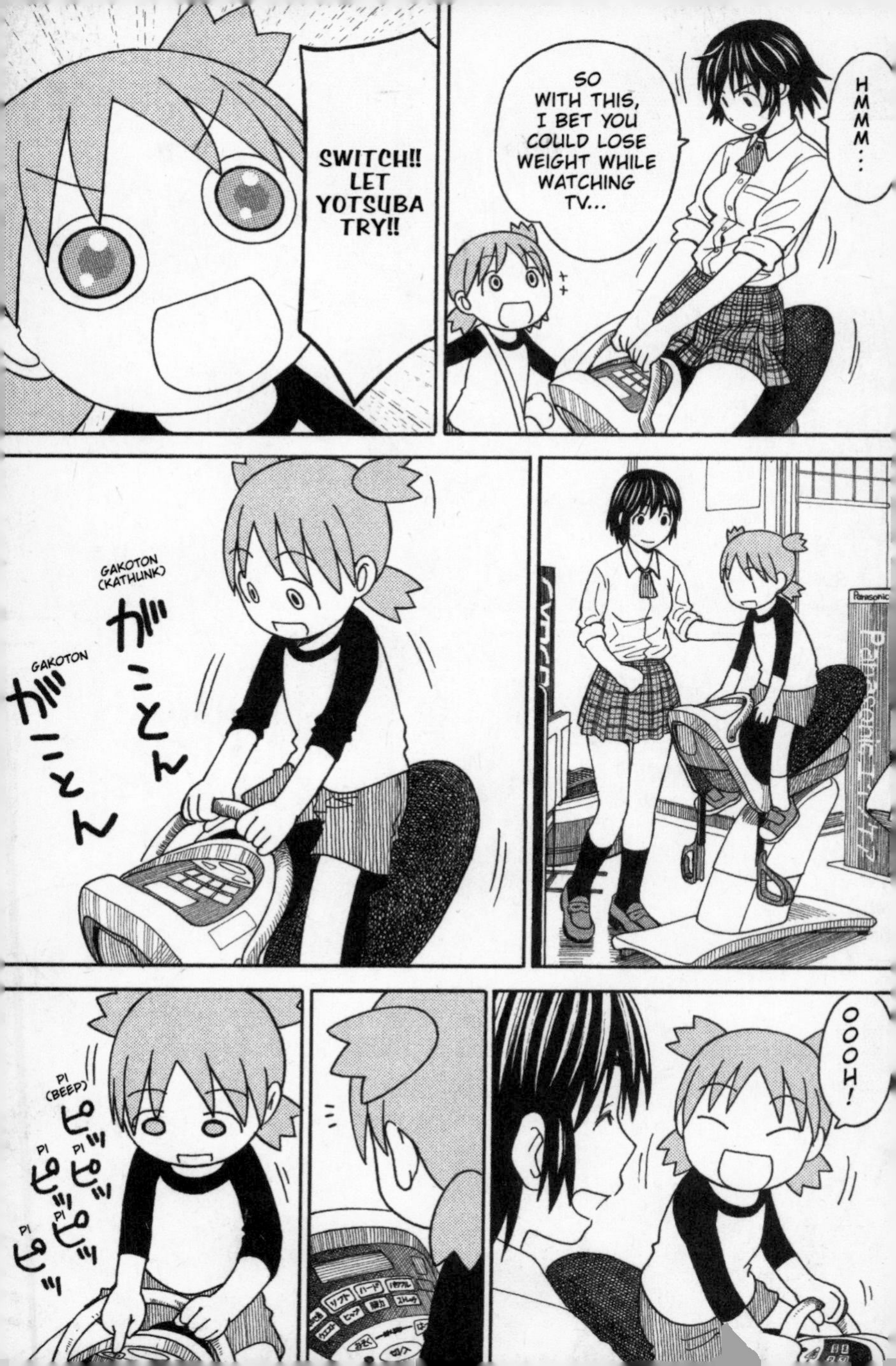
HMMM...
SO WITH THIS, I BET YOU COULD LOSE WEIGHT WHILE WATCHING TV...
SWITCH!! LET YOTSUBA TRY!!
Panasonic
GAKOTON (KATHUNK)
がことん
GAKOTON
がことん
OOOH!
PI (BEEP)
ピッ
PI
ピッ
PI
ピッ
PI
ピッ
PI
ピッ

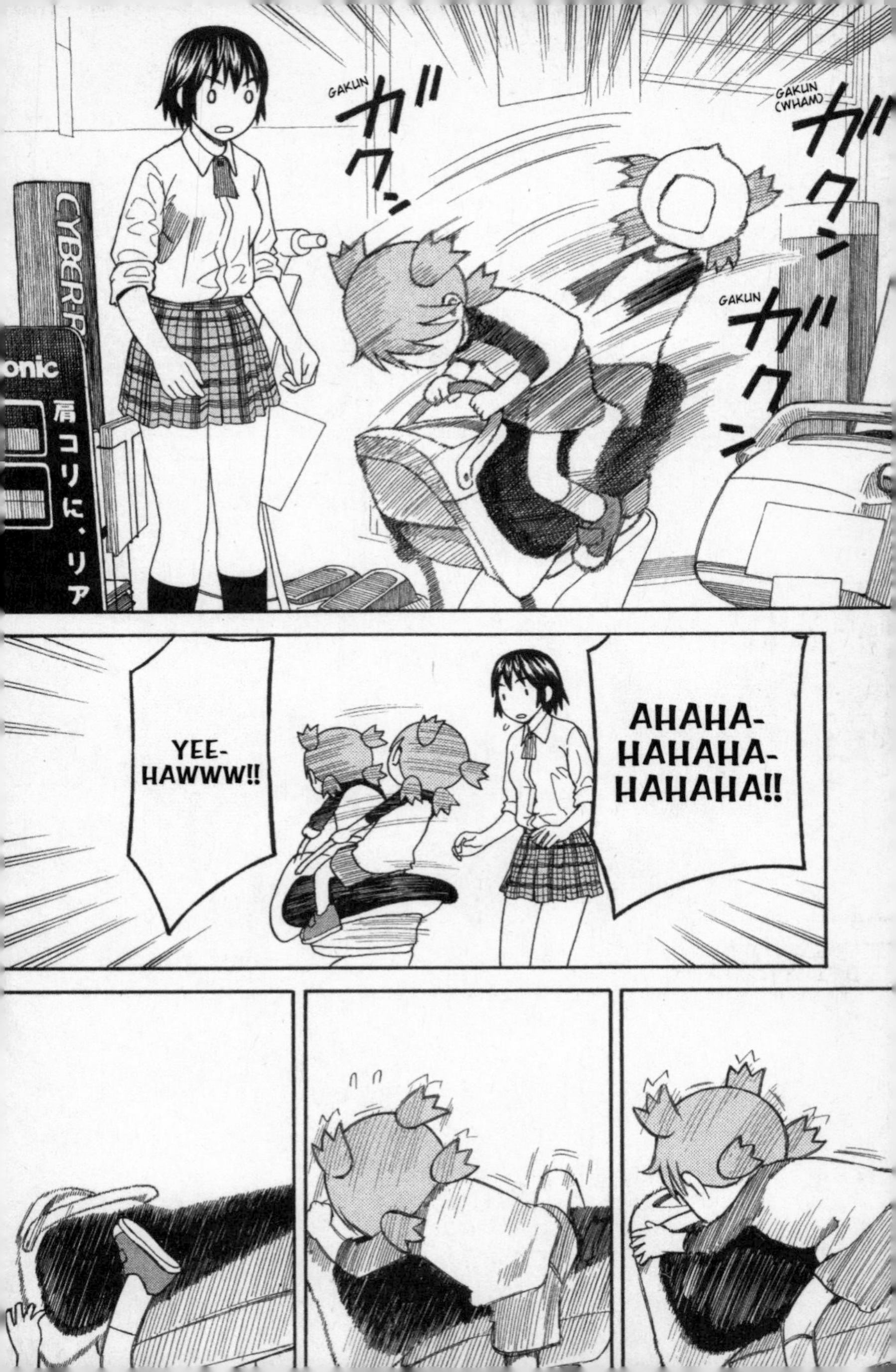

GAKUN (WHAM)
ガクン
GAKUN
ガクン
GAKUN
ガクン
CYBER-R
onic
肩コリに、リア
AHAHA-HAHAHA-HAHAHA!!
YEE-HAWWW!!

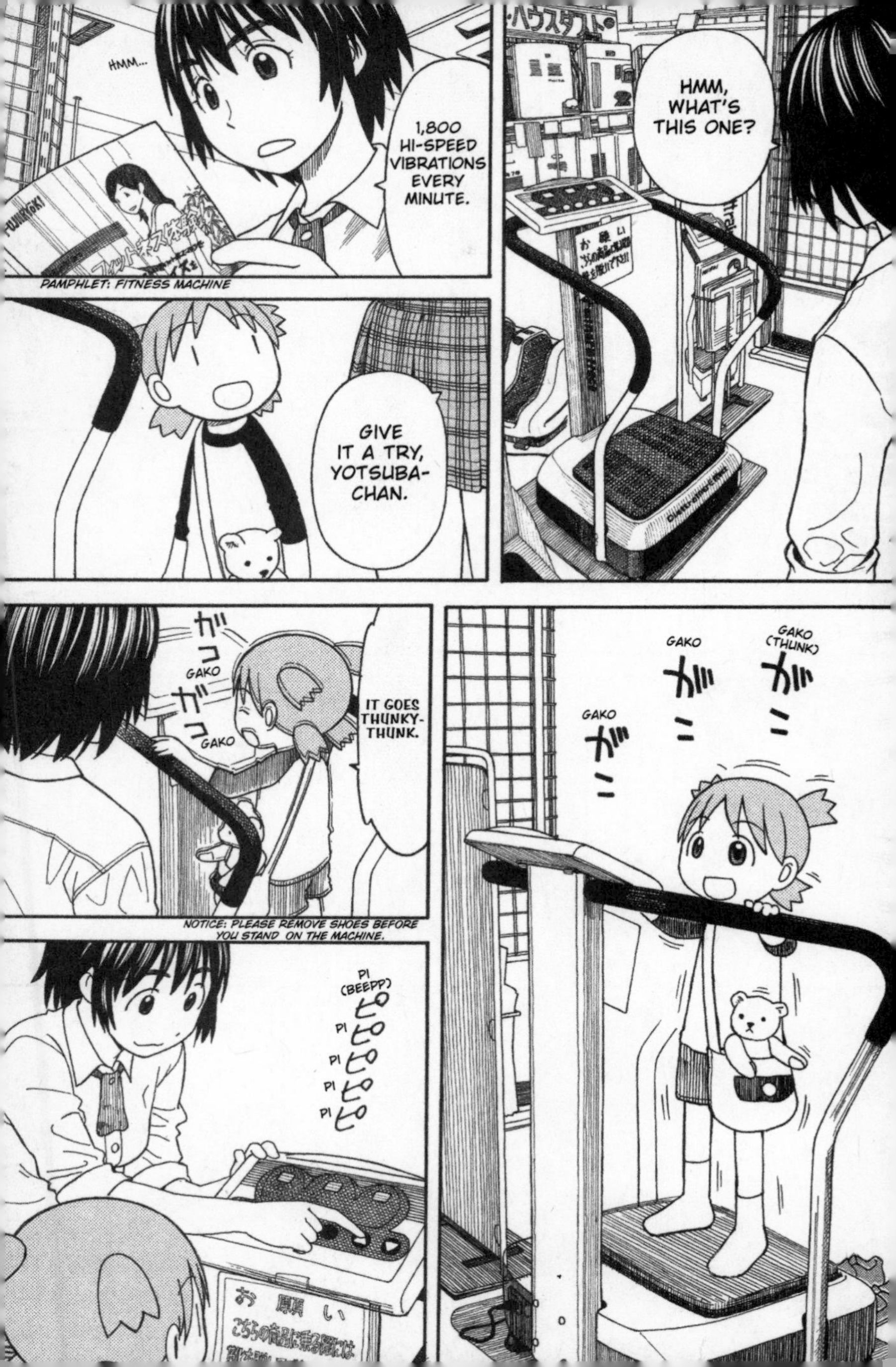
HMM, WHAT'S THIS ONE?
HMM...
1,800 HI-SPEED VIBRATIONS EVERY MINUTE.
PAMPHLET: FITNESS MACHINE
GIVE IT A TRY, YOTSUBA-CHAN.
GAKO (THUNK) がこ
GAKO がこ
GAKO がこ
がこ GAKO
がこ GAKO
IT GOES THUNKY-THUNK.
NOTICE: PLEASE REMOVE SHOES BEFORE YOU STAND ON THE MACHINE.
PI (BEEPP) ピ
PI ピ
PI ピ
PI ピ
PI ピ
お願い

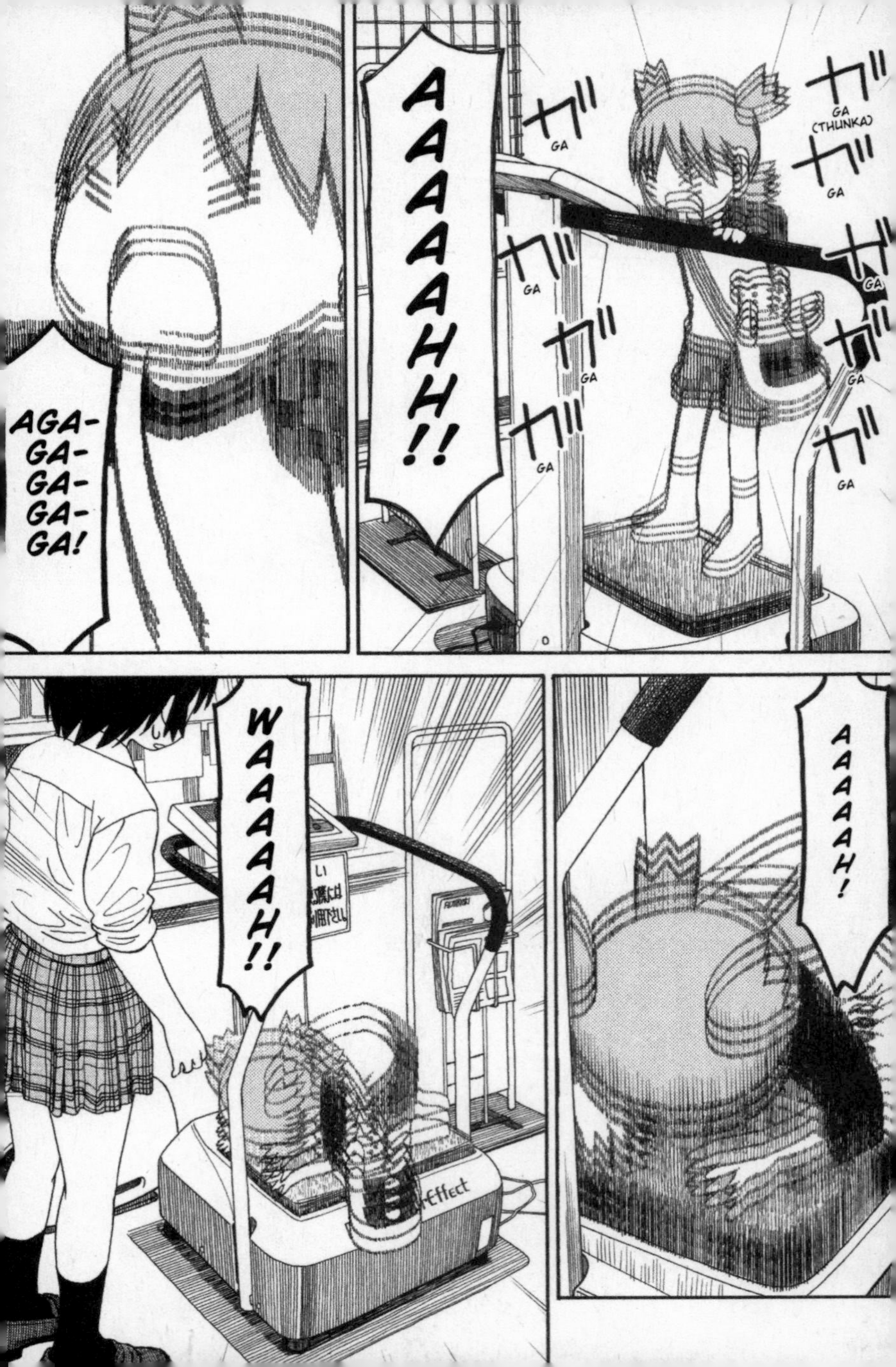

ガ
GA (THUNKA)
ガ
GA
ガ
GA
ガ
GA
ガ
GA
ガ
GA
AAAAAHH!!
ガ
GA
ガ
GA
ガ
GA
AGA-GA-GA-GA-GA!
AAAAAH!
WAAAAAH!!
rEffect

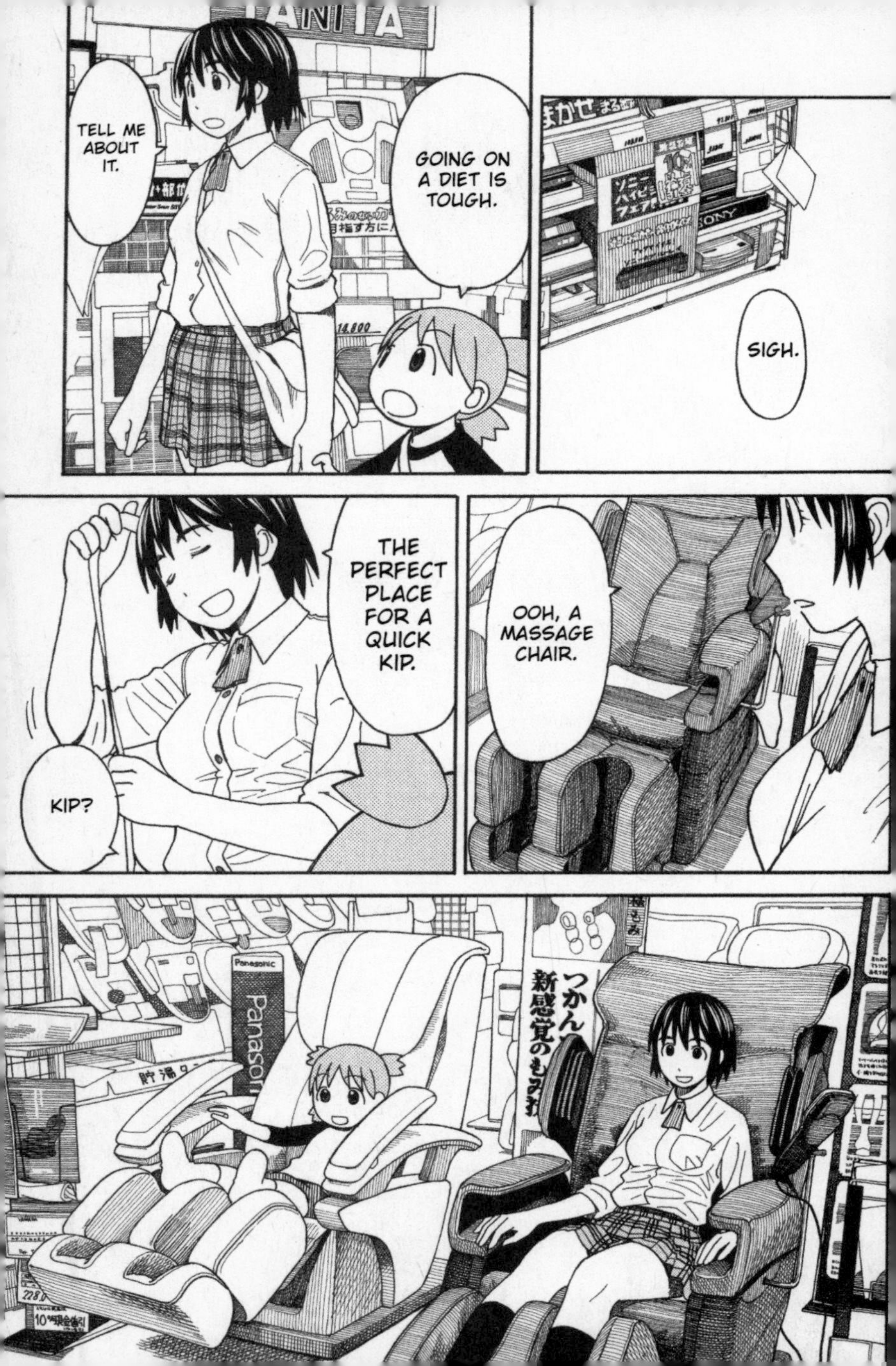
SIGH.
GOING ON A DIET IS TOUGH.
TELL ME ABOUT IT.
OOH, A MASSAGE CHAIR.
THE PERFECT PLACE FOR A QUICK KIP.
KIP?

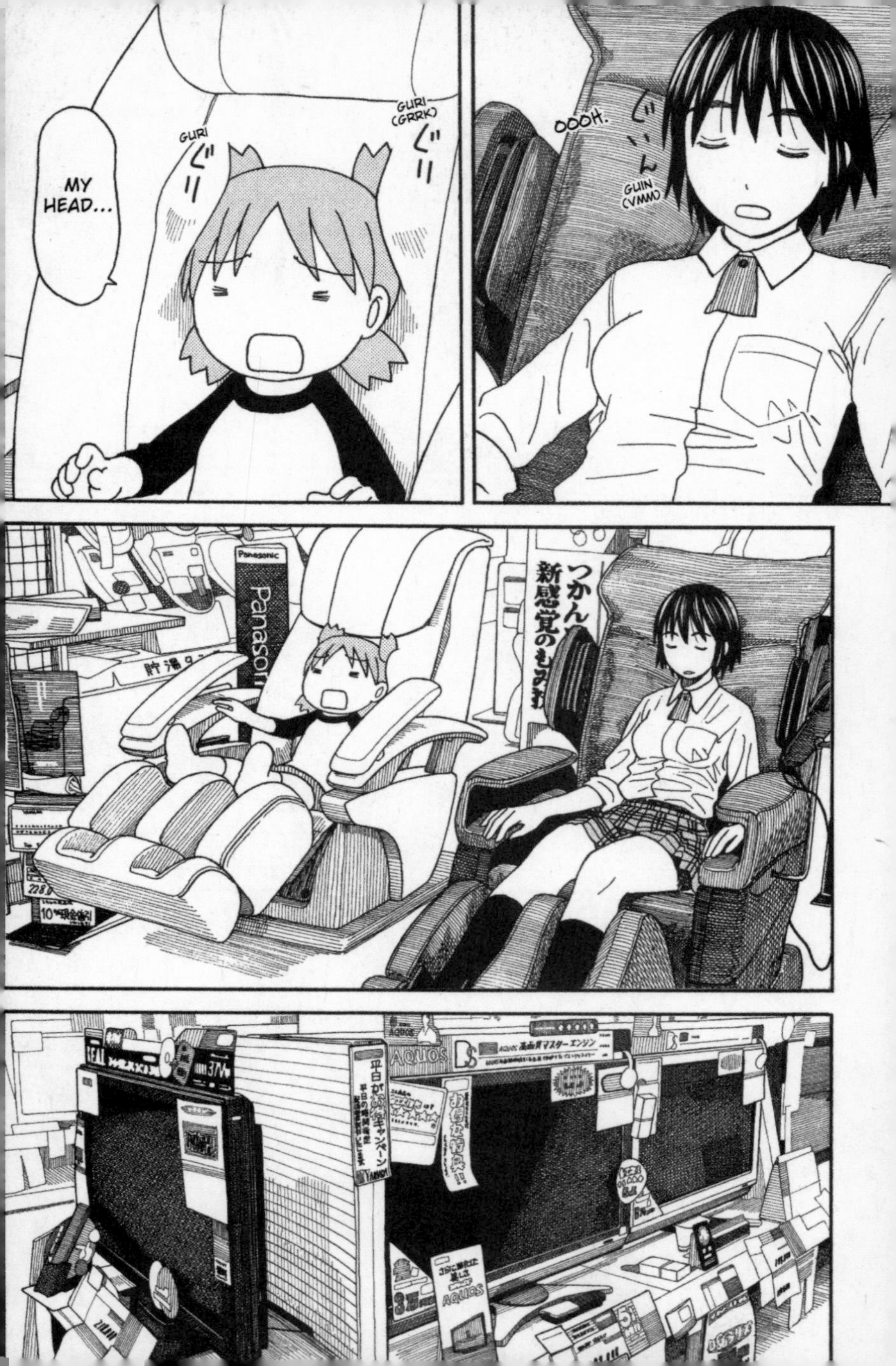
OOOH.
GUIN (VMMM)
GURI (GRRK)
GURI
MY HEAD...
Panasonic
AQUOS

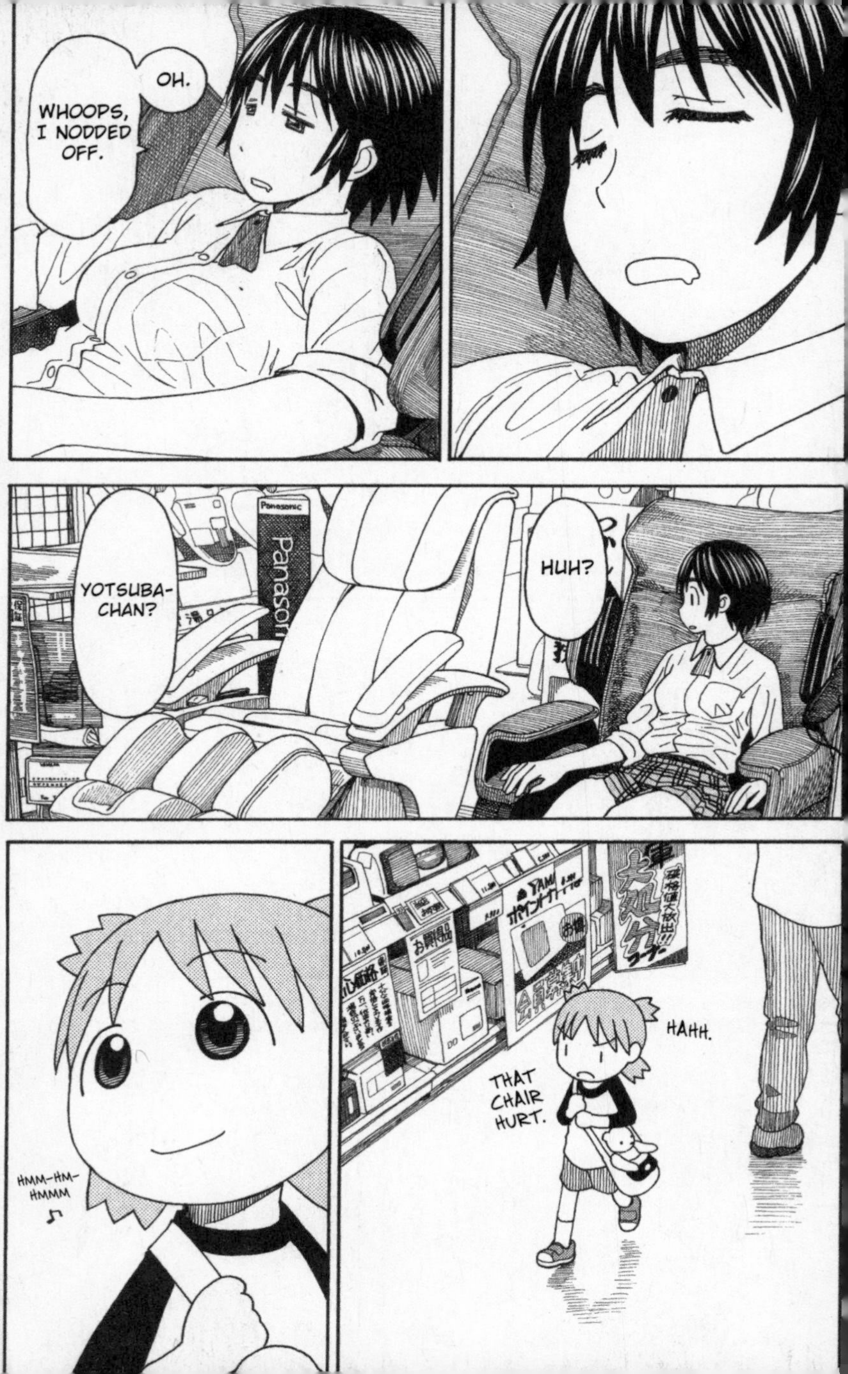
OH.
WHOOPS, I NODDED OFF.
HUH?
YOTSUBA-CHAN?
Panasonic
HAHH.
THAT CHAIR HURT.
HMM-HM-HMMM ♪

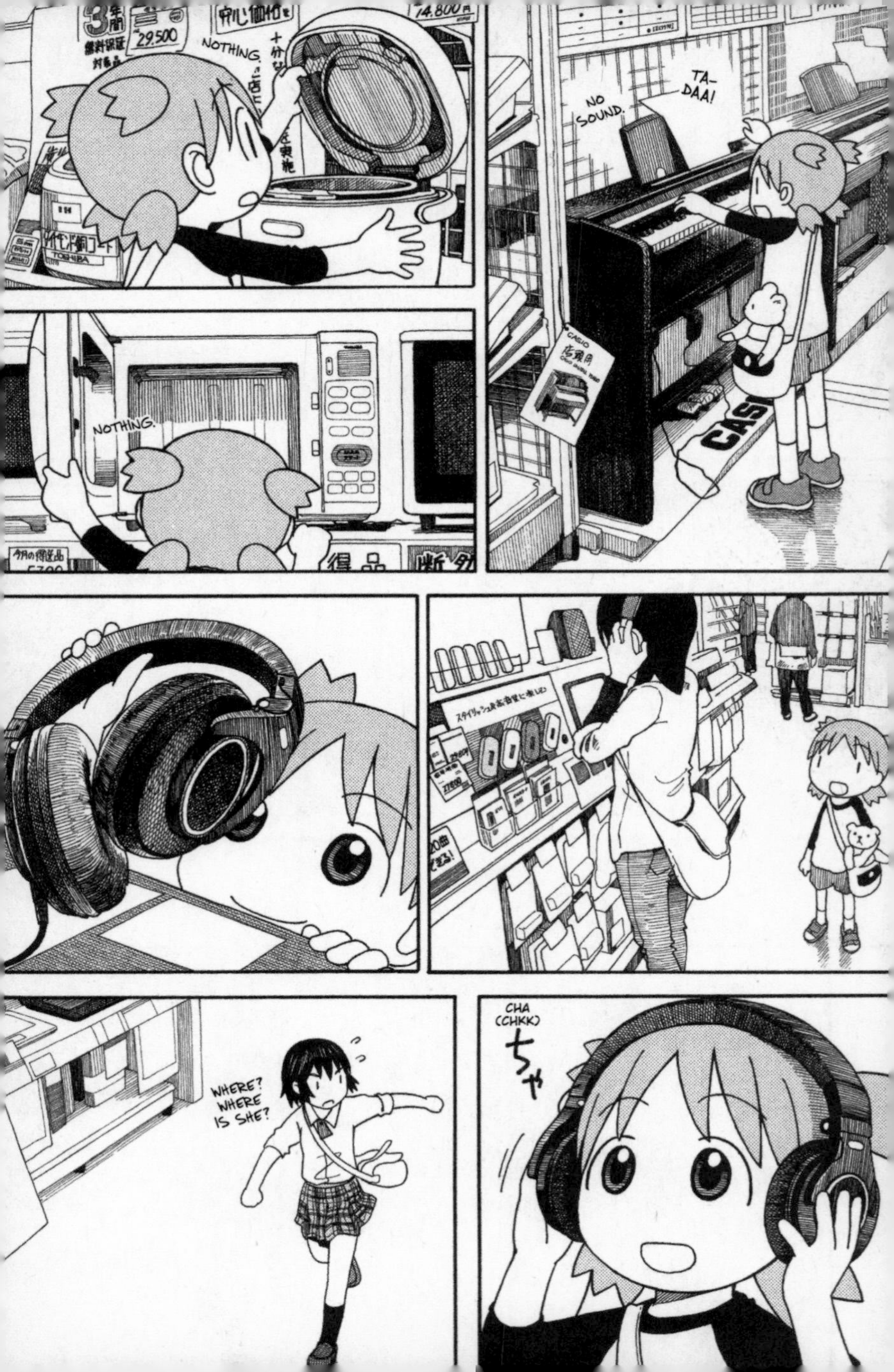
TA-DAA!
NO SOUND.
NOTHING.
NOTHING.
CHA (CHKK)
ちゃ
WHERE? WHERE IS SHE?

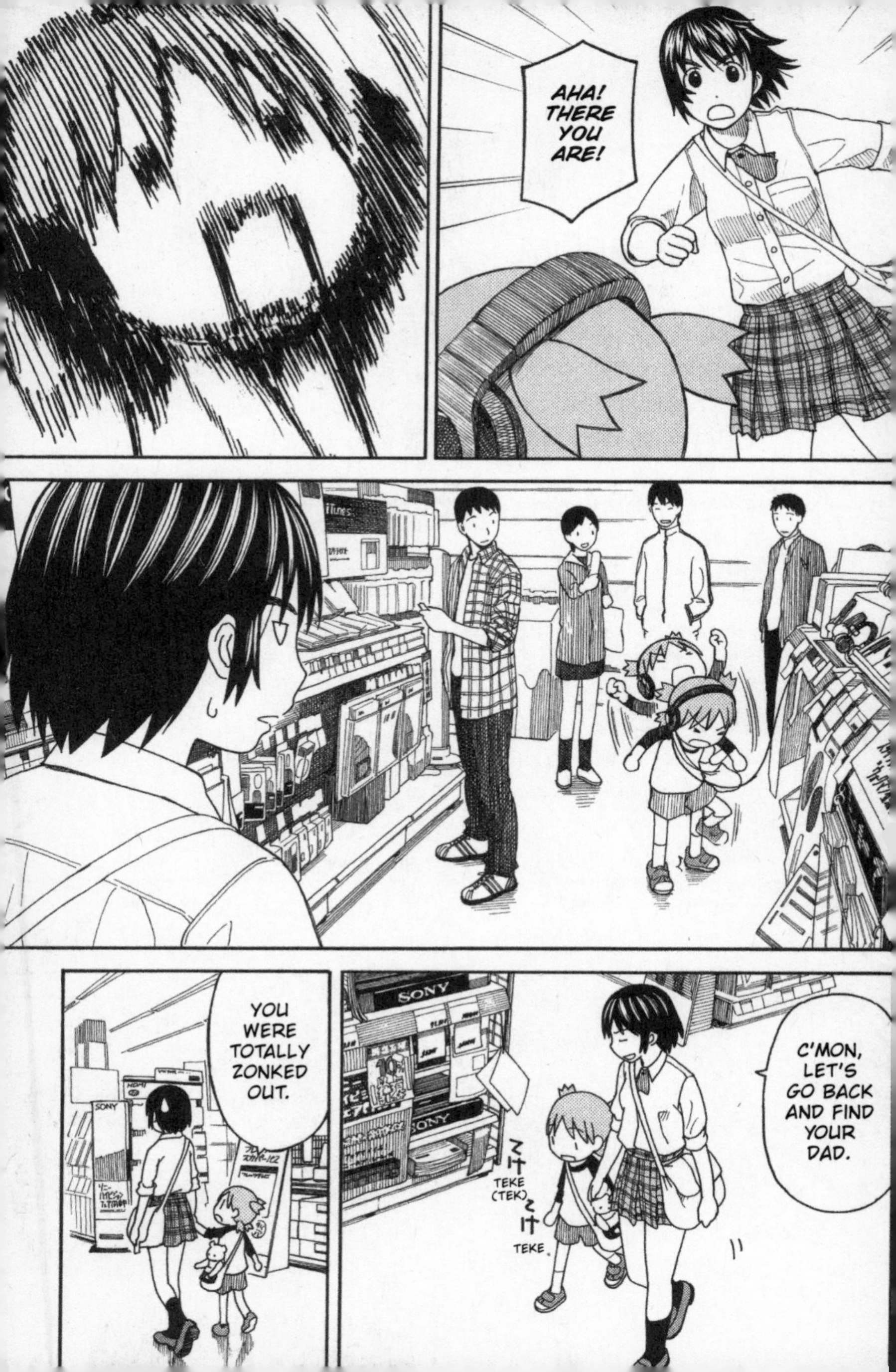
AHA! THERE YOU ARE!
C'MON, LET'S GO BACK AND FIND YOUR DAD.
TEKE (TEK)
TEKE
YOU WERE TOTALLY ZONKED OUT.

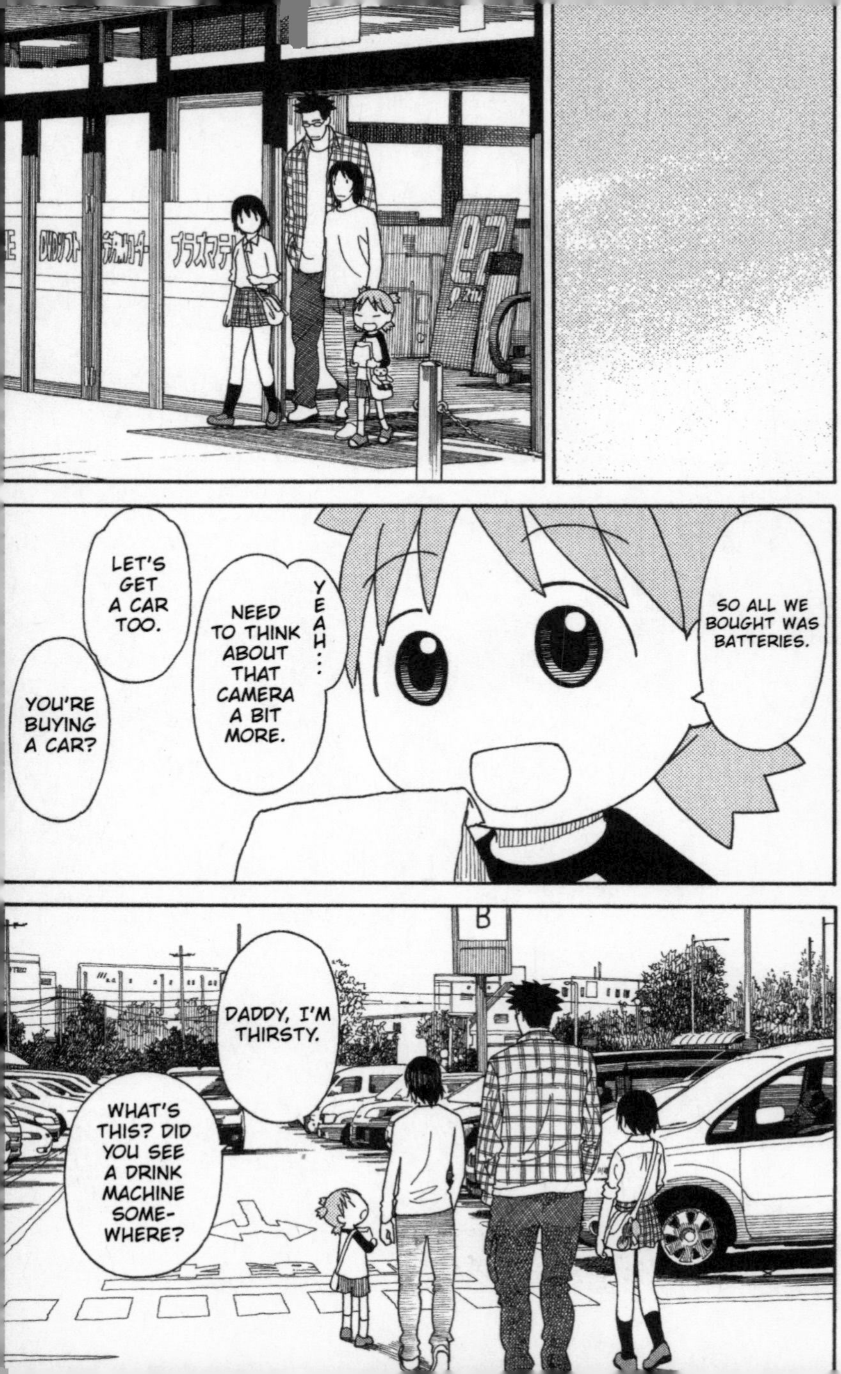
SO ALL WE BOUGHT WAS BATTERIES.
YEAH...
NEED TO THINK ABOUT THAT CAMERA A BIT MORE.
LET'S GET A CAR TOO.
YOU'RE BUYING A CAR?
DADDY, I'M THIRSTY.
WHAT'S THIS? DID YOU SEE A DRINK MACHINE SOME-WHERE?

YOTSUBA&!

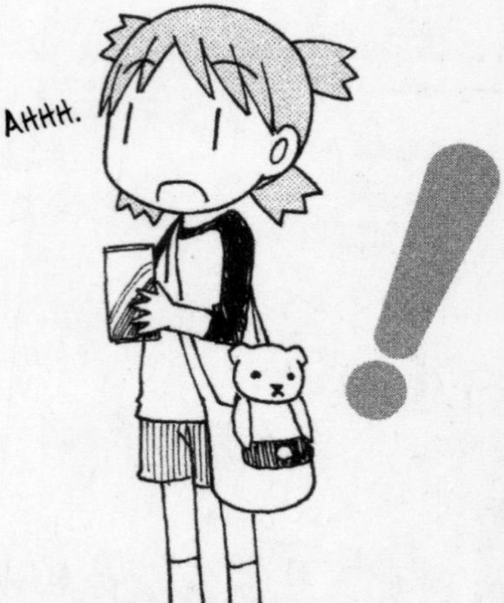
AHHH.

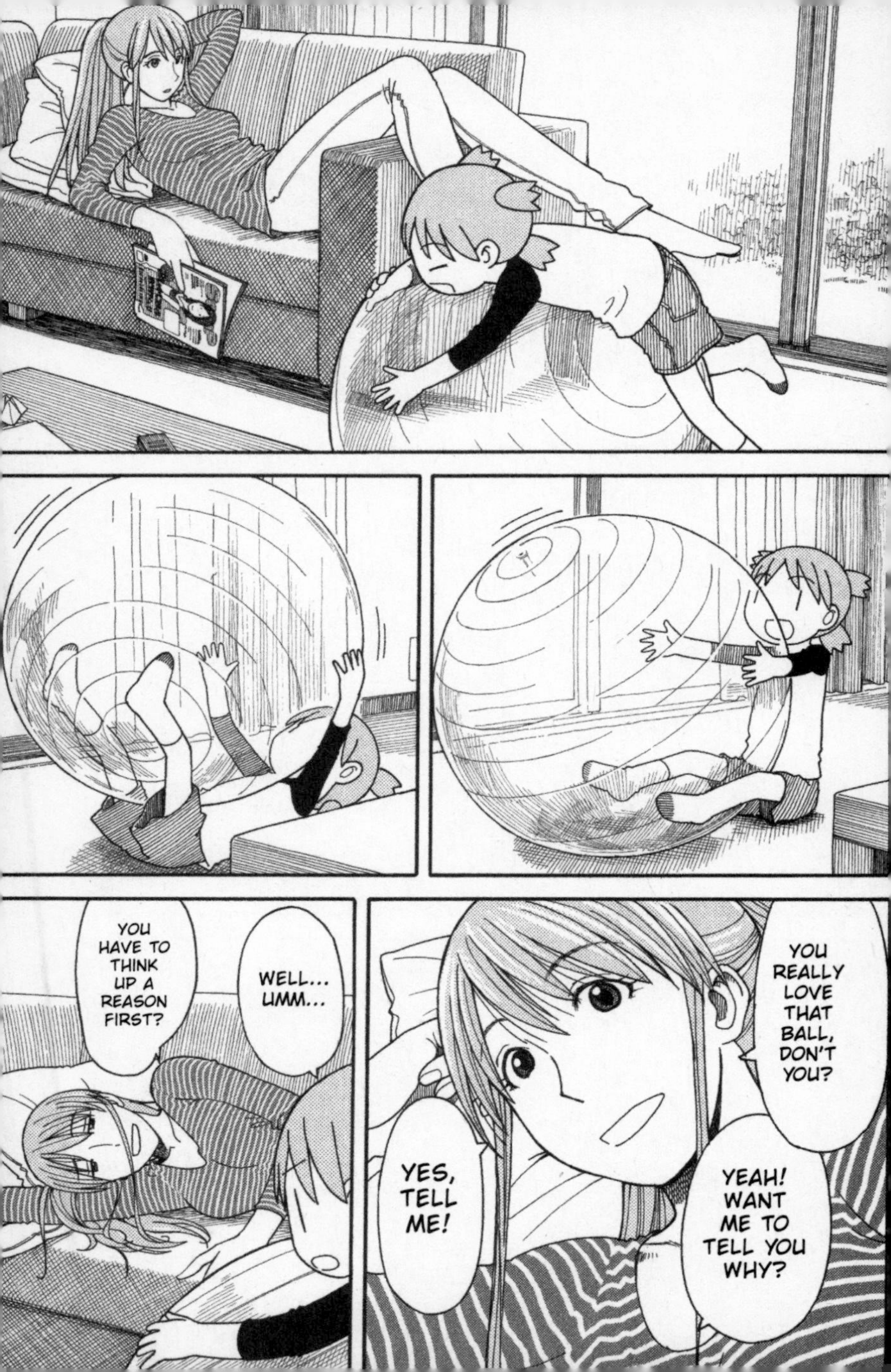
YOU REALLY LOVE THAT BALL, DON'T YOU?
YEAH! WANT ME TO TELL YOU WHY?
YES, TELL ME!
WELL... UMM...
YOU HAVE TO THINK UP A REASON FIRST?

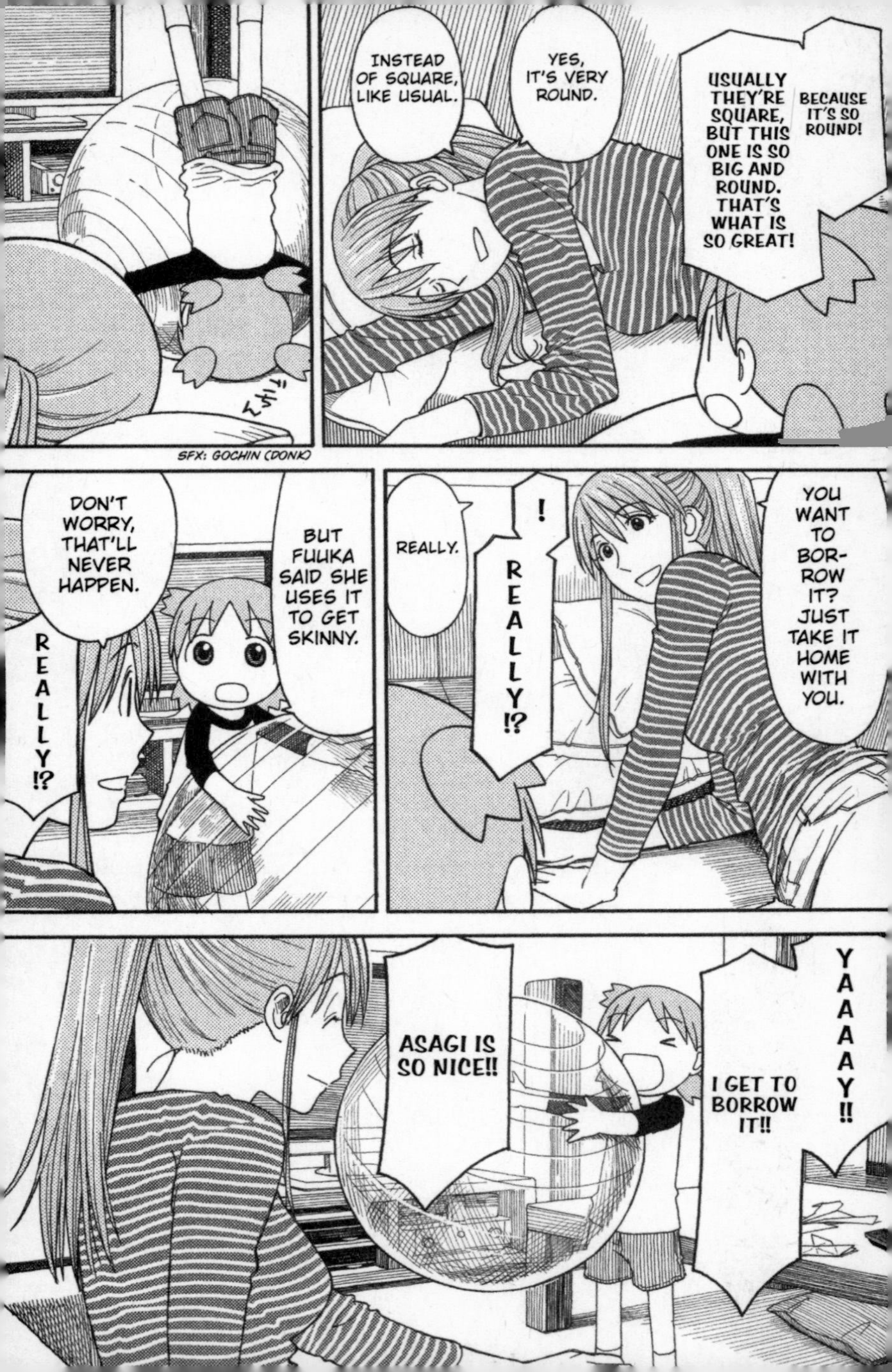
BECAUSE IT'S SO ROUND!
USUALLY THEY'RE SQUARE, BUT THIS ONE IS SO BIG AND ROUND. THAT'S WHAT IS SO GREAT!
YES, IT'S VERY ROUND.
INSTEAD OF SQUARE, LIKE USUAL.
ゴチン
YOU WANT TO BOR-ROW IT? JUST TAKE IT HOME WITH YOU.
!
REALLY!?
REALLY.
BUT FUUKA SAID SHE USES IT TO GET SKINNY.
DON'T WORRY, THAT'LL NEVER HAPPEN.
REALLY!?
YAAAAAY!!
I GET TO BORROW IT!!
ASAGI IS SO NICE!!

SFX: GOCHIN (DONK)

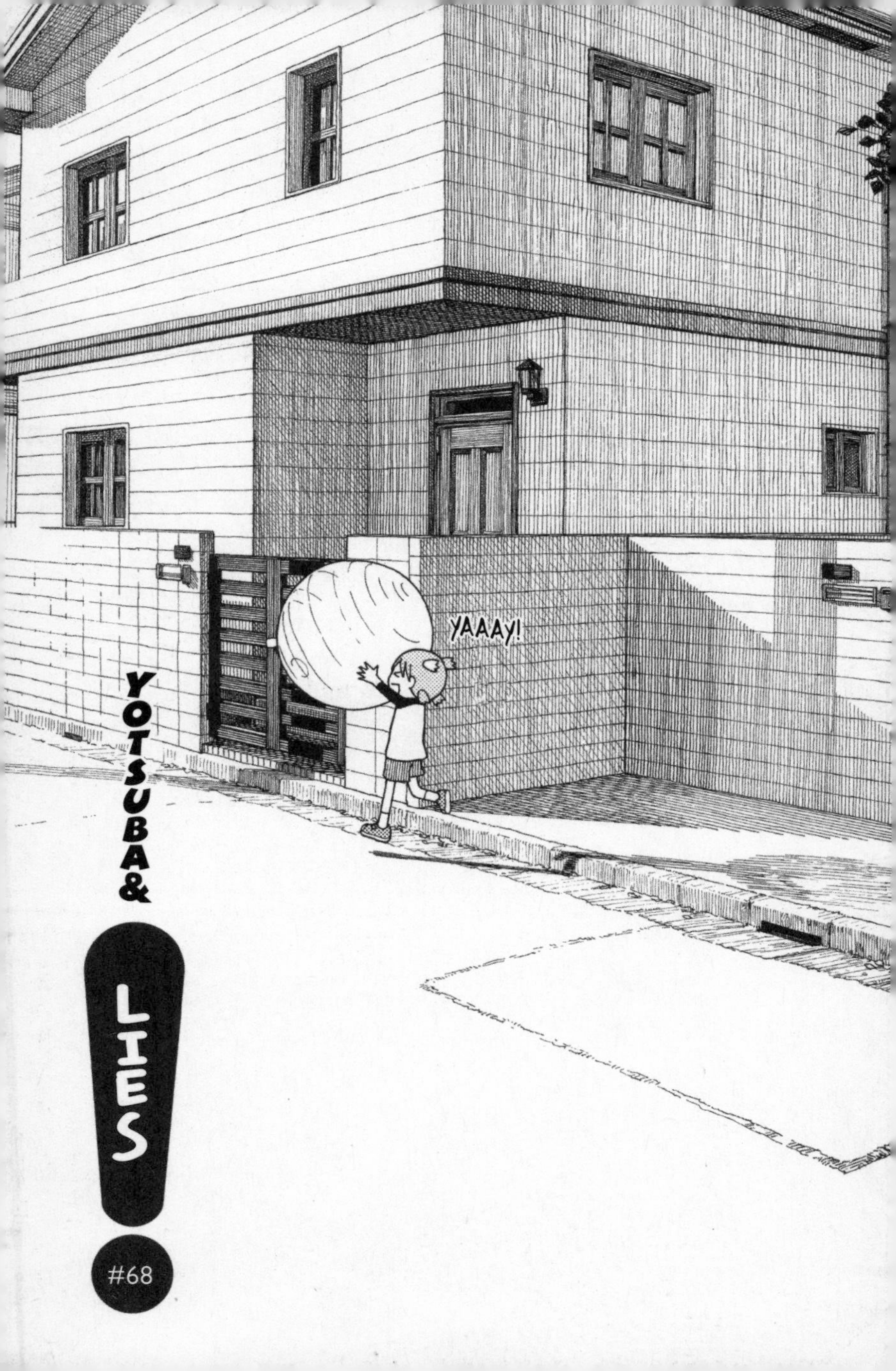
YAAAY!
YOTSUBA&
LIES
#68

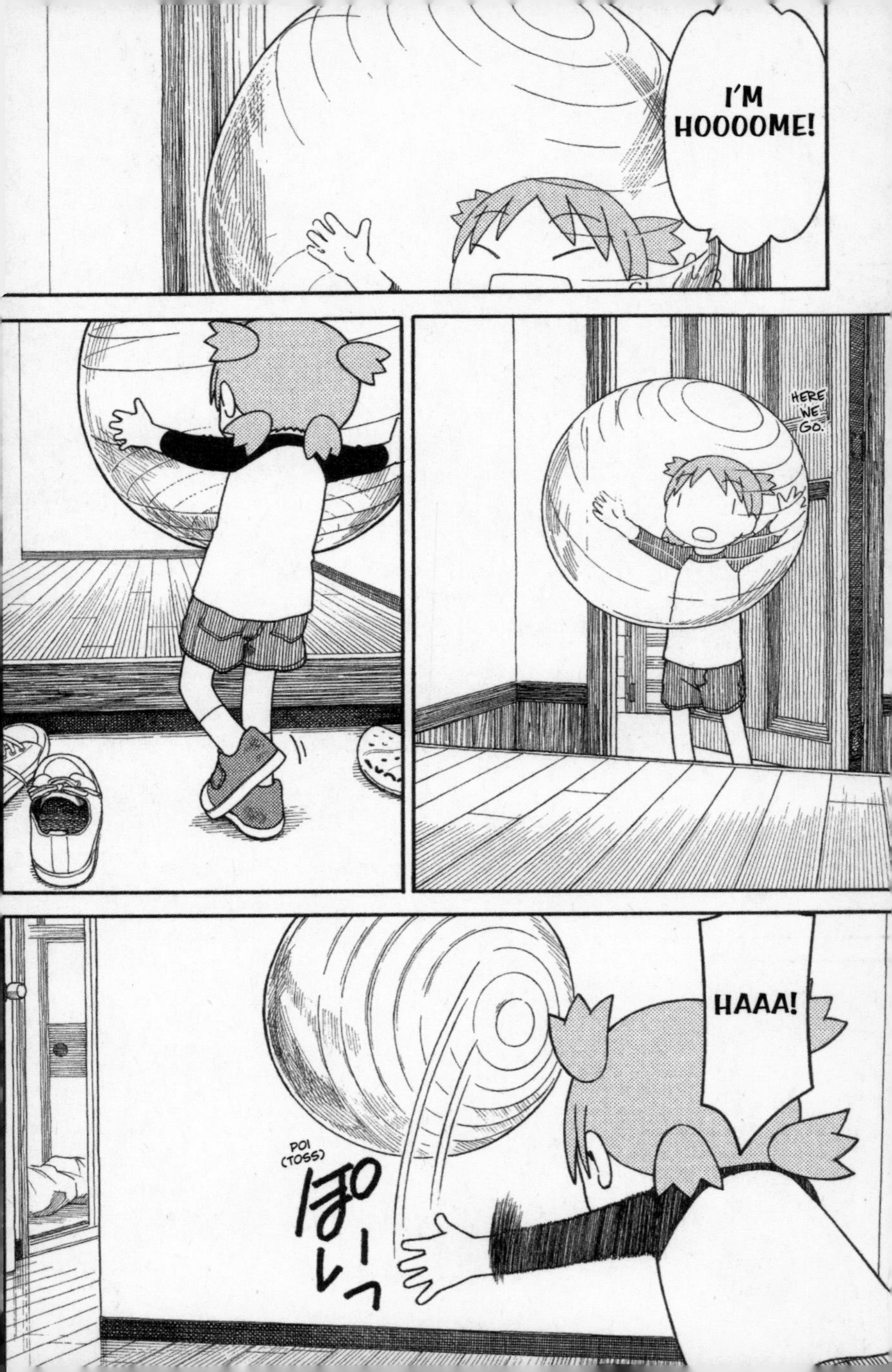
I'M HOOOOME!
HERE WE GO.
HAAA!
POI (TOSS)
ぽーいっ

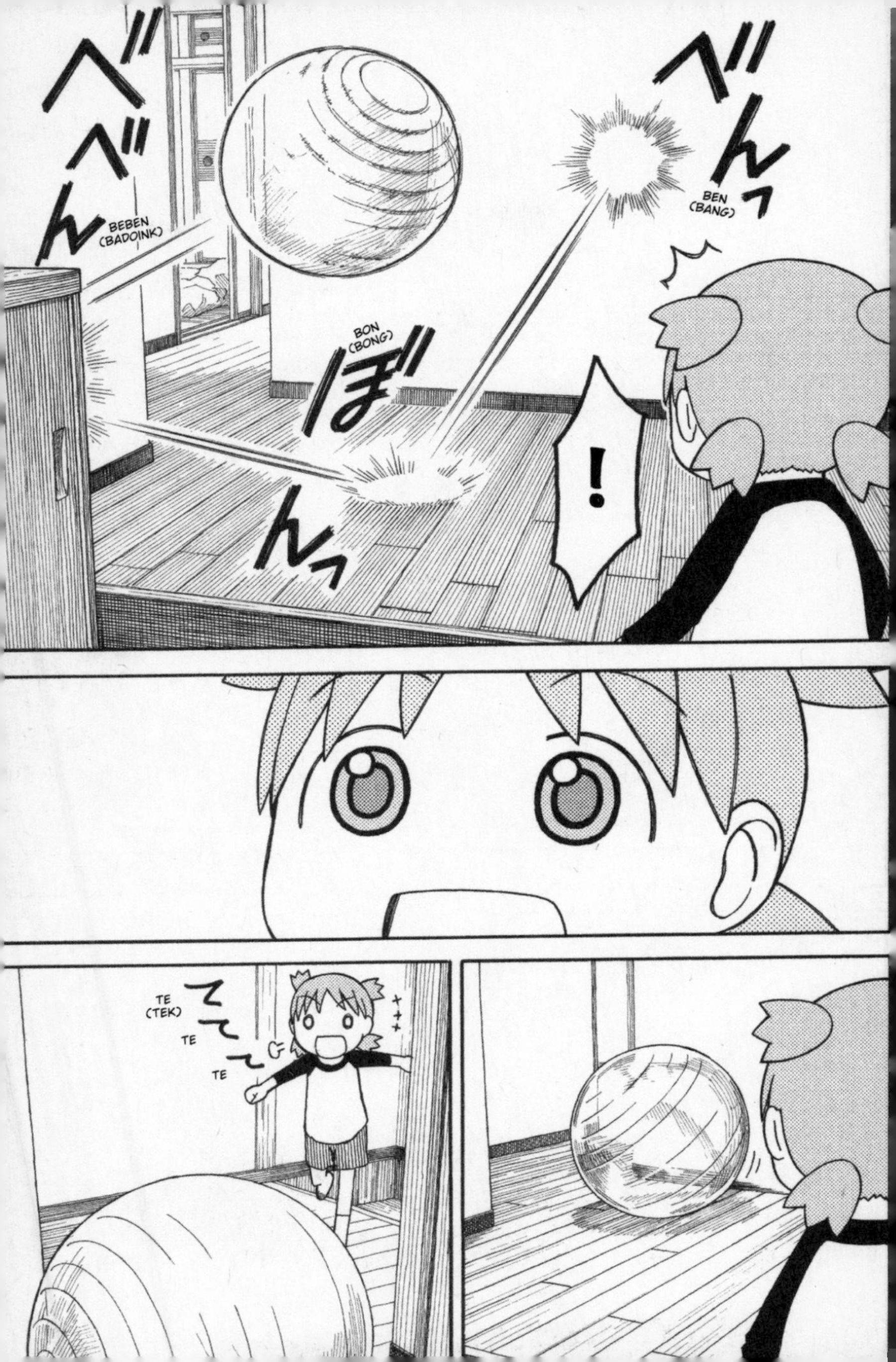

べんっ
BEN (BANG)
べべん
BEBEN (BADOINK)
BON (BONG)
ぼんっ
!
ててて
TE (TEK)
TE
TE

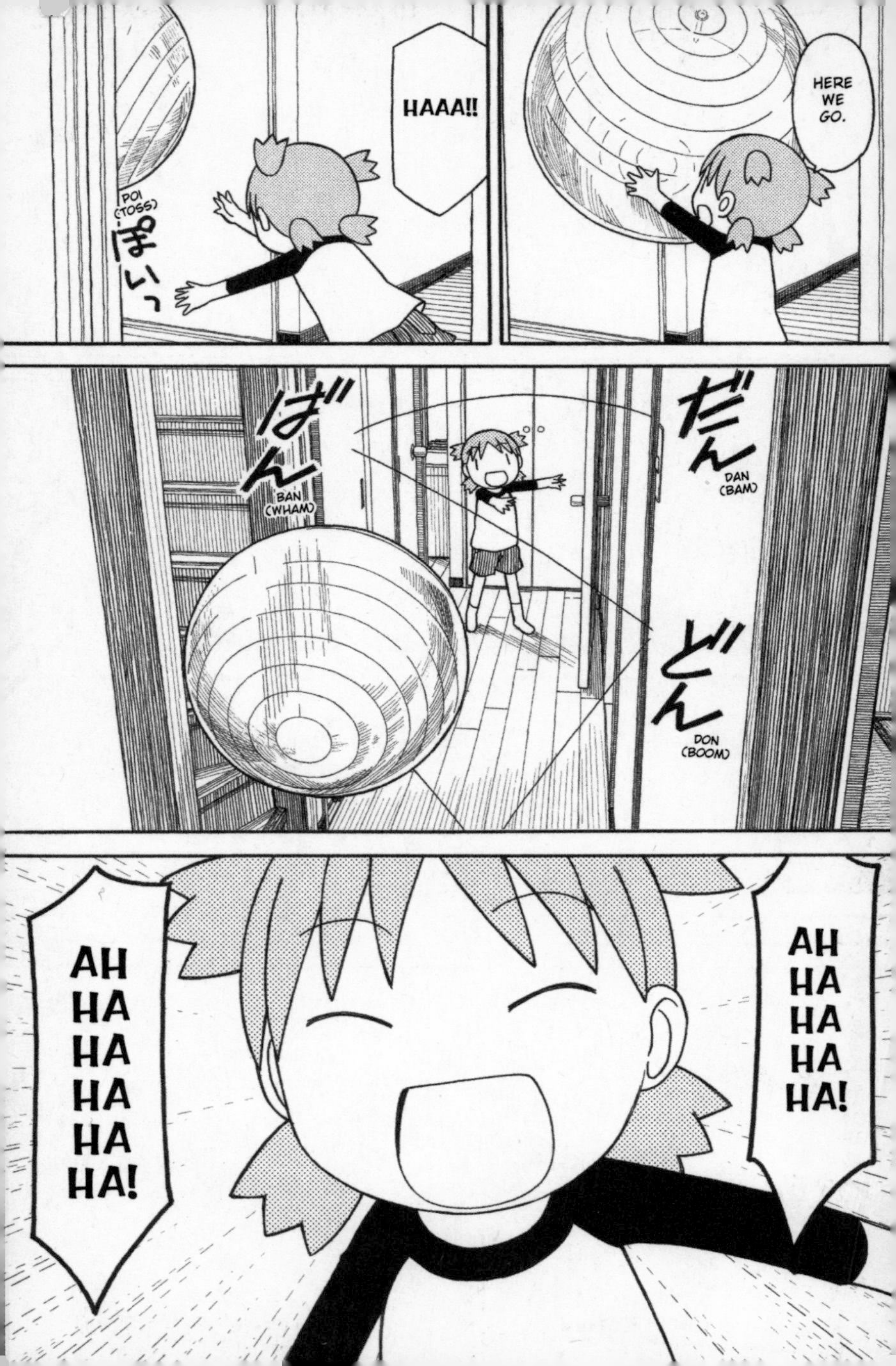
HERE WE GO.
HAAA!!
ぽいっ
POI (TOSS)
だん
DAN (BAM)
ばん
BAN (WHAM)
どん
DON (BOOM)
AH HA HA HA HA!
AH HA HA HA HA HA HA!

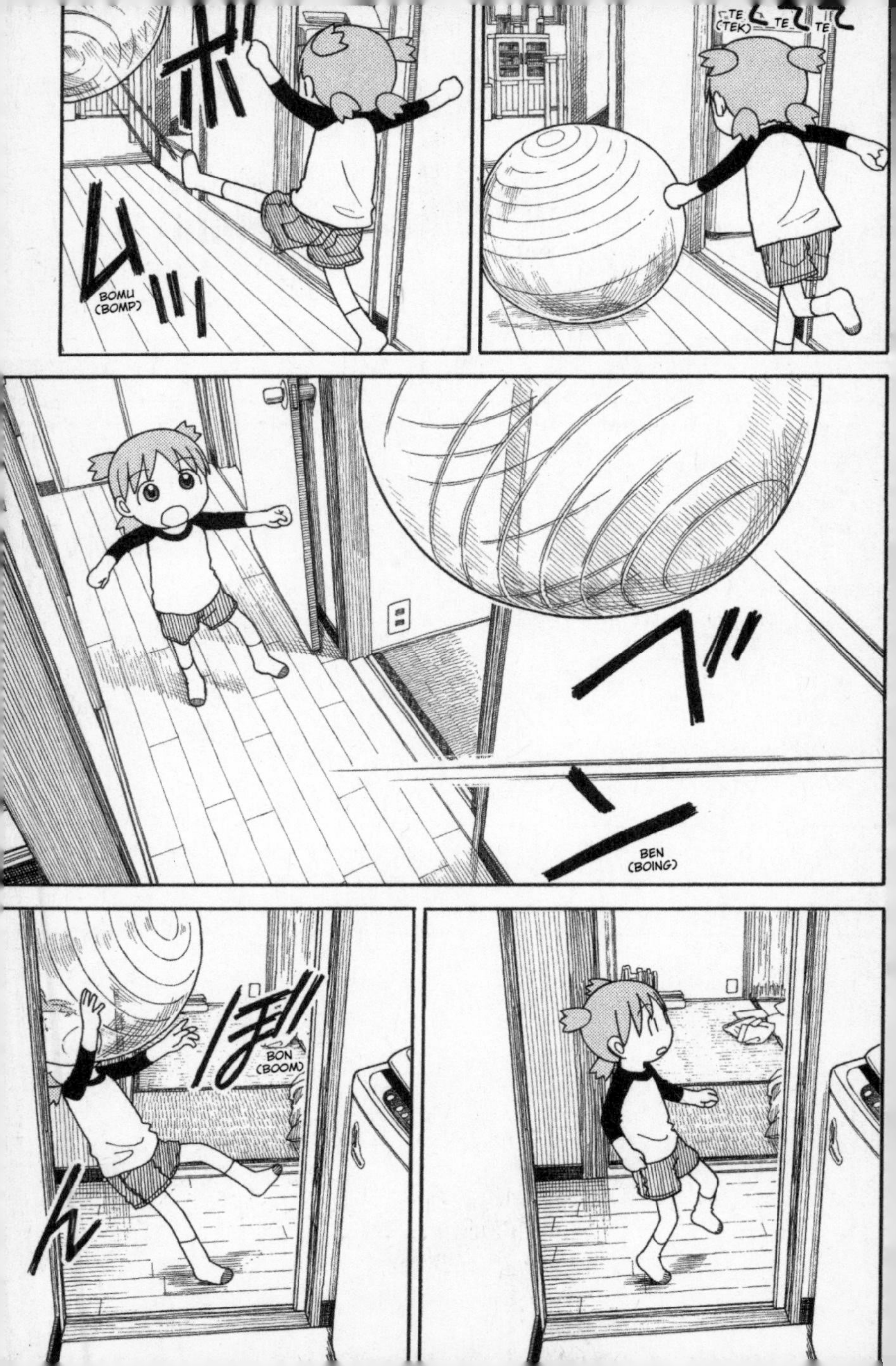
TE (TEK) TE TE
BOMU (BOMP)
BEN (BOING)
BON (BOOM)

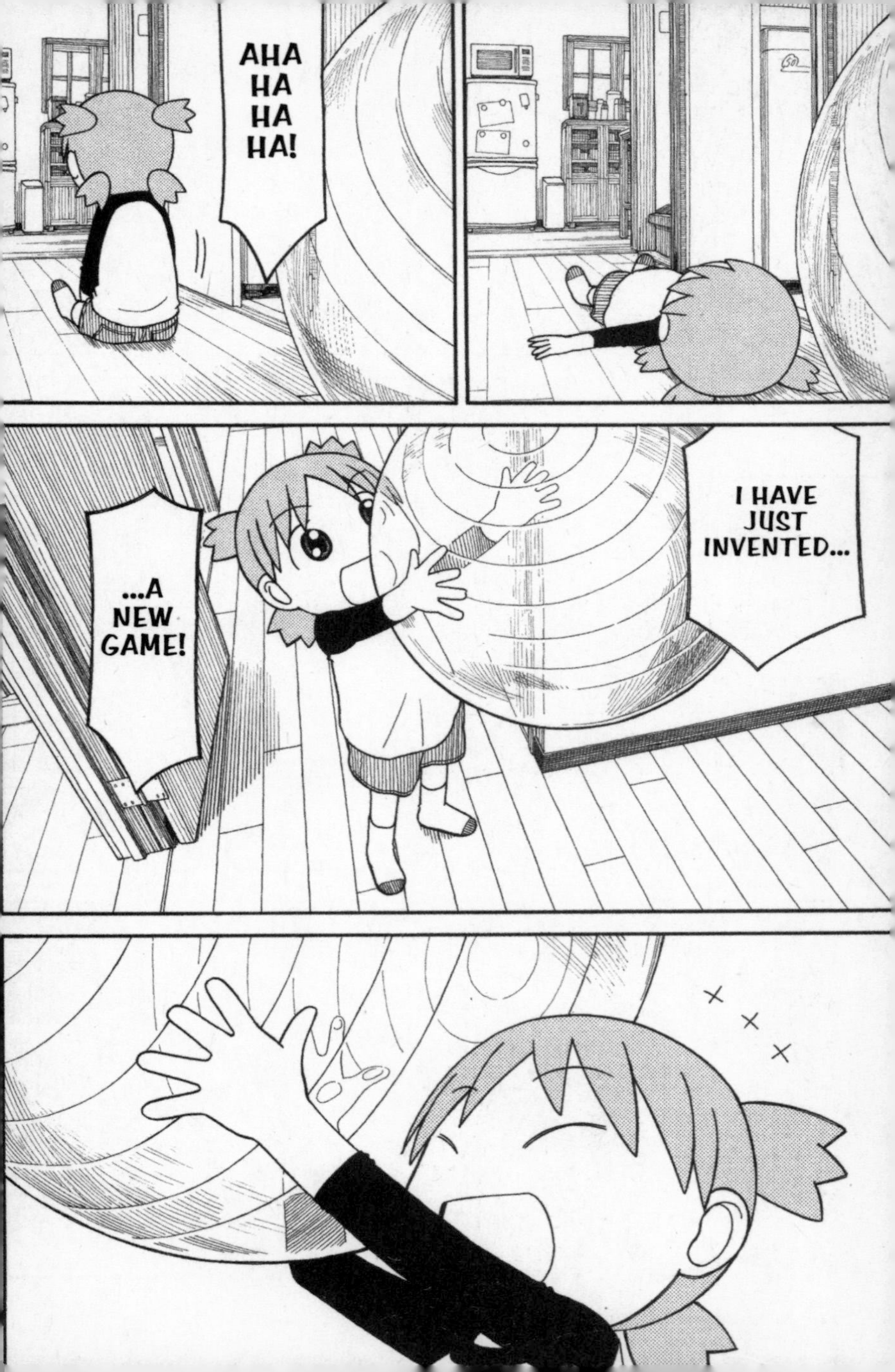
AHA HA HA HA!
I HAVE JUST INVENTED...
...A NEW GAME!

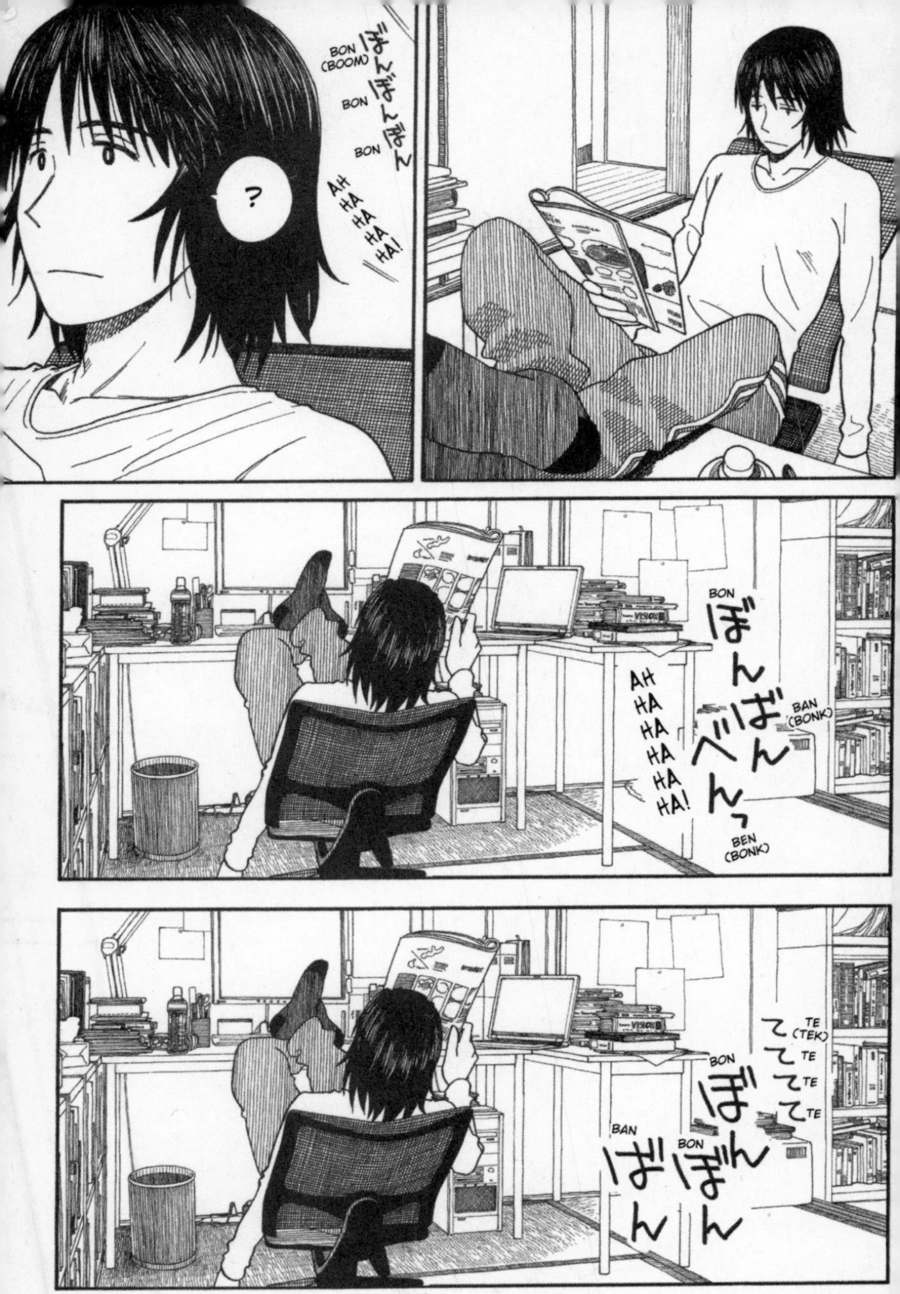
ぼんぼんぼん
BON (BOOM) BON BON
?
AH HA HA HA HA!
ぼんぼんべん
BON BAN (BONK) BEN (BONK)
AH HA HA HA HA HA HA!
てててて
TE (TEK) TE TE TE
ぼんぼんばん
BON BON BAN

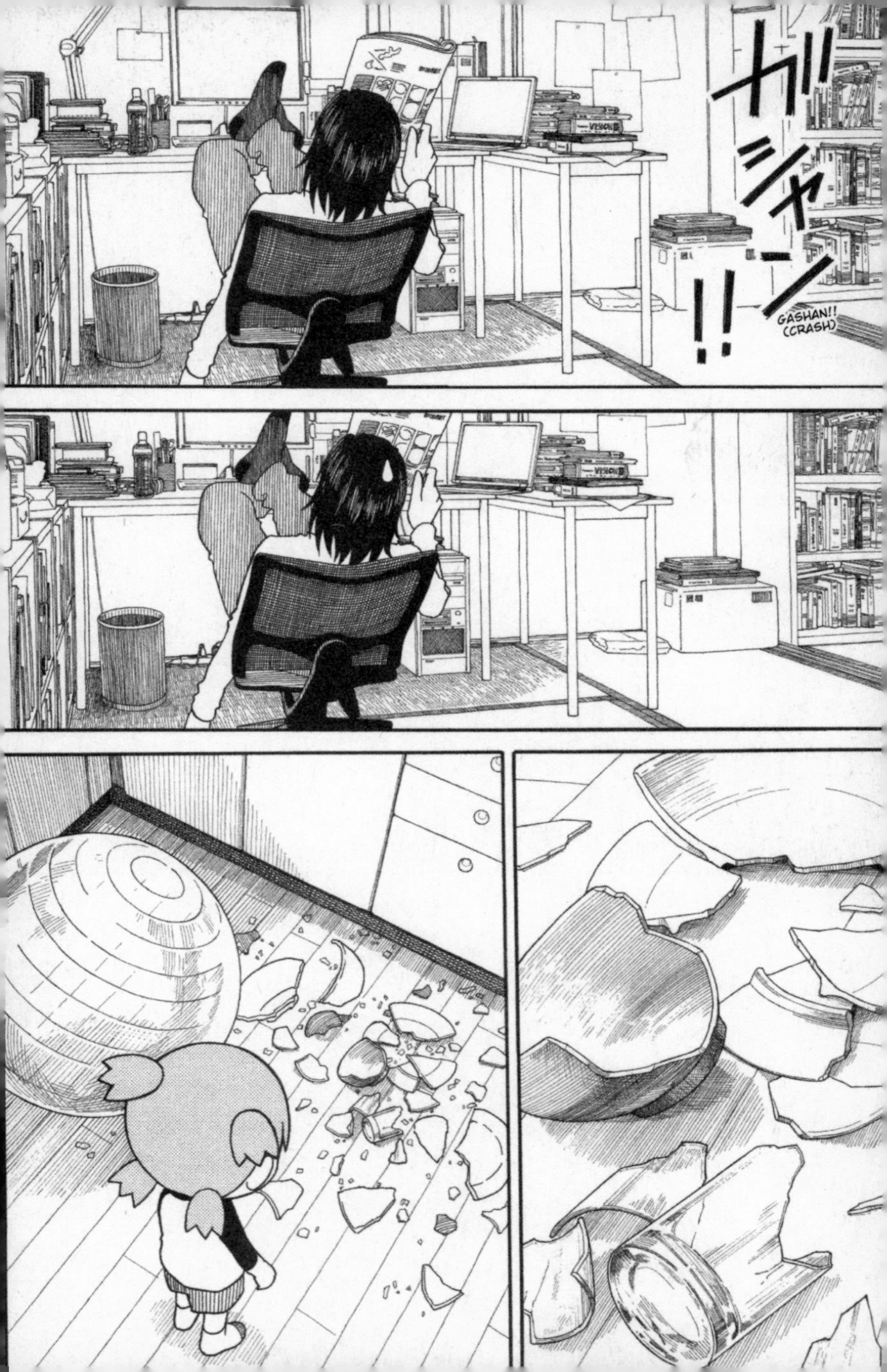
ガシャーン!!
GASHAN!! (CRASH)

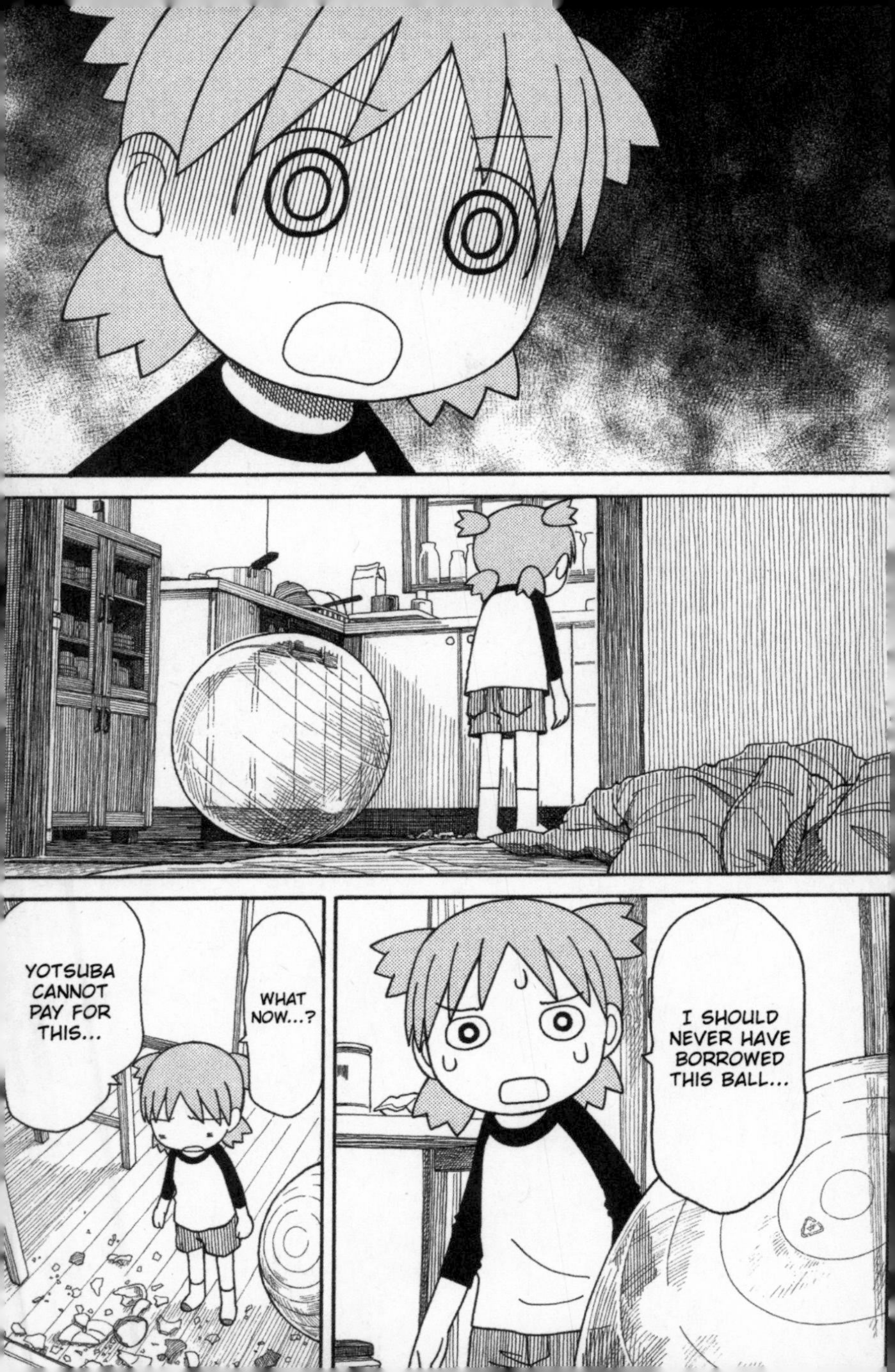
I SHOULD NEVER HAVE BORROWED THIS BALL...
WHAT NOW...?
YOTSUBA CANNOT PAY FOR THIS...

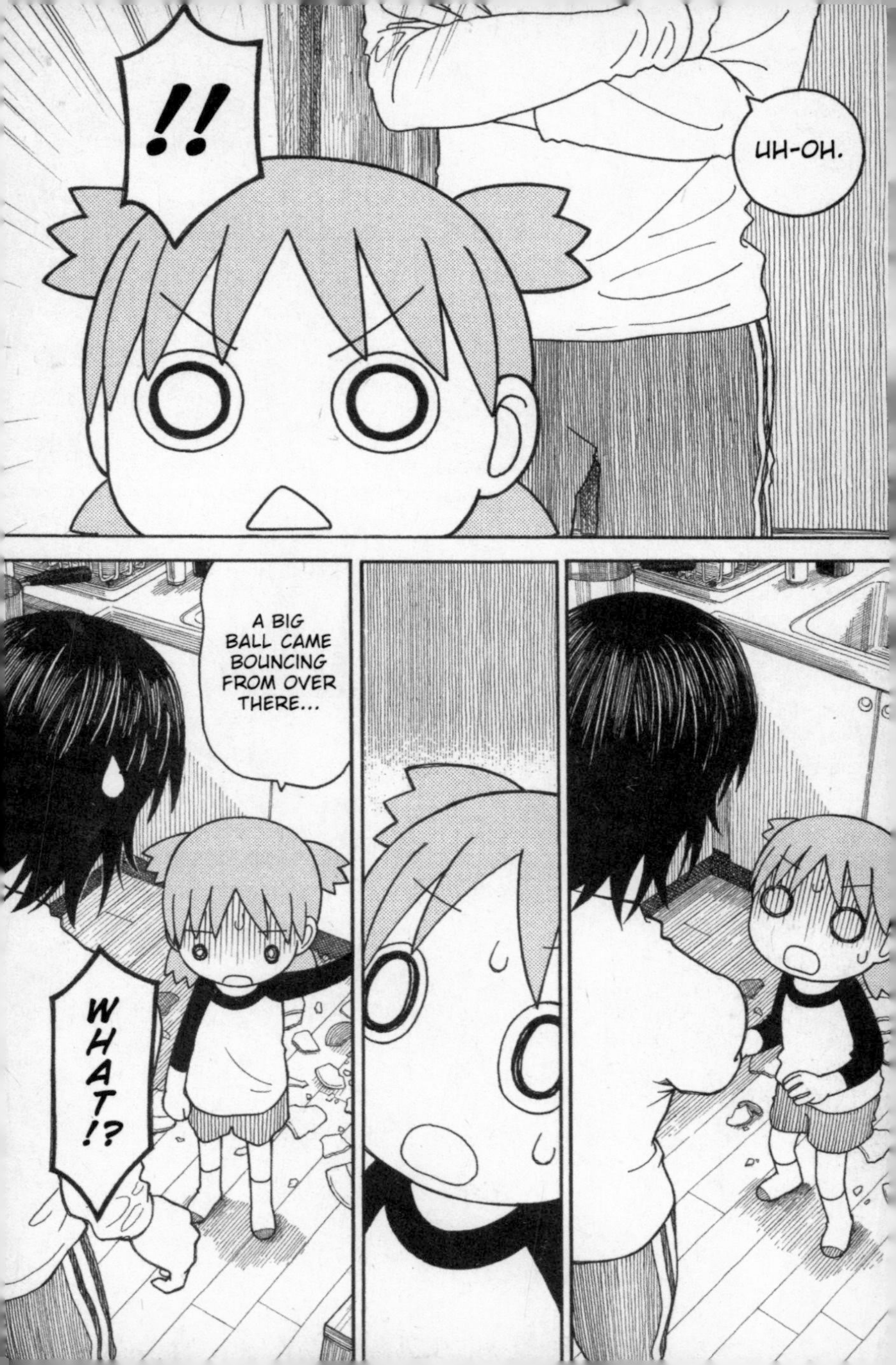
UH-OH.
!!
A BIG BALL CAME BOUNCING FROM OVER THERE...
WHAT!?

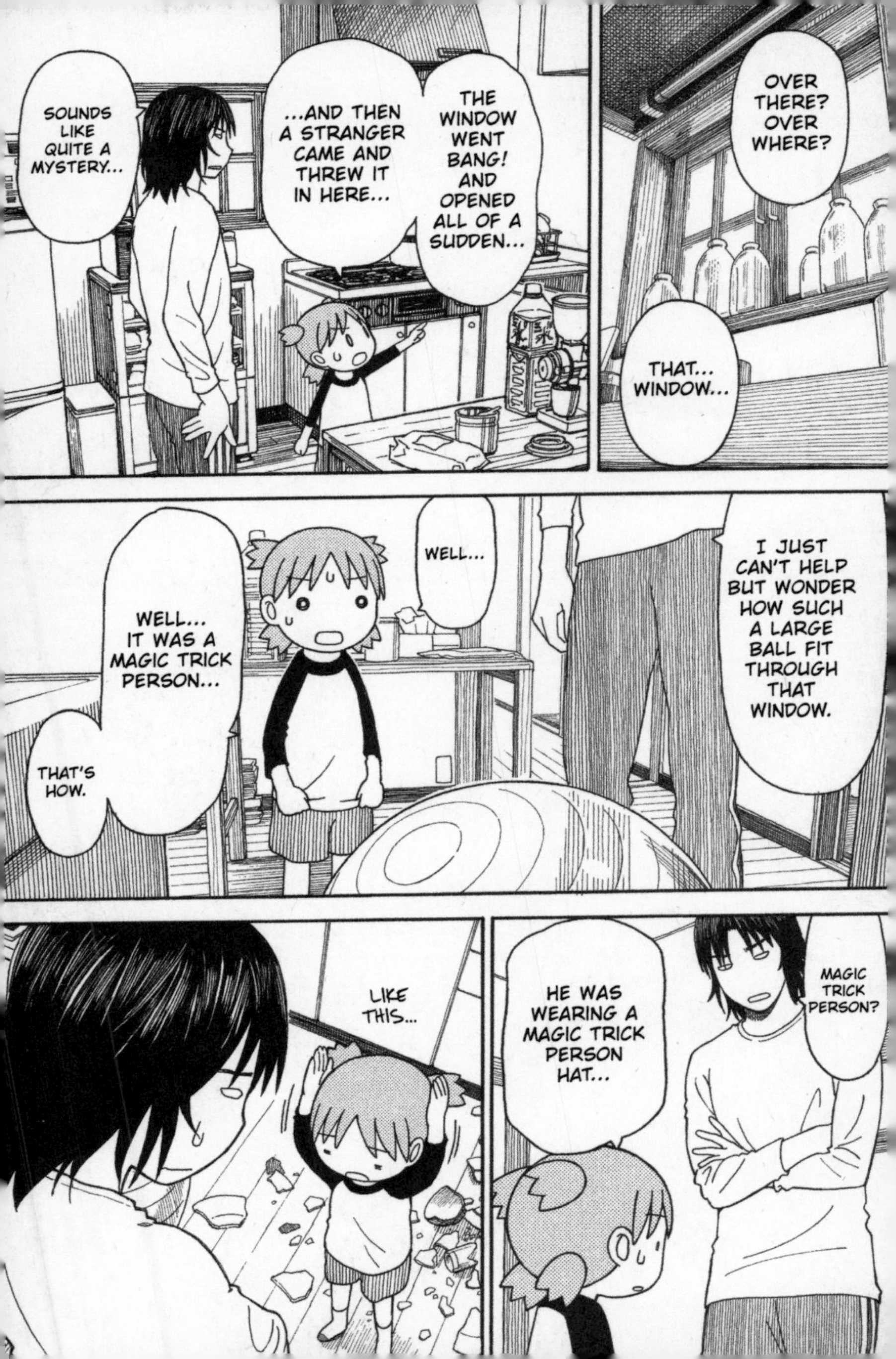
OVER THERE? OVER WHERE?
THAT... WINDOW...
THE WINDOW WENT BANG! AND OPENED ALL OF A SUDDEN...
...AND THEN A STRANGER CAME AND THREW IT IN HERE...
SOUNDS LIKE QUITE A MYSTERY...
I JUST CAN'T HELP BUT WONDER HOW SUCH A LARGE BALL FIT THROUGH THAT WINDOW.
WELL...
WELL... IT WAS A MAGIC TRICK PERSON...
THAT'S HOW.
MAGIC TRICK PERSON?
HE WAS WEARING A MAGIC TRICK PERSON HAT...
LIKE THIS...

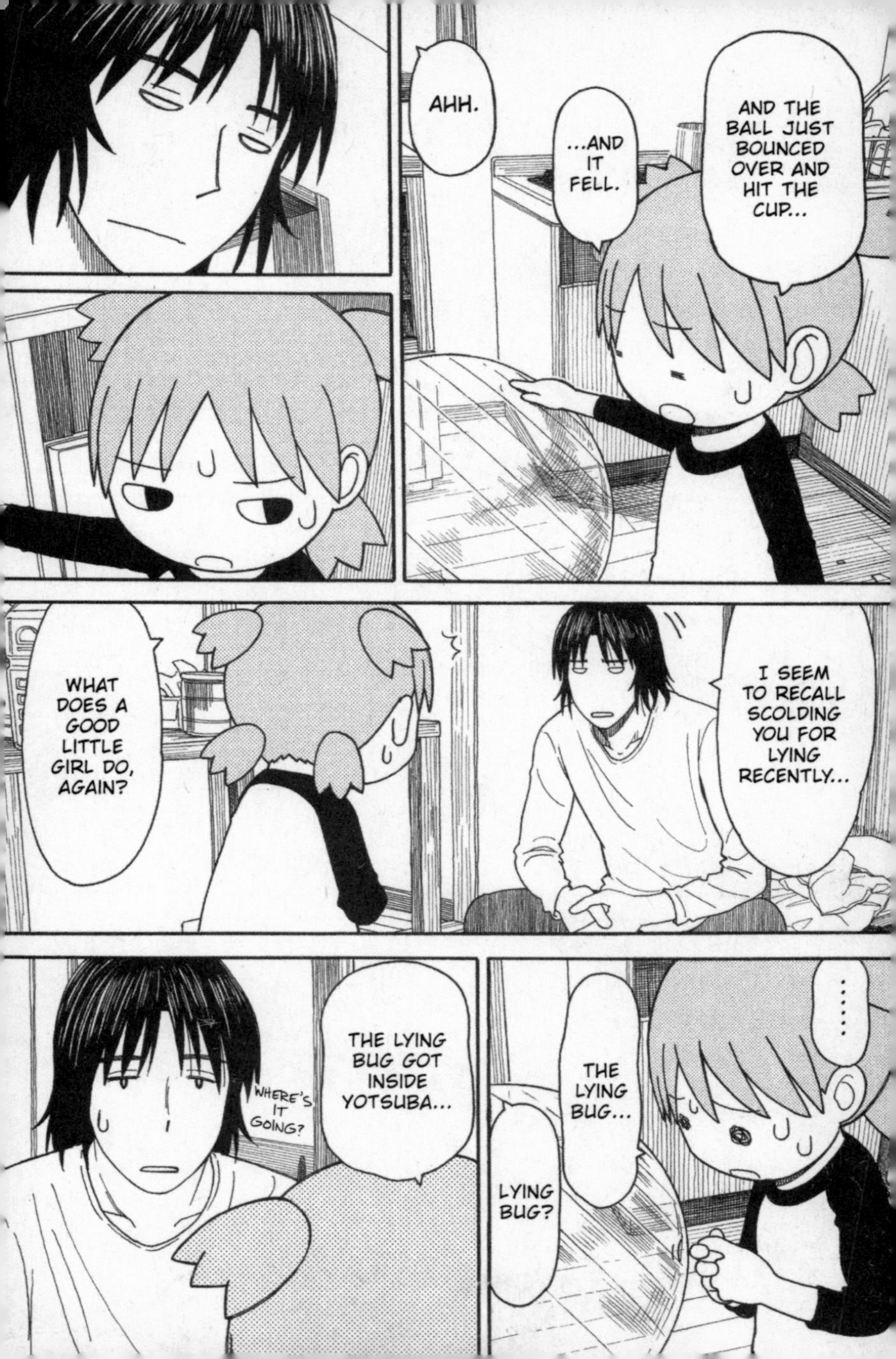
AND THE BALL JUST BOUNCED OVER AND HIT THE CUP...
...AND IT FELL.
AHH.
I SEEM TO RECALL SCOLDING YOU FOR LYING RECENTLY...
WHAT DOES A GOOD LITTLE GIRL DO, AGAIN?
......
THE LYING BUG...
LYING BUG?
THE LYING BUG GOT INSIDE YOTSUBA...
WHERE'S IT GOING?

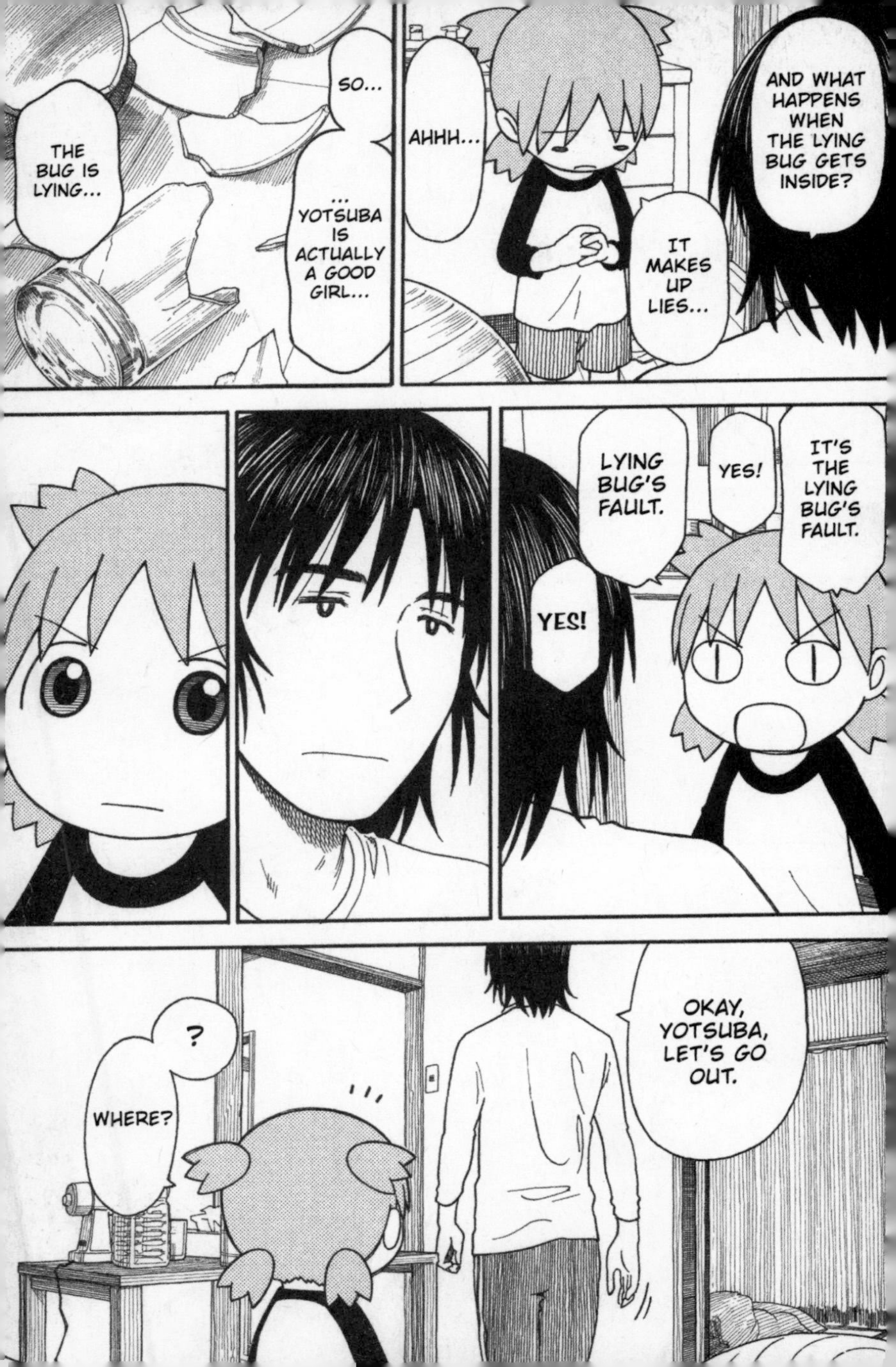
AND WHAT HAPPENS WHEN THE LYING BUG GETS INSIDE?
IT MAKES UP LIES...
AHHH...
SO...
... YOTSUBA IS ACTUALLY A GOOD GIRL...
THE BUG IS LYING...
IT'S THE LYING BUG'S FAULT.
YES!
LYING BUG'S FAULT.
YES!
OKAY, YOTSUBA, LET'S GO OUT.
?
WHERE?

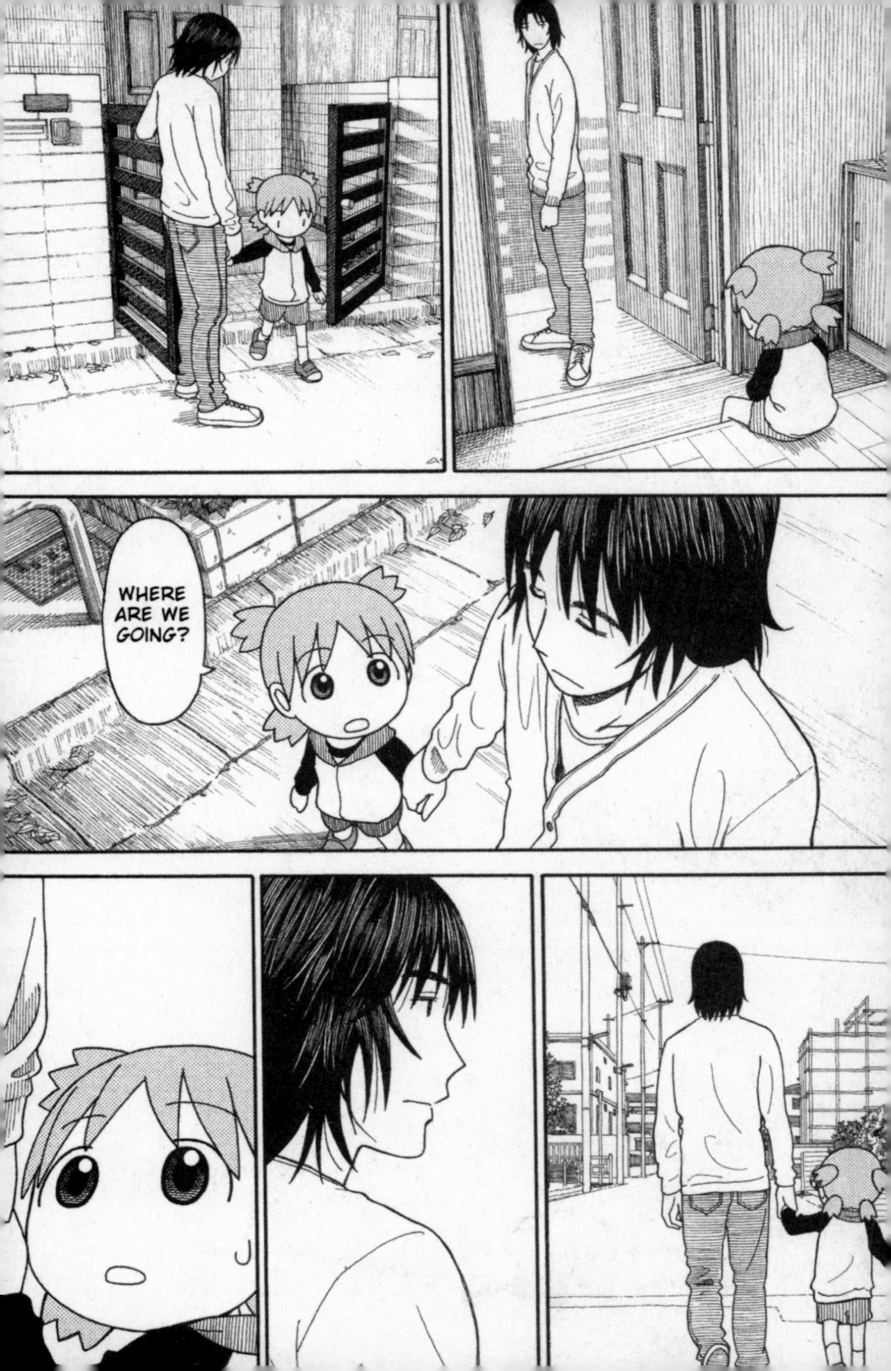
WHERE ARE WE GOING?

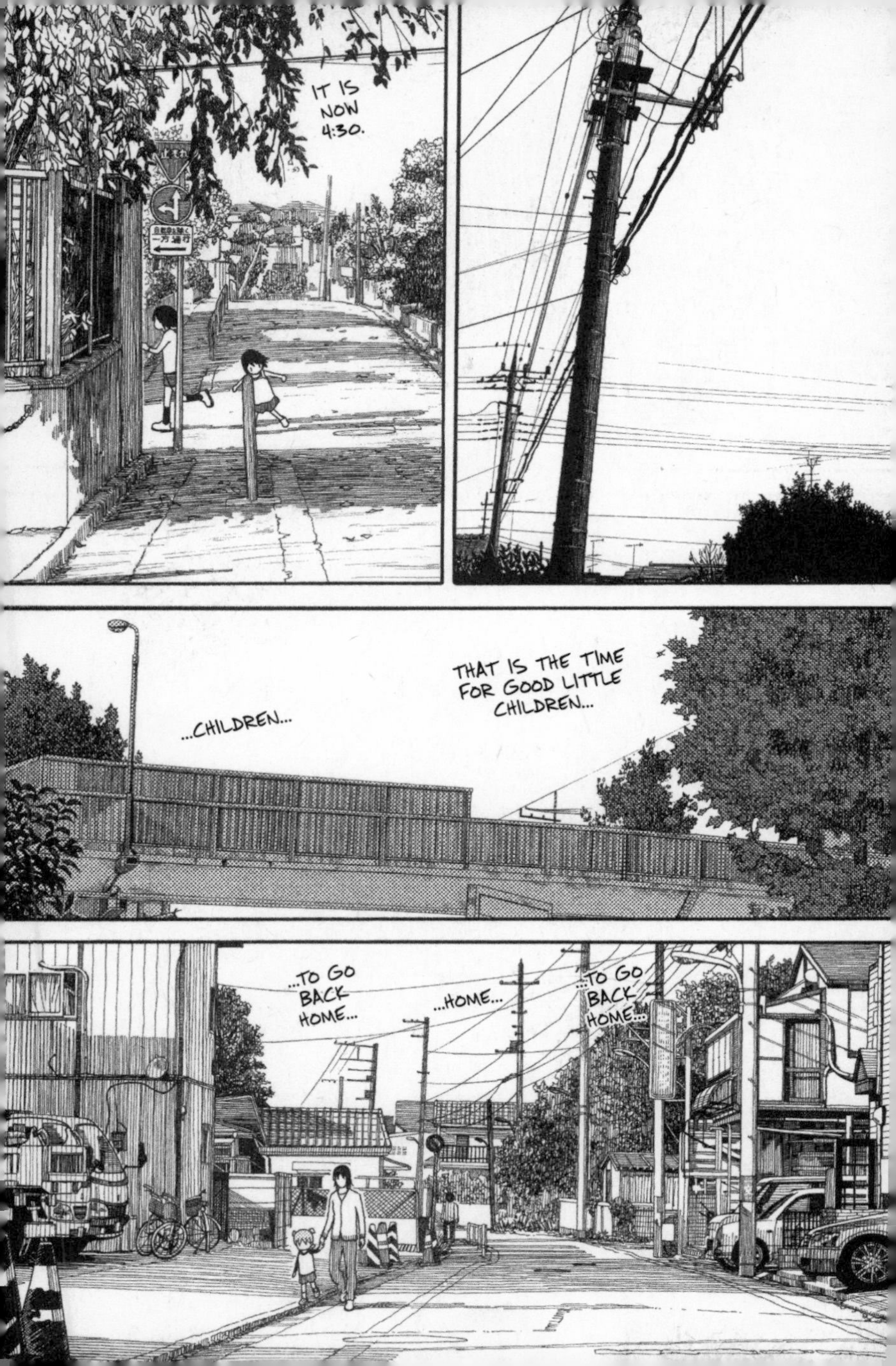
IT IS NOW 4:30.
THAT IS THE TIME FOR GOOD LITTLE CHILDREN...
...CHILDREN...
...TO GO BACK HOME...
...HOME...
...TO GO BACK HOME...

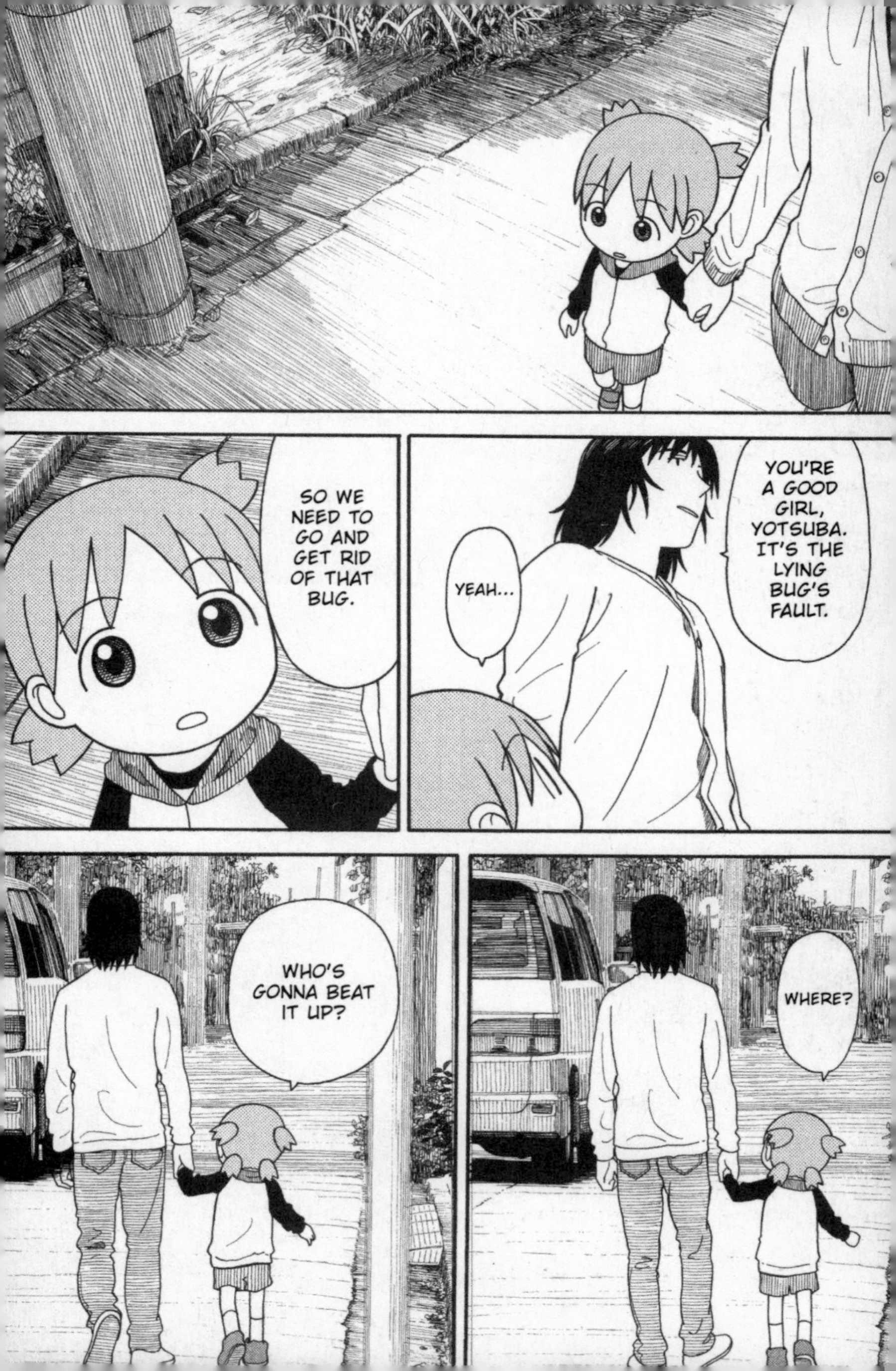
YOU'RE A GOOD GIRL, YOTSUBA. IT'S THE LYING BUG'S FAULT.
YEAH...
SO WE NEED TO GO AND GET RID OF THAT BUG.
WHERE?
WHO'S GONNA BEAT IT UP?

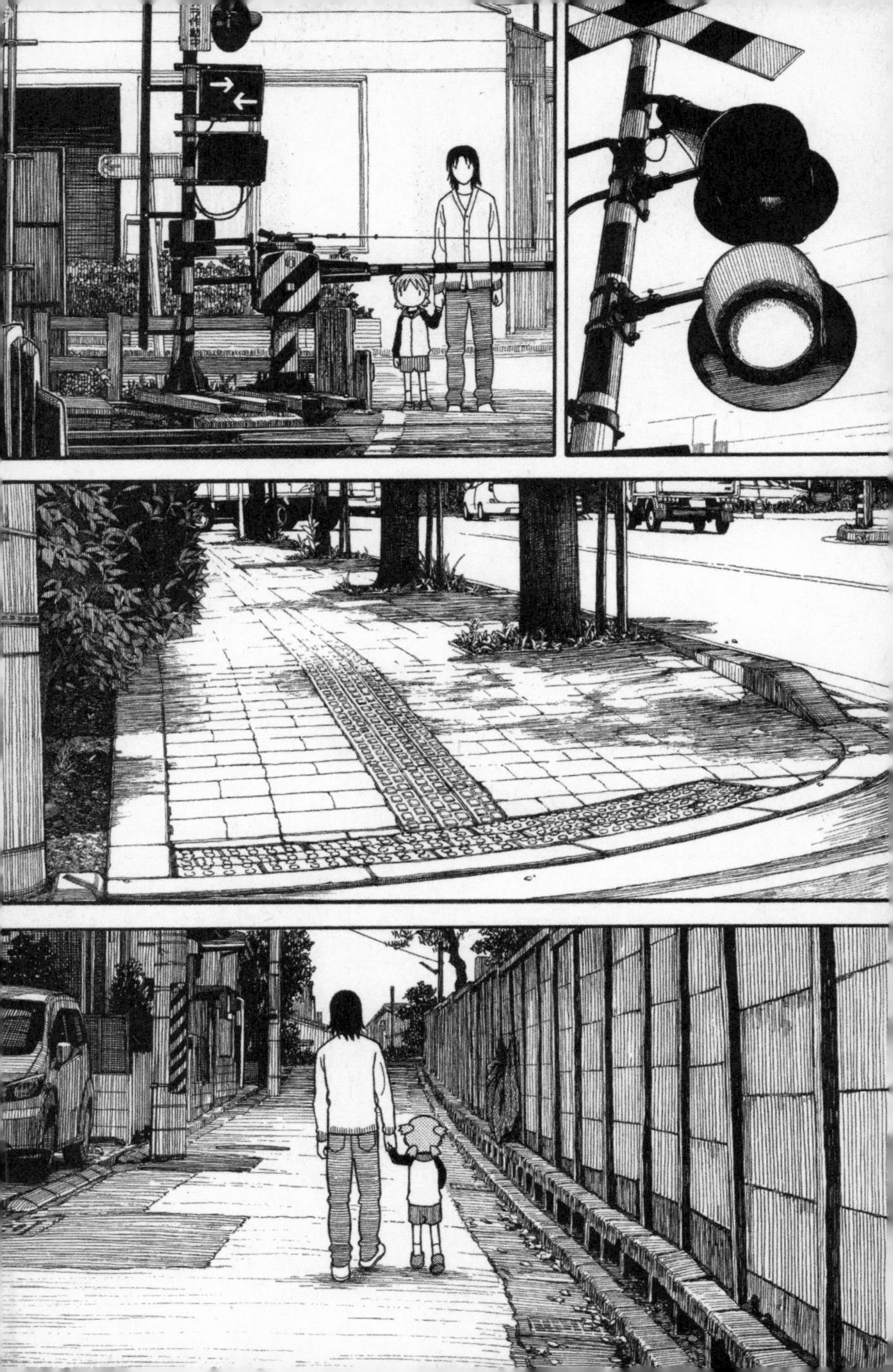

作動中

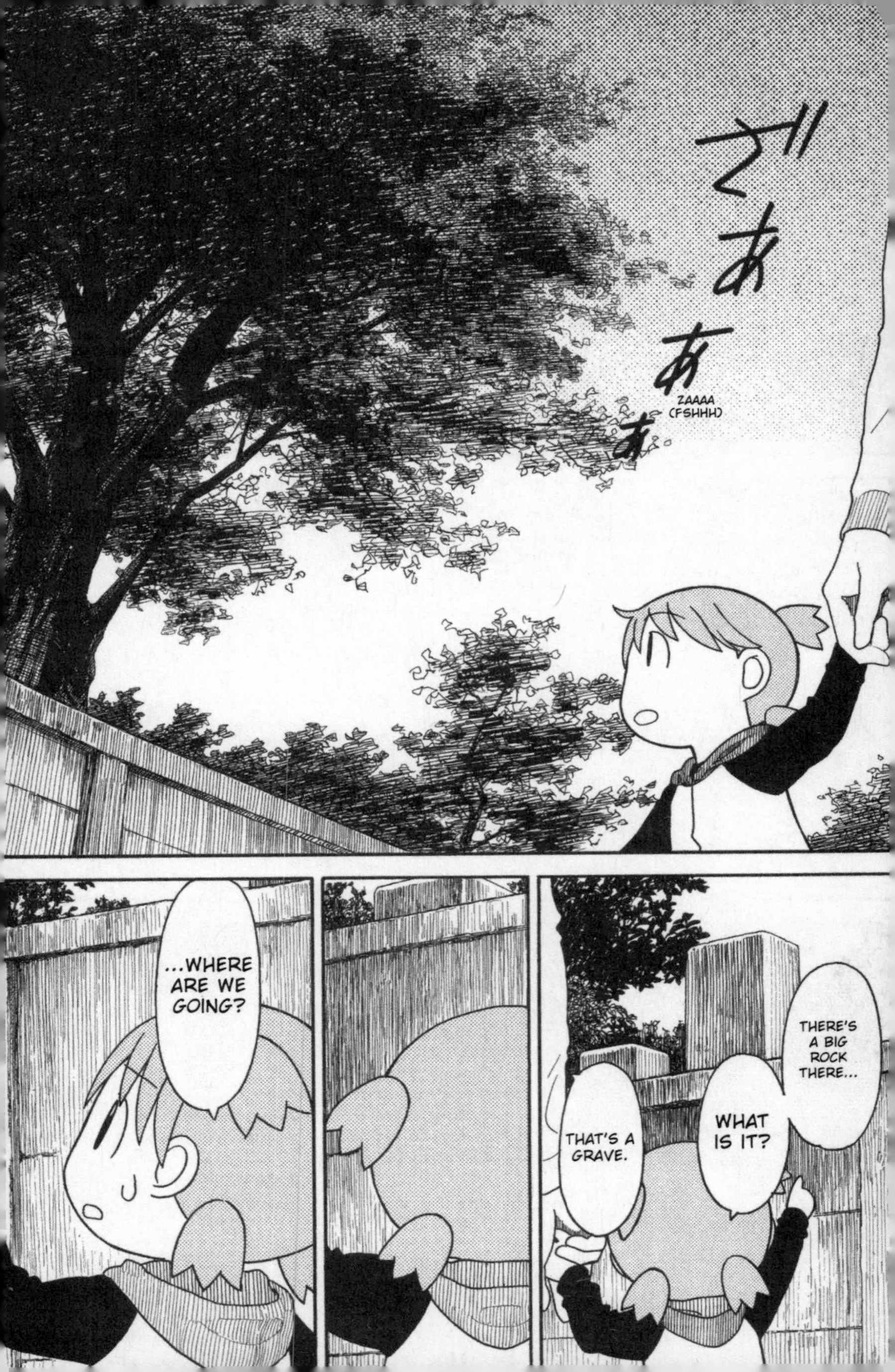
ざあああ
ZAAAA (FSHHH)
THERE'S A BIG ROCK THERE...
WHAT IS IT?
THAT'S A GRAVE.
...WHERE ARE WE GOING?

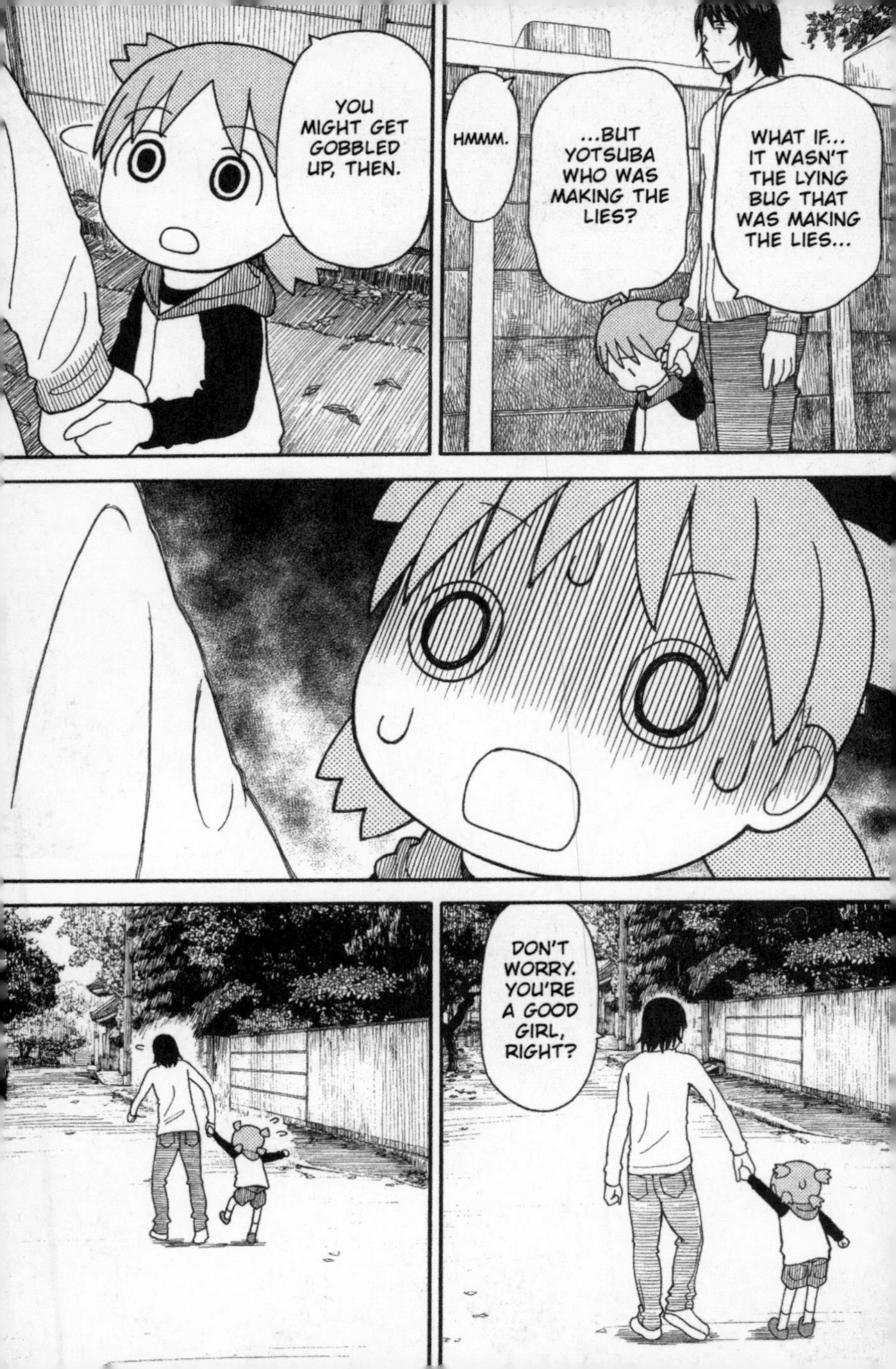
WHAT IF... IT WASN'T THE LYING BUG THAT WAS MAKING THE LIES...
...BUT YOTSUBA WHO WAS MAKING THE LIES?
HMMM.
YOU MIGHT GET GOBBLED UP, THEN.
DON'T WORRY. YOU'RE A GOOD GIRL, RIGHT?

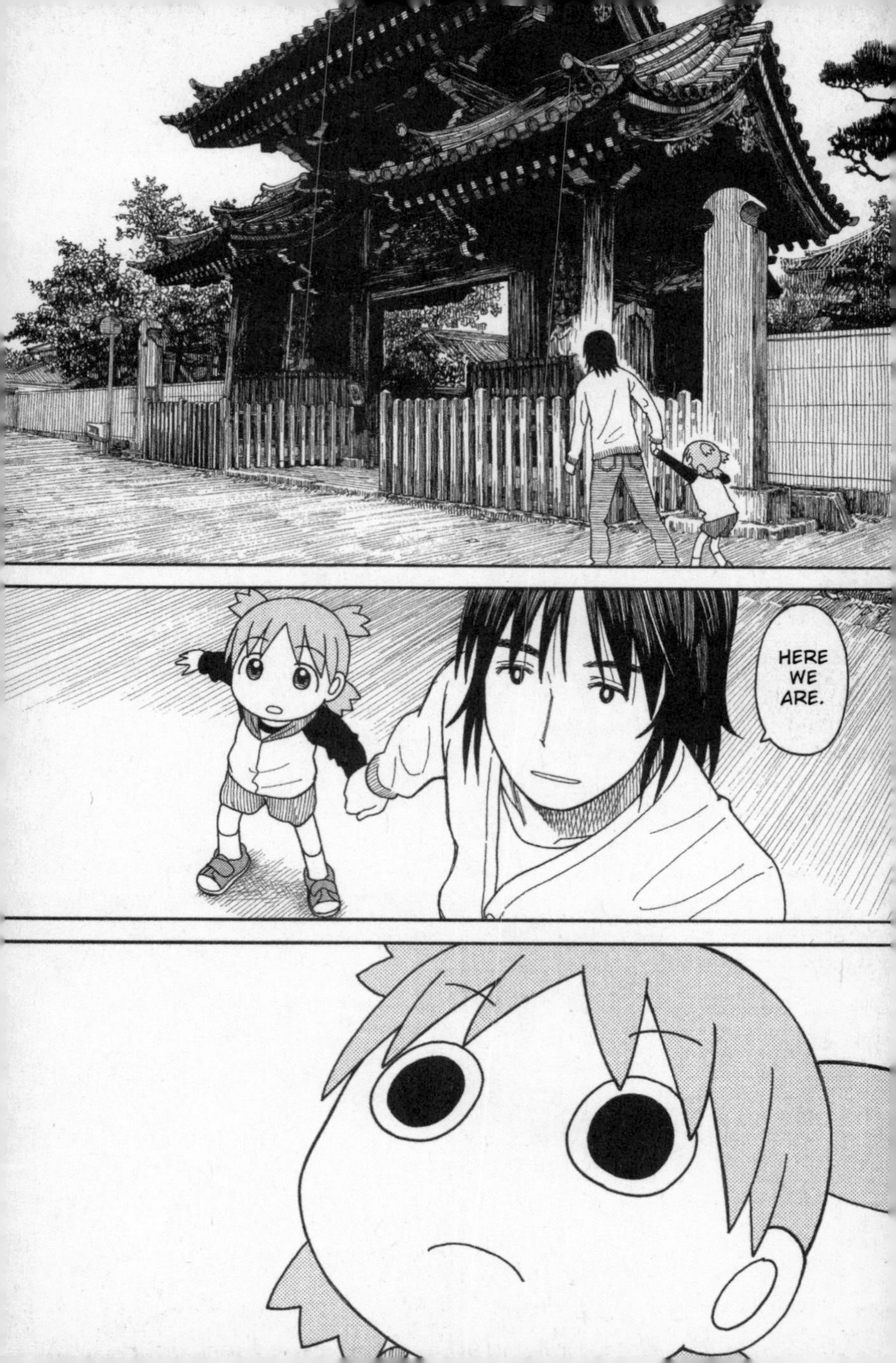
HERE WE ARE.

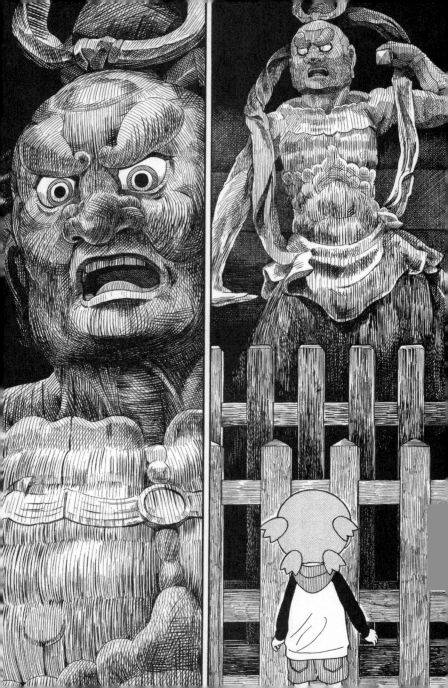

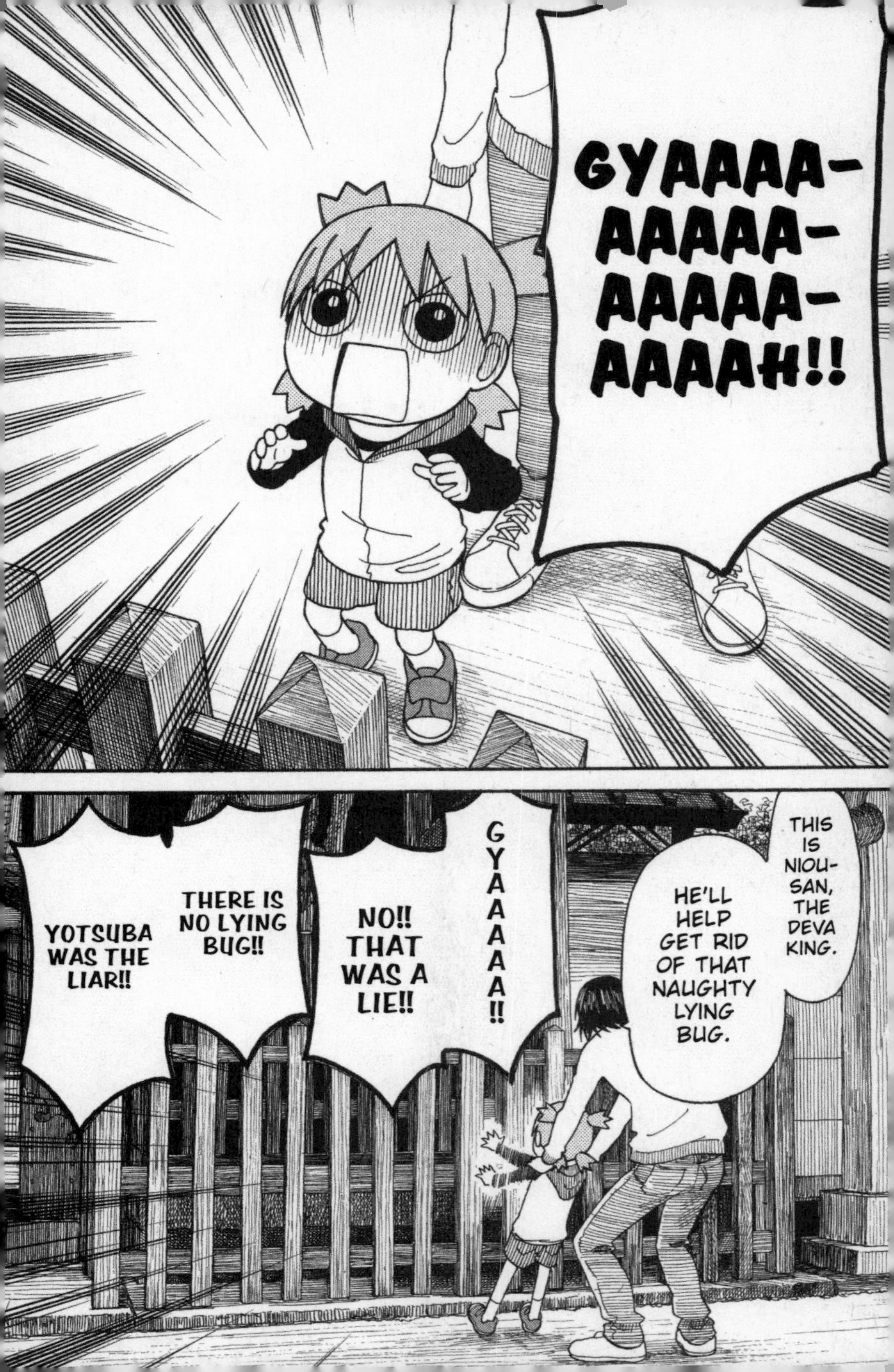
GYAAAA-AAAAA-AAAAA-AAAAH!!
THIS IS NIOU-SAN, THE DEVA KING.
HE'LL HELP GET RID OF THAT NAUGHTY LYING BUG.
GYAAAAAA!!
NO!! THAT WAS A LIE!!
THERE IS NO LYING BUG!!
YOTSUBA WAS THE LIAR!!

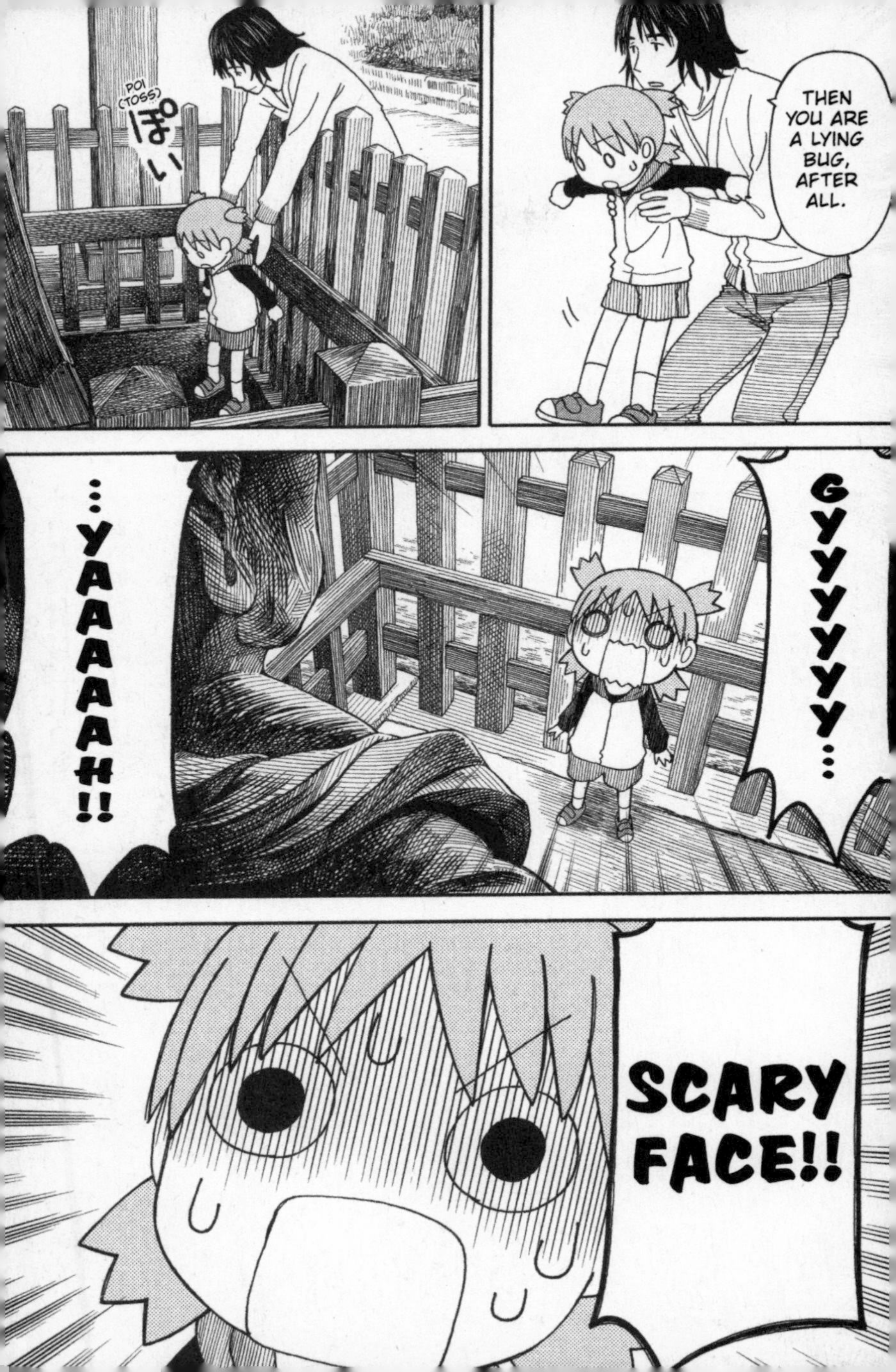
THEN YOU ARE A LYING BUG, AFTER ALL.
POI (TOSS)
ぽい
GYYYYYY...
...YAAAAAH!!
SCARY FACE!!

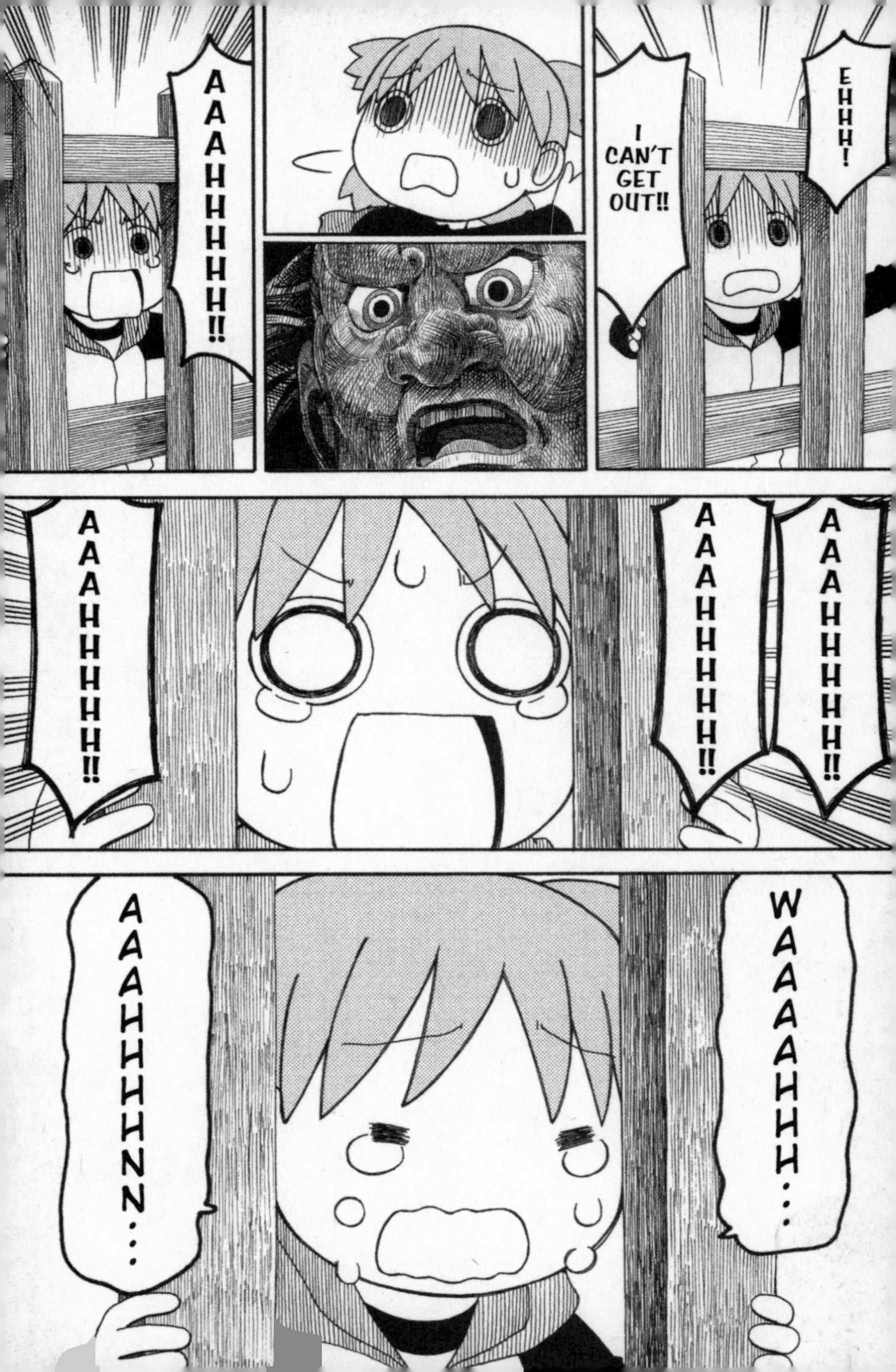
EHHH!
I CAN'T GET OUT!!
AAAHHHHH!!
AAAHHHHHH!!
AAAHHHHHH!!
AAAHHHHHH!!
WAAAAAHHH...
AAAHHHHNN...

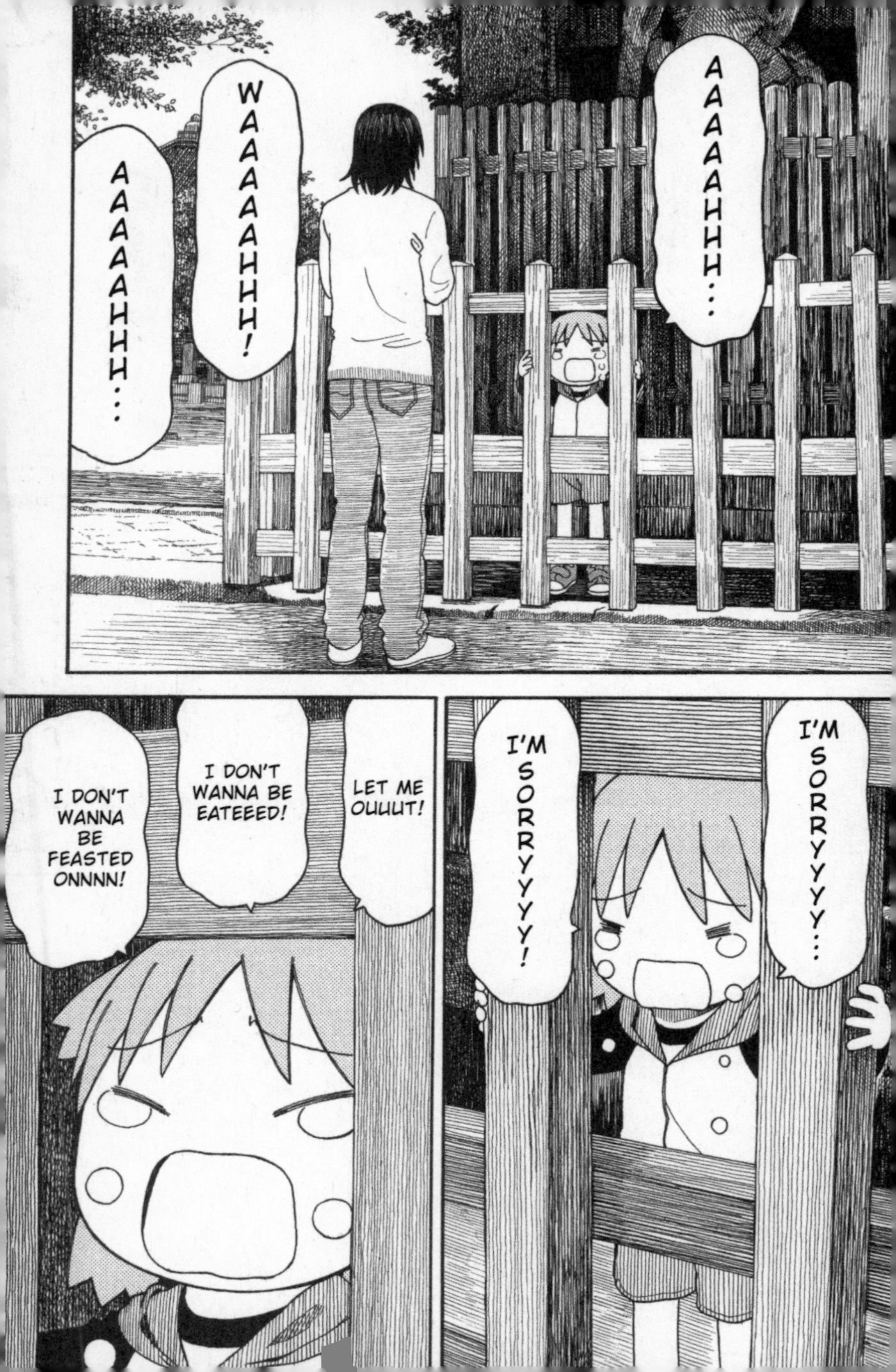
AAAAAHHH...
WAAAAAHHH!
AAAAAHHH...
I'M SORRYYYY...
I'M SORRYYYY!
LET ME OUUUT!
I DON'T WANNA BE EATEEED!
I DON'T WANNA BE FEASTED ONNNN!

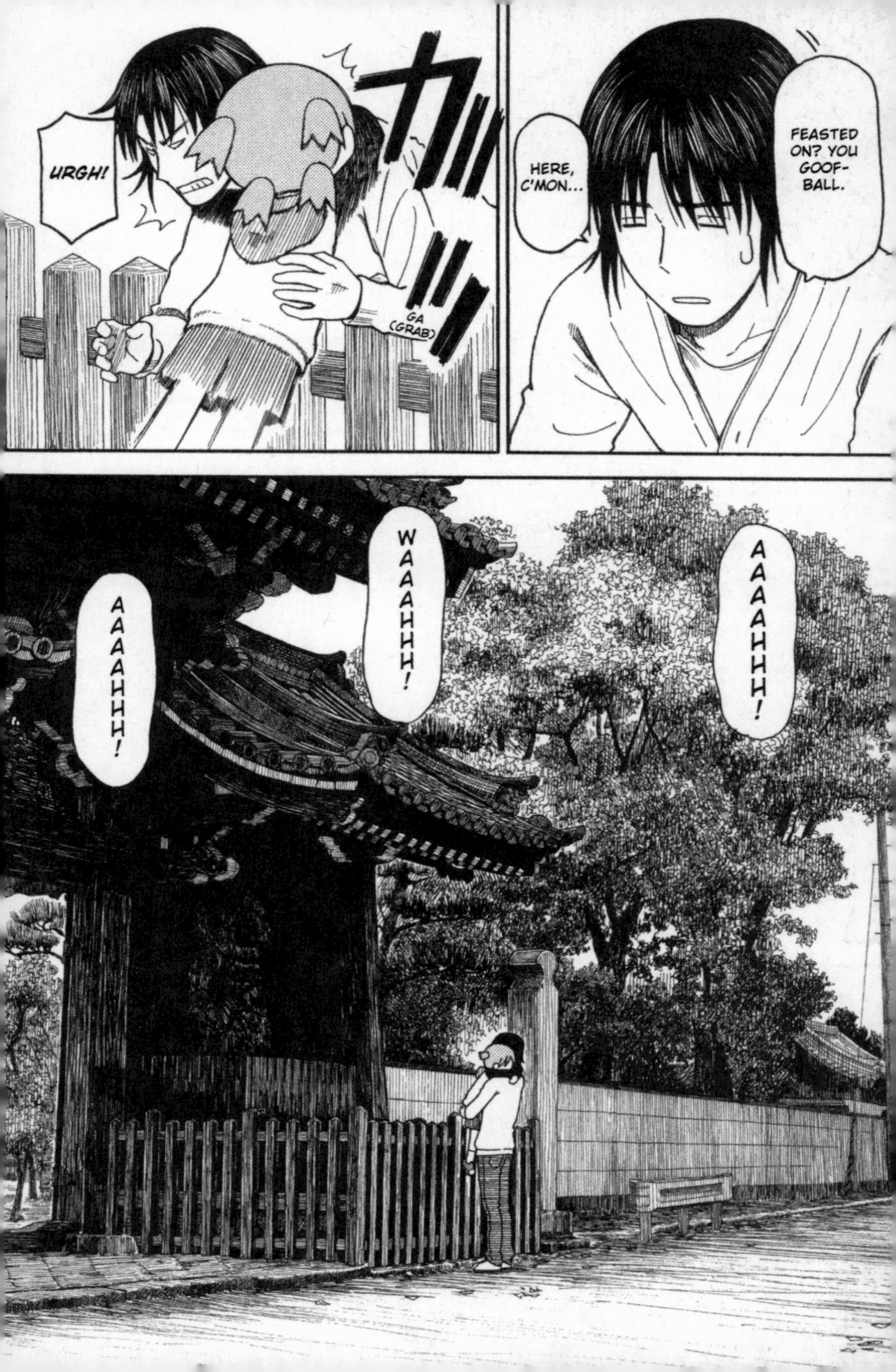
FEASTED ON? YOU GOOF-BALL.
HERE, C'MON...
GA (GRAB)
URGH!
AAAAAHHH!
WAAAAHHH!
AAAAAHHH!

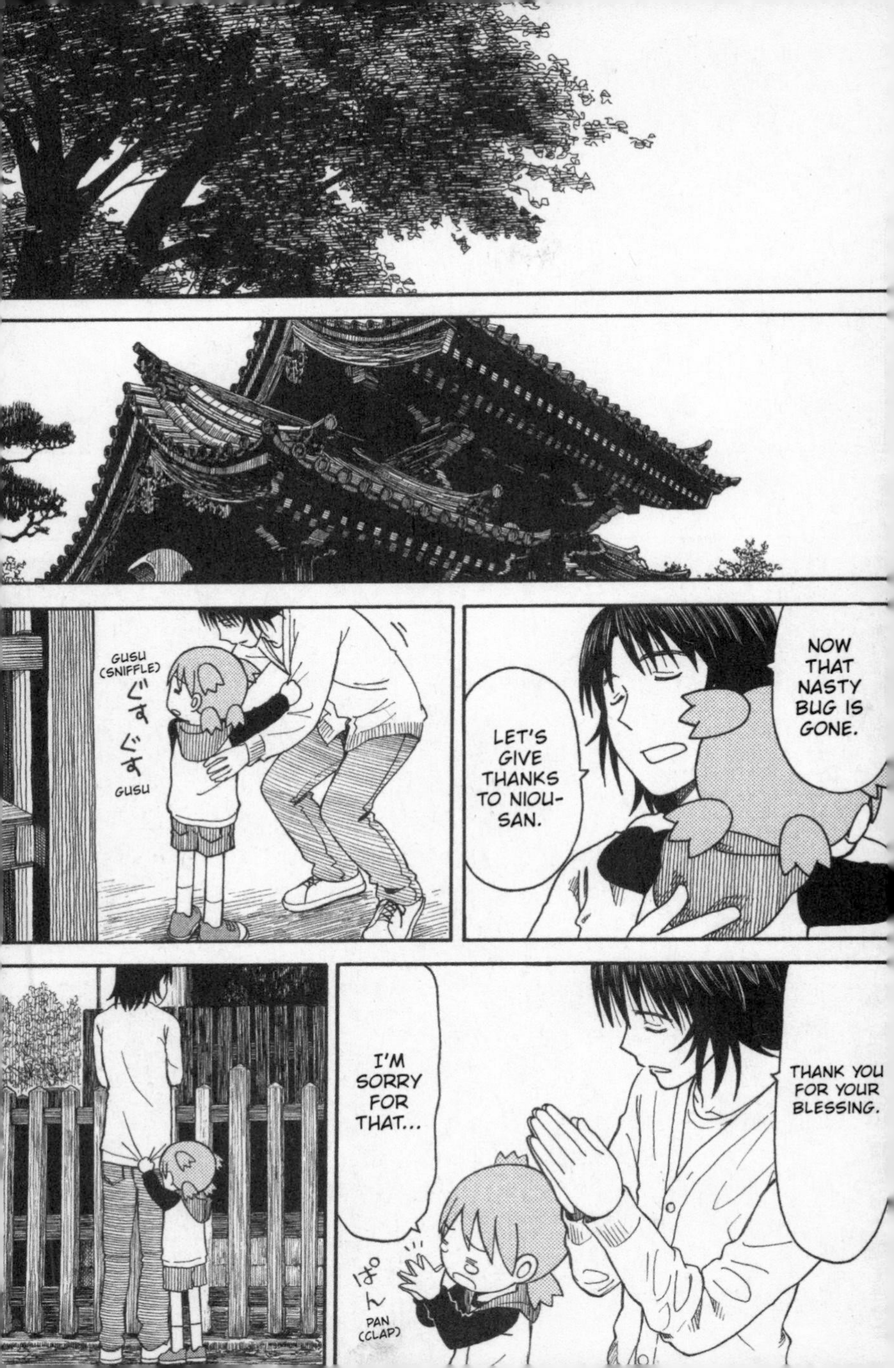
NOW THAT NASTY BUG IS GONE.
LET'S GIVE THANKS TO NIOU-SAN.
ぐすぐす
GUSU (SNIFFLE)
GUSU
THANK YOU FOR YOUR BLESSING.
I'M SORRY FOR THAT...
ぱん
PAN (CLAP)

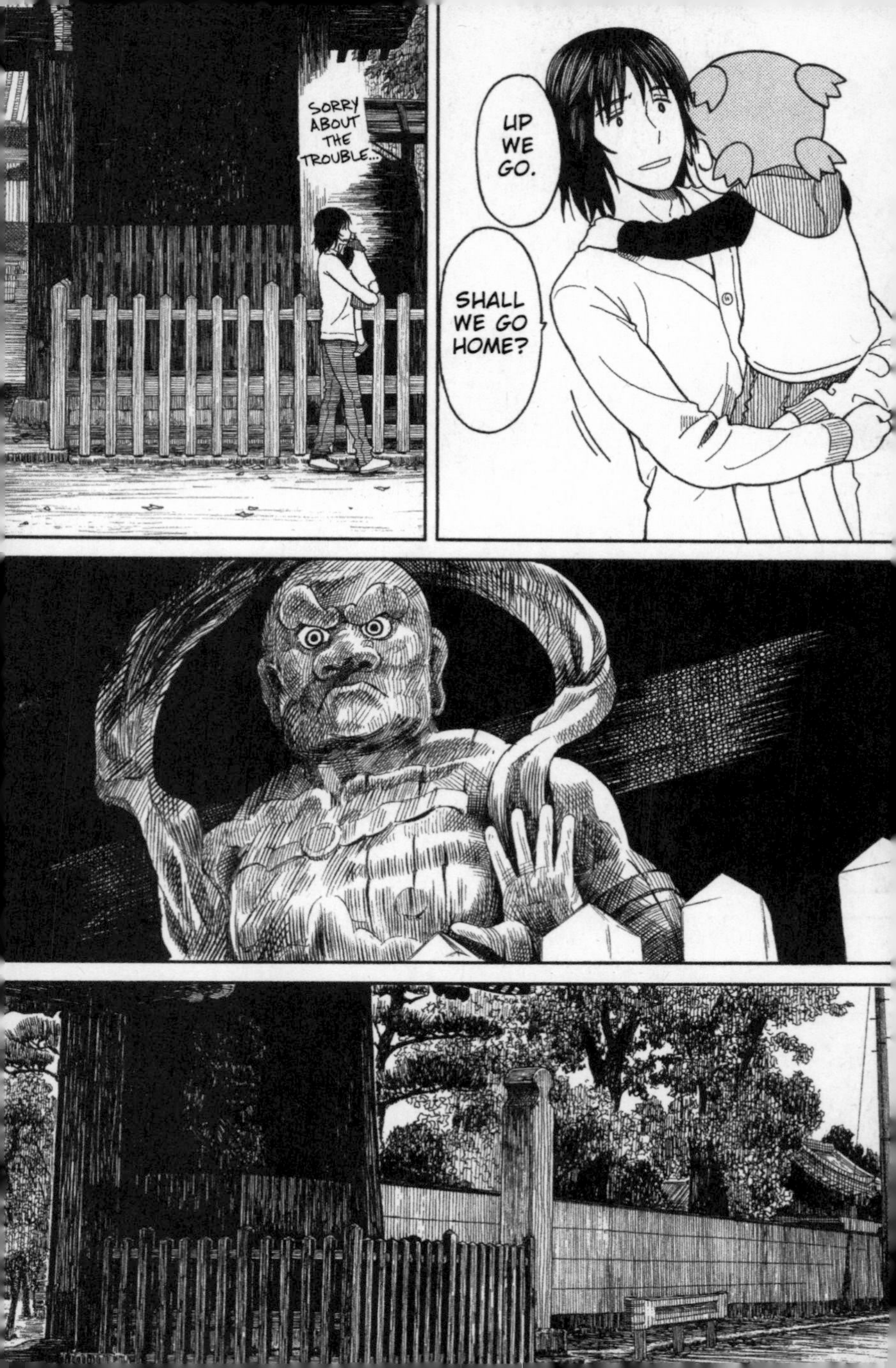
UP WE GO.
SHALL WE GO HOME?
SORRY ABOUT THE TROUBLE...

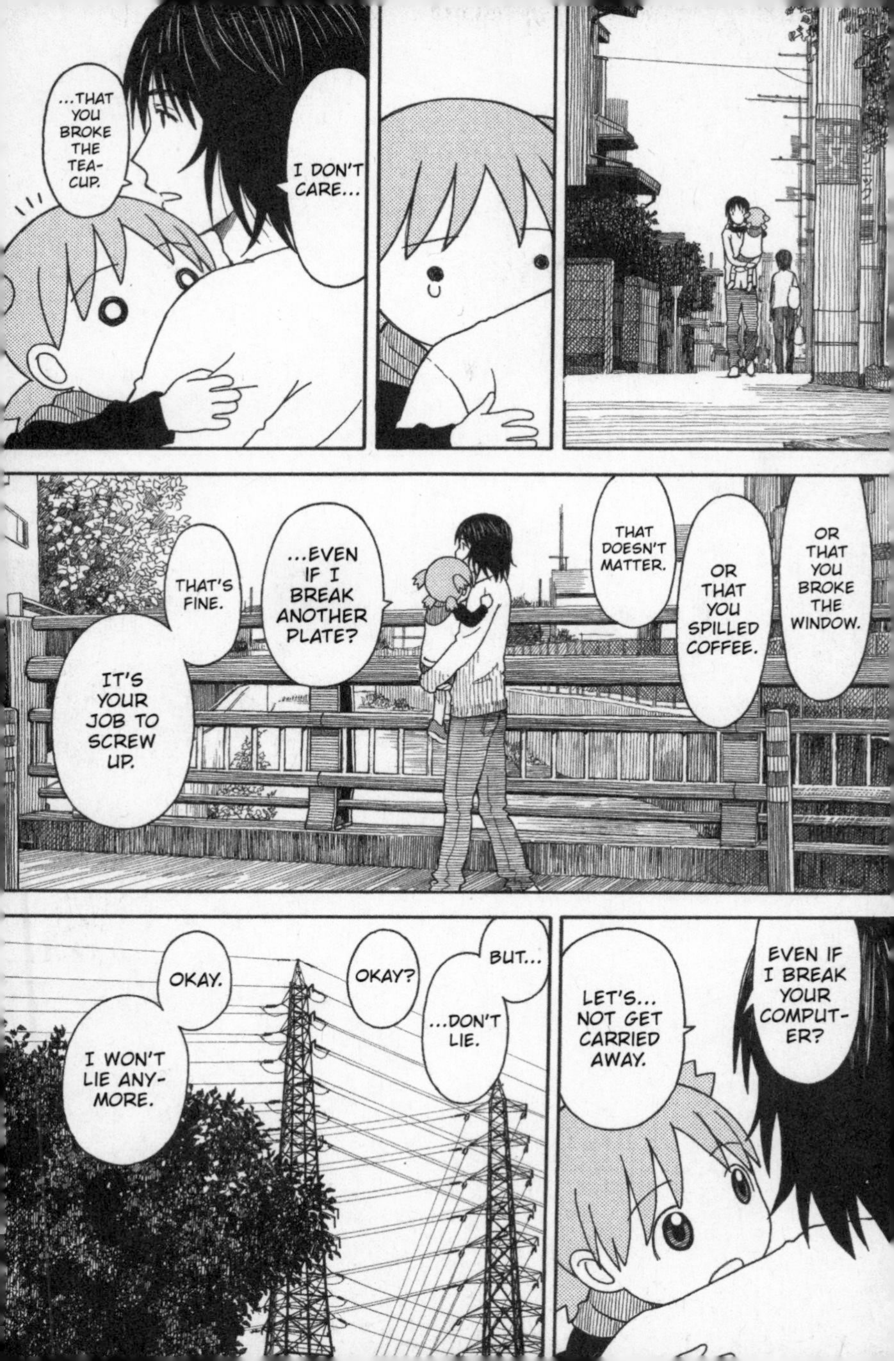
I DON'T CARE...
...THAT YOU BROKE THE TEA-CUP.
OR THAT YOU BROKE THE WINDOW.
OR THAT YOU SPILLED COFFEE.
THAT DOESN'T MATTER.
...EVEN IF I BREAK ANOTHER PLATE?
THAT'S FINE.
IT'S YOUR JOB TO SCREW UP.
EVEN IF I BREAK YOUR COMPUTER?
LET'S... NOT GET CARRIED AWAY.
BUT...
...DON'T LIE.
OKAY?
OKAY.
I WON'T LIE ANYMORE.

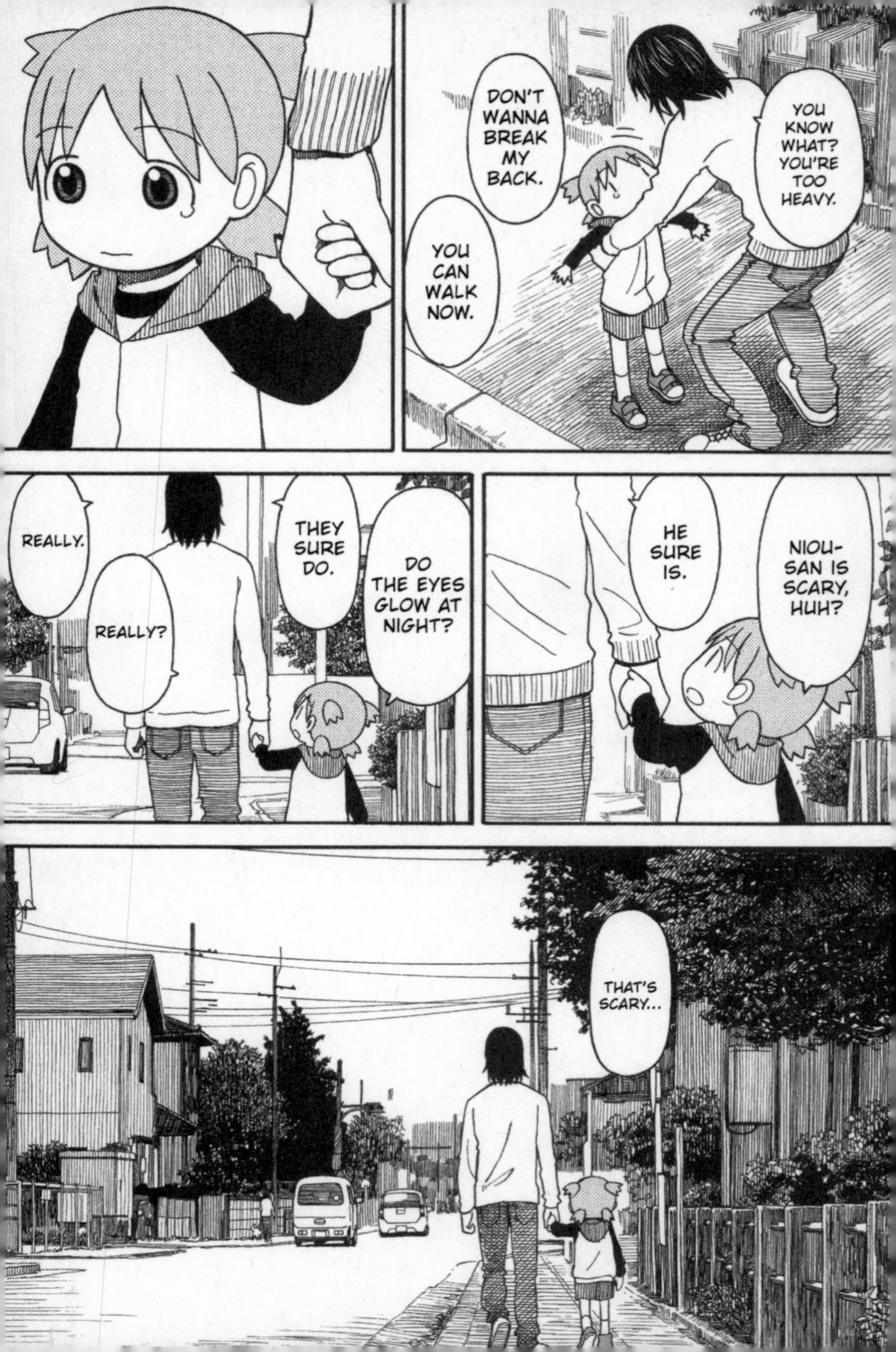
YOU KNOW WHAT? YOU'RE TOO HEAVY.
DON'T WANNA BREAK MY BACK.
YOU CAN WALK NOW.
NIOU-SAN IS SCARY, HUH?
HE SURE IS.
DO THE EYES GLOW AT NIGHT?
THEY SURE DO.
REALLY?
REALLY.
THAT'S SCARY...

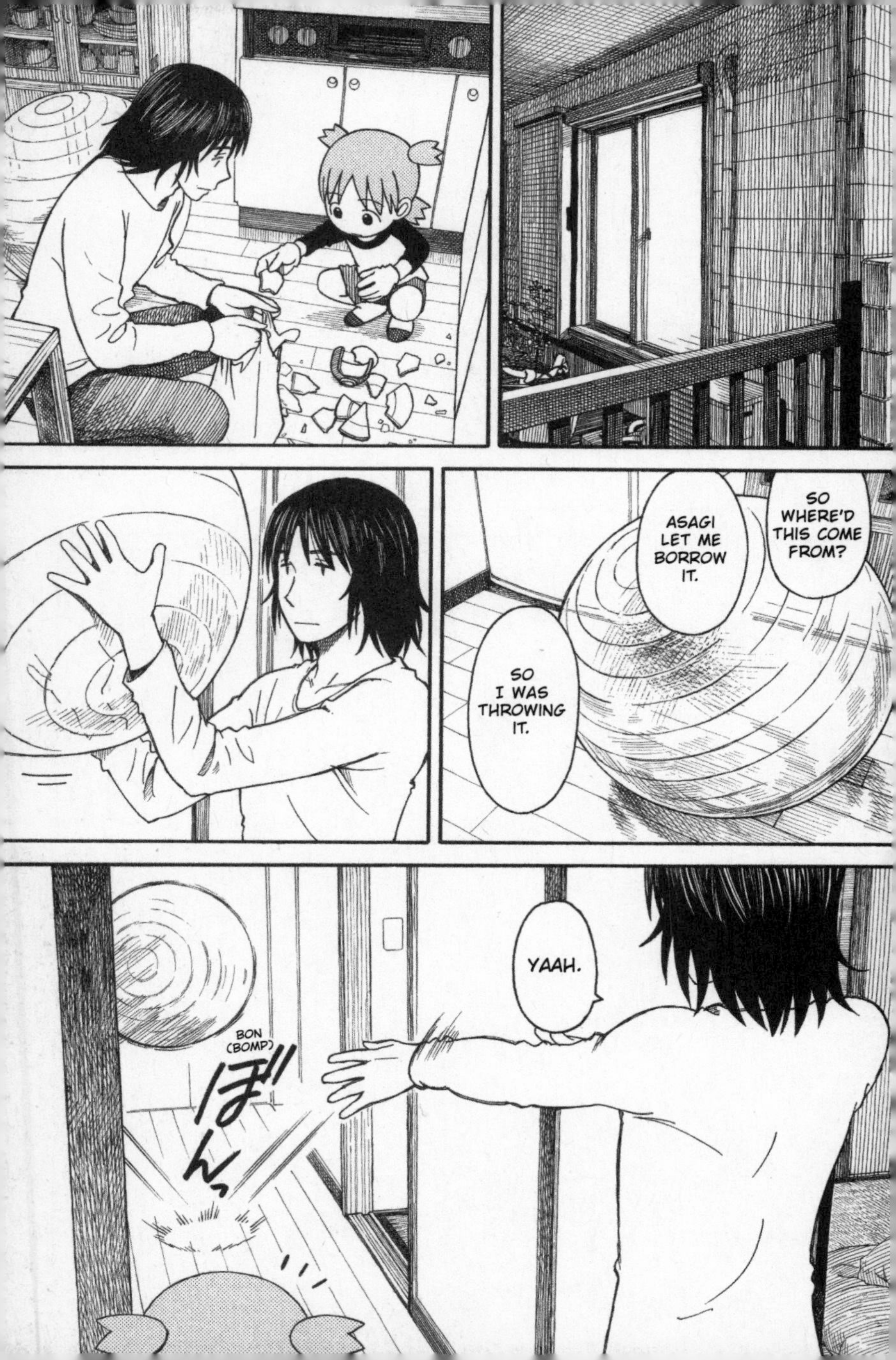
SO WHERE'D THIS COME FROM?
ASAGI LET ME BORROW IT.
SO I WAS THROWING IT.
YAAH.
BON (BOMP)
ぼん

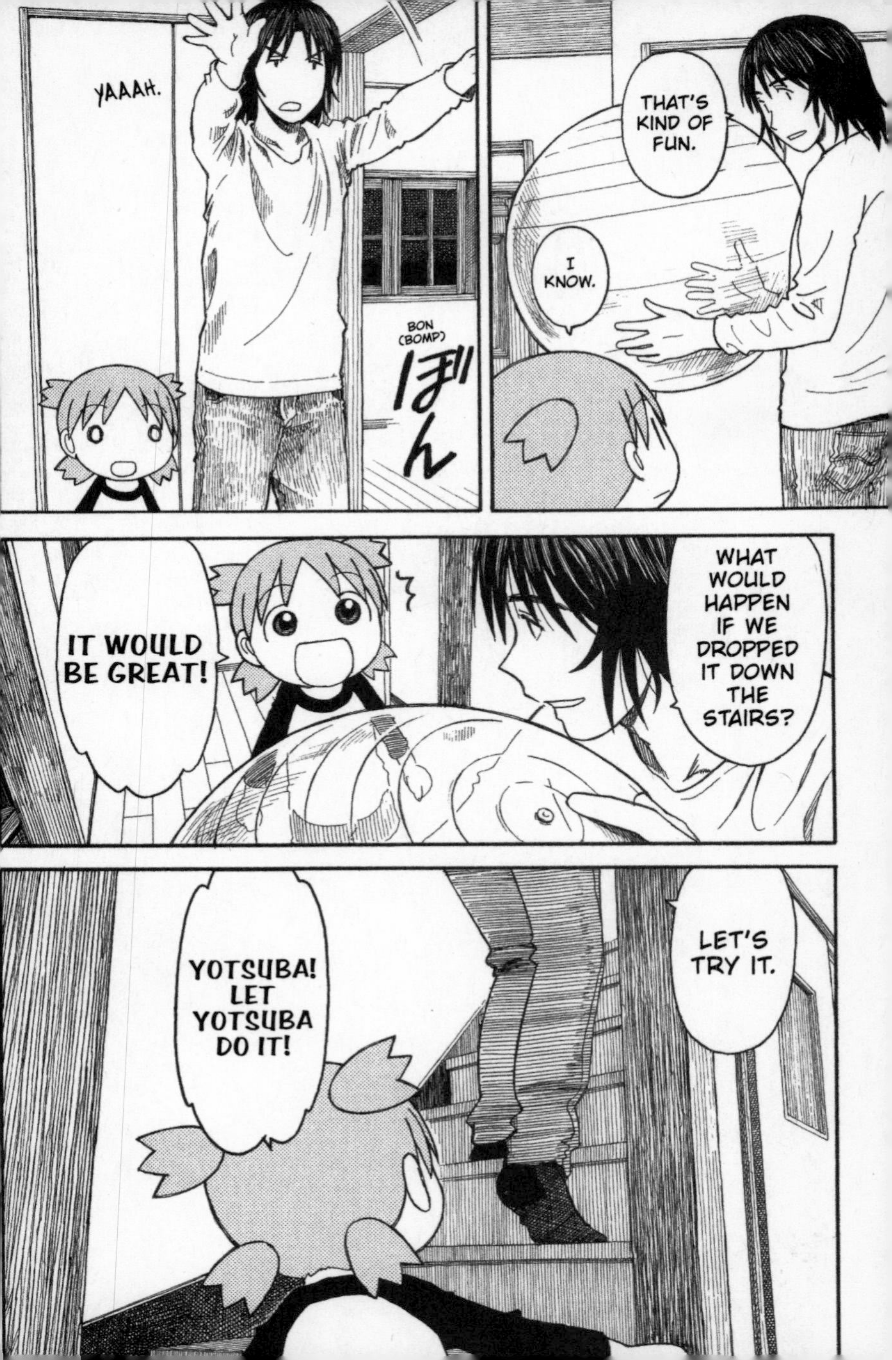
THAT'S KIND OF FUN.
I KNOW.
YAAAH.
BON (BOMP)
ぼん
WHAT WOULD HAPPEN IF WE DROPPED IT DOWN THE STAIRS?
IT WOULD BE GREAT!
LET'S TRY IT.
YOTSUBA! LET YOTSUBA DO IT!

YOTSUBA&!

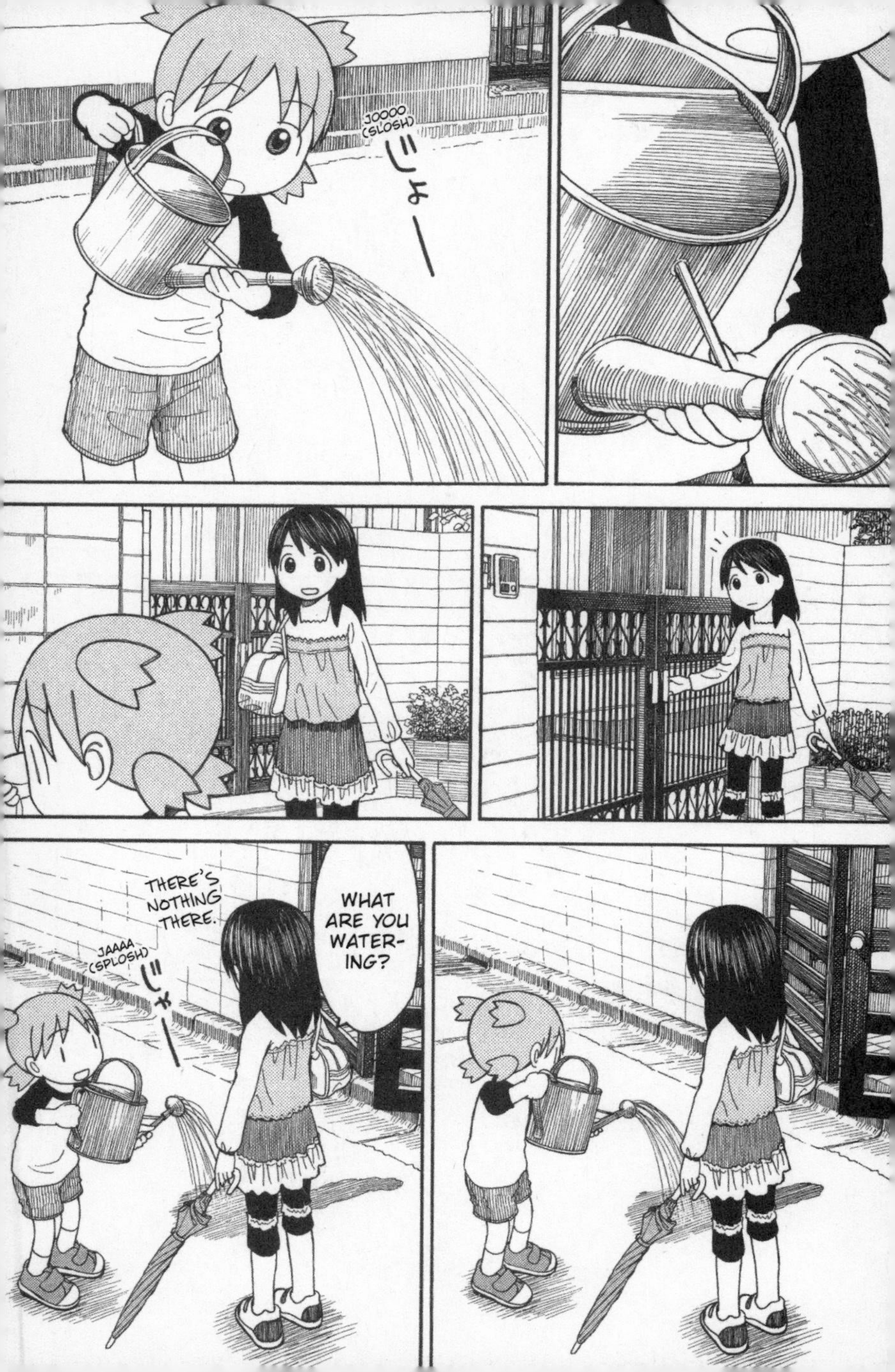
JOOOO (SLOSH)
じょー
WHAT ARE YOU WATERING?
THERE'S NOTHING THERE.
JAAAA (SPLOSH)
じゃー

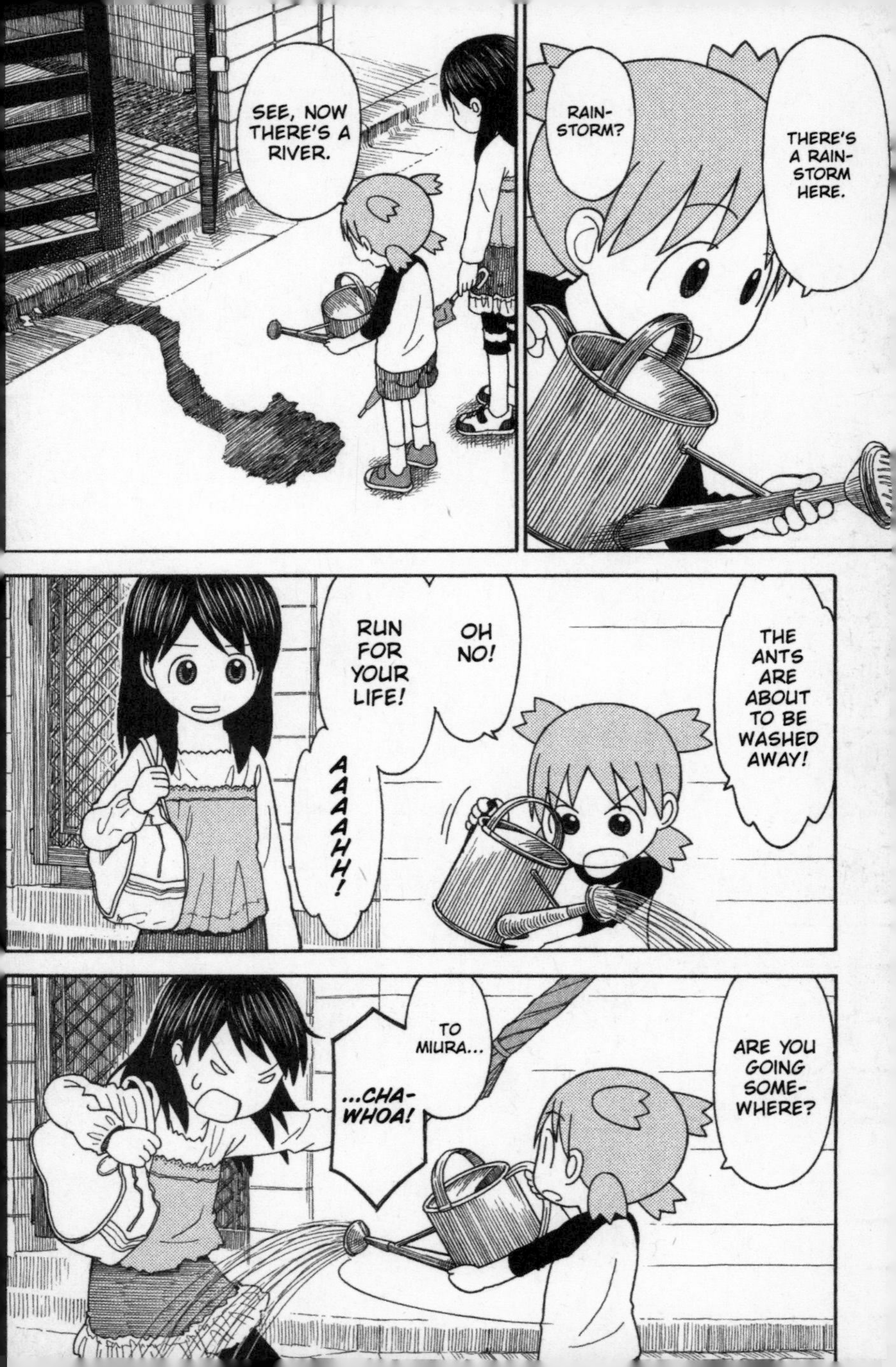
THERE'S A RAIN-STORM HERE.
RAIN-STORM?
SEE, NOW THERE'S A RIVER.
THE ANTS ARE ABOUT TO BE WASHED AWAY!
OH NO!
RUN FOR YOUR LIFE!
AAAAAHH!
ARE YOU GOING SOME-WHERE?
TO MIURA...
...CHA-WHOA!

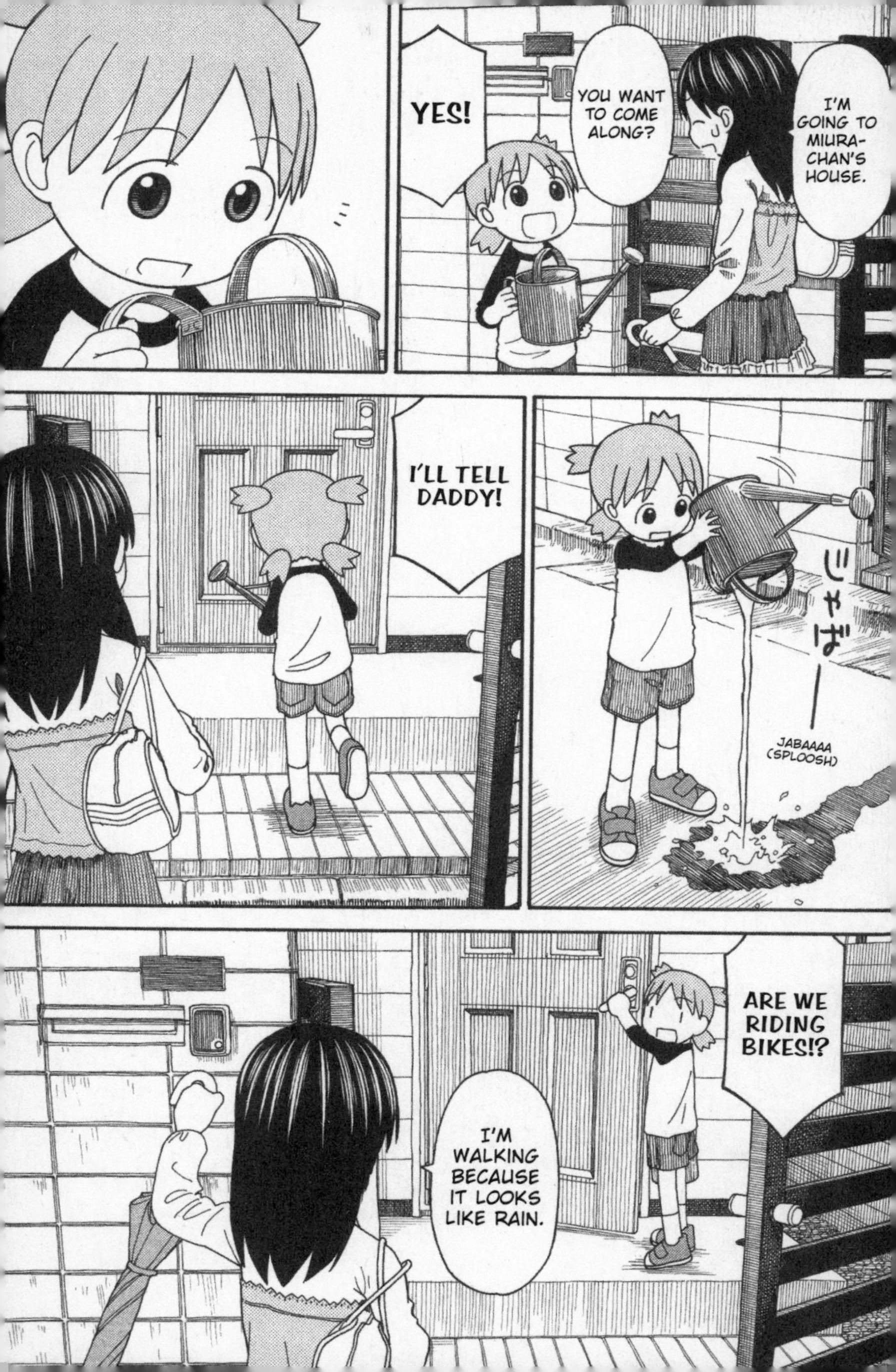
I'M GOING TO MIURA-CHAN'S HOUSE.
YOU WANT TO COME ALONG?
YES!
じゃばー
JABAAAA (SPLOOSH)
I'LL TELL DADDY!
ARE WE RIDING BIKES!?
I'M WALKING BECAUSE IT LOOKS LIKE RAIN.

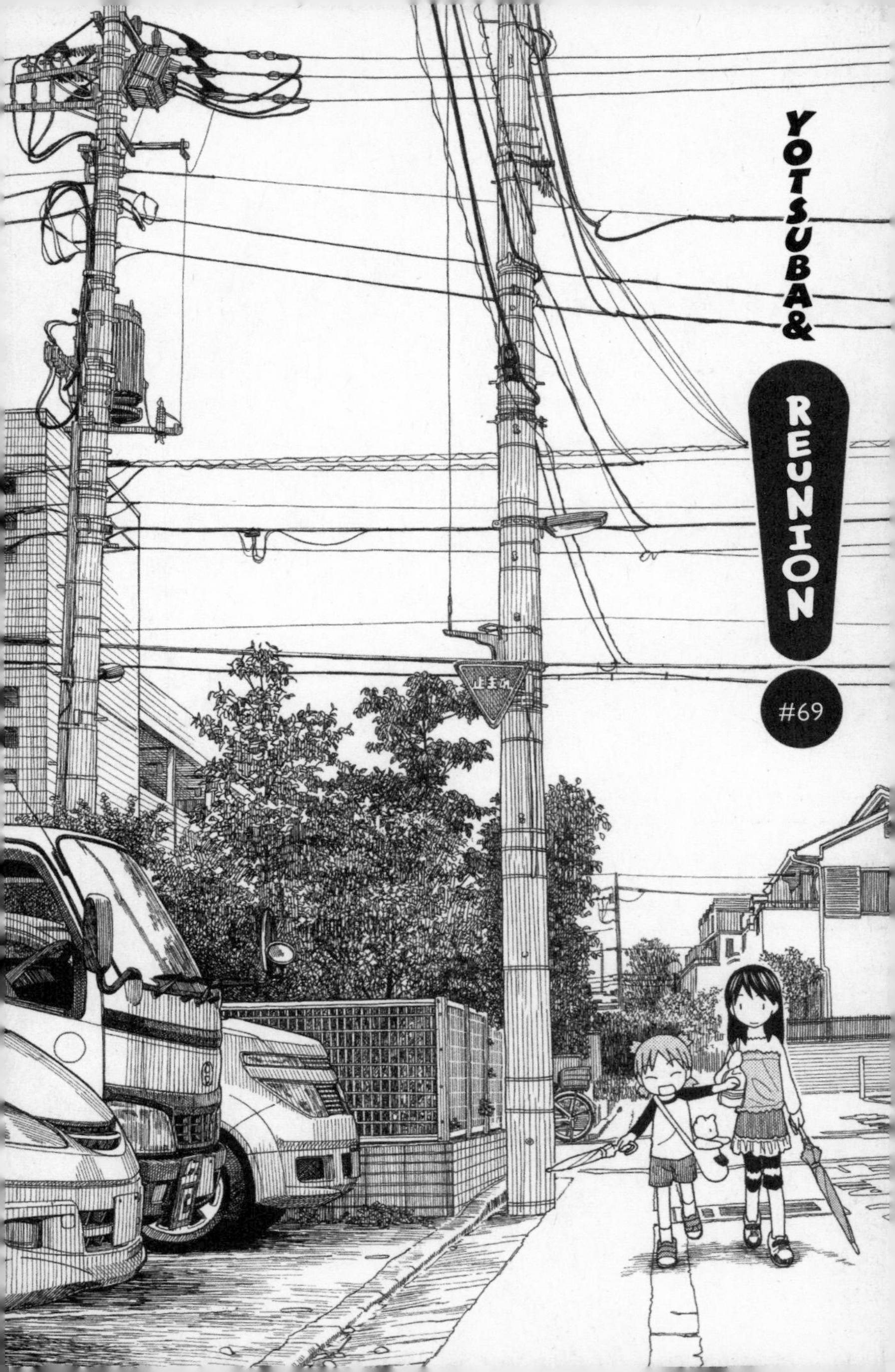
YOTSUBA&
REUNION
#69
止まれ

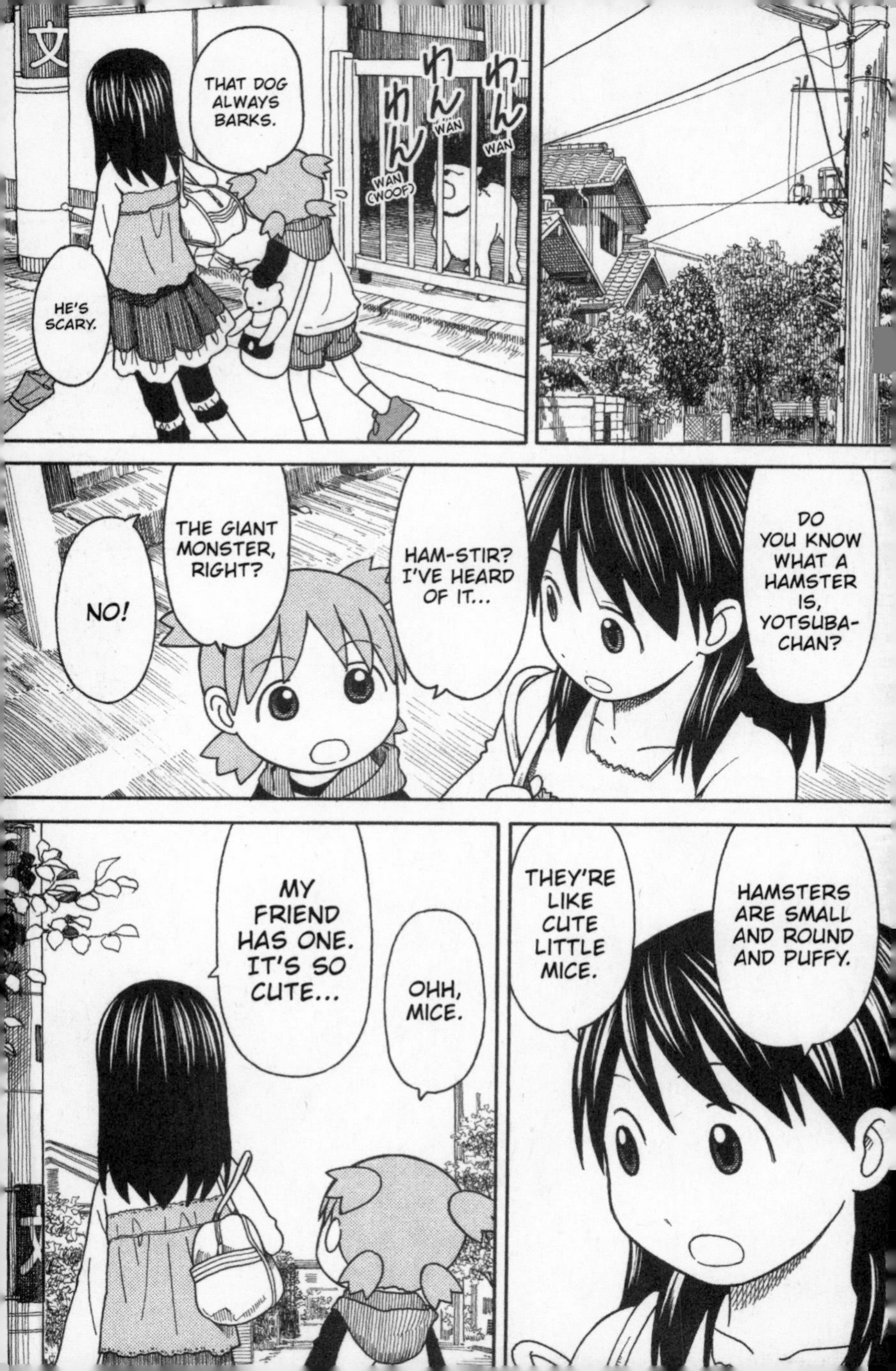
わん
WAN
わん
WAN
わん
WAN (WOOF)
THAT DOG ALWAYS BARKS.
文
HE'S SCARY.
DO YOU KNOW WHAT A HAMSTER IS, YOTSUBA-CHAN?
HAM-STIR? I'VE HEARD OF IT...
THE GIANT MONSTER, RIGHT?
NO!
HAMSTERS ARE SMALL AND ROUND AND PUFFY.
THEY'RE LIKE CUTE LITTLE MICE.
OHH, MICE.
MY FRIEND HAS ONE. IT'S SO CUTE...

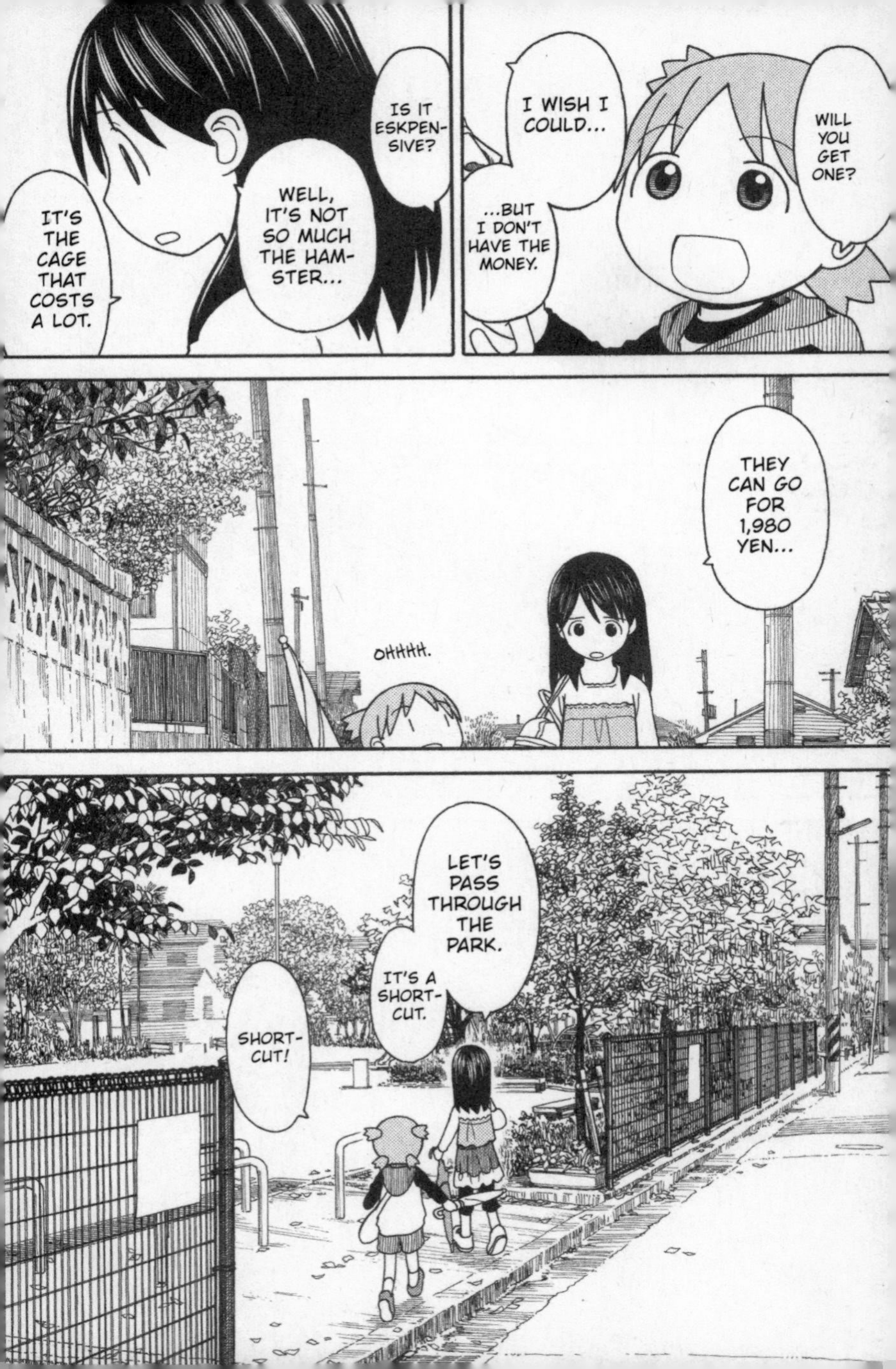
WILL YOU GET ONE?
I WISH I COULD...
...BUT I DON'T HAVE THE MONEY.
IS IT ESKPENSIVE?
WELL, IT'S NOT SO MUCH THE HAMSTER...
IT'S THE CAGE THAT COSTS A LOT.
THEY CAN GO FOR 1,980 YEN...
OHHHH.
LET'S PASS THROUGH THE PARK.
IT'S A SHORTCUT.
SHORTCUT!

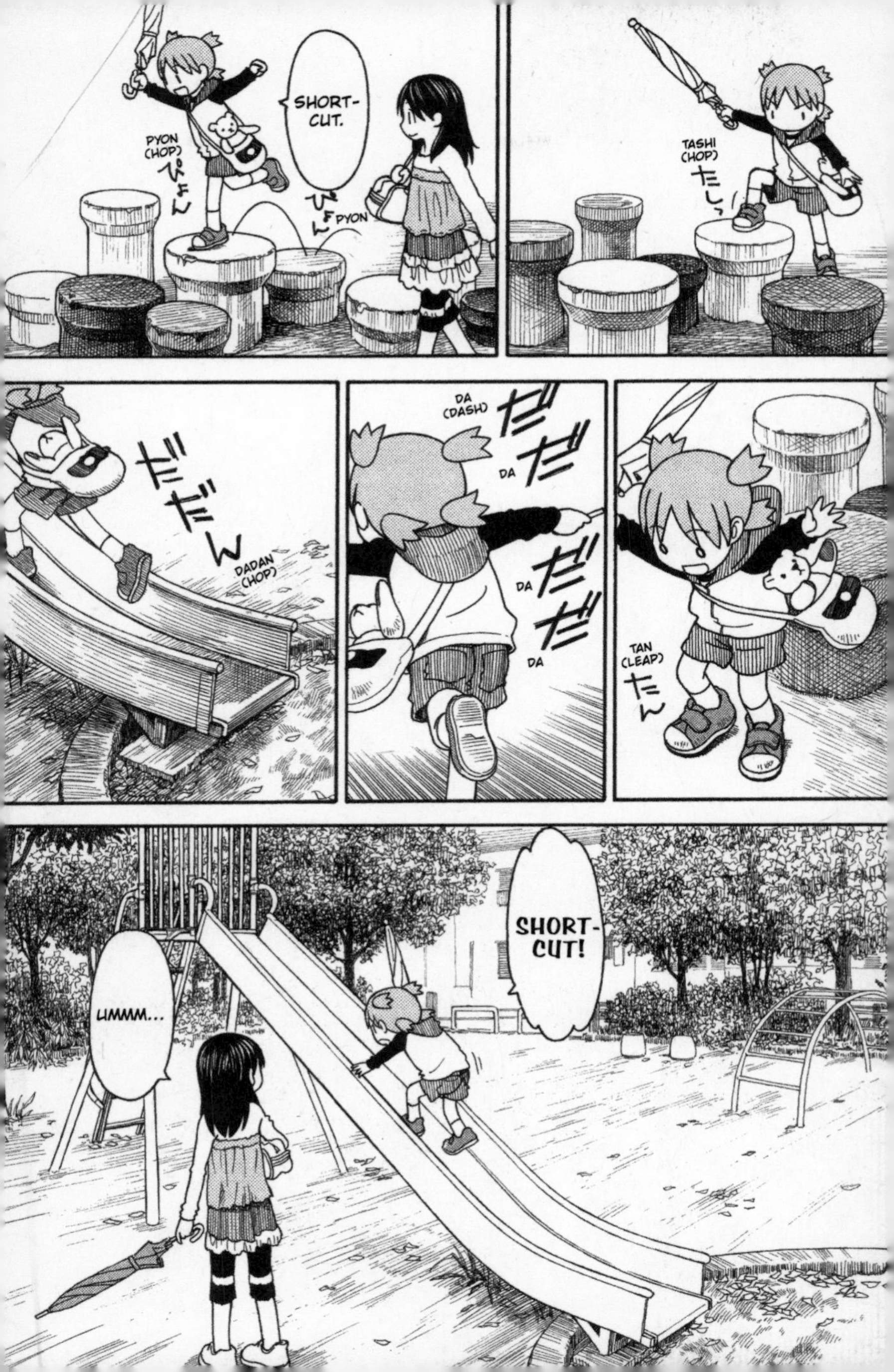
TASHI (HOP)
たしっ
SHORT-CUT.
PYON (HOP)
ぴょん
ぴょん
PYON
TAN (LEAP)
たん
DA (DASH)
だ
DA
だ
DA
だ
DA
だ
DADAN (HOP)
だだん
SHORT-CUT!
UMMM...

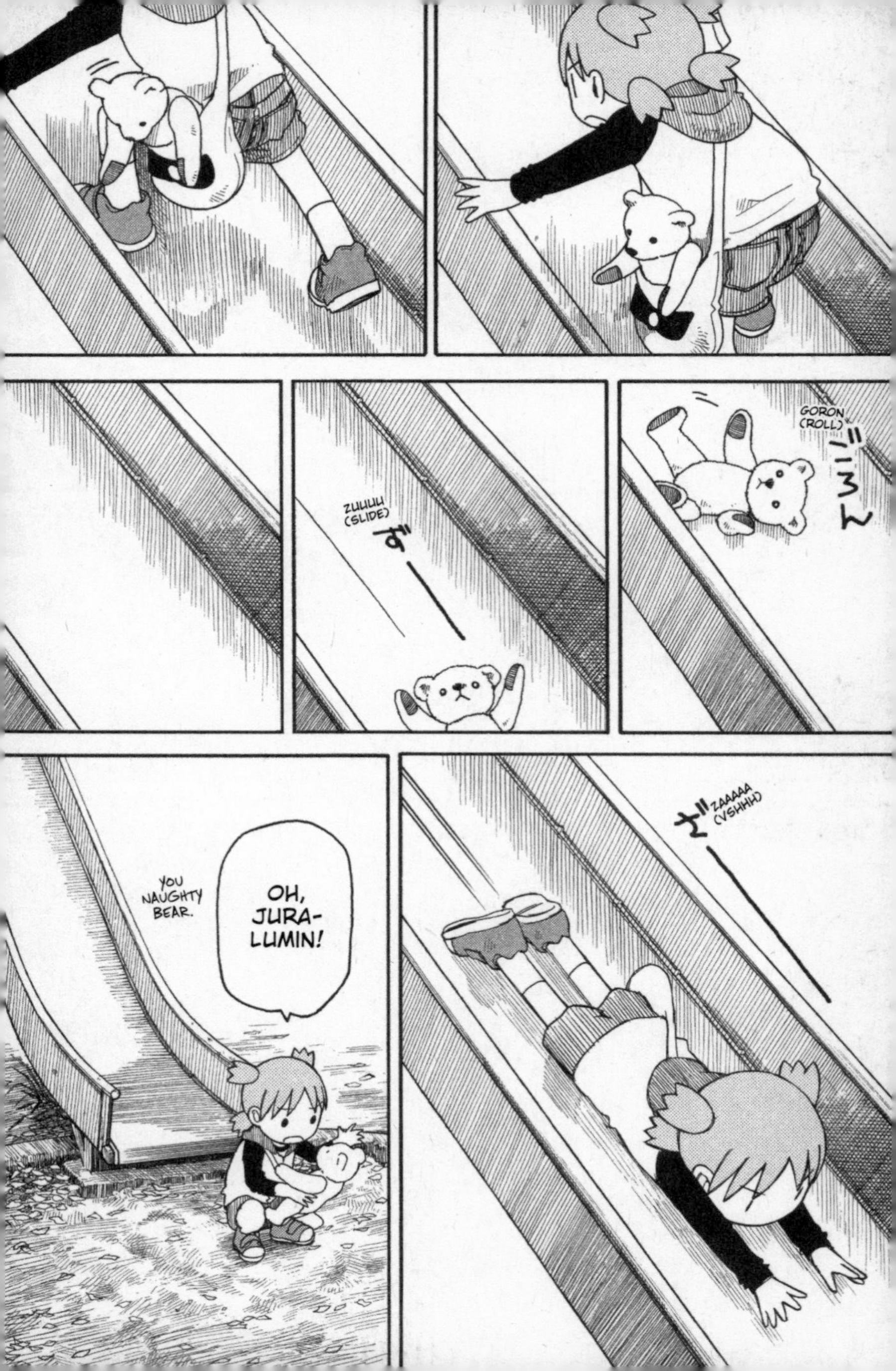
GORON (ROLL)
ごろん
ZUUUU (SLIDE)
ず
ZAAAAA (VSHHH)
ざ
OH, JURA-LUMIN!
YOU NAUGHTY BEAR.

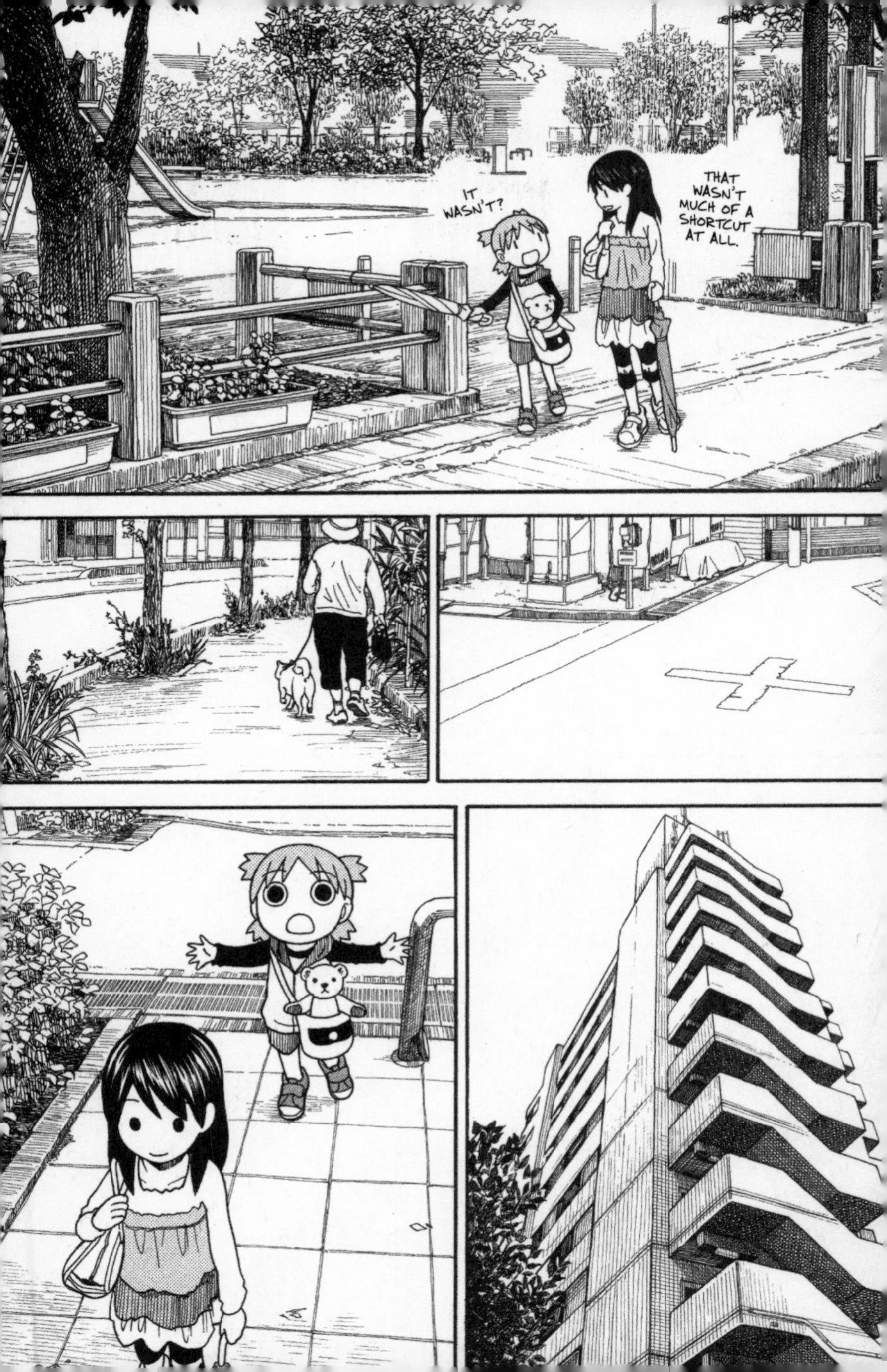
THAT WASN'T MUCH OF A SHORTCUT AT ALL.
IT WASN'T?

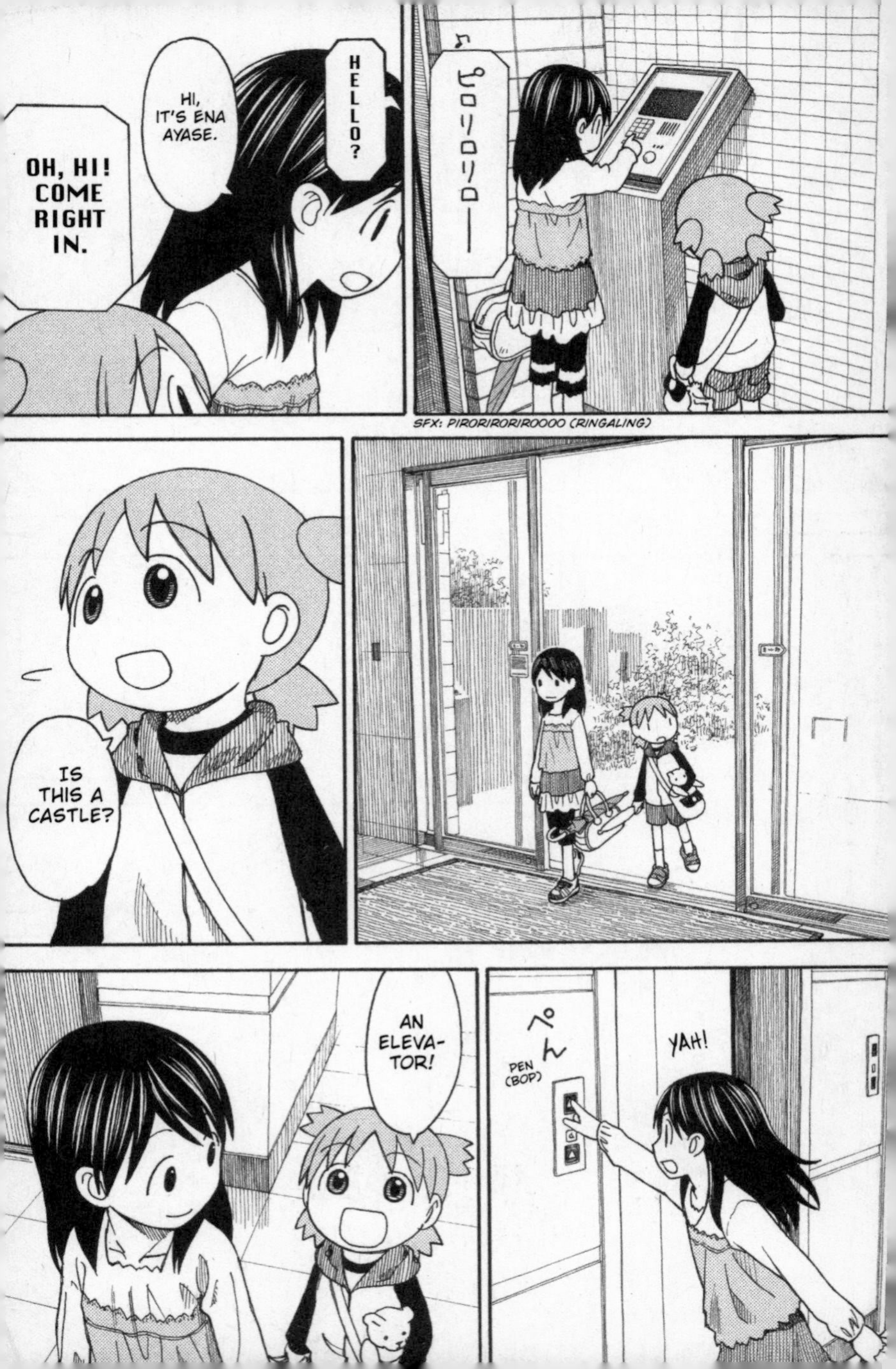
ピロリロリロー
SFX: PIRORIRORIROOOO (RINGALING)
HELLO?
HI, IT'S ENA AYASE.
OH, HI! COME RIGHT IN.
IS THIS A CASTLE?
YAH!
ぺん
PEN (BOP)
AN ELEVATOR!

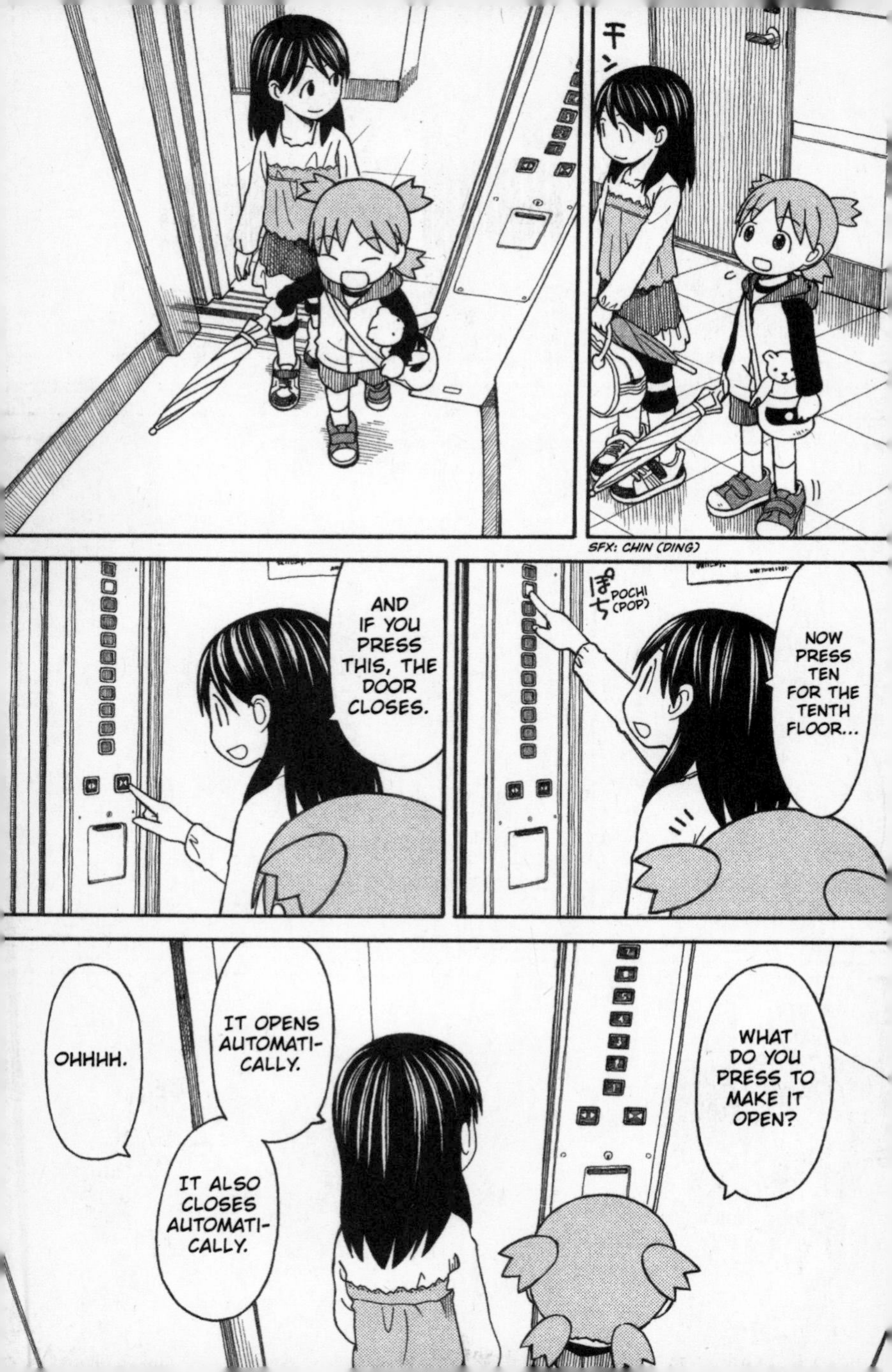
キン
SFX: CHIN (DING)
ぽち POCHI (POP)
NOW PRESS TEN FOR THE TENTH FLOOR...
AND IF YOU PRESS THIS, THE DOOR CLOSES.
WHAT DO YOU PRESS TO MAKE IT OPEN?
IT OPENS AUTOMATI-CALLY.
IT ALSO CLOSES AUTOMATI-CALLY.
OHHHH.

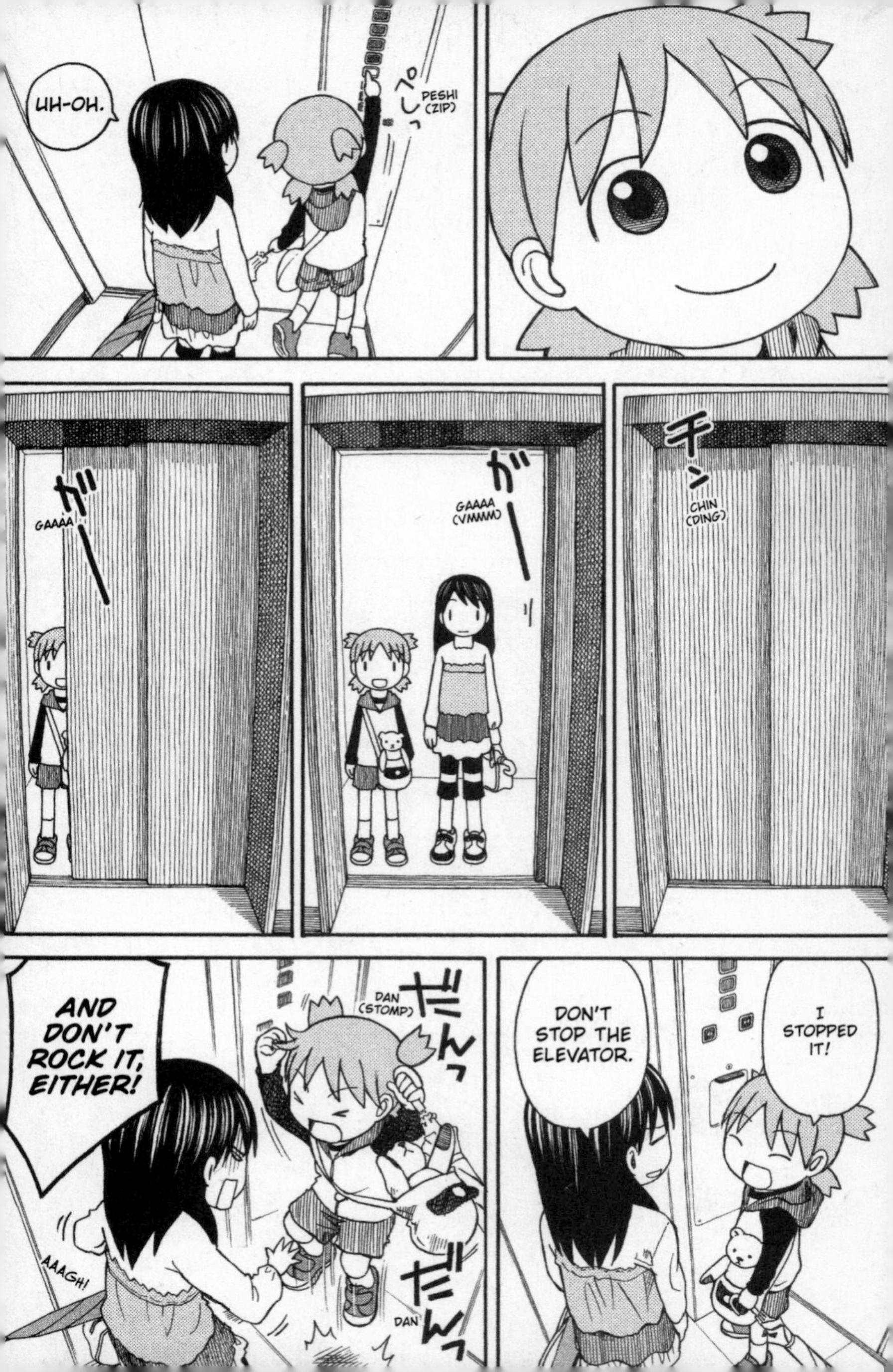
ぺしっ
PESHI (ZIP)
UH-OH.
チン
CHIN (DING)
がー
GAAAA (VMMM)
がー
GAAAA
I STOPPED IT!
DON'T STOP THE ELEVATOR.
だんっ
DAN (STOMP)
AND DON'T ROCK IT, EITHER!
だんっ
DAN
AAAGH!

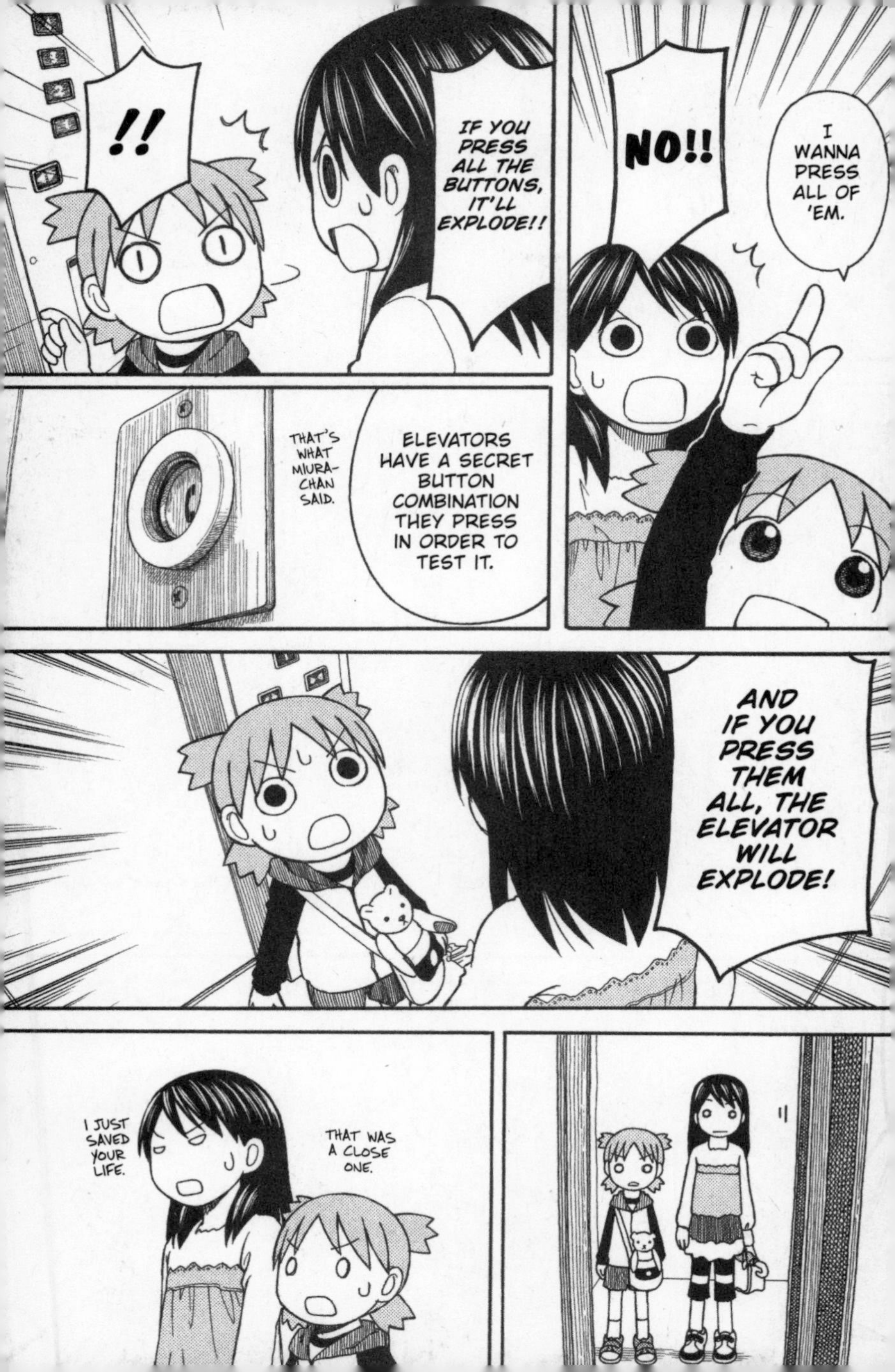
I WANNA PRESS ALL OF 'EM.
NO!!
IF YOU PRESS ALL THE BUTTONS, IT'LL EXPLODE!!
!!
ELEVATORS HAVE A SECRET BUTTON COMBINATION THEY PRESS IN ORDER TO TEST IT.
THAT'S WHAT MIURA-CHAN SAID.
AND IF YOU PRESS THEM ALL, THE ELEVATOR WILL EXPLODE!
THAT WAS A CLOSE ONE.
I JUST SAVED YOUR LIFE.

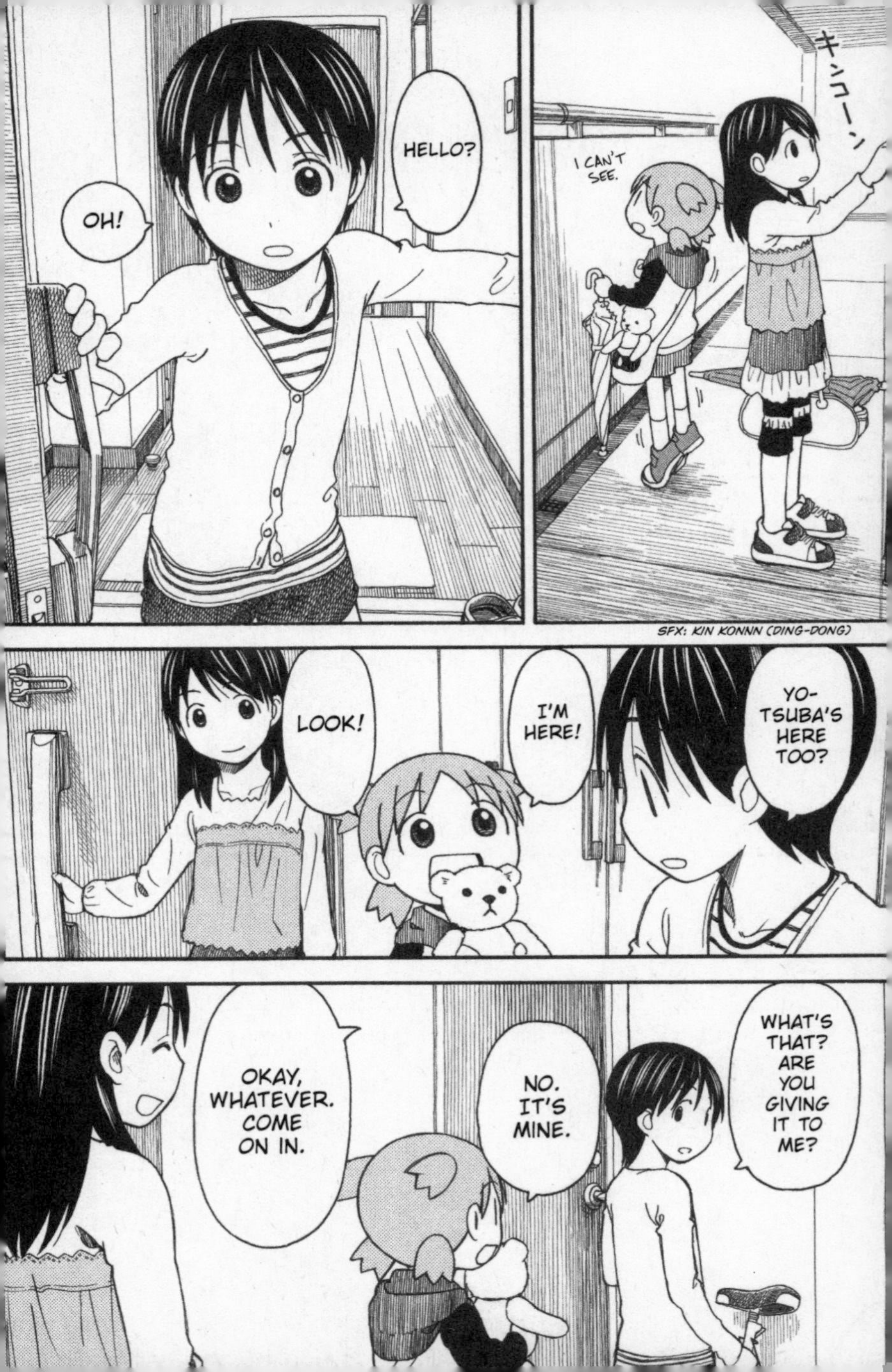
キンコーン
I CAN'T SEE.
SFX: KIN KONNN (DING-DONG)
HELLO?
OH!
YO-TSUBA'S HERE TOO?
I'M HERE!
LOOK!
WHAT'S THAT? ARE YOU GIVING IT TO ME?
NO. IT'S MINE.
OKAY, WHATEVER. COME ON IN.

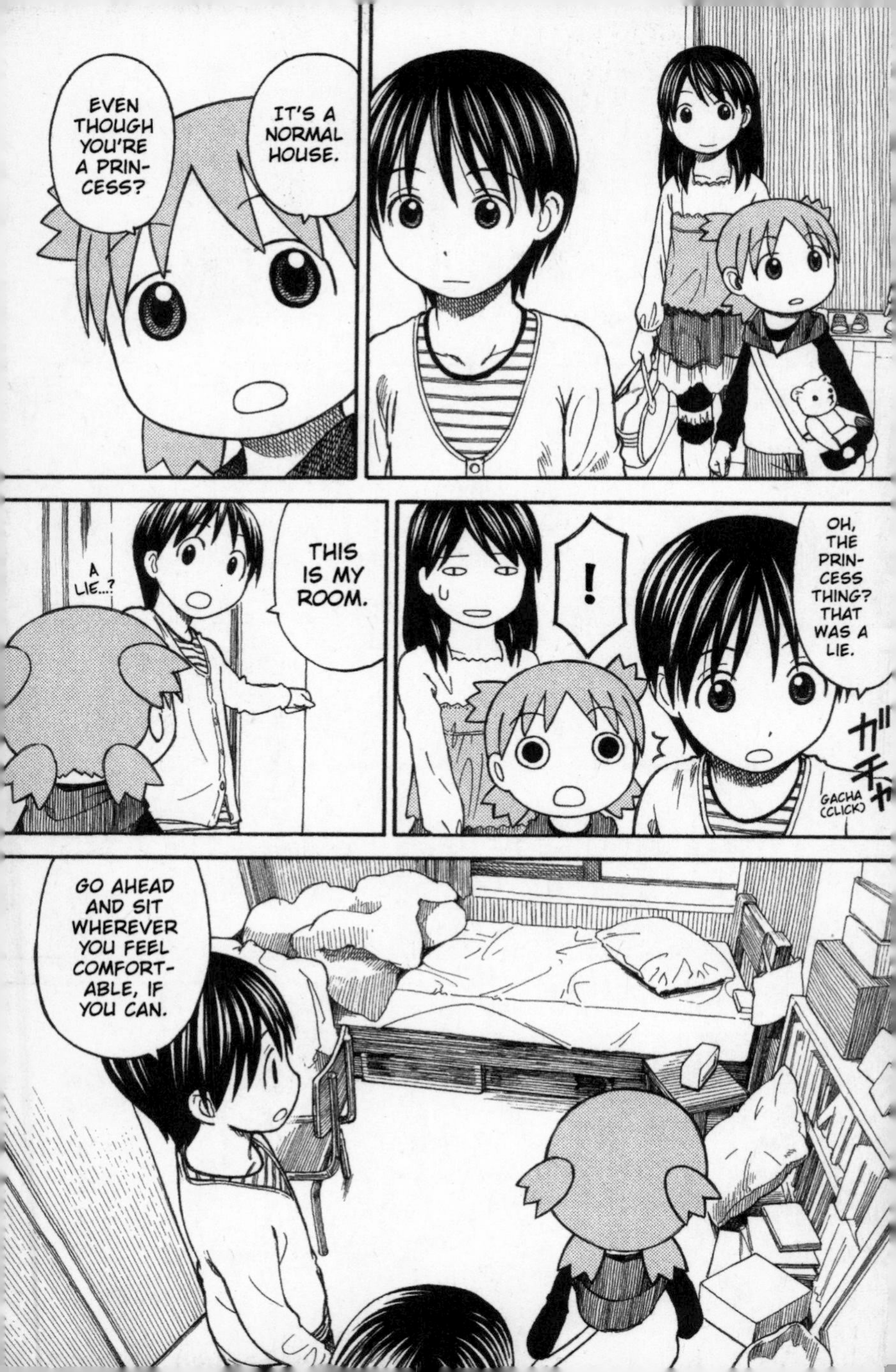

IT'S A NORMAL HOUSE.
EVEN THOUGH YOU'RE A PRIN-CESS?
OH, THE PRIN-CESS THING? THAT WAS A LIE.
ガチャ
GACHA (CLICK)
!
THIS IS MY ROOM.
A LIE...?
GO AHEAD AND SIT WHEREVER YOU FEEL COMFORT-ABLE, IF YOU CAN.

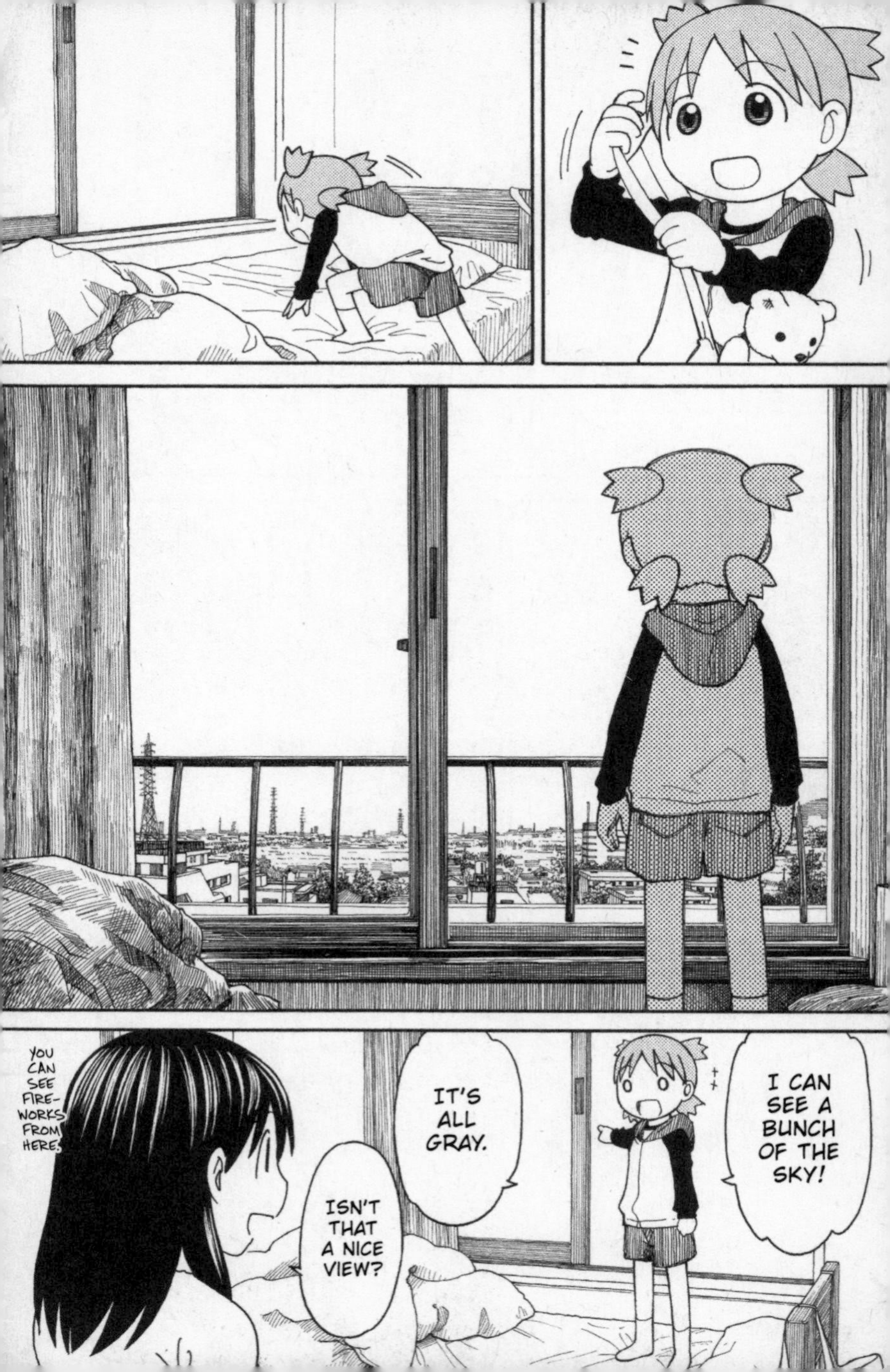
I CAN SEE A BUNCH OF THE SKY!
IT'S ALL GRAY.
ISN'T THAT A NICE VIEW?
YOU CAN SEE FIRE-WORKS FROM HERE.

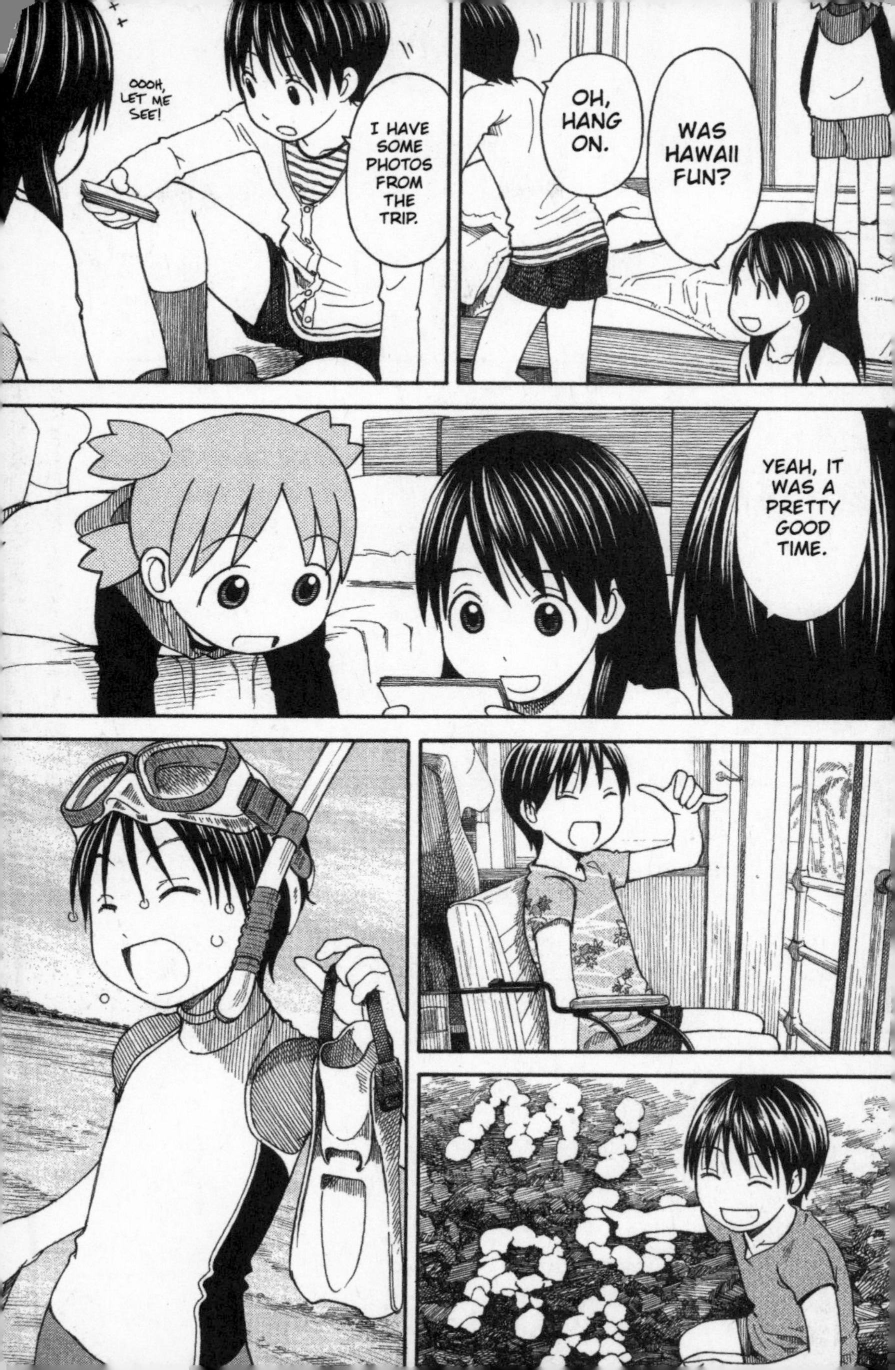
WAS HAWAII FUN?
OH, HANG ON.
I HAVE SOME PHOTOS FROM THE TRIP.
OOOH, LET ME SEE!
YEAH, IT WAS A PRETTY GOOD TIME.

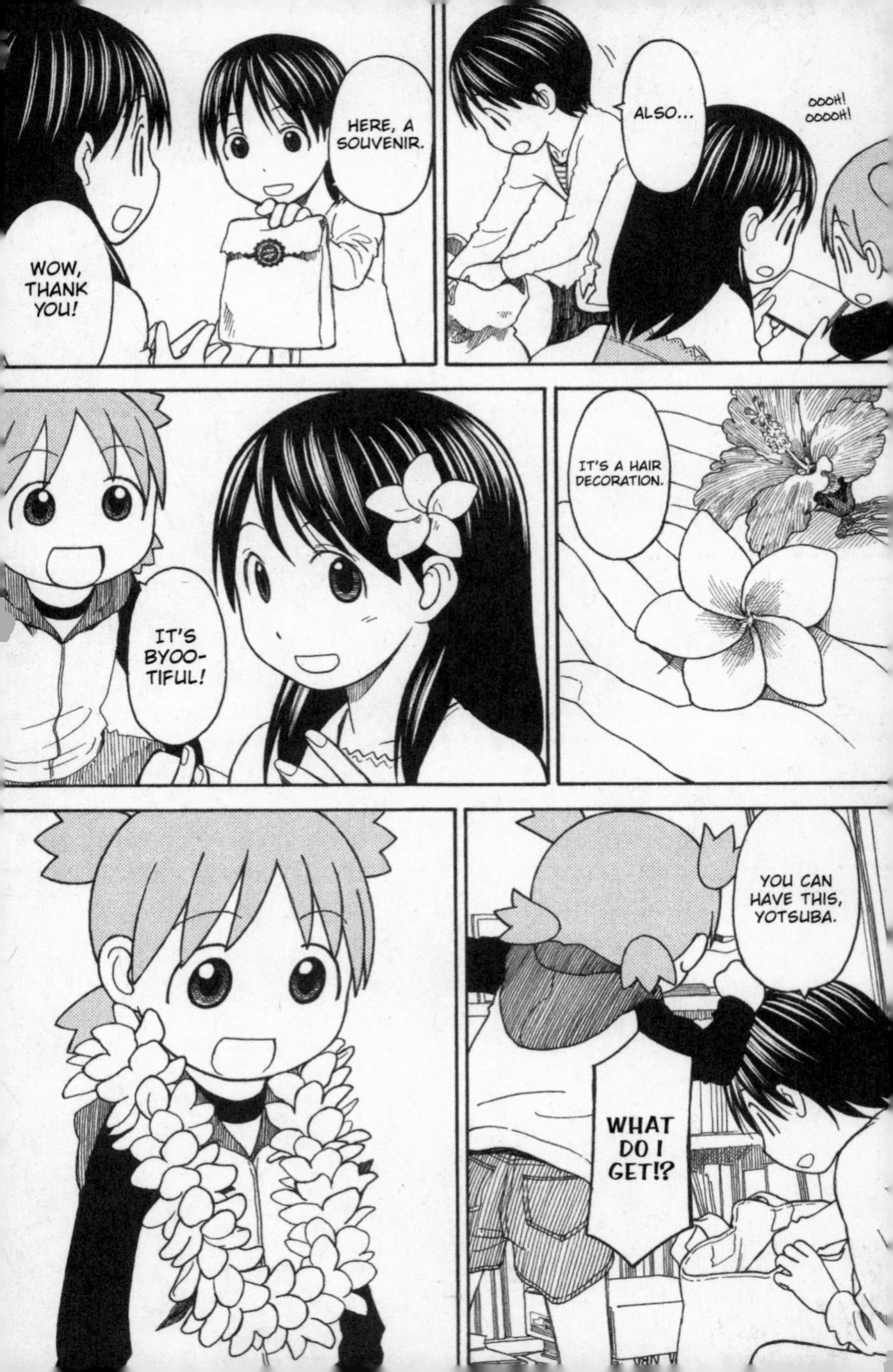
ALSO...
OOOH! OOOOH!
HERE, A SOUVENIR.
WOW, THANK YOU!
IT'S A HAIR DECORATION.
IT'S BYOO-TIFUL!
YOU CAN HAVE THIS, YOTSUBA.
WHAT DO I GET!?

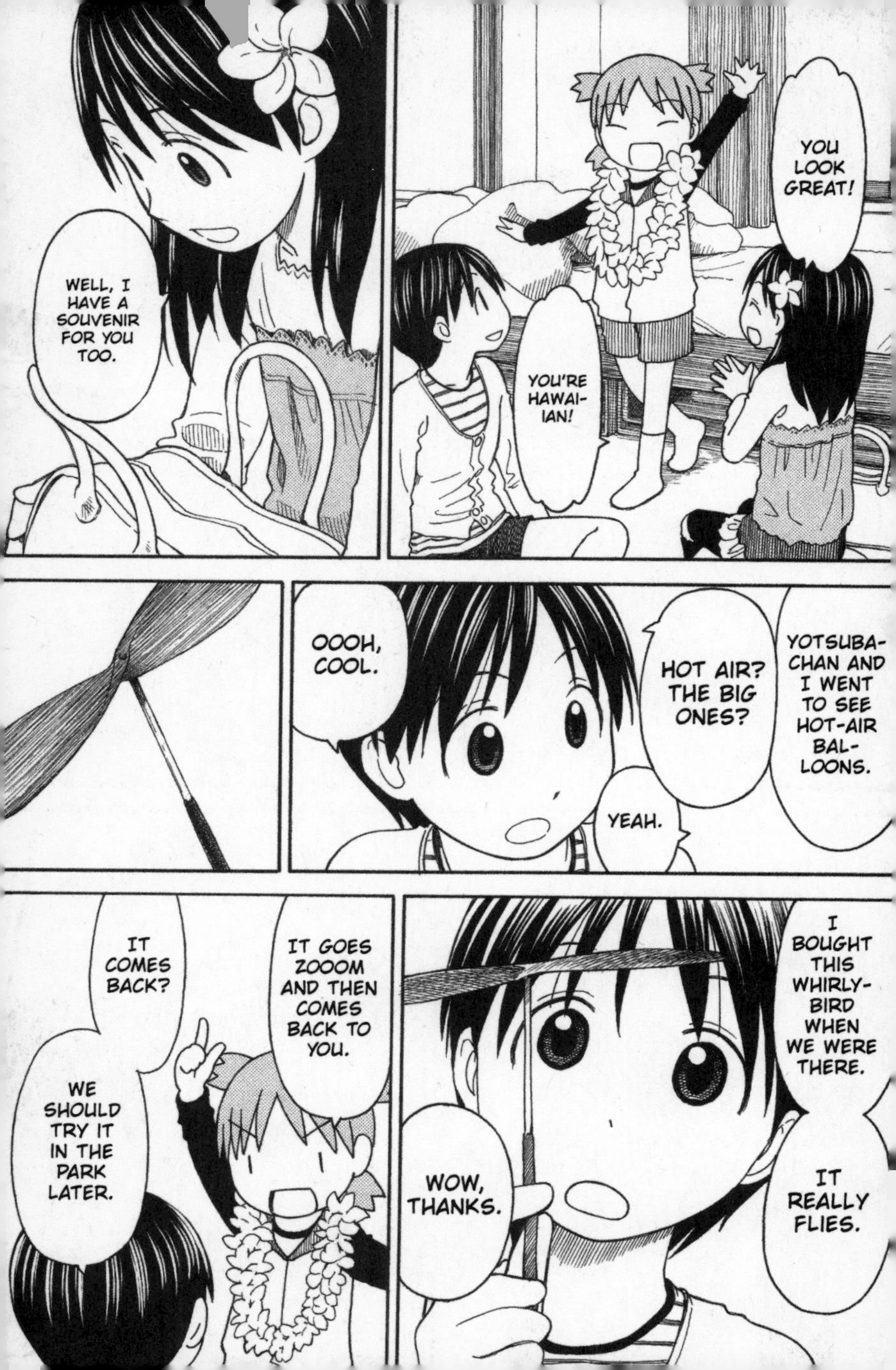
YOU LOOK GREAT!
YOU'RE HAWAIIAN!
WELL, I HAVE A SOUVENIR FOR YOU TOO.
YOTSUBA-CHAN AND I WENT TO SEE HOT-AIR BALLOONS.
HOT AIR? THE BIG ONES?
YEAH.
OOOH, COOL.
I BOUGHT THIS WHIRLYBIRD WHEN WE WERE THERE.
IT REALLY FLIES.
WOW, THANKS.
IT GOES ZOOOM AND THEN COMES BACK TO YOU.
IT COMES BACK?
WE SHOULD TRY IT IN THE PARK LATER.

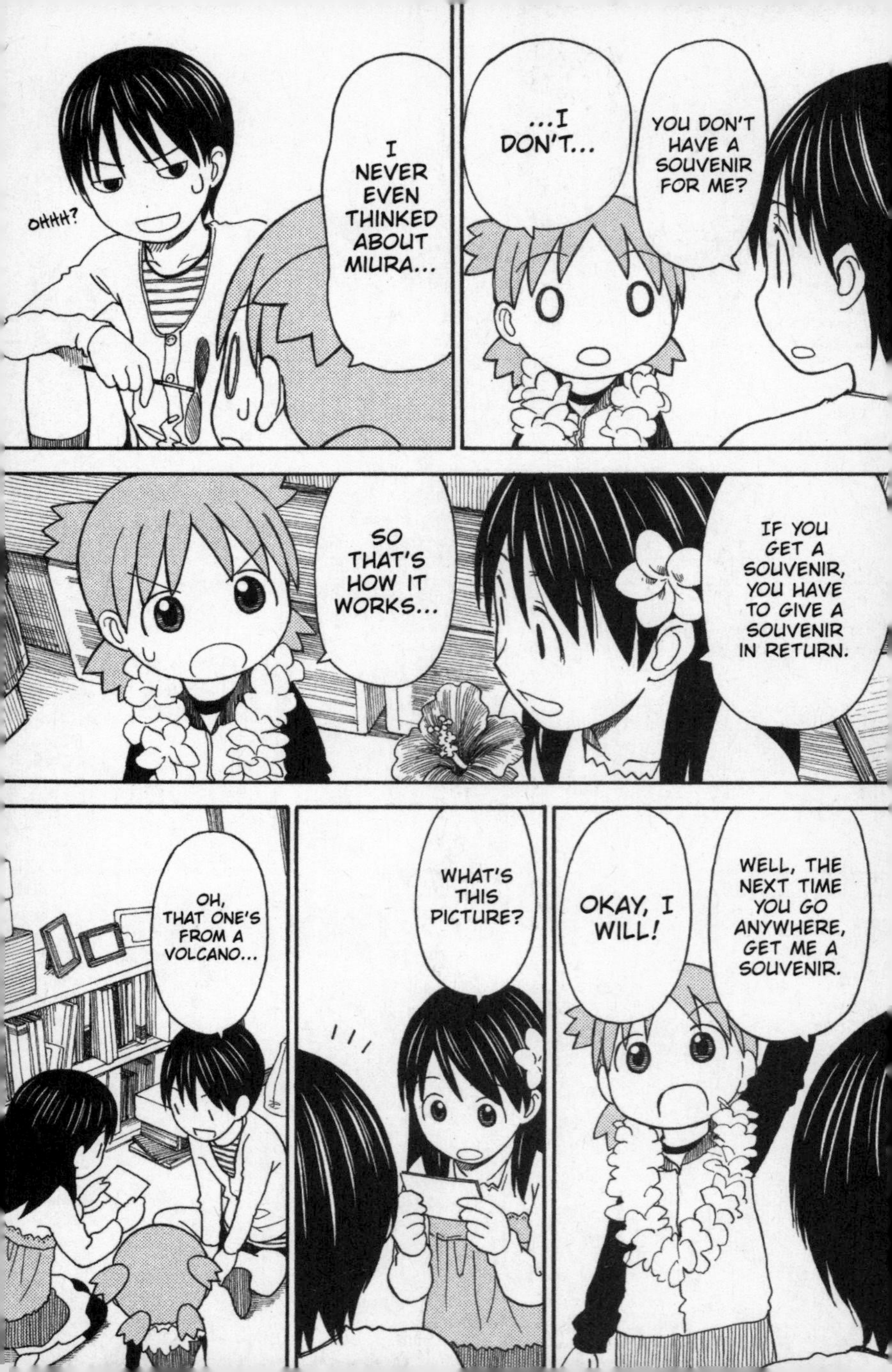
YOU DON'T HAVE A SOUVENIR FOR ME?
...I DON'T...
I NEVER EVEN THINKED ABOUT MIURA...
OHHH?
IF YOU GET A SOUVENIR, YOU HAVE TO GIVE A SOUVENIR IN RETURN.
SO THAT'S HOW IT WORKS...
WELL, THE NEXT TIME YOU GO ANYWHERE, GET ME A SOUVENIR.
OKAY, I WILL!
WHAT'S THIS PICTURE?
OH, THAT ONE'S FROM A VOLCANO...

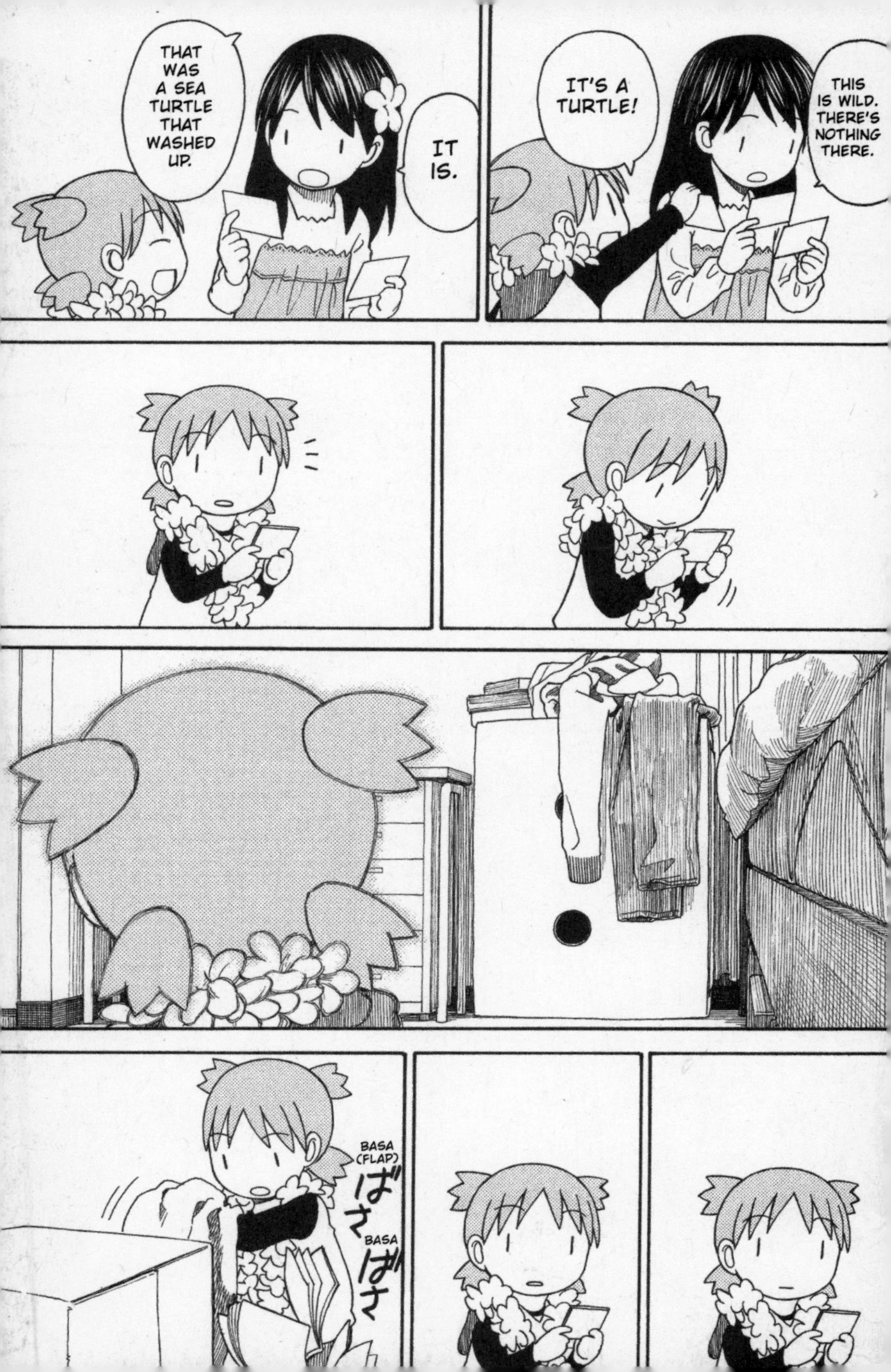
IT'S A TURTLE!
THIS IS WILD. THERE'S NOTHING THERE.
THAT WAS A SEA TURTLE THAT WASHED UP.
IT IS.
BASA (FLAP)
ばさ
BASA
ばさ

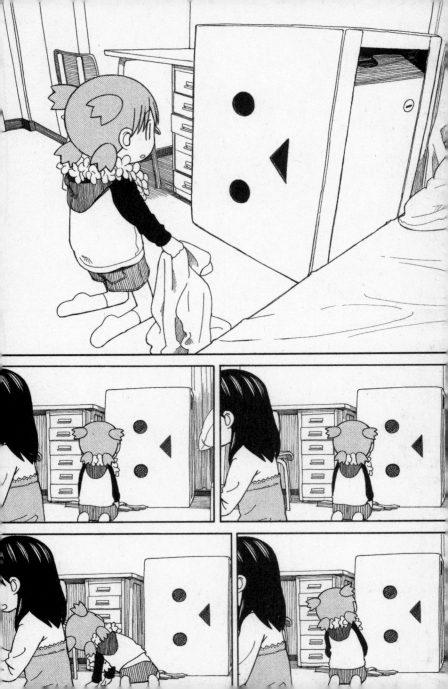

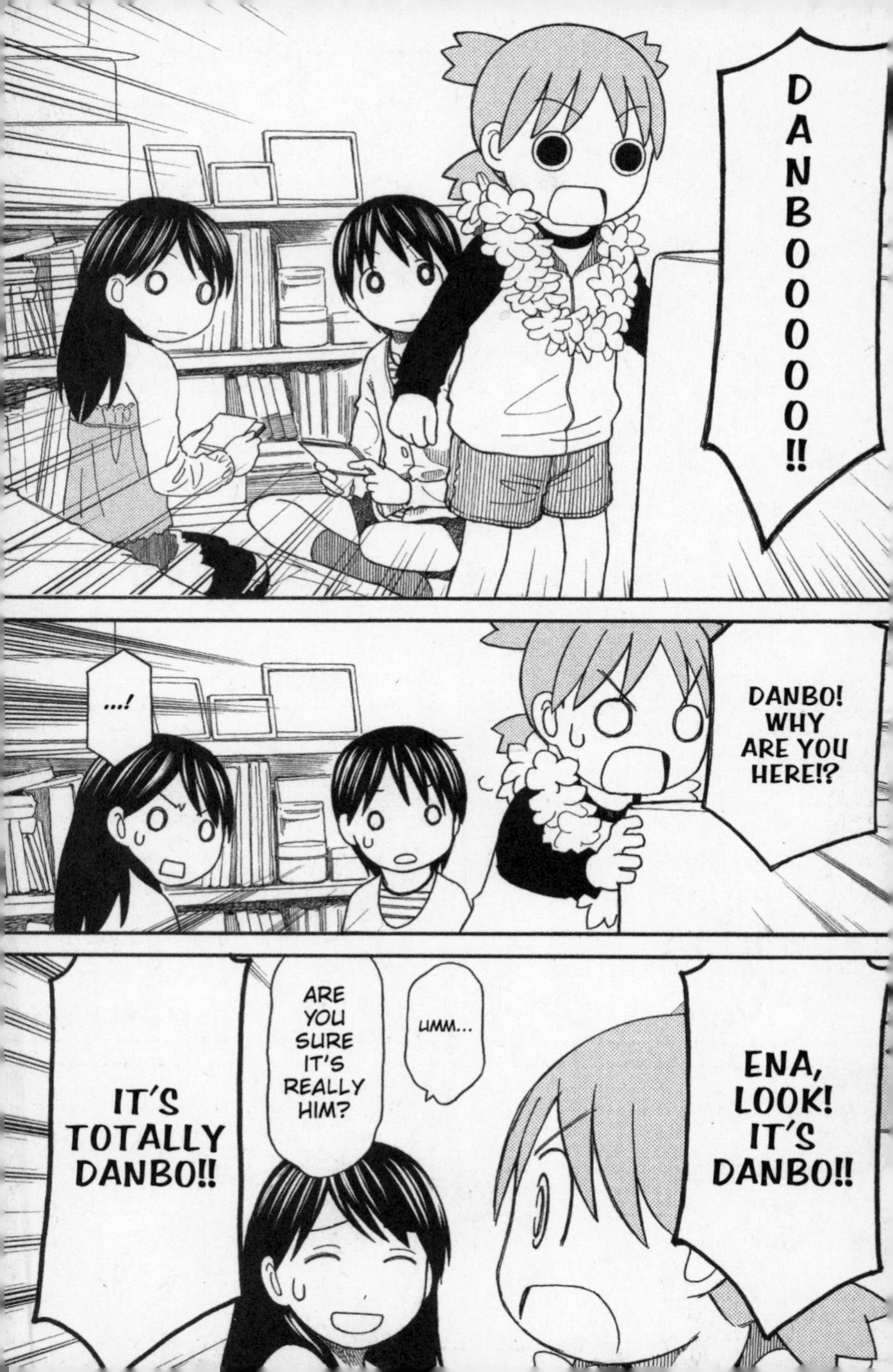
DANBOOOOOOO!!
DANBO! WHY ARE YOU HERE!?
...!
ENA, LOOK! IT'S DANBO!!
UMM...
ARE YOU SURE IT'S REALLY HIM?
IT'S TOTALLY DANBO!!

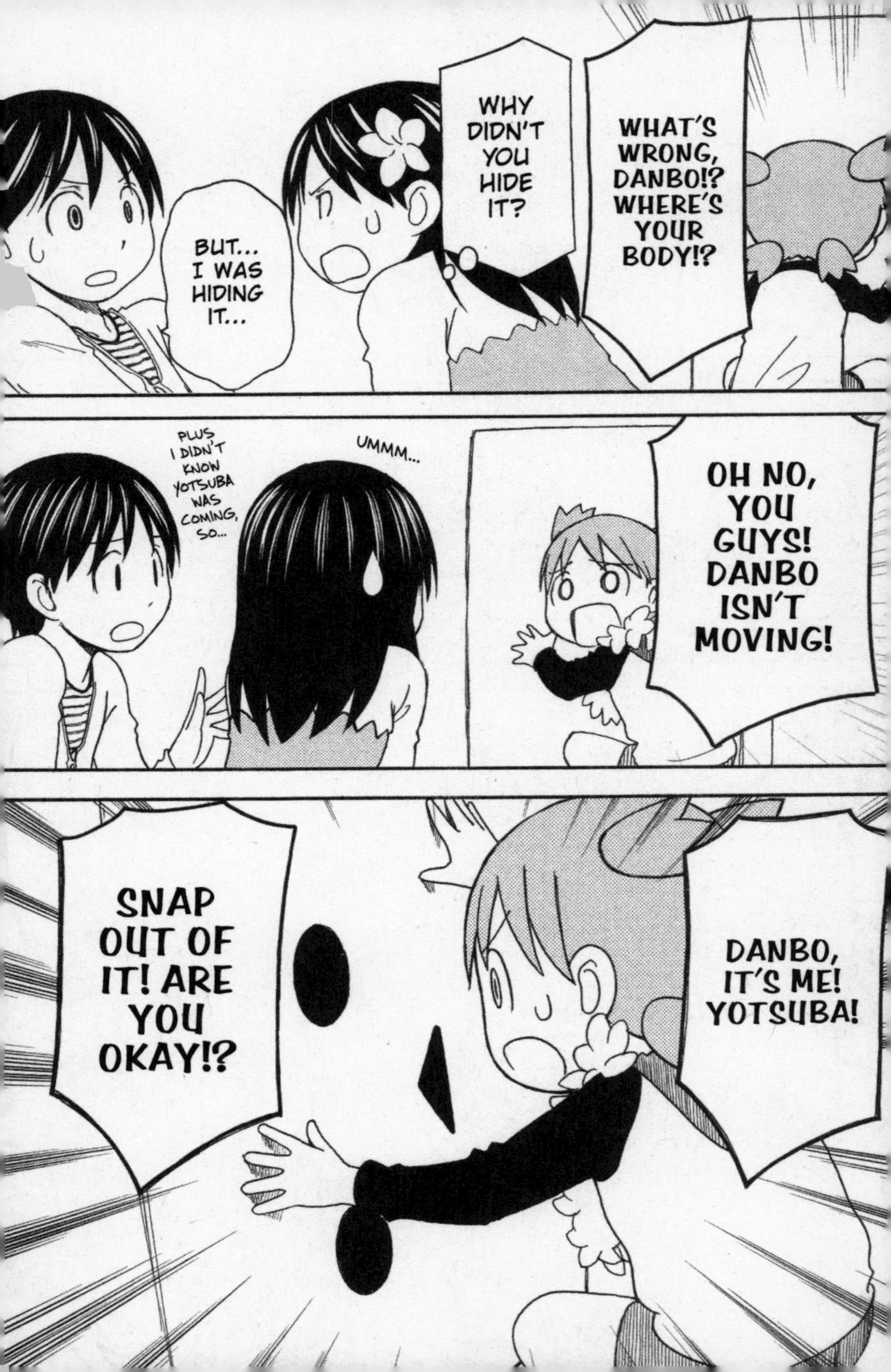
WHAT'S WRONG, DANBO!? WHERE'S YOUR BODY!?
WHY DIDN'T YOU HIDE IT?
BUT... I WAS HIDING IT...
OH NO, YOU GUYS! DANBO ISN'T MOVING!
UMMM...
PLUS I DIDN'T KNOW YOTSUBA WAS COMING, SO...
DANBO, IT'S ME! YOTSUBA!
SNAP OUT OF IT! ARE YOU OKAY!?

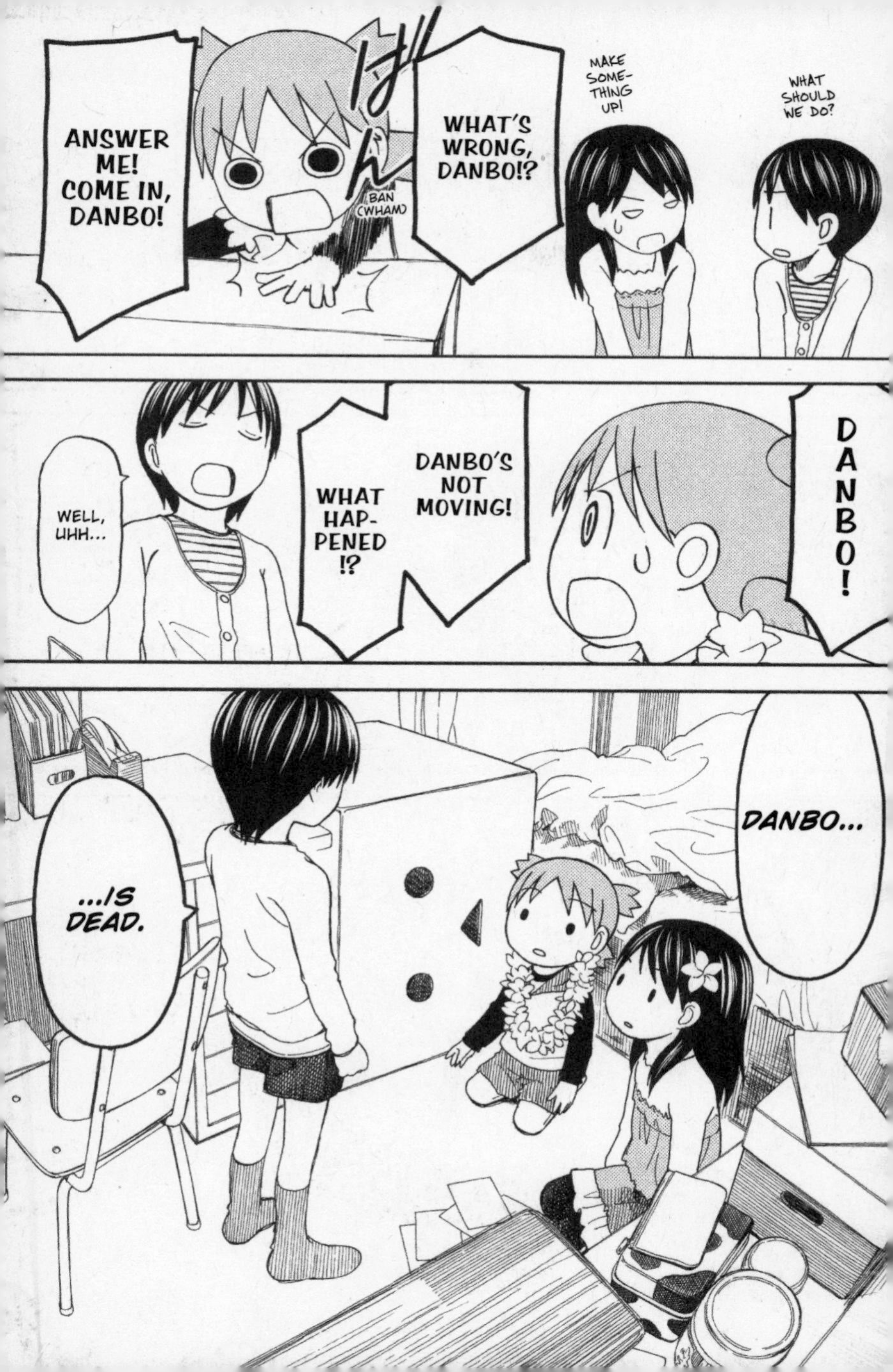
WHAT SHOULD WE DO?
MAKE SOME-THING UP!
WHAT'S WRONG, DANBO!?
BAN (WHAM)
ANSWER ME! COME IN, DANBO!
DANBO!
DANBO'S NOT MOVING! WHAT HAP-PENED!?
WELL, UHH...
DANBO...
...IS DEAD.

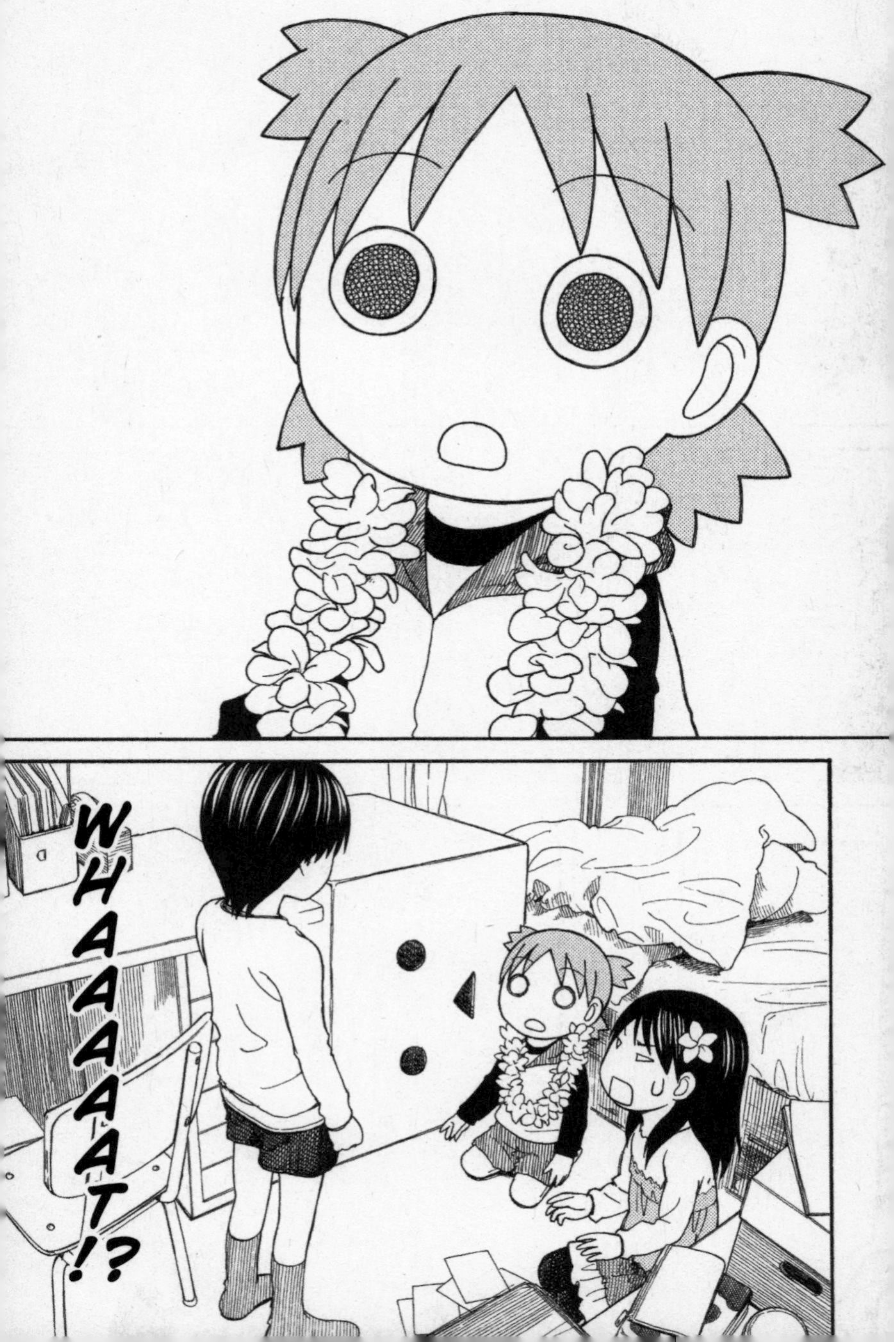
WHAAAAAT!?

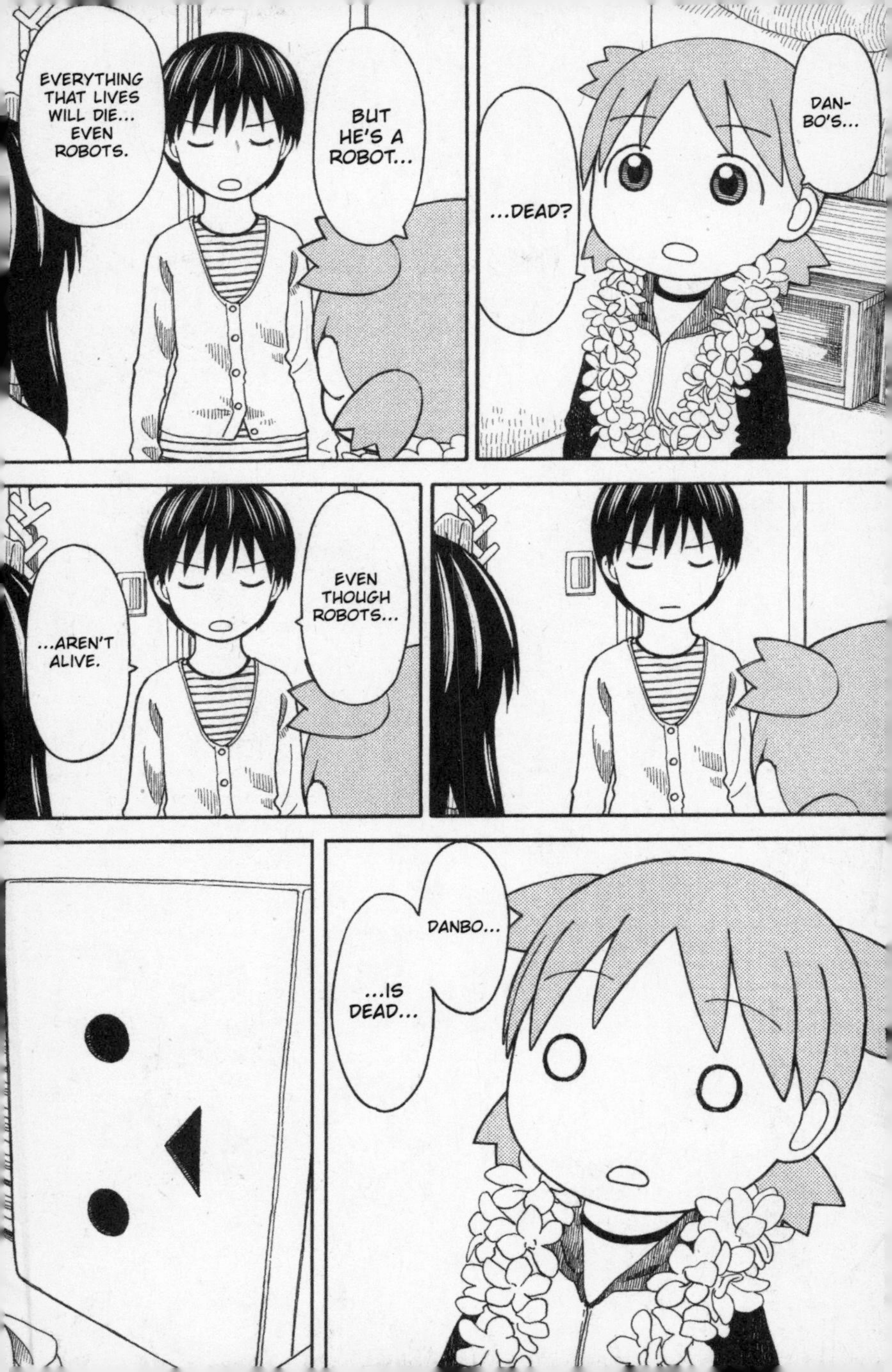
DAN-BO'S...
...DEAD?
BUT HE'S A ROBOT...
EVERYTHING THAT LIVES WILL DIE... EVEN ROBOTS.
EVEN THOUGH ROBOTS...
...AREN'T ALIVE.
DANBO...
...IS DEAD...

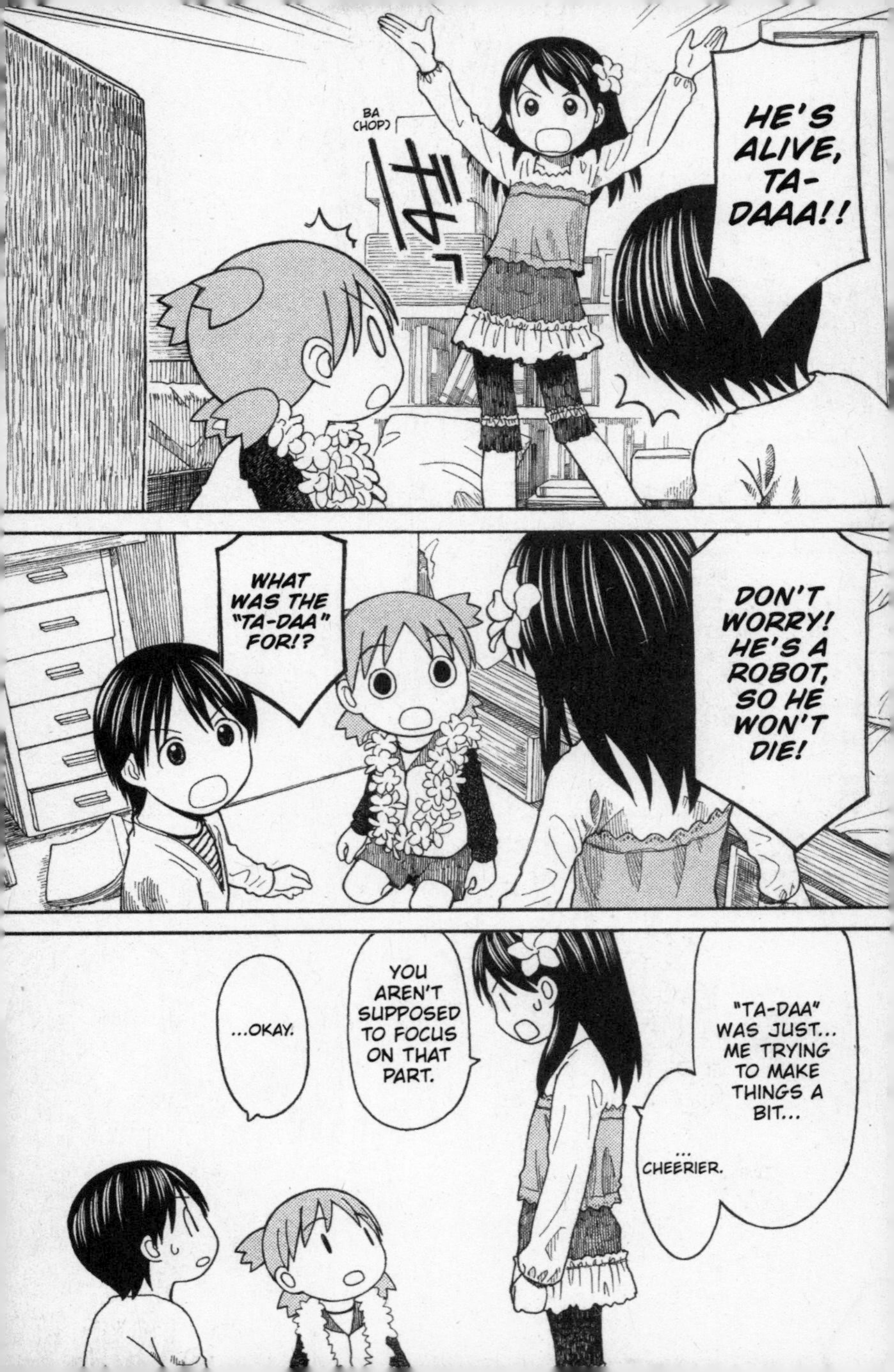
HE'S ALIVE, TA-DAAA!!
BA (HOP)
DON'T WORRY! HE'S A ROBOT, SO HE WON'T DIE!
WHAT WAS THE "TA-DAA" FOR!?
"TA-DAA" WAS JUST... ME TRYING TO MAKE THINGS A BIT...
... CHEERIER.
YOU AREN'T SUPPOSED TO FOCUS ON THAT PART.
...OKAY.

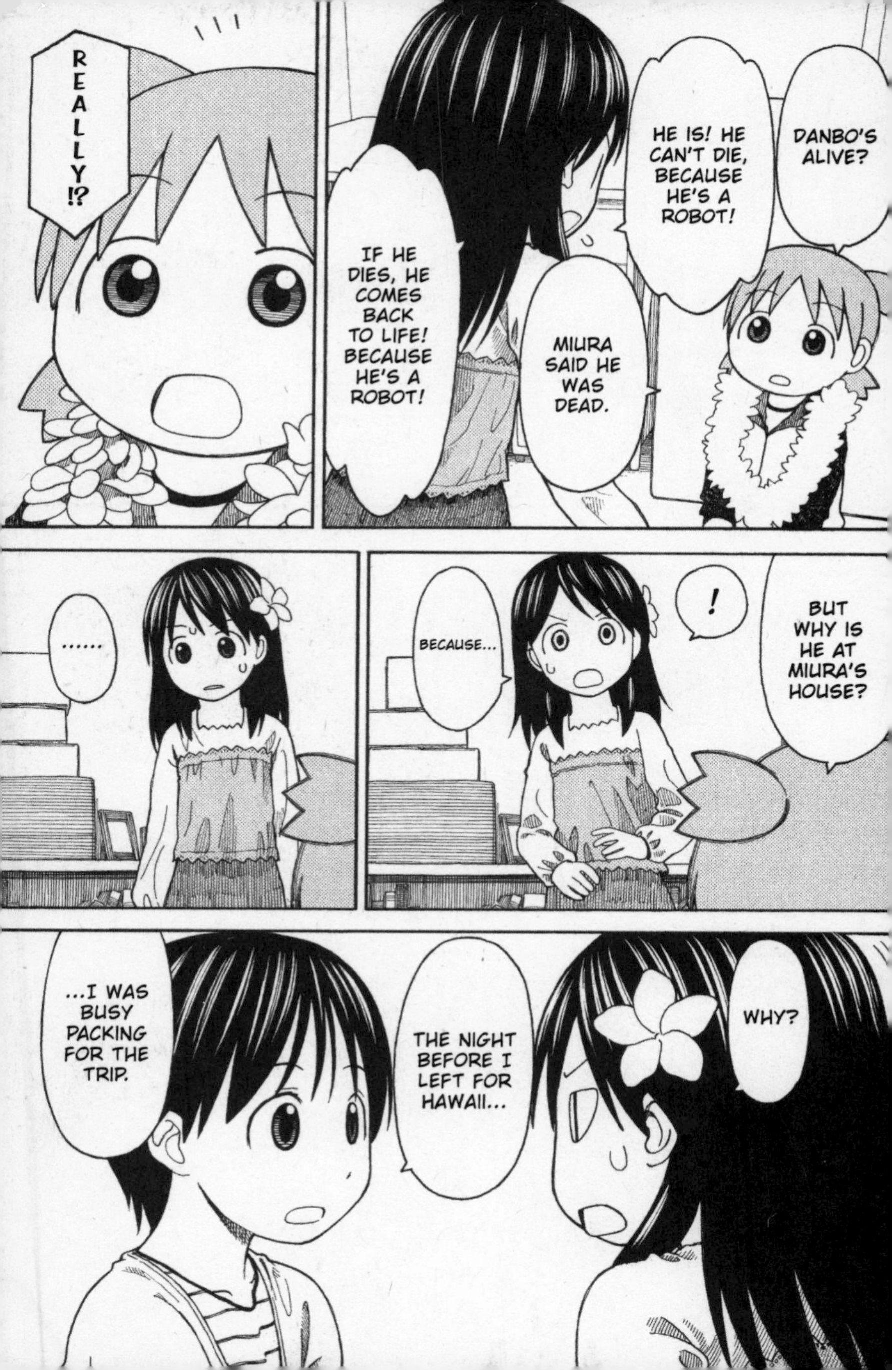
DANBO'S ALIVE?
HE IS! HE CAN'T DIE, BECAUSE HE'S A ROBOT!
MIURA SAID HE WAS DEAD.
IF HE DIES, HE COMES BACK TO LIFE! BECAUSE HE'S A ROBOT!
REALLY!?
BUT WHY IS HE AT MIURA'S HOUSE?
!
BECAUSE...
......
WHY?
THE NIGHT BEFORE I LEFT FOR HAWAII...
...I WAS BUSY PACKING FOR THE TRIP.

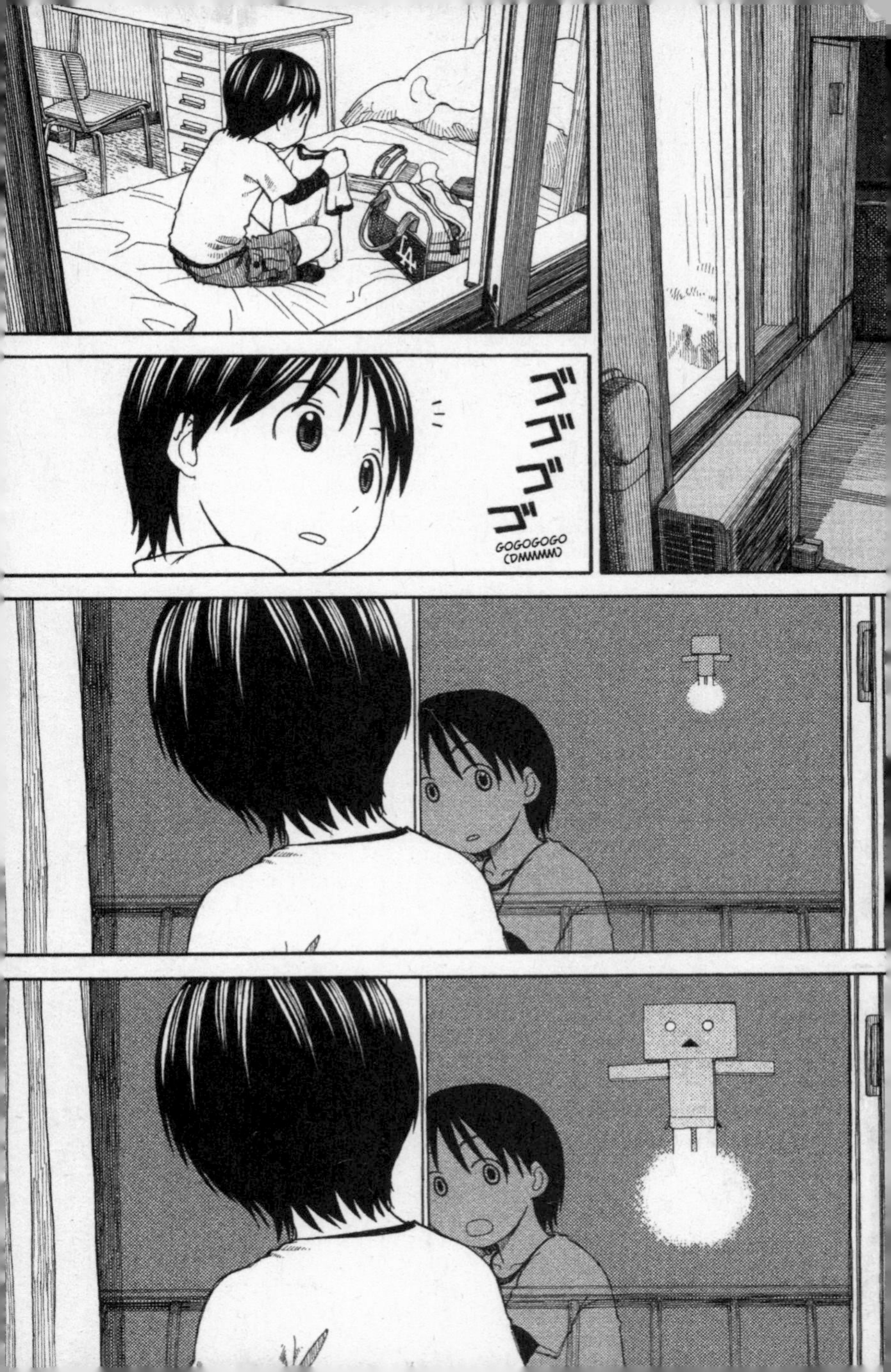
ゴゴゴゴ
GOGOGOGO
(DMMMM)

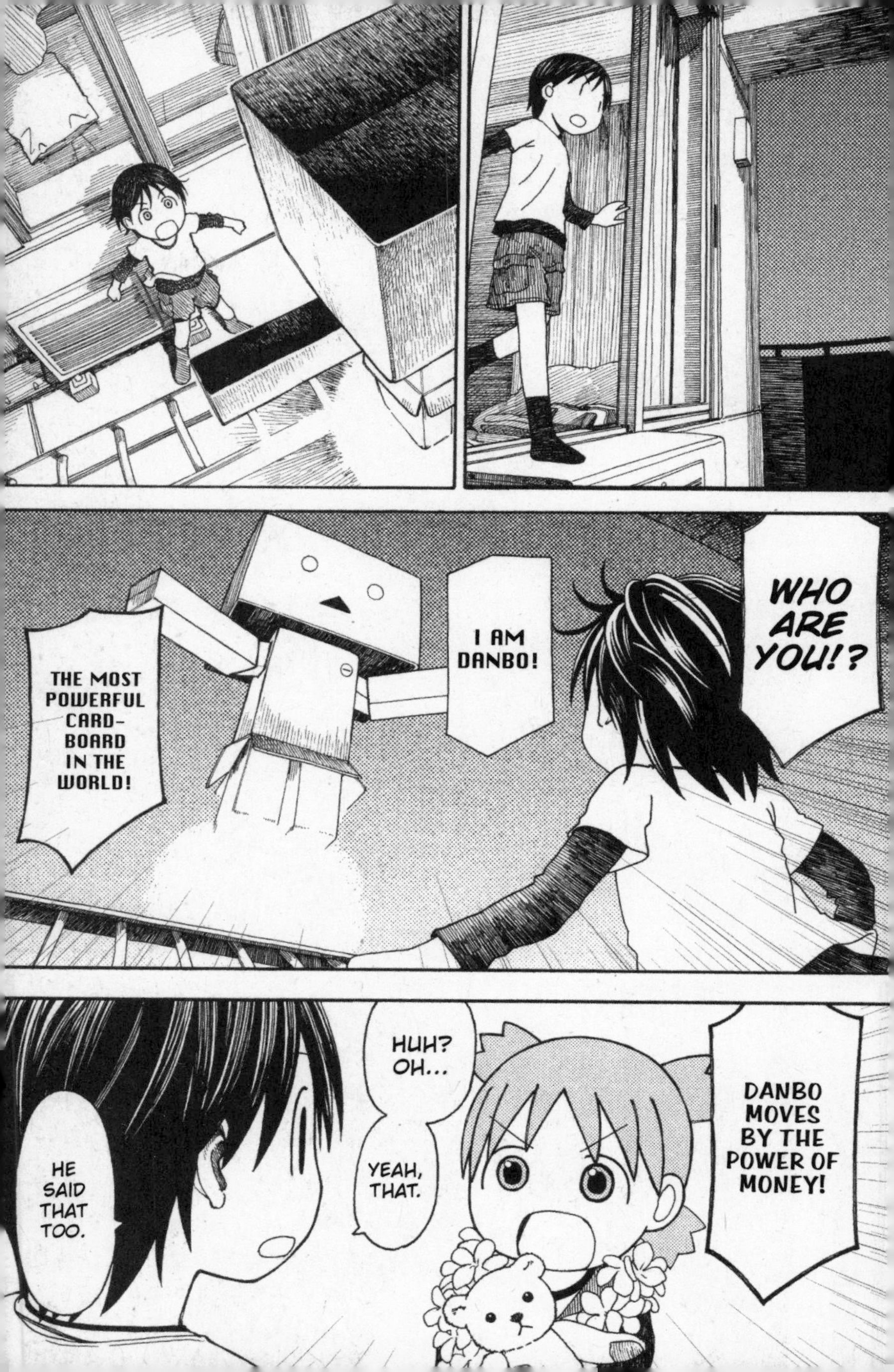
WHO ARE YOU!?
I AM DANBO!
THE MOST POWERFUL CARD-BOARD IN THE WORLD!
DANBO MOVES BY THE POWER OF MONEY!
HUH? OH...
YEAH, THAT.
HE SAID THAT TOO.

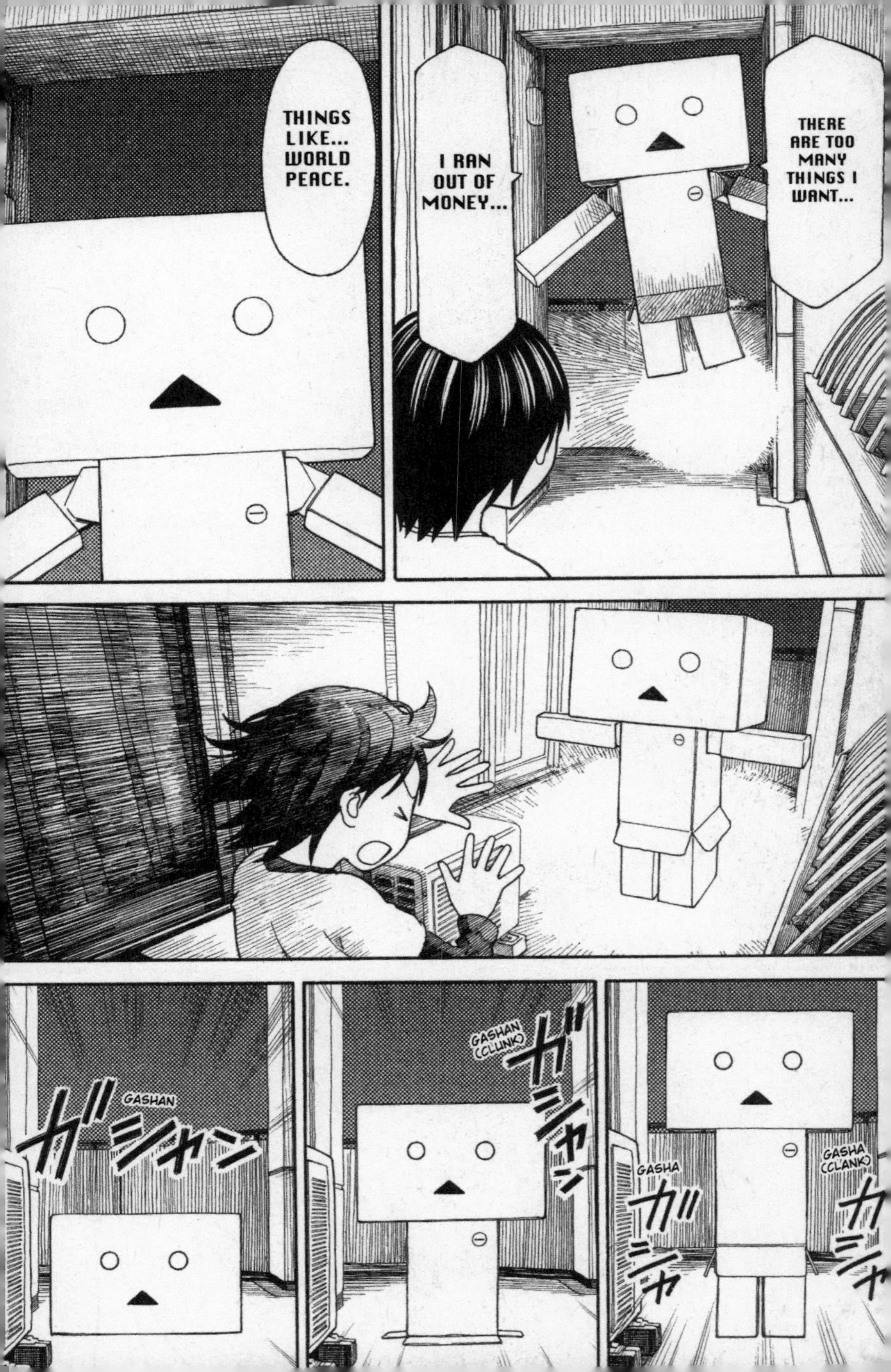
THERE ARE TOO MANY THINGS I WANT...
I RAN OUT OF MONEY...
THINGS LIKE... WORLD PEACE.
GASHA (CLANK)
カシャ
GASHA
ガシャ
GASHAN (CLUNK)
ガシャン
GASHAN
ガシャン

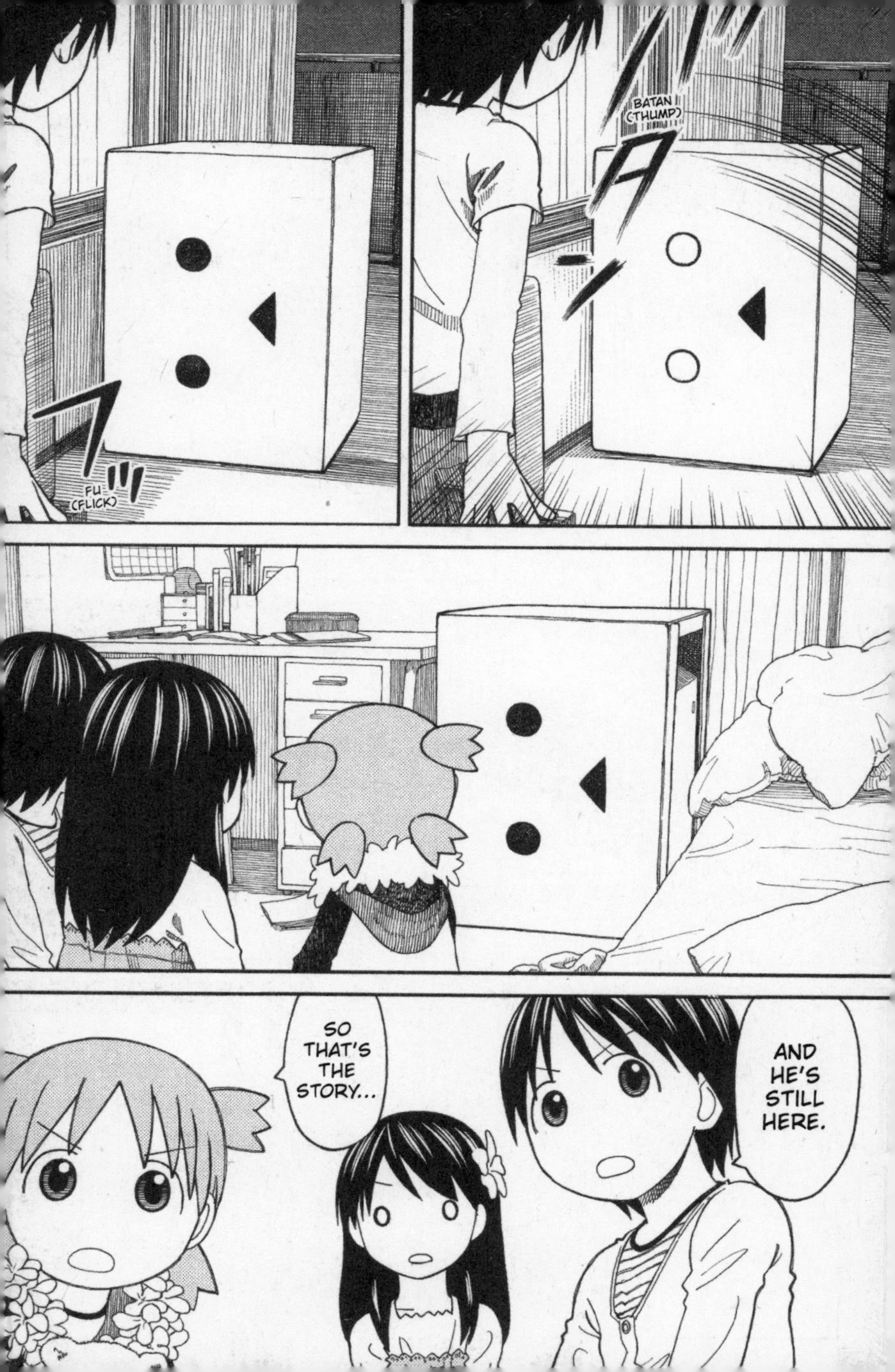
BATAN (THUMP)
FU (FLICK)
AND HE'S STILL HERE.
SO THAT'S THE STORY...

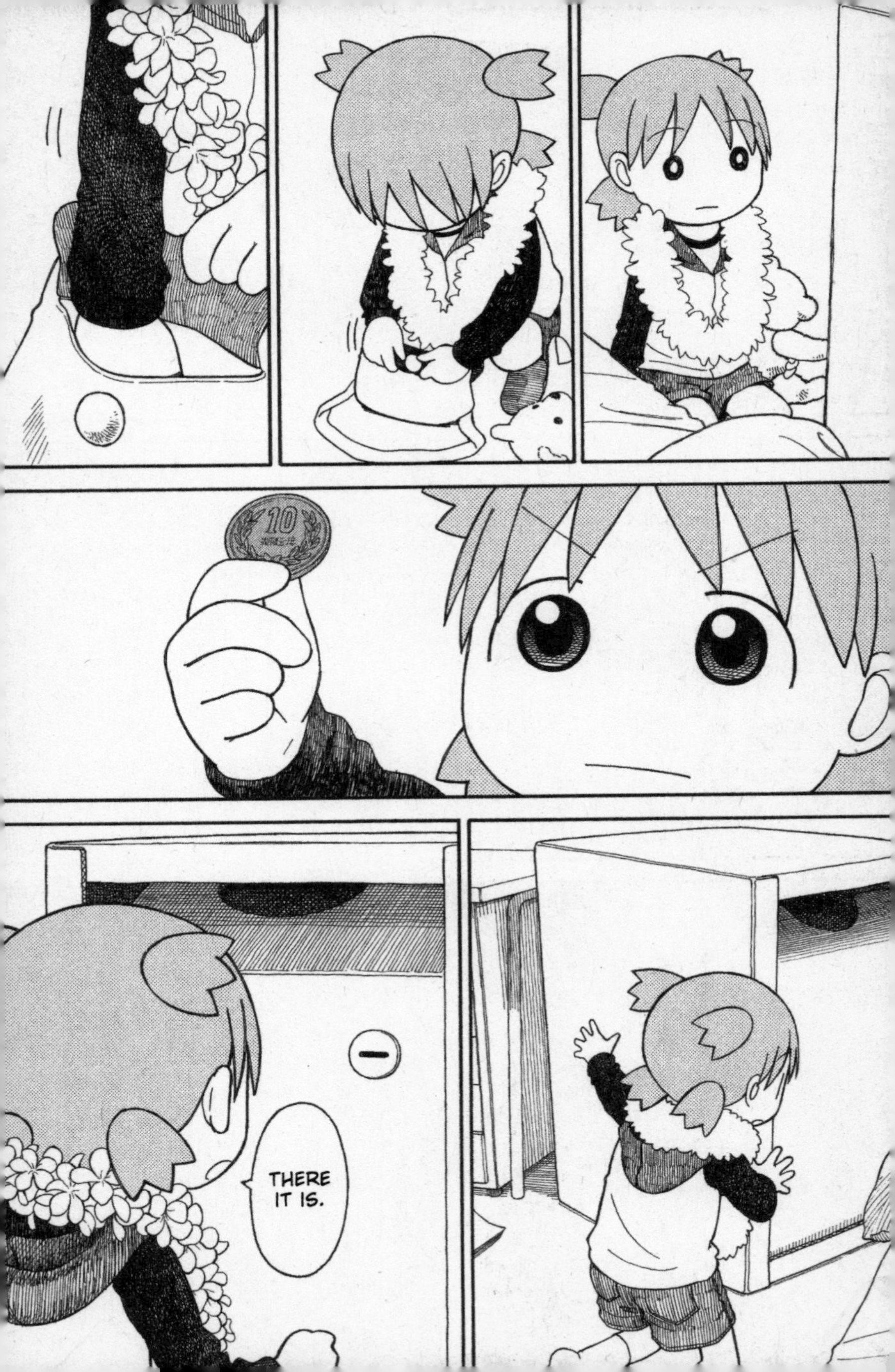
THERE IT IS.

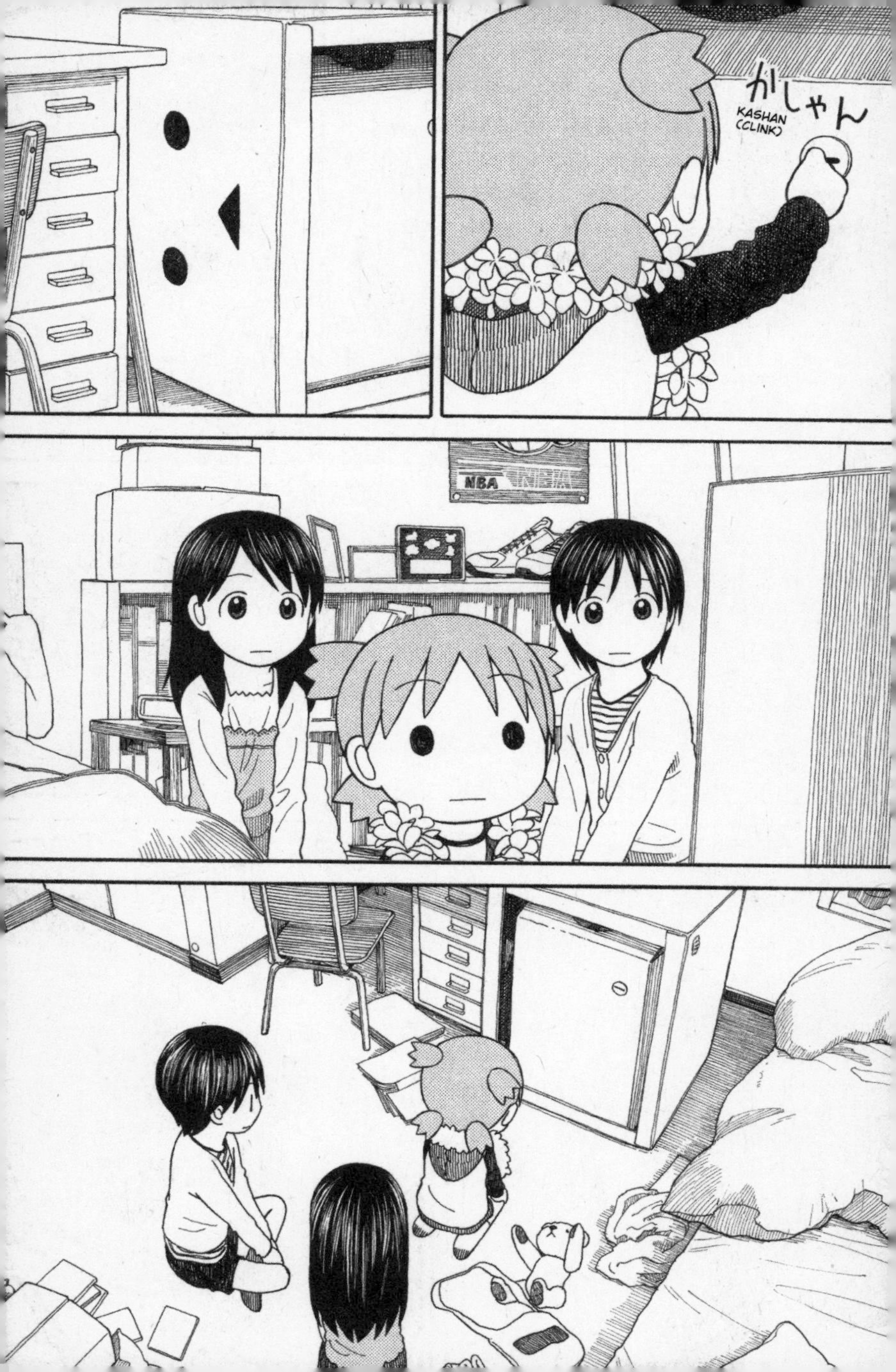
がしゃん
KASHAN
(CLINK)
NBA

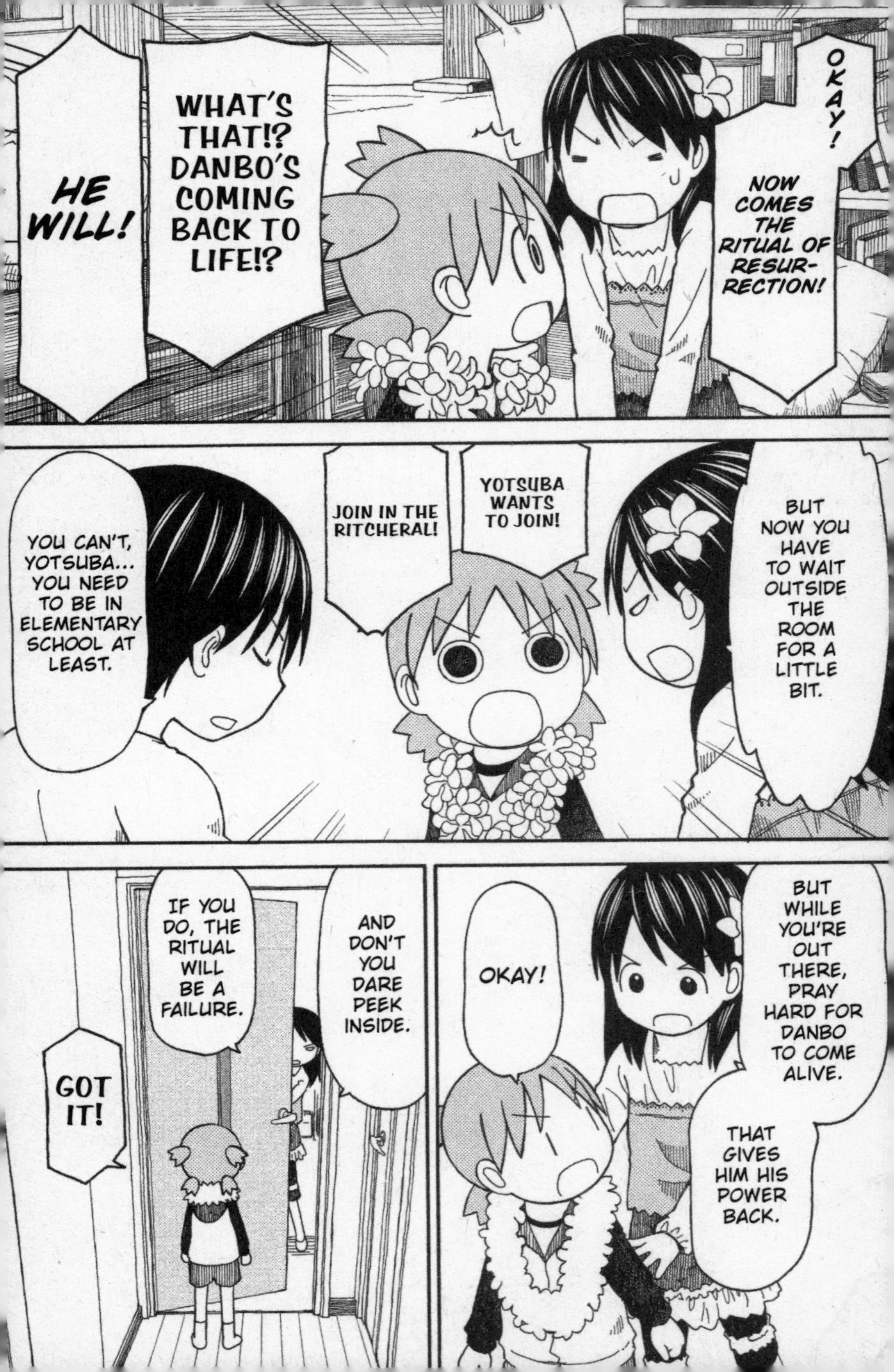
OKAY!
NOW COMES THE RITUAL OF RESUR-RECTION!
WHAT'S THAT!? DANBO'S COMING BACK TO LIFE!?
HE WILL!
BUT NOW YOU HAVE TO WAIT OUTSIDE THE ROOM FOR A LITTLE BIT.
YOTSUBA WANTS TO JOIN!
JOIN IN THE RITCHERAL!
YOU CAN'T, YOTSUBA... YOU NEED TO BE IN ELEMENTARY SCHOOL AT LEAST.
BUT WHILE YOU'RE OUT THERE, PRAY HARD FOR DANBO TO COME ALIVE.
THAT GIVES HIM HIS POWER BACK.
OKAY!
AND DON'T YOU DARE PEEK INSIDE.
IF YOU DO, THE RITUAL WILL BE A FAILURE.
GOT IT!

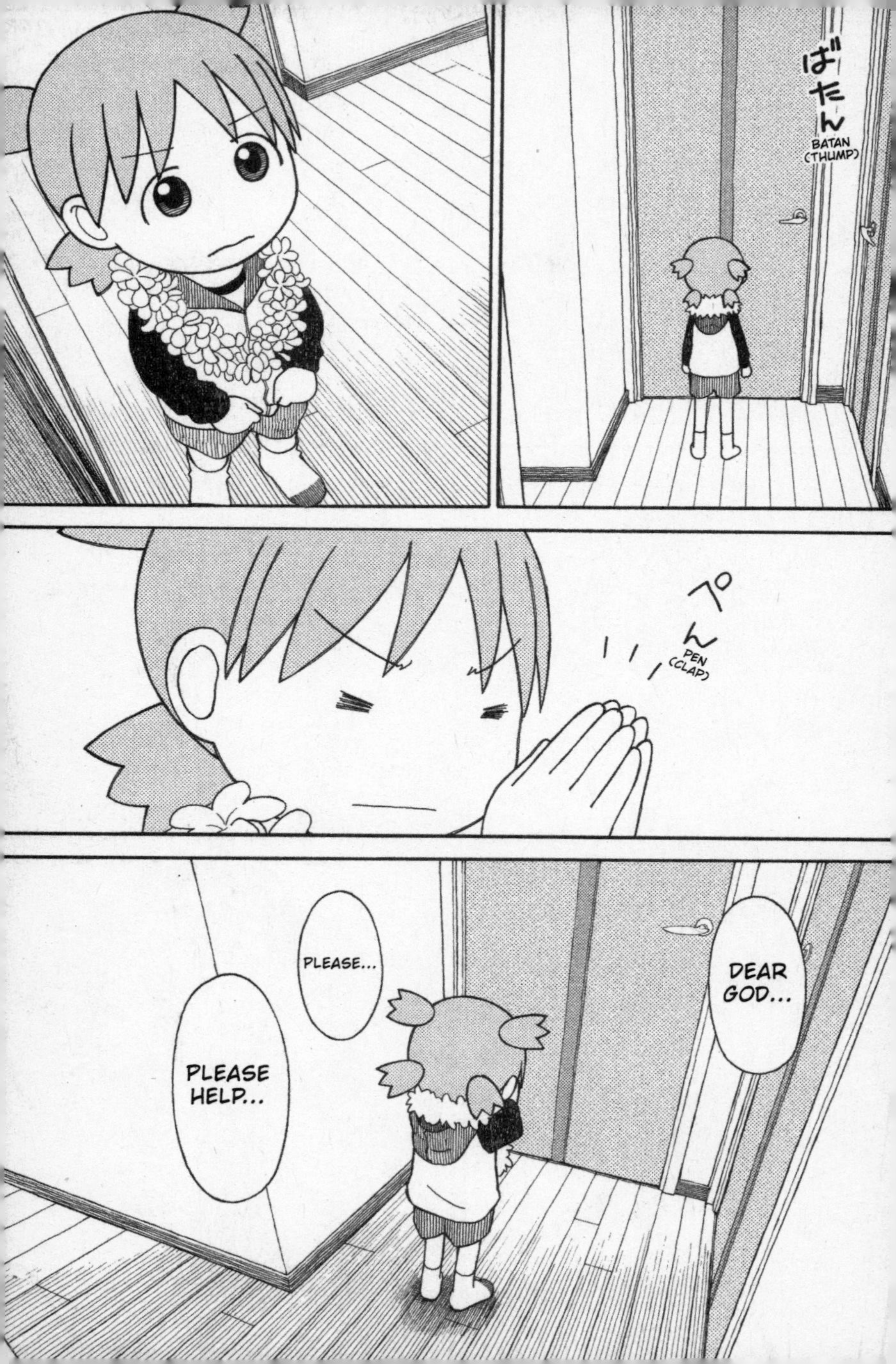
ばたん
BATAN (THUMP)
ぺん
PEN (CLAP)
DEAR GOD...
PLEASE...
PLEASE HELP...

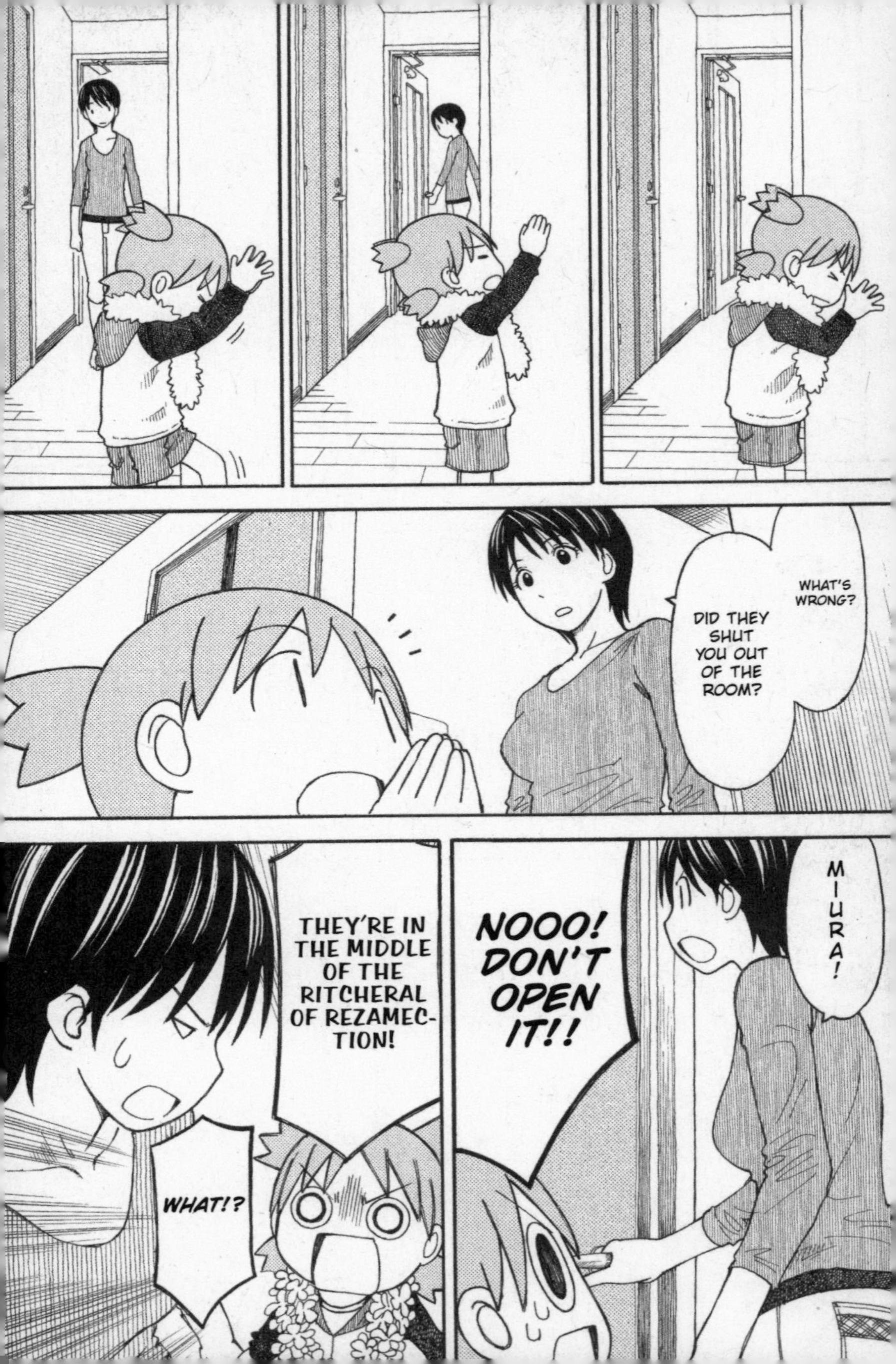
WHAT'S WRONG?
DID THEY SHUT YOU OUT OF THE ROOM?
MIURA!
NOOO! DON'T OPEN IT!!
THEY'RE IN THE MIDDLE OF THE RITCHERAL OF REZAMEC-TION!
WHAT!?

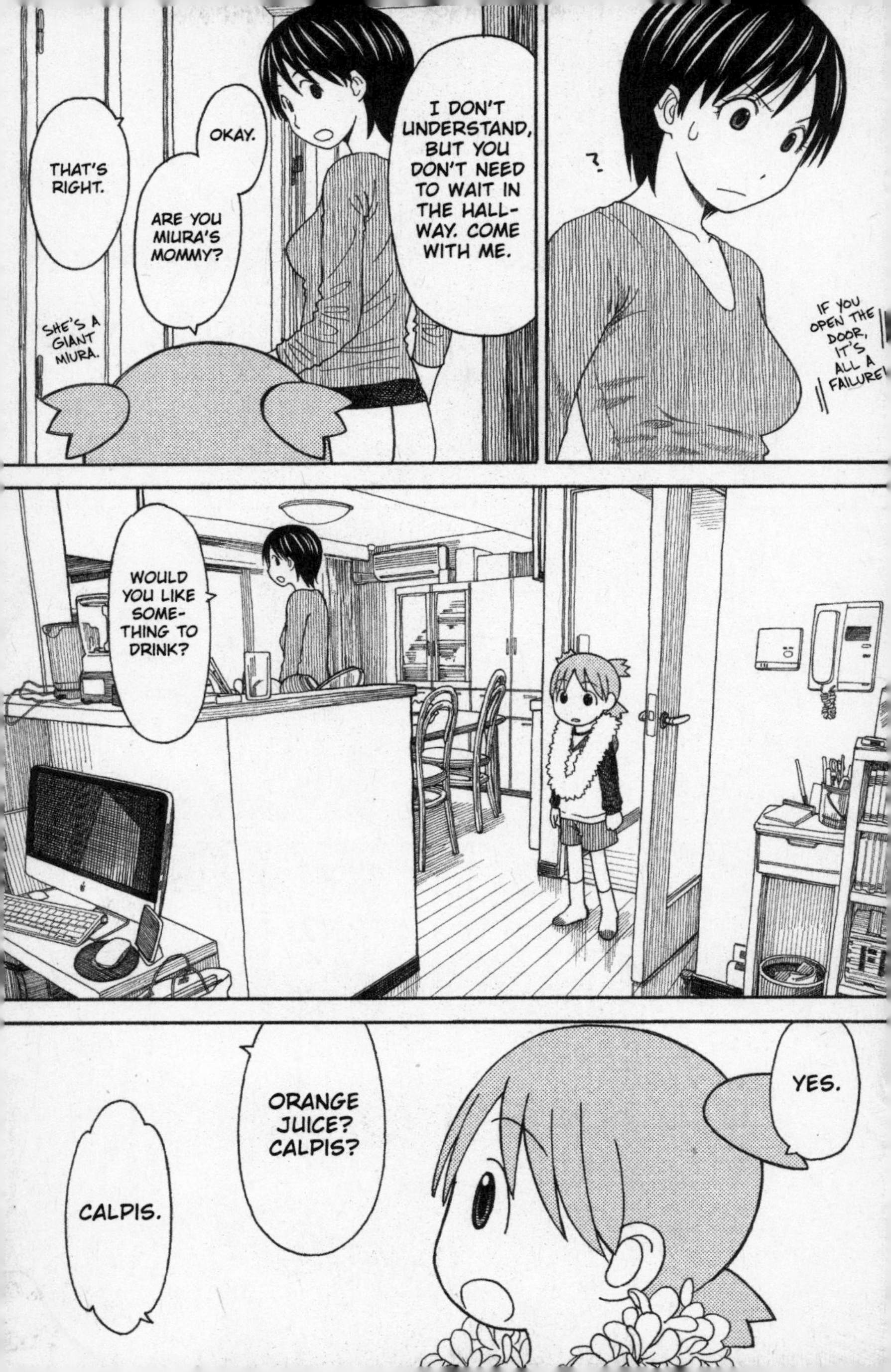
?
IF YOU OPEN THE DOOR, IT'S ALL A FAILURE!
I DON'T UNDERSTAND, BUT YOU DON'T NEED TO WAIT IN THE HALL-WAY. COME WITH ME.
OKAY.
ARE YOU MIURA'S MOMMY?
THAT'S RIGHT.
SHE'S A GIANT MIURA.
WOULD YOU LIKE SOME-THING TO DRINK?
YES.
ORANGE JUICE? CALPIS?
CALPIS.

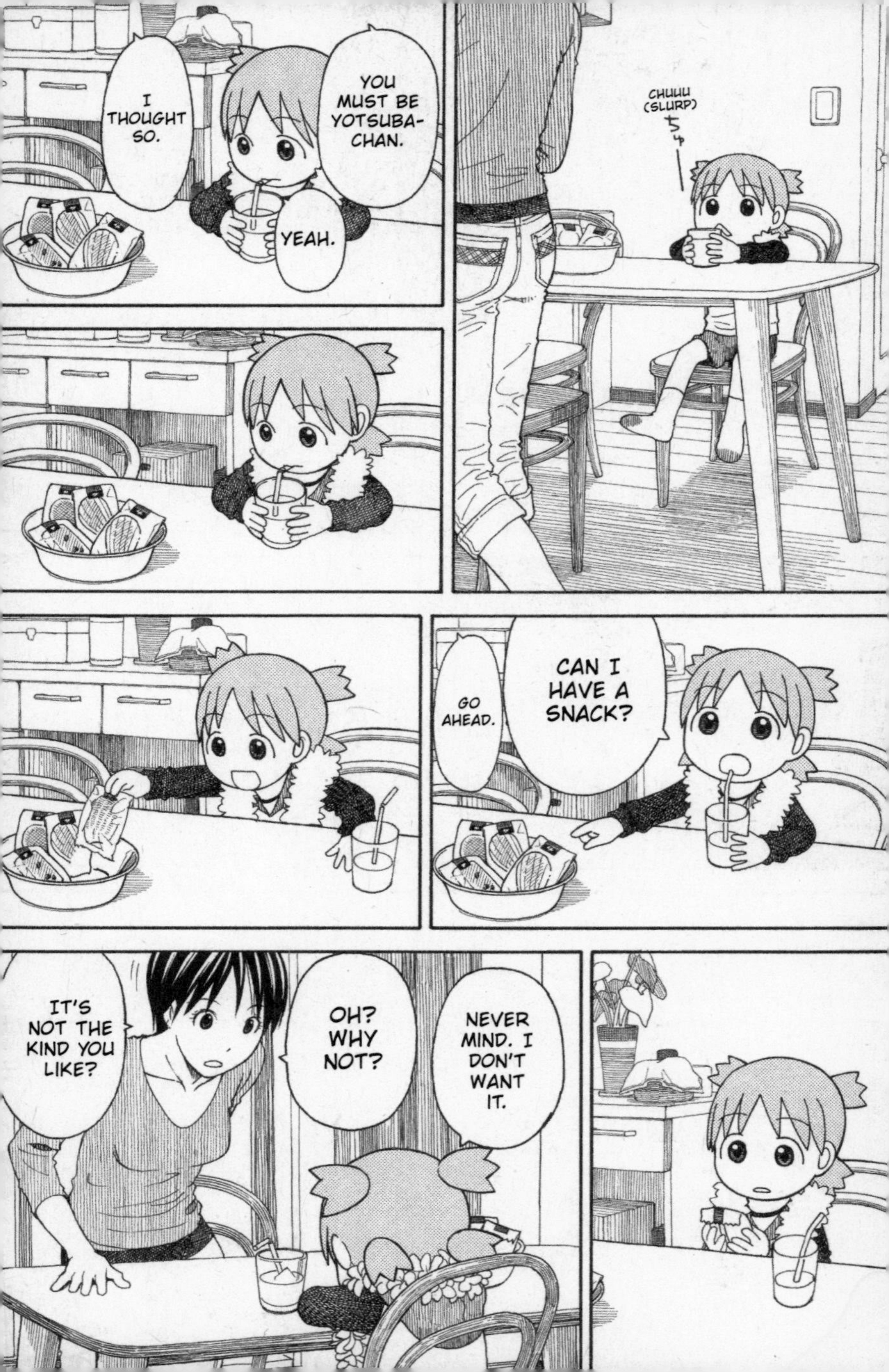
CHUUU (SLURP)
ちゅー
YOU MUST BE YOTSUBA-CHAN.
YEAH.
I THOUGHT SO.
CAN I HAVE A SNACK?
GO AHEAD.
NEVER MIND. I DON'T WANT IT.
OH? WHY NOT?
IT'S NOT THE KIND YOU LIKE?

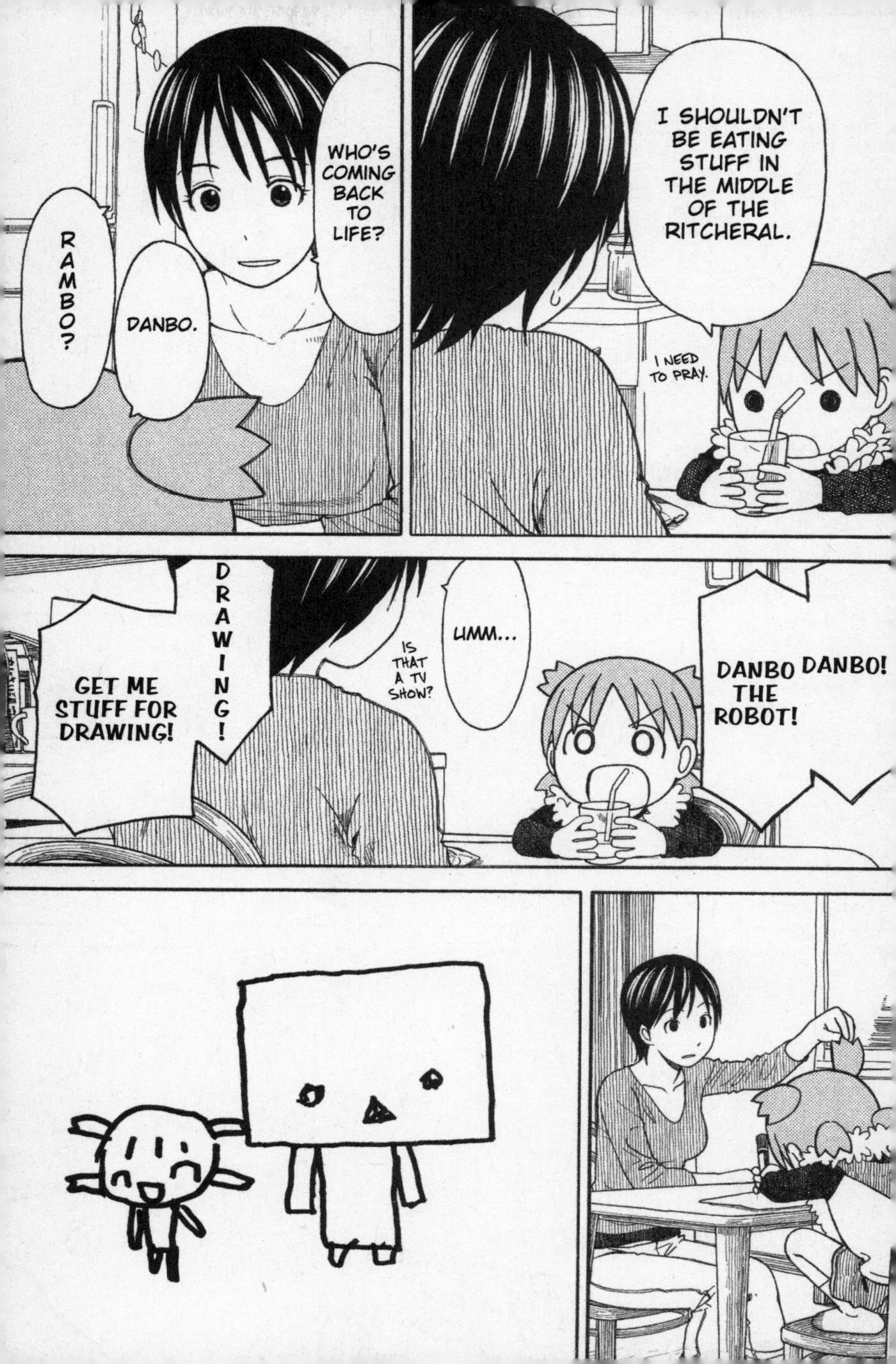
I SHOULDN'T BE EATING STUFF IN THE MIDDLE OF THE RITCHERAL.
I NEED TO PRAY.
WHO'S COMING BACK TO LIFE?
DANBO.
RAMBO?
DANBO!
DANBO THE ROBOT!
UMM...
IS THAT A TV SHOW?
DRAWING!
GET ME STUFF FOR DRAWING!

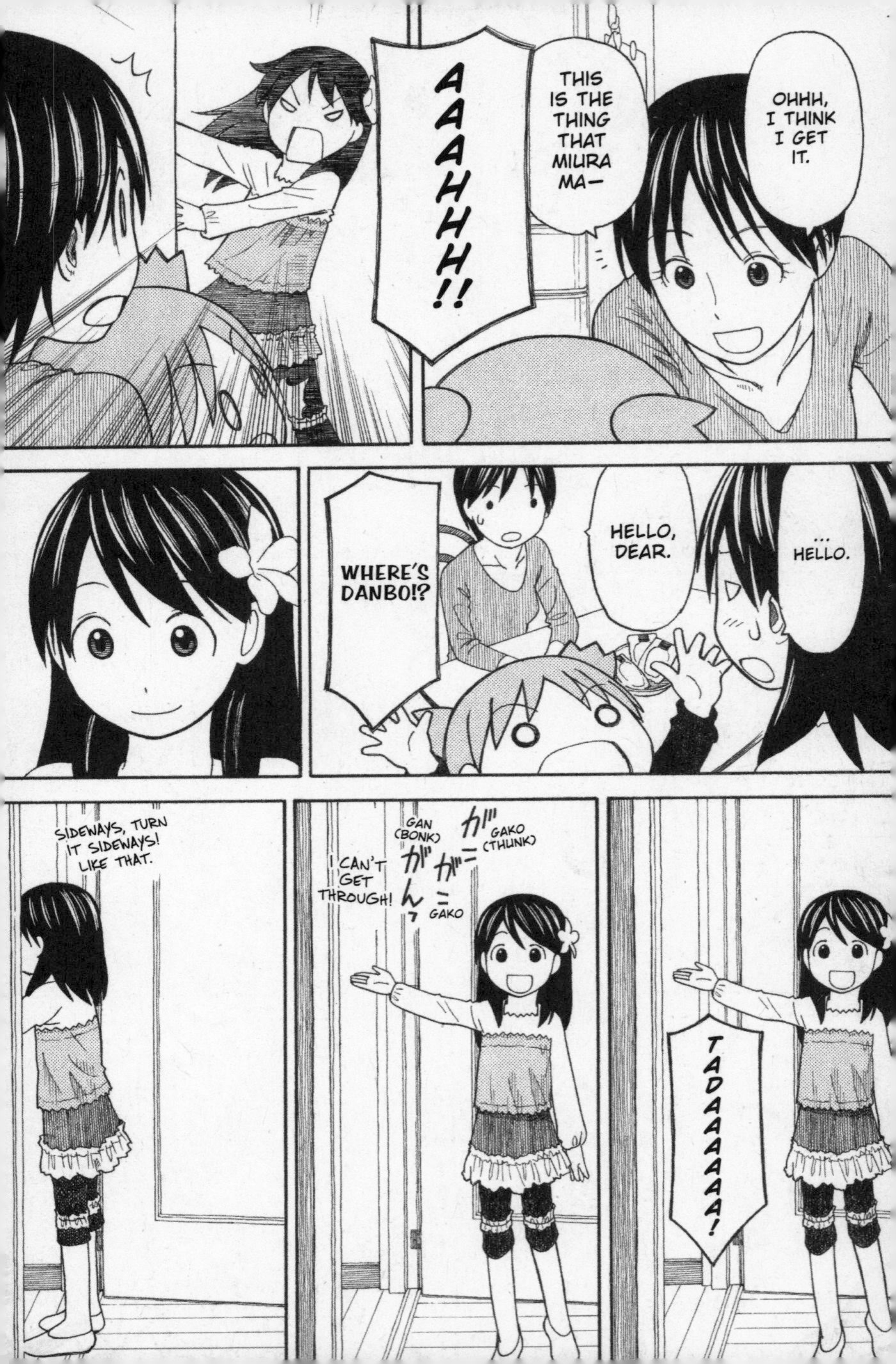
OHHH, I THINK I GET IT.
THIS IS THE THING THAT MIURA MA—
AAAAHHHH!!
... HELLO.
HELLO, DEAR.
WHERE'S DANBO!?
TADAAAAAAA!
がこ
GAKO (THUNK)
がん
GAN (BONK)
がこ
GAKO
I CAN'T GET THROUGH!
SIDEWAYS, TURN IT SIDEWAYS! LIKE THAT.

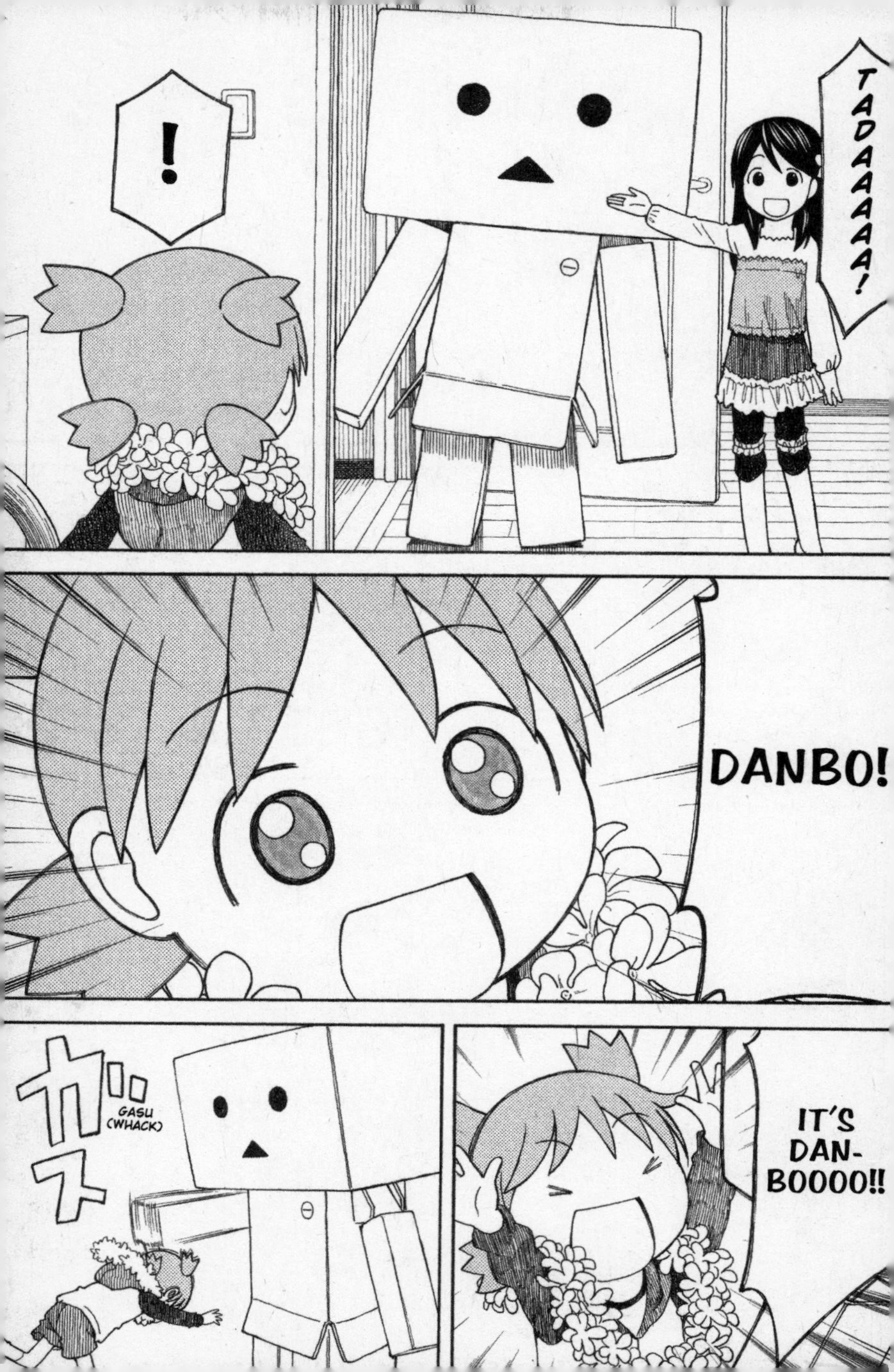
TADAAAAAA!
!
DANBO!
IT'S DAN-BOOOO!!
GASU (WHACK)

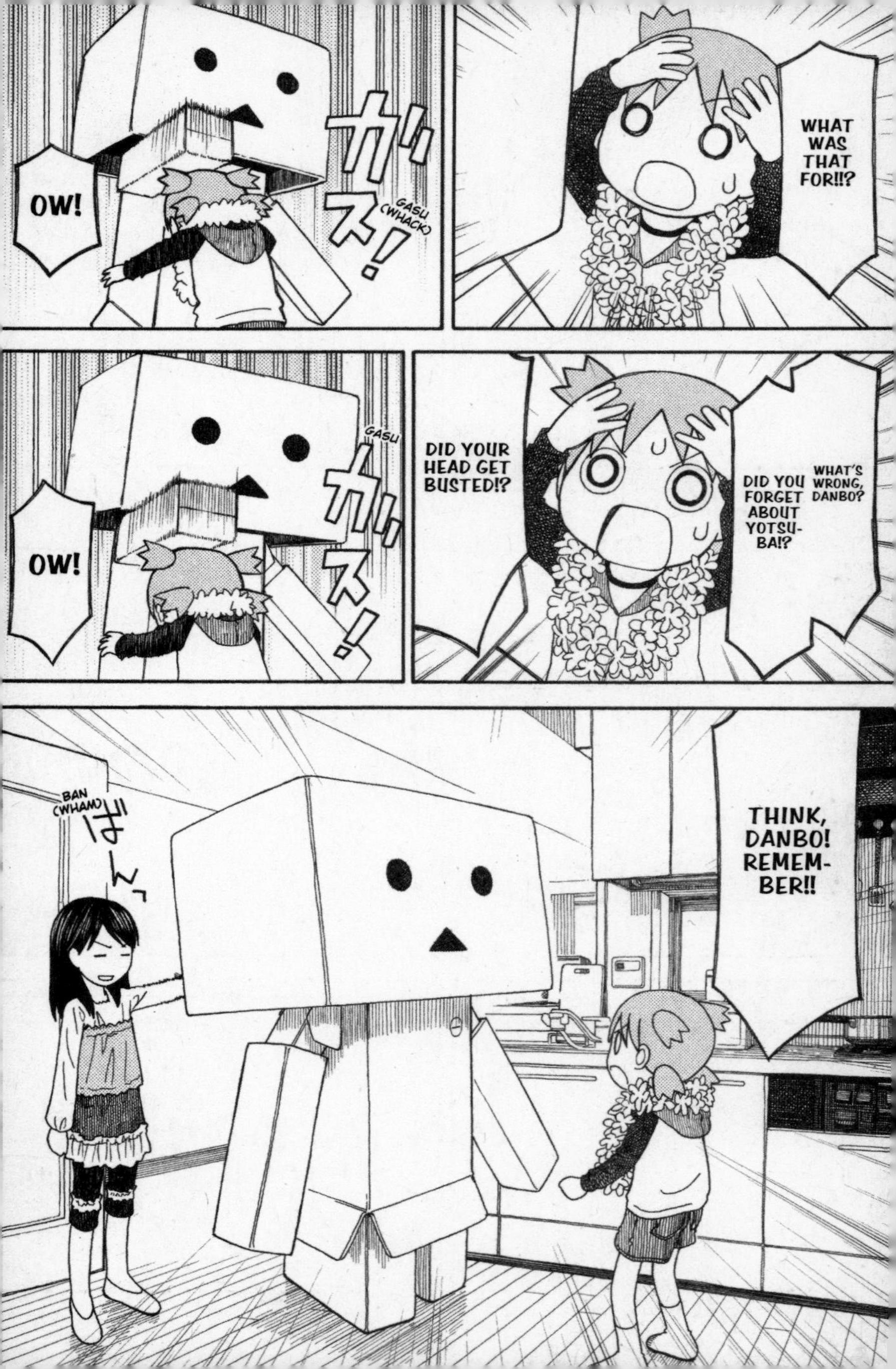
WHAT WAS THAT FOR!!?
ガス!
GASU (WHACK)
OW!
WHAT'S WRONG, DANBO?
DID YOU FORGET ABOUT YOTSU-BA!?
DID YOUR HEAD GET BUSTED!?
ガッス!
GASU
OW!
THINK, DANBO! REMEM-BER!!
ばんっ
BAN (WHAM)

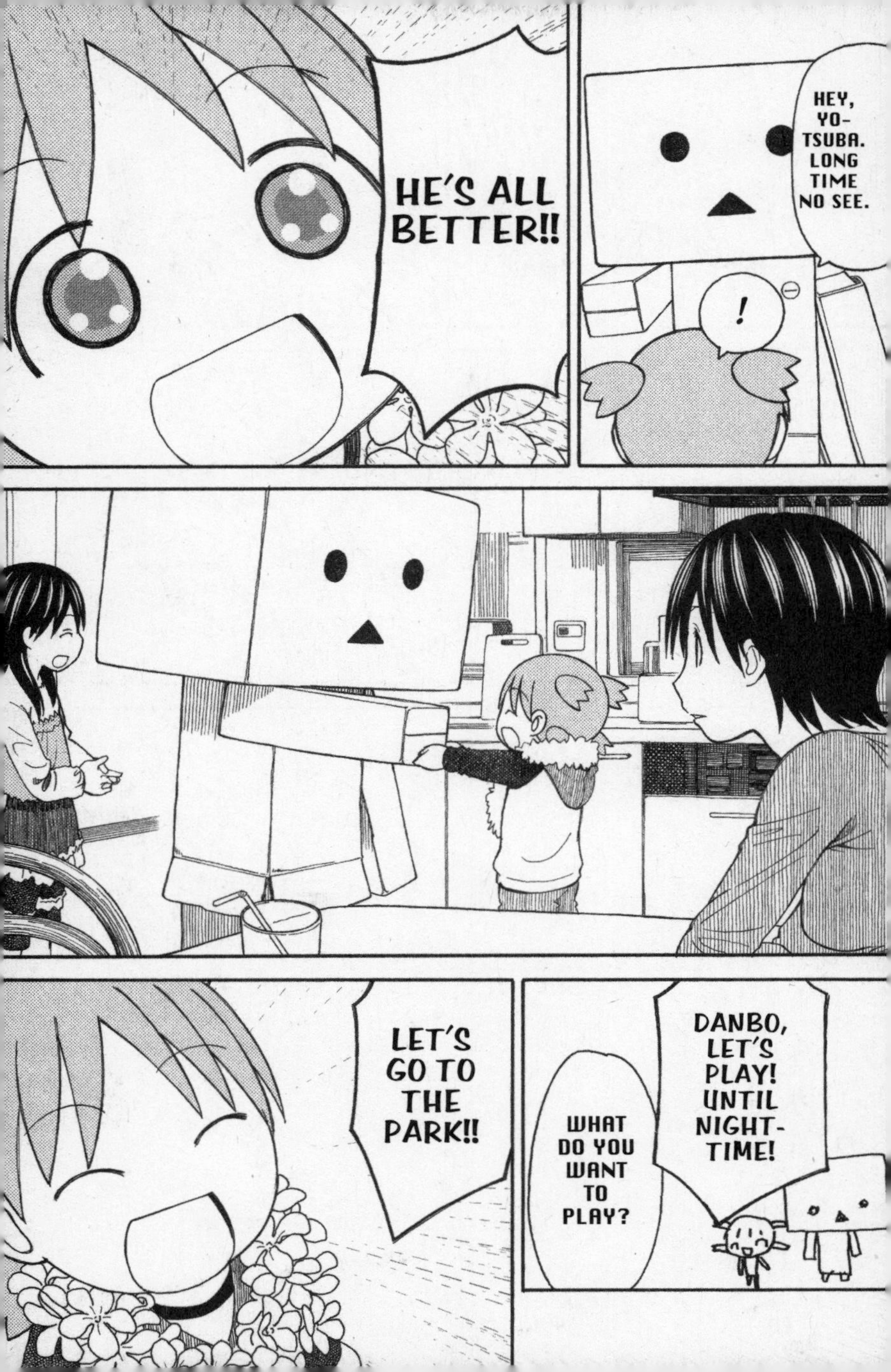
HEY, YO-TSUBA. LONG TIME NO SEE.
!
HE'S ALL BETTER!!
DANBO, LET'S PLAY! UNTIL NIGHT-TIME!
WHAT DO YOU WANT TO PLAY?
LET'S GO TO THE PARK!!

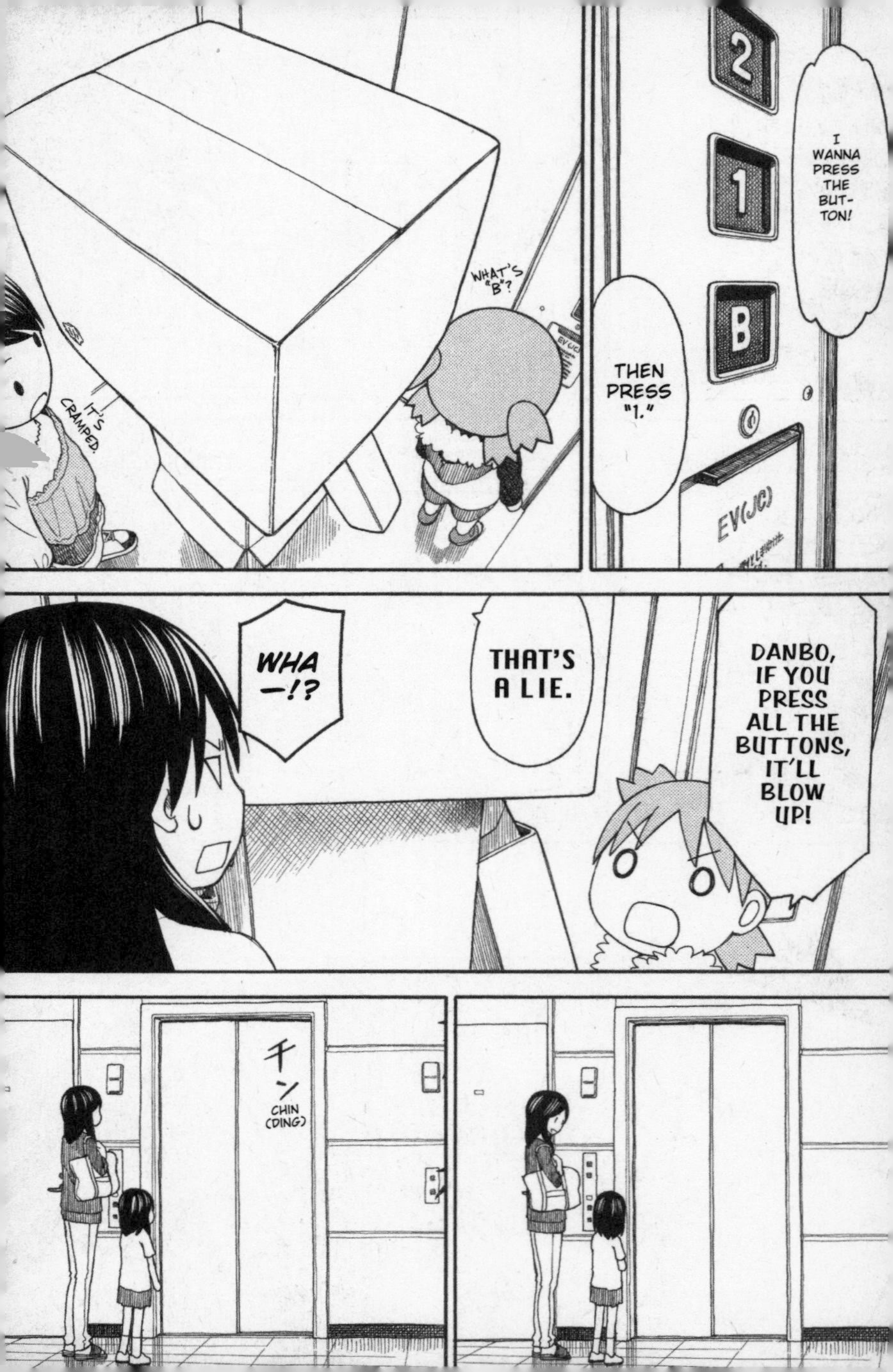
I WANNA PRESS THE BUT-TON!
THEN PRESS "1."
EV(JC)
WHAT'S "B"?
IT'S CRAMPED.
DANBO, IF YOU PRESS ALL THE BUTTONS, IT'LL BLOW UP!
THAT'S A LIE.
WHA—!?
チン
CHIN (DING)

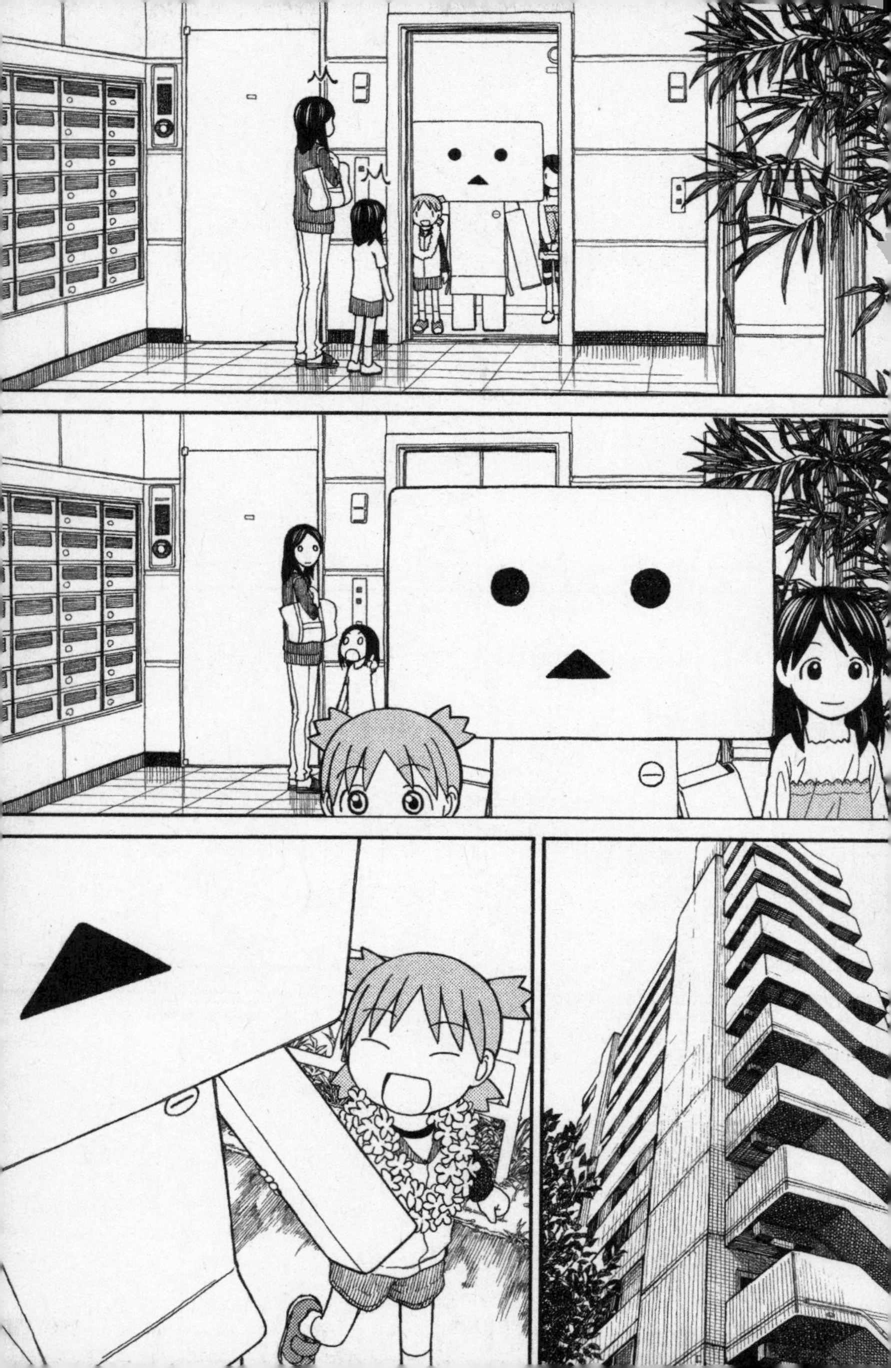

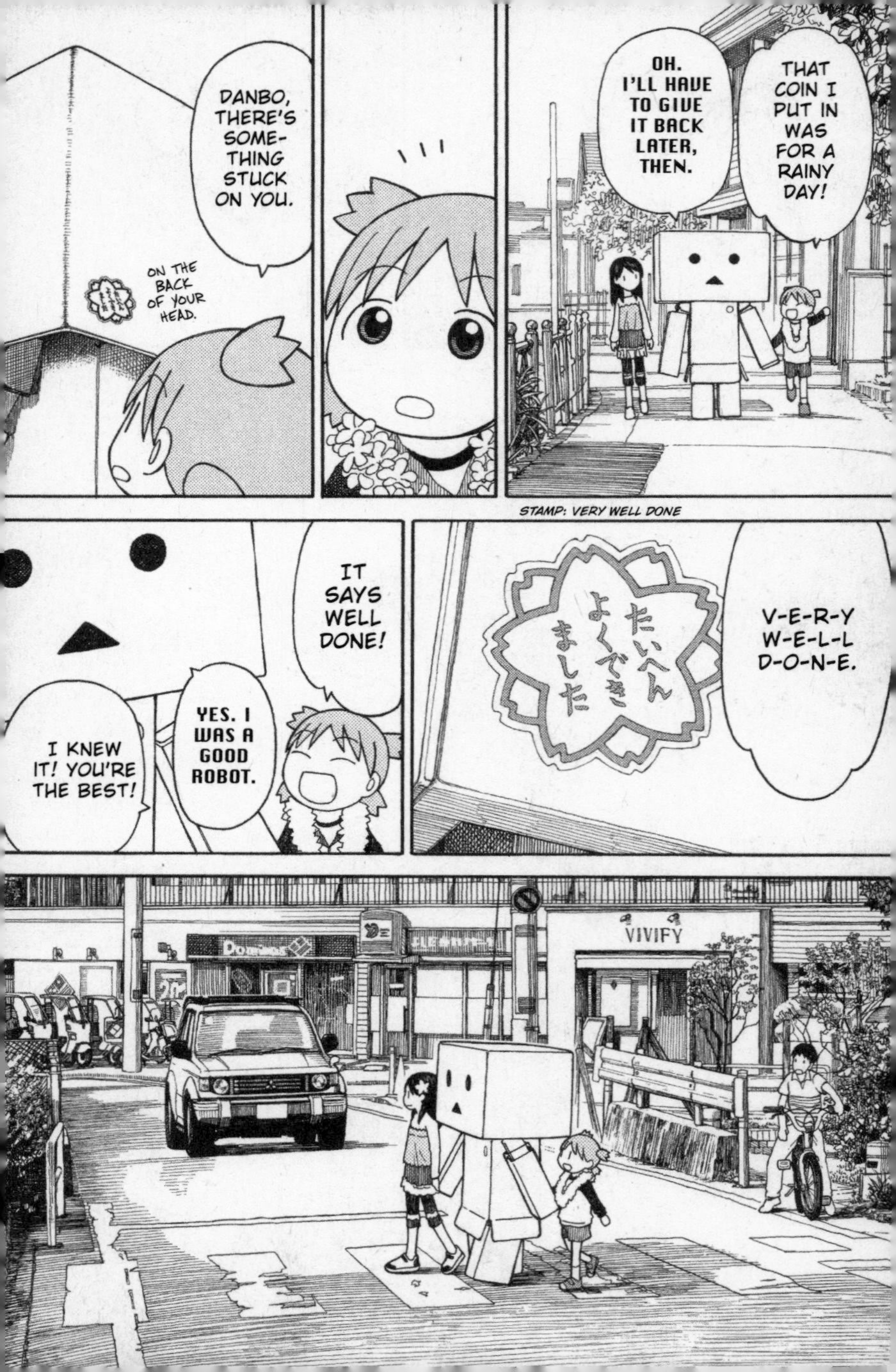
THAT COIN I PUT IN WAS FOR A RAINY DAY!
OH. I'LL HAVE TO GIVE IT BACK LATER, THEN.
DANBO, THERE'S SOME-THING STUCK ON YOU.
ON THE BACK OF YOUR HEAD.
STAMP: VERY WELL DONE
V-E-R-Y W-E-L-L D-O-N-E.
たいへんよくできました
IT SAYS WELL DONE!
YES. I WAS A GOOD ROBOT.
I KNEW IT! YOU'RE THE BEST!
VIVIFY

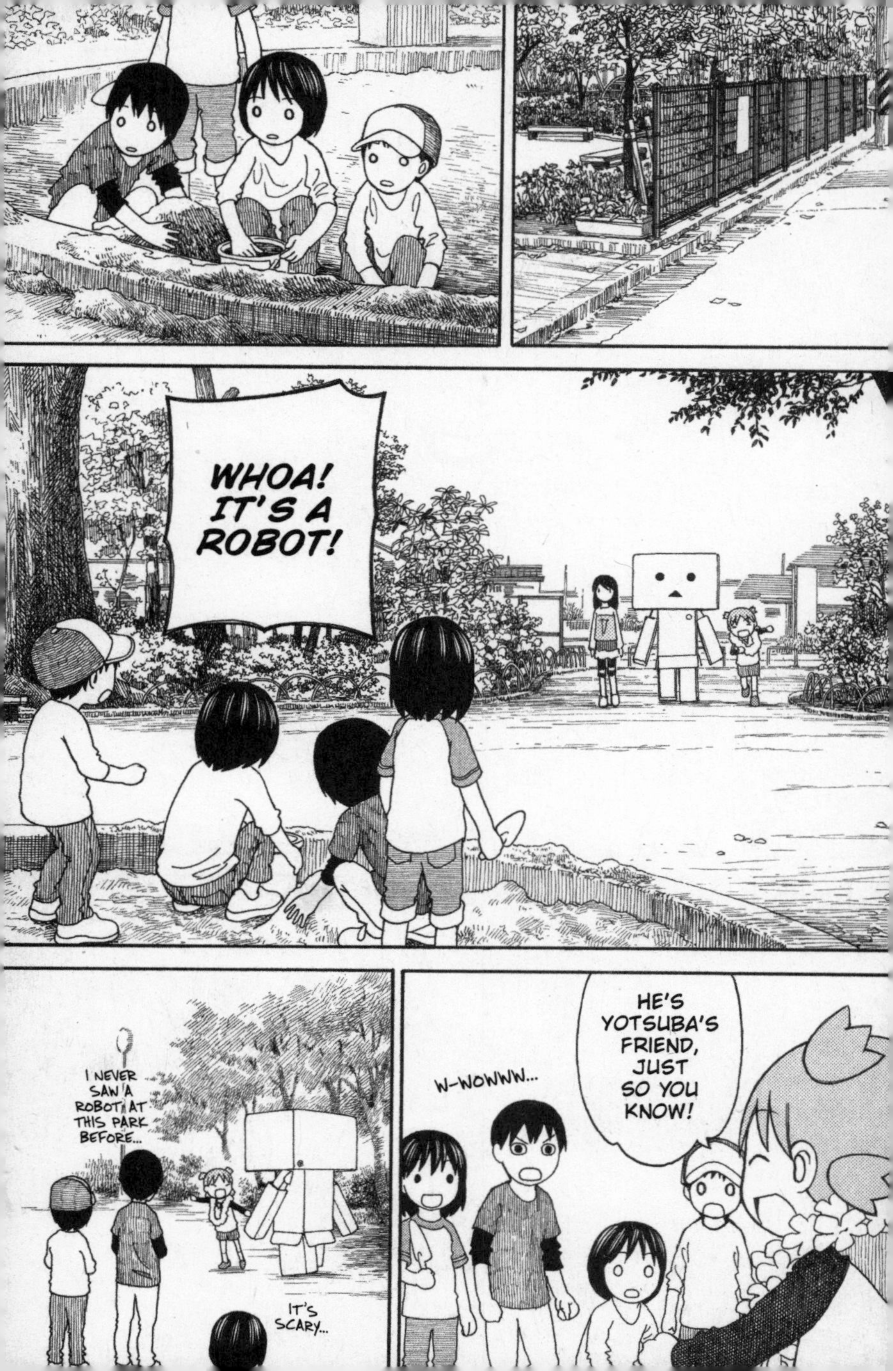
WHOA! IT'S A ROBOT!
HE'S YOTSUBA'S FRIEND, JUST SO YOU KNOW!
W-WOWWW...
I NEVER SAW A ROBOT AT THIS PARK BEFORE...
IT'S SCARY...

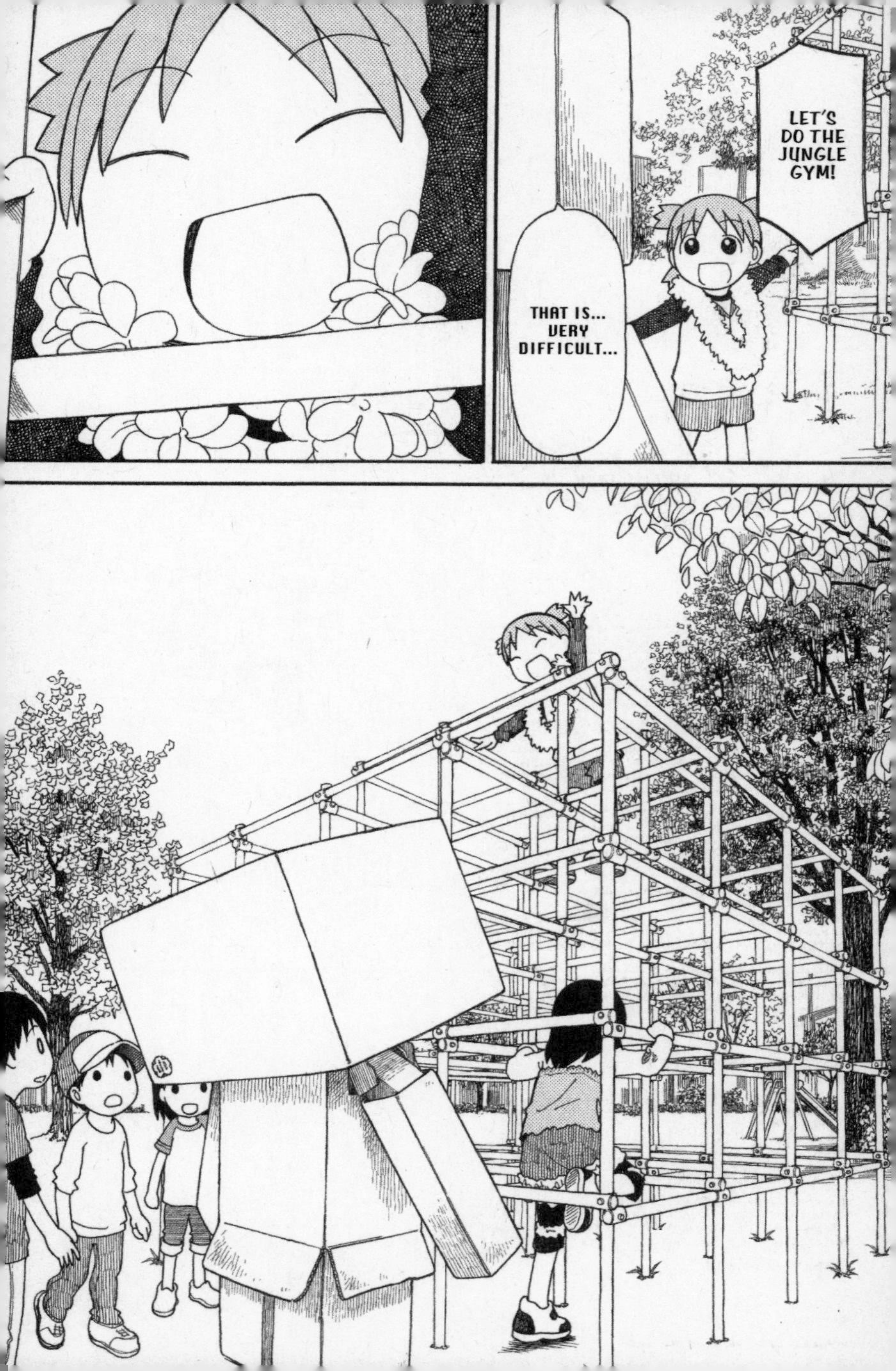
LET'S DO THE JUNGLE GYM!
THAT IS... VERY DIFFICULT...

YOTSUBA&! 10

KIYOHIKO AZUMA

Translation: Stephen Paul
Lettering: Terri Delgado

YOTSUBA&! Vol. 10 © KIYOHIKO AZUMA / YOTUBA SUTAZIO 2010. All rights reserved. First published in Japan in 2010 by ASCII MEDIA WORKS INC., Tokyo. English translation rights in USA, Canada, and UK arranged with ASCII MEDIA WORKS INC. through Tuttle-Mori Agency, Inc., Tokyo.

English translation © 2011 by Yen Press, LLC

Yen Press
1290 Avenue of the Americas
New York, NY 10104

Visit us at yenpress.com
facebook.com/yenpress
twitter.com/yenpress
yenpress.tumblr.com
instagram.com/yenpress

First Yen Press Edition: October 2011

Yen Press is an imprint of Yen Press, LLC.
The Yen Press name and logo are trademarks of Yen Press, LLC.
The publisher is not responsible for websites (or their content) that are not owned by the publisher.

ISBN: 978-0-316-19033-6

10

BVG

Printed in the United States of America

YOTSUBA&!

ENJOY EVERYTHING.

TO BE CONTINUED!